FOREIGN WORKERS AND LAW ENFORCEMENT IN JAPAN

Japanese Studies
General Editor: Yoshio Sugimoto

FOREIGN WORKERS AND LAW ENFORCEMENT IN JAPAN

Wolfgang Herbert

KEGAN PAUL INTERNATIONAL
London and New York

First published in 1996 by
Kegan Paul International
UK: P.O. Box 256, London WC1B 3SW, England
Tel: (0171) 580 5511 Fax: (0171) 436 0899
E-mail: books@keganpau.demon.co.uk
Internet: http://www.demon.co.uk/keganpaul/
USA: 562 West 113th Street, New York, NY 10025, USA
Tel: (212) 666 1000 Fax: (212) 316 3100

Distributed by
John Wiley & Sons Ltd
Southern Cross Trading Estate
1 Oldlands Way, Bognor Regis
West Sussex, PO22 9SA, England
Tel: (01234) 779 777 Fax: (01234) 820 250

Columbia University Press
562 West 113th Street
New York, NY 10025, USA
Tel: (212) 666 1000 Fax: (212) 316 3100

Copyright © Wolfgang Herbert 1996

Phototypeset in Times
by Intype London Ltd
Printed in Great Britain by TJ Press, Padstow, Cornwall

British Library Cataloguing in Publication Data

Herbert, Wolfgang.
   Foreign workers and law enforcement in Japan. (Japanese
   studies series)
   1. Alien labor – Japan – Crimes   2. Criminal justice,
   Administration of – Japan   3. Mass media and criminal justice
   – Japan
   I. Title
   364'.0952

   ISBN 0–7103–0555–9

Library of Congress Cataloging-in-Publication Data

Herbert, Wolfgang.
   Foreign workers and law enforcement in Japan / Wolfgang Herbert.
   375 pp. 22 cm. — (Japanese studies series)
   Includes bibliographical references and index.
   ISBN 0–7103–0555–9 (alk. paper)
   1. Alien labor—Japan—Social conditions.   2. Illegal aliens—
Japan.   3. Law enforcement—Japan.   I. Title.´   II. Series:
Japanese studies.
   HD8728.5.H47   1996
   305.5'62—dc20   96–15452
                                                        CIP

Contents

Figures

Tables

Preface

This work is the result of a stay in Japan of over two years (late 1988 to early 1991). It could only have been completed with the help and support of many people. Firstly, I express my thanks to my supervisors; to Professor Sepp Linhart for much advice and encouragement, and to Dr Arno Pilgram for fruitful discussions and valuable instructions on the theoretical framework and reference material. Concerning my work 'in the field', I am indebted to many, but most of all to Niwa Masao, who was always ready to provide advice on the law, even on trifling matters, and who provided literature for my use. Further useful information was provided by members of the 'Asian Friends', and here I especially thank Koyanagi Nobuaki, Mizuno Ashura and Nakajima Fumio. Many other informants' conversations and insights have helped form this thesis. I thank all of you.

To the Commission for Scholarships at the Faculty of Humanities at the University of Vienna, and to the efforts of Professor Linhart, I owe thanks for a scholarship which provided the freedom and mobility that is so important in intercultural studies. I also thank friends and colleagues who were victims of many discussions, and who were not so easily impressed: to name just a few, Sabine Frühstück, Martin Kaneko, Manfred Ringhofer, Corinna Tettinger, and Fleur Wöss.

My very deep thanks go to those closest to me: to my wife Yōko, and to my son Kenji, who painfully had to accept that I often played more with my computer than with him. For material and spiritual support, I am forever indebted to my parents and parents-in-law. For the wonderful music that was always in the background while working, I thank my brother Peter.

As for the English edition, my thanks go to Professor Yoshio Sugimoto, of La Trobe University, who encouraged me to perform the translation and had so much confidence in my work. Without him this book would not exist. Special thanks go to Dr Michael Dix for his invaluable and insightful editing work upon my appalling English. Without him this book would have been unreadable. And to all the others whose names I cannot list here, all those who accompanied me in some way or other during my work on this project, I also offer my thanks.

This study was completed early in the decade, though it is, I believe, still applicable, especially in relation to the theoretical framework of my feedback model, which describes the interaction between the organs of the state, judiciary, mass media and social actors. Certain details must be viewed in the light of recent developments. For example, the media coverage of illegal workers is no longer as topical as when this work was being carried out, but when this particular issue is viewed overall, it is still the case that the focus is on official data on deportations or crimes committed, and it can still be argued that this study provides a framework that could be applied to other societies subject to an influx of 'illegals'.

As a technical comment, Japanese terms have been transcribed using the Hepburn method, and are explained at the point of first occurrence in the text. The order of Japanese names follows Japanese convention: the family name is placed before the given name.

1 Preliminary Remarks

This study is an analysis *ex post facto*. However, the period under study (1981–90) is not wholly an arbitrary one of a neat ten-year span, for it was the period in which the 'problem' of foreign migrant workers surfaced to public awareness and led to political discussion, and it was in its closing year that this process was brought to a climax with the introduction of a new Immigration Control Act on 1 June 1990. No doubt some other time-slice could be equally well justified but in no case is socio-surgical precision possible. I therefore transgress this time-frame when it is necessary or heuristically useful to do so. The *ex post facto* nature of every thorough sociological analysis has the consequence that new developments cannot – or can only exceptionally, and with *ad hoc* interpretation – be taken into consideration.

The time-frame pertains mainly to my sources, since with the exception of several important later studies (for example, the extensive collection of treatises edited by Tezuka A.O. (1992) although this collection also chiefly covers the time up to 1990) I took into account only the literature published up to the end of 1990. An (admittedly superficial) examination of the post-1990 literature dealing with foreign workers, when I returned to Japan in the spring of 1992, revealed some two dozen new publications. Most of these were journalistic (except for the clearly scientific studies of Tezuka, A.O., 1992) and repeated the catch-phrases *kyōson* (coexistence) or *kyōsei* (living together), the keywords of the 'second round' in the debate on foreign workers. The 'first round' was dominated by arguments related to 'policy concerning whether to open or to close the country' (cf. Tezuka, 1992b:7), and I did not expect to find on my return any substantially new insights concerning the purpose of my inquiry.

With regard to my sources I shall make a brief global comment: characteristic of most of them is a usually uncritical presentation of official statistics and data pertaining to the situation of foreign migrants to Japan, illustrated by concrete examples from field studies or the press. This approach is found not only in the journal-

1

istic works, but also in the publications claiming to be scientific. The latter alone (but unfortunately not always) are careful to cite their sources. For longer quotations, I have noted the profession of the author (journalist, lawyer, scientist) at the first passage quoted, in order to identify the literary genre. However, a professorship at a university, for example, does not necessarily guarantee the scientific character of statements published *ex cathedra*.

Independent empirical research is the exception among the Japanese literature. This might be explained by the high credibility attributed to the official 'holy transcripts' of data, for example, those released by the Ministry of Justice. These data are 'recycled' in most of the publications. The cited cases (as a rule extreme ones) from the daily press are more indicative of standards of newsworthiness and of popular themes than of reality itself. The cases I have used for illustration are mostly drawn from the literature; in some passages original newspaper articles are quoted. I tried to collect all of the circulating (and sometimes discordant) data and to evaluate their reliability with something approaching pyrrhonic scepticism. The following section dealing with the phenomenology of 'illegal' migration of labour to Japan, therefore, is a *descriptio post festum*, a description primarily of, and also conditioned by, the Japanese *discourse*. This discourse, after all, generates what becomes visible as '*reality*', which is then describable in a second-order construction.

2 Phenomenology of the 'Illegal' Labour Migration to Japan

2.1 Theories of 'Illegal' Migration of Labour

To begin, I want to propose a theoretical framework within which some explanations may be offered for the 'illegal' migration of workers to Japan. I do not intend to propound a new sociological theory of migration; instead I want to present the models discussed in Japan. I will then attempt to carefully assess the relevance of these approaches and to identify universal characteristics of labour migration. This discussion will serve to introduce the theoretical concepts and to outline the (surface-)structure of migratory movement directed to Japan. It will provide a background for the Japanese discourse regarding the 'problem' of foreign workers.

Since the second half of the 1980s (at latest) there has been an 'irregular' migration of labour to Japan – mainly from Asian countries. This gained public attention through coverage by the mass media and political discussion as to whether an official 'guest worker policy' should be implemented or not. The term 'irregular' indicates that no official recruiting or dispatching of workers was involved, taken, and points to the circumvention of administrative rulings concerning stay and labour. Legally speaking, offences against regulations of the administrative law are committed, thus making applicable such legal descriptions as 'illegal entrance' (*fuhō nyūkoku*), 'illegal stay' (*fuhō zanryū*), or 'illegal work' (*fuhō shūrō*). However, by use of the term 'irregular', the criminal and stigmatizing connotations of 'illegal' are avoided. Nevertheless, the ascription of the term 'illegal' to the activities and existence of Asian migrant workers is ubiquitous in the Japanese discourse. For that reason, I adopt that label (without meaning to stigmatize cases to which it is applied) when quoting from the literature.

In contrast to European countries, the percentage of foreigners in Japan is very small – only 0.8 per cent in a population of approximately 122 million. Koreans constitute 69.3 percent of

3

(registered) foreigners (681,838 of the 984,455 non-Japanese residents). This group is comprised partly of second- and third-generation descendants of those who, after the annexation of Korea as a *de facto* colony in 1910, immigrated or were deported to Japan as forced labour. The Chinese minority (whose presence dates from the annexation of Taiwan in 1895) comprises roughly 14 per cent of foreigners. Only an estimated 5 per cent of foreigners originate from Western countries (data for 1989 from Yamazaki, 1991:138 and 151). Since Japan first opened itself to foreigners after a period of self-imposed isolation (around 1641 to 1854) it has always pursued a rigid and restrictive 'foreigner-policy', with its focus on control still symbolized in the obligation of every foreigner residing for more than three months to carry a 'certificate of alien registration'.

After Japan was able to conclude treaties with the foreign powers following that with England in July 1894, by which extraterritoriality was abolished, foreigners in Japan got the opportunity to move freely in the whole country in 1899 pursuant to an emperor's ordinance. Herewith a new regulation of the foreigner law became necessary. The newly promulgated regulations were to again provide far-reaching opportunities for control. Japanese accommodating foreigners were bound by another ordinance released at the same time to inform the local police thereof, and foreigners who stayed at least 90 days in Japan also had to notify the authorities. At first, mainly diplomatic delegations and students came into the country, attracted by Tokyo, the cultural center of East Asia of the time. Manual labourers as a rule did not get entry permission, because the Japanese authorities wanted to protect the domestic labour market from an invasion by cheap Chinese manpower. Therefore on principle only those foreigners were allowed to settle for a length of time, who were qualified for specified services. (Gohl, 1984:331f.)

Except in the case of temporary (coerced) migration from the colonies until the end of the Second World War, the latter regulation – preventing admission of manual labour, and allowing only restricted admission of 'qualified' foreigners into clearly circumscribed fields of activity – has remained in force. Since the 1970s, there has been a migration of South East Asian women who are illegally employed in the so-called 'services' (that is, in the sex industry). This has been justly described as a traffic in women. The bulk of this immigration is arranged by organized traffickers. In addition to this influx, there has been since the mid-1980s, larger scale, irregular migration of male 'working tourists', although not in the same pattern as recent 'tourism for work' (*Arbeitstourismus*) occurring in such countries as Austria since the opening of borders to former Eastern-bloc countries. In Japan, 'working tourists' are forced underground, since distance and financial burden prevent them from re-legalizing their residential status as tourists by first returning to their home country and then re-entering Japan. They therefore remain illegally. This 'unexpected' immigration of migrant workers jeopardizes a widely-accepted, semi-ideological view of Japan's 'identity' as a 'homogeneous island people with little experience in dealing with foreigners' (see, for example, Komai's (1992b) speculations as to whether Japan could become a 'multi-ethnic' country) and led to an over-heated debate about whether 'guest workers' should be welcome, and what sort of legislation would adequately control increasing migration from Asian countries.

2.1.1. The push-pull model

In the literature and public discussion dealing with 'illegal' Asian migrant workers, the question was repeatedly posed as to how and why Japan 'suddenly' became the target country of an irregular migration of labour. Neo-classical economic explanations gained particular popularity. According to this theoretical approach, labour is seen as a resource which 'freely' becomes mobile (or can be mobilized) depending on the supply-demand constellation. Existing disparities are assumed to be balanced through the 'flow' of labour. Push- and pull-factors are differentiated, and the attractiveness of labour migration is assessed according to their respective strength. The pull-factors are a cumulative combination of economic, demographic and social developments. For example, they could include falling birth rates, an increasing percentage of elderly (hence a decrease in the working population), and movement of indigenous workers into pleasant, better-paying (that is, white-collar) jobs. The push-factors which cause migrants to leave their countries of origin are overpopulation, pauperism, under-development and unemployment (cf. Castles and Kosack,

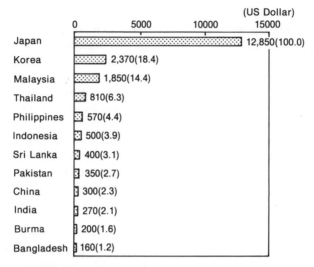

Source: World Bank 'World Tables', 1987 edition, data of 1986.
In brackets are percentage comparison figures with Japan being 100.
(Herbert, 1991b: 34, based on Keizaikikakuchō sōgōkeikakukyoku 1989: 44)

Figure 1.1 International comparison of per capita GNP

1985:26f.). At the macro-level, exorbitant economic disparities
between Japan and its neighbours are evident. Gross national
product (GNP) per capita serves as one indicator of disproportion
in economic power, as shown in Figure 1. This economic imbalance
is regularly mentioned, although not always with such force as
here: 'The premise of international labour migration is always the
existence of smaller or bigger economic disparities' (Miyajima,
1989:10).

At the micro-level, the opportunity to earn a high income in
Japan – the result of the enormous wage gap between Japan and
its neighbours – lures 'illegal' migrants and makes work in Japan
attractive for them despite the risk of being repatriated. The prospect of earning money and the expectation of higher wages than
at home are the *manifest* motives most often expressed by migrant
workers. However, one should not overlook the possibility that
this might be regarded as a legitimatory *ascription* (from a profit
orientation) justifying toleration or shutting of one's eyes, and for
the employers it can help to aid and abet use of 'illegal' labour.
Moreover, migrant workers are not just 'profiteers' who can be
portrayed with 'gold-digger' metaphors. The decision to migrate

is very often made out of the necessity to secure mere survival, and as a last choice, to escape a wretched situation of extreme poverty and unemployment. It can also be claimed that 'cultural' motives such as wanting to get to know the 'success-country' Japan, or to acquire knowledge and skills, may have been influential in the decision to migrate as is noted in Komai's (1992a:285) analysis of 115 interviews of migrant workers in Japan.

The push-pull model is the dominant theory in Japan. A representative of the Ministry of Justice borrowed from this theory in enumerating several causes of migration, as he outlined and explained new legal measures and the position of his Ministry at a symposium. The causes mentioned were: economic imbalance (measured by per-capita GNP); revaluation of the yen, which makes migration of labour to Japan more profitable; economic depression in former target-countries of labour migration in the Middle East; worsening labour market conditions in the respective home countries; links between Japan and source countries organized by professional labour agents; and high demand for manual workers in middle- and small-scale enterprises and in services (or 'entertainment') (Yamazaki, 1991:142).

Demographic reasons are also given by pointing to the acute overpopulation in Asian developing countries, and the marked shortage of personnel in some sectors in Japan. Furthermore, calculations, such as that the wages for one month of work in Japan for a Pakistani are equivalent to wages for forty months of work at home, are well known (cf. Tezuka, 1989a:116–21).

Table 1.1a Differentials of GNP between Japan and other Asian countries

	Per capita income (1980)	Ratio between Japan and other countries (1980)	Per capita income (1987)	Ratio between Japan and other countries (1987)
Japan	9.890	1.00	15.770	1.00
Korea	1.520	6.51	2.690	5.86
Taiwan	2.269	4.36	5.075	3.11
Philippines	720	13.74	590	26.73
Thailand	670	14.76	840	18.77
Pakistan	300	32.97	350	45.06
Bangladesh	120	82.42	160	98.56
China			300	52.56

Compiled from World Bank Atlas, 1981, 1988 (Tezuka, 1991: 43).

Table 1.1b Differentials of GNP between the Federal Republic of
Germany (West) and other European and Middle-East
countries

	Per capita income (1972)	Ratio between Germany and other countries (1972)	Per capita income (1987)	Ratio between Germany and other countries (1987)
Germany (West)	3.738	1.00	14.460	1.00
Italy	1.988	1.88	10.420	1.31
Spain	1.235	3.03	6.010	2.41
Portugal	947	3.95	2.890	5.00
Greece	1.331	2.81	4.350	3.32
Turkey	440	8.50	1.200	12.05

Compiled from World Bank Atlas, 1988 (Tezuka, 1991: 43).

The industrial law specialist, Tezuka, compared the differences
in per-capita GNP between Germany at the beginning of the
1970s (before the ending of recruitment of guest-workers in that
country) and Japan at the present time. He sought to demonstrate
that the economic disparity between Japan and its neighbours is
many times that between, for example, Germany and Italy (1:1.88
differential in 1972) or Germany and Turkey (1:8.5 in 1972). In
comparison, the per-capita GNP in Japan (1987) was 13.7 times
that of the Philippines, and 82.4 times that of Bangladesh. These
disparities are seen as a reason for the increasing migration of
labour to Japan independently of official policies in Japan and the
'exporting' states. The high rate of 'underemployment' (up to 30
per cent) in neighbouring Asian countries, and their immense
population surpluses, provide a large pool of potential migrant
workers, and are also taken into account as causes of migration
(Tezuka, 1991:41ff.).

Another author presents the (too) simple calculation –
especially popular in journalism – that a migrant worker could
earn a living for between ten and twelve months (by the standard
of his home country) by working for one month in Japan (Gonoi
1989:1). A further study states that the lowest of the wage disparities is five to one (in the case of Korea), while in the highest case
(Bangladesh) it is as high as sixty to one (KKSK, 1989:43;
numerical differences between these and the earlier-given figures
are a result of using differing years as the bases of computation).

The investigative reporter, Gonoi, summarizes the already-mentioned factors as the backdrop for the 'illegal' migration of labour; they are: the gap in economic power; the diminished attractiveness of previously popular target countries (oilstates in the Middle East); the deterioration of the labour market situation in the supplying countries; the existence of labour agents; the demand for labour in the small-business and services sector in Japan; and the increase in profit due to the high yen-rate since the mid-1980s (Gonoi, 1989:179). Analogous, more or less complete, enumerations of push-pull-factors are presented in Tezuka, 1989a:116, Yorimitsu, 1989:11, and critically by Kuwahara (1989:137ff.), KKSK (1989:36 and 41ff.), the head of the Bureau for Measures for Employment of Foreign Workers in the Ministry of Labour, Yoshimen (1990:42), Mori (1989:8 and 1990:62), Yashima (1989:17) and others. Karthaus-Tanaka (1990:6 and 27) provides a plain 'flow-model' representing the basic pattern of international labour migration as movement from countries of low income to those with high income. This, decorated with per-capita GNP figures as an indicator of economic divergences, and including official data, offers an English introduction to the Japanese theoretical perspective.[1]

2.1.2 Complementary theoretical fragments

There are other aspects of the discussion which are not considered in the neoclassically-inspired economic theories, or which are deemed merely to be 'intervening variables'. One scholar, for instance, points out that distances have become considerably 'shorter' due to modern transport (the variable of geographical distance). He hints also at the increase in flow of information, amplified not least by the intensified operations of Japanese capital in foreign countries (cf. Kuwahara, 1989:132f.).[2]

Repeatedly, one finds remarks attributing the internationally-known phenomenon of chain migration to the fact that migrants induce their relatives, friends and acquaintances to follow them to work in Japan. When they temporarily return to their home country they present success stories (even in cases of failure) and stage 'uncle-from-America appearances' (Hofer, 1992:19) by bringing back consumer goods. Word-of-mouth and the emergence in time of ethnic networks mediate and facilitate travel and work for others from the migrant's place and group of origin. Thus

9

Sawahata (1989:28ff.) tells of a village in Pakistan, from which 500, or according to other sources 1,000, young men left to seek jobs in Japan. It is claimed that there were 'emigration villages' in Pakistan (Komai, 1992a:287; and Yonemoto, 1990:39. See also Hinago, 1990a:91, concerning networks amongst Philippinos. The common multi-staged migration pattern of rural exodus to big cities (and often to the slums of these cities) as a starting point for foreign migration is also mentioned (for example, Mori, 1989:8).

2.1.3 Critique of the neoclassical model

The pure push-pull model, which treats labour migration reductionistically and only in economic terms, also became an object of critique in Japan. It attracted the following criticisms: (1) That the subjective side of motivation is ignored (the author here obviously did not know of the survey conducted in 1990 by GRJCK, 1992). It was objected (2) That its approach is too static, and simply looks at labour as a resource such as capital or land (labour 'flowing' from countries of low income to those of high income). If a process of migration is underway, one should also consider the three 'R-variables': recruiting, (prospects on) return, and (the possibility of sending) remittances (to relatives). Psychological moments in the act of deciding whether to migrate or not should also be taken into account. (3) That a plain push-pull model is ahistorical and sociologically deficient, and endorses the naive fiction of a 'free economic subject' reflecting rationally upon advantages and disadvantages. (4) That the postulated balancing of power-gaps is not necessarily brought about by labour migration. Restrictions and interventions by the state and legislation are not taken into account. However, the author, a professor of economics, concedes that a comprehensive synthesis of theory is hard to provide (Kuwahara 1991:182–5). (5) That labour does not 'function' according to the law of supply and demand or through political liberalization (as in trade or flow of capital). Instead, ethnic criteria differentiate workers and bring about a segmented labour market. Migrants will occupy the lowest stratum, and this will retard modernization and structural change of an economy. Therefore, a more extensive theory of migration is needed (Hara, 1990:17, who rejects the 'naive' neoclassical theory after first giving an historical overview of labour migration in Asia). This critique resembles the concept of *Unterschichtung* (boosting the lower social strata) of Hoffman-Nowotny, who speaks *inter alia* of 'a relative conservation of economic structures' and attenuation of the pressure for social change (cf. Hoffman-Nowotny, 1973:307, and the outline of his theses below).

2.1.4. Western migration theories and 'migration universals'

Several parallels are evident between the Japanese theoretical discussion and that found in Western publications. I want to distil some insights from selected classics of the sociology of migration which may be deemed to be of transnational validity, and therefore pertinent to Japan. In these classics, it is noted that while only modest progress has been made toward a theory of migration, a plethora of isolated factors and findings is available, together with numerous explanatory hypotheses (Albrecht 1972:4). It is recognized, moreover, that migration be seen not only as problem-generating (a view that could be claimed to be predominant in Japan), but also as a problem-solving social phenomenon.

Internationally as well as nationally, migration is understood as reaction to existing and emerging chances for the fulfilment of unsatisfied needs (material and immaterial) of the migrating persons. Migration thereby – for industrialized societies as well as developing countries – maintains an important role in the process of economic growth (Albrecht, 1972:8).

Albrecht attempts to assess inquiries into variables of migration and comes to the conclusion that investigations into the selectivity of migration lack 'integration into a sociological theory which could "explain" migration'. Push-factors of an economic nature, according to Albrecht, often are decisive, 'but the assertion that migration proceeds in the direction of the highest wage-level is much too generic to even approximately do justice to reality' (Albrecht, 1972:11 and 12). Statisticians often have proposed in 'distance-opportunity theories' dealing with the connections between distance, structure of chances and migratory streams. A host of surveys investigate the consequences of migration, and the integration and assimilation of migrants (Albrecht, 1972:13f.). Like Kuwahara, Albrecht critically urges that while traditionally migration studies are predicated on data of the official statistics, 'only interviews broadly designed – if necessary in connection with

11

census data – can provide a sound basis from which one could make statements in regard to motives, normative patterns and other social features of migrants'. He further objects that economists are mainly preoccupied with the migration of labour, and employ the 'fiction of a purely rational and economically calculating single person without considering the multiple social relations in which the decision to migrate is taken or prepared and in which the respective consequences emerge' (Albrecht, 1972:18 and 19). The author offers a remark which is, I suggest, particularly relevant for scientists from highly-industrialized countries and salient to the discussion of economic differences (and exclusively economic taxonomies) 'the postulated culture or civilization gap often represents a "creation" out of the ethnocentrism of the researcher' (Albrecht, 1972:28).

Albrecht advances a push-pull theory of the causes of migration (supporting it with a study from 1936!), but adds that concepts of this kind are likely to result in mere description without explanatory value. Nevertheless, 'economic incentives to migrate will always exist in an evolutionary economy' (Albrecht, 1972:42 and 45). He cites over-population and rural exodus as causal factors, and describes labour migration as a 'phenomenon ensuing in almost all societies, which modernize with high speed or just industrialize'. In summary, he states that 'Labour migration in developing countries has very strong economic reasons, arising from the process of development. The functionality for the further economic and social development is questionable' (Albrecht, 1972:50 and 55). He differentiates three types of migration models: 'distance theories' (gravitation models), 'push-pull models' and 'probabilistic' theories (mostly 'simulation models'), and is sceptical regarding their explanatory potential: 'The majority of these models proceed from very unrealistic premises and are therefore useless alone' (Albrecht, 1972:109).

The phenomenon of chain migration, Albrecht comments, demonstrates 'what immense importance can be attributed to communication and interaction for the triggering off and direction of migration streams' (Albrecht, 1972:118). Albrecht examines a multitude of narrower studies and piecemeal theories with the intention of expounding a general theory of migration. However, he concludes that this ambition is not achievable:

according to the constellation of the releasing conditions and social organization of the respective societies, the course-pattern of migration processes turns out to be very diverse. For the time being it is not possible to provide precise information on which factors the determining impacts result from. *The* theory of migration, for this reason, does not exist and probably can never exist' (Albrecht, 1972:278f.).

This refutation of a 'universal theory' implies that, in the case of Japan, the relevant factors for immigration would have to be assessed as peculiar to it. Nevertheless, *ex post facto* one can identify in the migration that occurred several 'universals' with equivalents and homologies in analogous migratory movements. The debate on guest-workers in Western Europe is in a number of respects similar to that in Japan.

It is held true that labour migration as a consequence of national and international developmental differences is a historical phenomenon and the actual immigration of labour force with foreign nationality into regions and states with a higher level of development is no specific or novel type of our era (Leitner, 1983:14).

However, modern movements are fostered by better transport systems to overcome distances, and by the mass media transmitting information about living standards, production modes and habits of other countries. Through the relaxation of traditional bonds in the countries of origin, mobility is also boosted, and the international economic interlinking, together with mass tourism, promote the liberalization of passport regulations and lead to a higher permeability of state borders (cf. Leitner, 1983:16f).

In the well known and much discussed study of Hoffmann-Nowotny it is maintained that, from a theoretical perspective, migration 'can be interpreted as interaction between societal systems, which serve the transfer of tensions and thereby the balancing of power and prestige' (Hoffmann-Nowotny, 1973:13). According to this migration specialist, the 'developmental differences' produce a proportionate migration movement. The central thesis is that a 'boosting of the lower strata' (*Unterschichtung*) is the outcome; for example, 'immigrants enter the lowest ranks of the employment structure and hereby allow an expansion there'.

[The result] for the status line employment [is] a greater openness and accessibility. On the individual level, boosted chances for mobility are provided for, primarily for the indigenous population belonging to the lower classes. Many natives, therefore, automatically reach higher rungs of employment and therewith higher income, without this advancement being preceded by an elevation of educational position (Hoffmann-Nowotny, 1973:24).

By virtue of this *Unterschichtung*, a certain conservation of structures is brought about. Enterprises in the production sector long due for closing down in the rationalization process can survive because the labour positions offered there are occupied by immigrants. Expansion of the tertiary sector puts pressure on the economic structure – an indicator of technological and economic change – having already initiated a reduction of the 'ground stratum' before immigration occurs. Subsequently, a 'neo-feudal disengagement' of the indigenous workers follows; for example, immigrants are assigned to marginal positions and to positions inferior with regard to income and profession (Hoffman-Nowotny, 1973:128ff.). Immigration primarily brings a country's structural problems to the fore. The problem of foreign labourers, therefore, should be analyzed from the point of view of a sociology of the immigration country, rather than by focussing on the foreign workers (Hoffmann-Nowotny, 1973,151f.).[3] This approach permits the social position of foreign workers in Japan to be located. However, in Japan, the phenomenon is, in terms of mere numbers, much too slight to speak of a general 'boosting of the lower strata'.

In yet another attempt (Ronzani, 1980) to expound a theoretical framework for labour migration, it is again stated that a lack of an overall social scientific vision exists. Thus the availability of a host of theories and explanation models in separate disciplines rather nullifies the aim of envisaging migration comprehensively (Ronzani, 1980:1). Ronzani too conceives migration as interaction between societies to be comprehended on four levels of action: 1) the level of the individual; 2) the level of societal subsystems; 3) the level of societies at large; and 4) the level of the supersystem formed by the involved societies (Ronzani, 1980:3). As far as I know, a truly integrative approach doing justice to these analytical demands exists in Japan only in the study of the Economic Planning Agency (KKSK, 1989). But this is abstract and descriptive

14

(rather than explanatory), still neglects the level of the individual, and is hardly conclusive.

'The economic connections between different societies manifest themselves predominantly in flows of goods and money as well as in streams of the population (migrations)' (Ronzani, 1980:8). In Japan, it became a catch-phrase regarding 'internationalization' that, after the influx (and international exchange) of goods (*mono*) and capital (*kane*), the influx of 'human beings' (*hito*) followed (cf., for example, Tezuka, 1988:274 or 1992:3).

'Migration of labour is a phenomenon which affects particularly the lower social strata and is so designated because it is in the sense of the individual migration strategy practically determined *only* by the search for a place to work. (The international mobility of members of middle or upper classes – university graduates, technicians, managers – has, for qualitative reasons, to be distinguished from labour migration; the notion of a brain drain is clear and adequate.) (Ronzani, 1980:8f.).

This remark has some relevance for the Japanese situation. In Japan, the irregular migration of 'unqualified' or 'unskilled' workers (*tanjun rōdōsha*) has come to dominate the discourse. Not only are 'qualified' workers employed with a safe legal status for their stay, but they also are not considered problematic; this form of employment is rather promoted than labelled a 'social problem'.

According to Ronzani again, migration follows a pattern of development-gaps, so to speak, 'from poor to rich'.

A migration potential arises not only for demographic reasons, but also in closest connection with socio-economic developmental differences, if corresponding societal conduits and mechanisms of information are existent and the perception of this information is guaranteed for the individual (Ronzani, 1980:9).

The author realistically comments:

The individual migrant is, as regards information about the potential receiving country, dependent mainly on very one-sided, distorted and deficient sources (for example, oral

15

propaganda, exaggeration, showing-off), or sources which are too closely bound by their own interests (for instance, recruitment bureaus). At certain times virtual myths about the receiving societies circulate which are pertinent to those stages in which short-term positive effects boost the enthusiasm of actual and potential migrants (Ronzani, 1980:207).

Similarly, in Asian countries at present, myths abound about Japan being a place where one can become rich. This inspired the title of the book, *Jipangu* (Sawahata, 1989) – an intentional allusion to the thirteenth-century reports on the country Zipangu (Chin. Jih-pen-kuo) by the Venetian merchant Marco Polo, who spoke of houses roofed with gold. Regarding the explanation of migration processes in terms of push-pull factors, Ronzani comments that, in addition to this, individual- and socio-psychological factors of the perception, and macro-sociological and – economic expla-nations of the existence and dynamics of these forces should be theoretically amalgamated (Ronzani, 1980:17). He then constructs a basic situation of labour migration in which he lists all the relevant variables (see Table 1.2).

Table 1.2 Basic situations of labour migration

Society of origin	Receiving society
situation/phase 1 *before migration*	situation/phase 2 *emigration time*
confrontation with modern life-style, hiking expectations	presence as 'foreign' manpower
partly deficient satisfaction of material basic wants	satisfaction of urgent material wants, supporting of family
perception: examples, offers (recruitment), social expectations	perception: higher living standard, own socially low position
situation/phase 4 *remigration* (possibly further migration)	situation/phase 3 *staying* (integration)
re-integration: (a) inactive (e.g. as old age pensioner, jobless) (b) active: with additional experiences *innovative*	(a) integration positive: *participation* with equal chances (b) integration negative: underprivileged, accepted discrimination, marginal position in receiving society

Ronzani, 1980: 28.

Migration processes, on the one hand, emerge on the individual level through the perception of a relative deprivation in comparison with (real or imagined) groups in one's own or other societies and, in the end, aid the individual conflict solution. On the other hand, societal-level migration fulfils diverse tasks: 'the "demographic function" (reduction of "overpopulation"), the political function (reduction of social and political tensions) and the economic function (acquisition of income from foreign countries, that is, export of the production factor labour)' (Ronzani, 1980:62). To illustrate the complexity of migratory processes, I cite a micro-sociological survey of the problems migrants face (see Table 1.3).

In a further classic of migration sociology (Esser, 1980), the author laments the existence of a chaos of disconnected single studies. In the search for *the* theory of migration – which neither exists nor will ever exist – these findings are liable to be induced 'up' into a general theory pertinent to a specific field (Esser, 1980:12). Without examining Esser's view in detail,[4] I want to introduce some of his conclusions, which seem to be of general interest for the understanding of migratory processes. According to Esser, four groups of migration theories could be roughly distinguished: distance-models, opportunity theories, decision-theoretical approaches and sociological migration theories (where 'structural imbalances', 'system problems' and the like are seen as causes). In maintaining his methodological paradigm, he states:

> But attempts of this kind to infer 'system problems', for example, from intra- or inter-societal disparities can in the final analysis be reduced to the – more or less successful – acting of persons who are linked together in relations of interaction and power (and respectively represent 'environment' for each other) (Esser, 1980:27).

Regarding the selectivity of migrations, he reiterates that males are more likely to migrate than females, younger people migrate more often than older people, and that migrants are more performance-oriented, psychologically more mobile and of stronger universalistic orientation than immobile persons. But with a strong push, this selectivity is further diminished:

> With a great push, which increasingly makes migration the

17

Table 1.3 Problems, goals, strategies of main actors

	Society	Migrant	Society 2
Primary problems:	overpopulation: general and structural unemployment, underemployment, disparities in economic development, local and sectoral	lack of income-chances, low education, increasing economic and social wants (extrinsically induced), personal development	persistent labour shortage, locally and sectorally concentrated, professional mobility upwards (drain below)
Strategy:	toleration or promotion of (mass) emigration	labour migration temporarily/unclear/ permanently	employment of foreign labourers
Goals and expectations:	defusement of population pressure. Additional returns locally (transfer) and nationally (remittances). Social and political easing of tensions developmental effect by processes of learning	source of income intensive saving and saving security establishment of existence 'at home' 'abroad' re-integration integration social advancement	short term solution for local and sectoral labour market problems, flexible labour market (buffer for economic ups/ downs) wage pressure, extensive growth, fast accumulation of capital
Secondary problems:	erosion of population-structure, local and sectoral manpower shortages; impediments to development measures socio-structural involution non-solving of longterm problems (education, politics, life quality etc.), mass remigration	'life as guest-worker' (exacerbation of individual and social problems: communication, orientation, integration, legal and political position) unplanned unexpected staying remigration failed investments, failure of re-integration	secondary demand for infrastructure, additional extensive growth (self-reinforcement) retardation of structural adaptation in economy. Socio-political problems ('guest-worker-problem'), difficulties with integration, political reactions, problems of second generation

Ronzani, 1980: 200.

only acceptable alternative for action without consideration of other motives and the nature of specific target regions, the individual differences between migrants and non-migrants diminish more and more (Esser, 1980:28f.).

If, however, the pull is strong, the more 'active' part of the population emigrates (Esser, 1980:113). Much of Esser's work is dedicated to research on integration and he concludes that successful 'assimilation' depends more upon characteristics of the environment in the receiving system than on personality features: 'Environmental factors prevail in their importance over personality factors inasmuch barriers to acting, or exclusion from alternatives, emerge' (Esser, 1980:102, cf. also 92). Esser too deems migration to be functional. It leads to a compensation in differentials, restricted by such factual conditions as 'political restrictions, [and] selectivity of the migrating populace, in a way that makes one doubt the thesis of the possibility of pulling off labour potential' (Esser, 1980:112). He describes these compensative effects extensively, and partly with metaphors from the field of physics (for example, 'removal of pressure').

Functionally migration therefore has three basic patterns: Firstly, (psychological) mobilization and marginalization of persons, and diffusion of knowledge, norms and skills; that is, social change, social differentiation and modernization in general. Secondly, redistribution for optimal allocation, and to compensate for marginal productivities and (perceived) gaps in the supply of resources (for example, real wage differentials). And thirdly, in consequence of such redistributions, a balancing of tensions within and between the interacting systems, stabilizing (even while exacerbating) existing internal and external inequalities through tension absorption, and effecting stress-transfer by 'breaking up' collective conflict front-lines (into individual anomie, individual opportunism or 'neo-feudal' ethnic stratification).

> The general hypothesis, therefore, suggests that under certain
> preconditions (primarily formal freedom of movement,
> individual-specific motivation to migrate, and subsequent
> subordinate integration of the migrants) migration makes a
> contribution to the solution of the basic problems of modern
> societies, this contribution being the realization of
> differentiation, the enhancement of capacities and the
> stabilization of social systems (Esser, 1980:106 and 107).

Other publications, while referring to developmental disparities as causes for migration, note that securing material subsistence for oneself and one's family is one of the prime motives for migrating (poll in Kremer and Spangenberg, 1980:27f.; similar responses were obtained by an Austrian poll among guest-workers, whose main motive was stated to be 'better income opportunities', Bauböck, 1986a:331).

In standard English works (the two cited below are quoted, for instance, in Miyajima, 1989), labour migration is also analyzed in terms of push-pull factors and economic inequalities (Castles and Kosack, 1985:27f.). A weighting of the factors is attempted, and it is stated that 'under conditions of economic migration control, "push" factors assume no significance unless there is at the same time a specific "pull" ' (Böhning, 1984:64). The richer a state, the stronger is its economic pull. To regard flow of labour as a 'free' production factor in the future international division of labour would be anachronistic. Human laws can attempt to regulate migration but they cannot suppress it: 'Anthropologically speaking, migration is an irrepressible human urge' (Böhning, 1984:12f.).

For Castles and Kosack (see bibliography in Kuwahara and Hanami, 1989:213), migrants have a specific socio-economic function. They have become structurally indispensable, having been recruited because they were willing (or circumstances compelled them) to accept the least desirable jobs, jobs deserted by indigenous labour. Class solidarity with native workers is prevented by prejudices and hindered by the perception of immigrants as new competitors on the (bottom of the) labour market. But the presence of a lower stratum of immigrant labourers allows social advancement to large sections of the indigenous working class. Labour migration must be understood in the historical context of the international capitalist system. Today migration is highly profitable for Western European capitalism. At the same time, it does nothing to alleviate the backwardness of the regions from which migrants come; indeed it is often a hindrance to development. *Labour migration is a form of development aid given by poor countries to rich countries* (Castles and Kosack 1985:7f.; my emphasis).

The mobilization of labour is seen by these authors as a precondition for European industrialization in the 19th century. The same is true of the Japanese situation.

Once local labour reserves were used up, labour migrants were induced to come from further afield. Often they crossed national frontiers in search of employment. The social history of industrialization is that of mass movements from country to town; international migration is a special case within this general pattern (Castles and Kosack, 1985:15).

This (very limited) selection of Western scientific findings and statements concerning labour migration shows that the discussion in Japan resembles that in Western Europe in many ways. However, in Japan push-pull models enjoy high acceptance and are over-emphasized. Questions pertinent to the functionality of 'irregular' migration for the Japanese labour market, and of labour migration as a problem-solving strategy for the emigrants are neglected. Instead – for political reasons – the focus is on 'social problems' which Japan might suffer as a result of immigration. In this way, the impact of Japanese capitalism on the countries of origin of the migrants may be ignored.

3 Some Historical Preliminaries

I shall very briefly sketch the historical situation of Japan regarding foreign workers, by referring to its presentation in the literature of the *Japanese discussion* (I cannot attempt here an exposition of the *factual* history of foreign workers in Japan). I intend to do this because, in Germany too, at the time of the signing of the first recruitment agreement with Italy (22 December 1955), 'a public debate on the tradition of the employment of foreigners, still a recent one ten years after the end of the war ... did not at this time take place' (Herbert, 1986:194). An historical survey noted that: 'in the numerous, most recent contributions to the discussion of the current "question of guest-workers", the historical perspective as a rule is lacking completely, if not dismissed with some sketchy remarks in an historicizing introduction' (Bade, 1983:9). This, despite Germany having a history of more than one hundred years of employing 'alien workers' (*Fremdarbeiter*), and despite its having channelled millions of forced labourers into the German (armaments) industry during World War II. The German discussion regarding guest-workers, therefore, commenced with the ahistorical fiction of a 'new beginning'.

A similar lament recurs in the Japanese discussion. Acknowledgement of the problem of permanently residing (*zainichi*) Koreans in Japan is said to be lacking almost totally and to be merely superficial where it occurs (Lee, 1989:37). An exception to this, however, is provided by Professor Tanaka Hiroshi of the prefectural University of Aichi, whose frequent comments on the issue in the media have raised public consciousness concerning the history and 'experience' of Japan in receiving (and dispatching) foreign labour. I therefore cannot assent to the sweeping assertion that the historical dimension is completely ignored in the discourse. Tanaka notes that Japan itself is a source of emigrants and labour, and comments on the coerced deportation and coerced recruitment of foreigners from the Japanese 'colonies' during Japan's imperialistic phase. The number of Koreans in Japan rose, for instance, from 790 in 1910 to almost two million in 1944 (Tanaka, 1988:17ff.). In further articles (Tanaka, 1990a and 1990b), he points also to Japan's foreign 'experience' with labour (that is, coerced recruitment of Chinese and Koreans) and presents a graph depicting the emigration situation of Japanese until the end of the Second World War (see Figure 2.1).

That Japan promoted an offensive emigration policy in order to dismantle social tensions and to obviate potential internal conflicts is also indicated elsewhere with reference to the 'importation' of Chinese and Korean forced labour (Yorimitsu 1989:2f.; Tezuka, 1989a:125). Ishitobi Jin prompts recollection of the revolt of Chinese forced labourers at Hanaoka, and maintains that the current question on Asian migrant workers has a one-hundred-year history in the history of Japan's relationship with Asian countries under conditions of exploration and colonization (including, nowadays, colonization by 'peaceful', that is, economic means) (Ishitobi, 1990:63). Mori Hiromasa, Professor of Economics at Hōsei University, reiterates that the migration of workers is not a 'new problem'. In the 1960s (the period of high economic growth under the 'income doubling plan'), the emerging shortage of labour was compensated for by inland migration; that is, graduates of junior-high and high schools from rural areas were induced to 'migrate' to big cities. And in the 1970s, the first nurses for training programs (*kenshūsei*) were brought to Japan from Korea, Singapore and the Philippines. On 14 March 1967, the first Japanese cabinet resolution was passed decreeing that there was no need for foreign workers. This decree was renewed on 30 January 1973 and 18 June 1976, and cemented the (still current) position of the government that 'guest-workers' were not to be accepted (Mori, 1989:2f.). Through inland migration from neighbouring regions, farmers and agricultural workers were contracted into short-term, wage-earner relations in the manufacturing and construction sector, providing them with a supplementary income (which often-times was essential for their subsistence). Moreover, labour shortages could easily be met with this flexible labour reserve. The term for this seasonal migratory work (which increasingly lost importance) was *dekasegi rōdōsha* (migrant workers), a term appearing again in the recent debate with the addition 'foreigner' (*gaikokujin*) designating irregular workers from Asian countries.

Mori distinguishes three types of foreigners in Japan: *zainichi*-Koreans and Chinese, 'Western' foreigners (from Europe, the

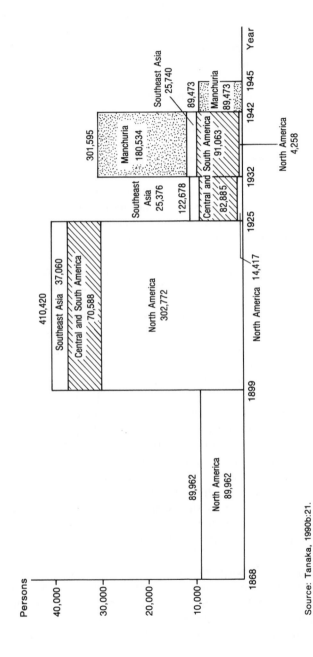

Source: Tanaka, 1990b:21.

Figure 2.1 Overseas emigration of Japanese before World War II

USA, Australia and New Zealand) and Asian workers (mostly 'unskilled' and irregular). The present discussion focuses mainly on the last-mentioned. The proportion of foreigners in the whole population is only approximately 0.8 per cent, and Mori draws attention to the fact that 92 per cent of these foreigners were from Asia and that 72 per cent of these Asian nationals were *zainichi* Koreans (Mori, 1990:62). In a discussion, Professor of Laws Ōnuma brought up the topic of *zainichi* Koreans and met with unanimous approval for his comment that this is a 'problem' which should be resolved with utmost priority before 'new' foreigners are to be accepted (Miyajima, 1987:14ff.). These historical references, however, are somewhat peculiarly interpreted in the debate: on the one hand it is stressed that the influx of irregular workers from Asian countries highlights the history of workers discriminated against in Japan (Tanaka, 1990:95; I A.O., 1990:5). On the other hand, this internal 'foreigner problem' is seen as an exemplary lesson with respect both to the handling of foreigners and to an unsuccessful integration (more correctly, 'assimilation') policy. Transformed into political small change, this means that an official guest-worker policy prior to the solution of the 'Korean question' would be premature; in other words, this serves as counter-argument to the acceptance of foreign workers (cf. statements by the economist Komai Hiroshi in KBR, 1990:34 or Komai, 1990:270).

This 'function as a lesson' was underscored by Ōnuma Yasuaki, Professor of Laws at Tokyo University, in his lecture at a symposium of the Goethe Institute Kyōto (at which I was present, and which I partly interpreted; the written report of the lecture was somewhat toned down, cf. Ōnuma, 1991). In an unusually, trenchant fashion, Professor Ōnuma attacked the whole concept of the symposium (on foreign workers in Germany and Japan). He dubbed it symptomatic of an overall state of consciousness and tradition in Japan in which the West was still to be adored as master. (German scientists were to be viewed as 'teachers', who were to teach the Japanese something about guest-workers and who were to be emulated.) However, the real lesson (the failure [*shippai*] of the assimilation of Koreans) was at hand and evident. The 'admiration of the West' (*ōbei sūhai*) was only the obverse of the 'disdain for Asia' (*Ajia besshi*), a prolonging of the Meiji-era policy of *datsua nyūō* (catching up with and joining the West), with its concomitant severing of Asian traditions (presumably, to avoid poverty and dependence). The discrimination against Asians was founded on the fact that other nations were assessed only according to their material wealth, educational systems and the value of their industrial production. The cultures of the countries surrounding Japan were hardly known. For example, Korean 'equivalents' of Goethe or Beethoven were unknown in Japan. (An analogous remark is made by a renowned ethnologist regarding racism: 'Racial prejudice is neither inherited nor spontaneously acquired; it is nothing but a prejudice, that is, not an objective but a culturally determined judgement of value ... [which] is essentially bound to antagonisms predicated on the economic structure of modern societies' (Leiris, 1985:118).) According to Ōnuma, one should rather become aware of the way in which Korean residents are treated in Japan than stare to the West as if spellbound. This appeal for emancipation from a one-sided 'West-orientation' can also be interpreted as a reflection of the boosted self-consciousness of Japan (as an economic superpower). This self-awareness has two aspects: on the one hand, Japan is perceived as part of Asia, no longer negatively defined in terms of the 'West', but now positively defined, with shared Asian traditions brought to consciousness and re-evaluated. On the other hand, a subliminal nationalism sneaks in, but goes unrecognized.[1]

The problem of Korean residents should be resolved in parallel with that of newly-entering foreigners (Miyajima, 1989:49, who also repeatedly points to the existence of the *zainichi*-Koreans). The still-precarious legal status of *zainichi*-Koreans entered the debate with the proposal that a 'labour permit' (*shūrō shikaku shōmeisho*) be introduced for all legally-admitted foreigners in order to allow employers to see at a glance whether the prospective employee is 'illegal' or not. It was objected that this measure could put permanent Korean residents under pressure to apply for this 'labour permit' too. It would exacerbate discrimination against them on the labour market (see, for example, Lee, 1989:49; see also SBHS, 1989:17). The objection was taken into consideration with respect to the amendment of the Immigration Control Act, inasmuch as acquisition of this 'labour permit' was stipulated to be 'voluntary' (Yamada and Kuroki, 1990:52).

4 Prelude: The *Japayuki* Question

Almost two decades before the immigration of male migrant workers began to be perceived as posing a 'problem', Asian women started coming to Japan (often through targeted recruitment and trafficking) in order to find employment in the so-called 'businesses affecting public morals' (*fūzoku eigyō*), for example, entertaining restaurant customers and sex-related trades. I must be brief and selective in describing the conflicts involved, since this topic is not the theme of this study although it is inseparably connected with it.

The notion *japayuki* is derived from its analogon *karayuki-san*. The latter denoted Japanese prostitutes in foreign countries who were carried off to South East Asian regions and as far as Russia after the 'opening of the country' in the late 19th century. Most of them came from 'poor' islands in Southern Japan (cf. Lenz, 1987; for the situation in Manchuria and Russia see Kurahashi, 1989). Philippino activists demanded that use of the term *japayuki-san* cease, because it has derogatory and discriminatory connotations (*Yomiuri shinbun*, 3 May 1988). However this did not diffuse into public consciousness, and in journalism in particular the term is still used frequently and with nonchalant inconsiderateness. I too shall use the term, but only because of its currency, and with no intention of demeaning those to whom it is applied. Recruitment methods, structural background, and patterns of exploitation of the *karayuki* are shockingly similar to the exploitation of Asian women 'coming to Japan' (the literal translation of *japaykui*). A tradition of sexual exploitation runs through the operations of Japan in foreign countries, and parallels its expansion and imperialism (military as well as economic). During World War II, women, mostly from Korea, were carried off (to China, Manchuria and so forth) to be at the 'disposal' of the army in theatres of war as so-called 'comfort women' (*ianfu*) serving the sexual 'needs' of soldiers. (Cf. Iwai, 1990; for a concise English presentation of the history of Japanese-promoted prostitution in foreign countries up to the sex-tourism of '*Kisaeng*-parties' in

Korea, see Kaji and Inglis, 1974). 'International power relations are expressed by the bodies of women. Prostitutes from poor, subordinated societies migrate in the 19th century into the centres of world trade or colonial economy and in the 20th century into the capitalist metropolises' (Lenz, 1987:69).

After World War II, it was not least the American military bases (for example, in Okinawa and the Philippines) which led to the establishment of 'entertainment areas' with bars, sex-show businesses and brothels. During the Vietnam War, American soldiers were sent to Thailand in ten-thousands for 'recreation'. This promoted and stabilized organised prostitution there, which remains today the focus of sex-tourism. From 1962 to 1967, there were seven major air-bases of the US-army in Thailand. The rest-and-recreation stays of the GIs marked the beginning of mass prostitution (cf. Latzka, 1989:239). The military bases and sex-tourism (from the USA, Europe, Australia, Arab States and Japan) to South East Asia (main targets: Thailand and the Philippines and, in the case of Japan, also South Korea) led to the existence of a 'recruitment pool of women prepared for mobility', whose majority had already experienced inland migration by being trafficked from country to urban areas for the urban sex-trade. They then sometimes become the object of recruitment to move them to foreign countries.

In the red light district of Manila, Ermita, an estimated 2,000 nightclubs, *kyabarê* (nightclubs mostly with strip-tease shows), disco-bars and Japanese restaurants exist in which roughly 10,000 women are said to be employed. Several dozens of the establishments are said to be under the control, if not the direct management, of big Yakuza-syndicates (Yamaguchi-gumi, Sumiyoshi-kai, Inagawa-kai). They channel women via the so-called 'Manila-connection' to Japan through *geinō–purodakushon* ('artists agencies'). The women are usually lured to Japan with worthless promises of jobs as dancers, singers or waitresses, and subsequently are often forced into prostitution (Yamatani, 1988:129ff.). In Ermita, there are several *karaoke*-bars in which sentimental Japanese tunes can be sung to background music. In these bars, Philippinas with work-experience in Japan or with the wish to go to Japan are often employed. It is said that it is relatively easy to recruit and 'dispatch' these women to Japan, and a considerable number of them are brought to Japan professionally by non-Yakuza (Ishiyama, 1989:154ff.; on the Bangkok counterpart of Ermita, the red-light district, Thaniya, where an exclusively Japanese clientele is served, see Hinago, 1989:147).

The women are channelled into Japan through use of a diverse range of visa categories. The most common method is to provide them with a tourist visa and 'show-money', hotel leaflets and the like, to underscore their tourist status at the Immigration Control. A *kōgyō–biza* ('entertainer' visa) is usually limited to sixty days and, in the case of the Philippines, is linked to an officially-issued 'artists permit' allowing work, for example as a dancer or musician. But virtually all of these women end up having to work as so-called 'hostesses', which is 'illegal' (that is, 'engagement in activities other than specified', *shikakugai katsudō*) and many also exceed the allowed period of stay ('overstay'). A visa obtained as the spouse of a Japanese national lifts all of the restrictions on gainful employment, and arranged 'fake-marriages' (*gisō kekkon*) are often organized. The acquisition of a 'student's visa' provides a semi-legal status, that is, the stay is legal but work is legally permitted only for up to twenty hours a week. The women coming to Japan usually have to pay high commissions for the necessary formalities, documents and travel expenses, and are forced to hand over monthly a portion of their wages to their agents or go-betweens (Matsuda, 1990:30f.).

With regard to the social profile of victimized women in Japan, it is noted that up to 70 percent are eldest daughters in poor families, who, out of 'sentiments of (filial) piety' support their parents and provide for the education of their siblings by their remittances (cf. case studies by Matsuda, 1990 and Sawahata, 1989:22–24; see also Yamatani, 1988:139, who points to the analogous situation of the *karayuki*). Quite often, these women are divorced, or are single with illegitimate children. In the rigid social context of their countries of origin (for example, the Philippines with its dogmatic-Catholic tradition), they are relegated to a marginal position with only slight chances of re-marriage (cf. Yamatani, 1988:159f.).

The backdrop of this coerced prostitution is not only poverty, but the generally restrictive labour market in Japan in which foreign women face a double disadvantage – as women and as foreigners. As long as they have no opportunity to obtain alternative, 'decent' work, the precarious situation of these women cannot be altered (Matsuda, 1990:41; Takeoka, 1990:1455; cf. Miyajima, who in this context calls for a vision that does not disconnect the problem of the 'hostesses' from that of male foreign workers: KBR, 1990:26). In this society, criminal prosecution through enforcement of the Anti-Prostitution Law (*baishun bōshihō*, proscribing abetment of prostitution, wooing of customers etc.) is very loose. Usually the foreign women, whose human rights have been violated and who are the actual victims, are simply deported; their recruiting agents or employers are not prosecuted or tried (Takeoka, 1990:139ff.).

The Philippines has the longest tradition of dispatching women to Japan. For more than twenty years women have been able to acquire qualification as 'artists' by attending 'auditions' established for this purpose, and in this way obtain relatively easily a *kōgyō*-visa for Japan. Roughly 90,000 Philippinas are reported to be proprietors of those 'artist qualification cards' (popularly called 'PECC-cards', the abbreviation is not explained). This card qualifies them to enter Japan and earn money there. In 1986, 60 percent of all the 'entertainer-visas' for Japan were granted to Philippinas (most qualifying as 'dancers', in contrast to Westerners with entertainer-visas, who are mostly sportspeople or musicians, cf. Ishiyama, 1989:78f.). The official statistics show a recent rise in the number of *kōgyō*-visas particularly for Philippine nationals (see Table 4.1).

Amongst the 'illegals', women face the worst exploitation, because they are not only exploited as labour but also are treated as objects and forced to sell their bodies (KBR, 1990:11). A host of 'loser-stories', life catastrophes and cases of crude exploitation are found in the literature. Even before the onset of 'irregular' migration of male foreign workers, the sad destiny and public scandal of the *japayuki-san* had been taken up by the media and

Table 4.1 New entries of persons in entertainment ('Old' visa status: 4–1–9)

	1982	1984	1986	1988
Philippines	9,103	11,941	25,996	41,357
Korea	2,691	7,091	375	994
China	1,554	1,563	3,021	3,105
USA	4,591	4,741	5,610	8,107
England	1,197	1,730	2,170	3,056
Others	4,708	5,886	7,817	14,407
Total	23,844	32,952	44,989	71,026

NTK, 1990: 53.

books. The series *Takarajima bessatsu* – always reacting quickly and sensitively to current events and to phenomena at the margins of society – published in 1986 the first edition of an anthology of reports on *japayuki-san*. The quality and content of the articles varied considerably, which is quite usual for this series, ranging from male fantasy to serious advocacy of the human rights of Asian women. The book offers an array of data (Ishii, 1989, chronology and data appendix: 273–86). Also in 1986, a shelter for victimized Asian women was founded in Tokyo by a Christian Women's Organization called HELP (House in the Emergency of Love and Peace). The organization's account of its activities is filled with the stories of victims (Ōshima and Francis, 1988). Two examples follow below.

In the first, a Philippine female agent promised a young woman a job as a receptionist for six months at a monthly salary of 100,000 yen (one month's pay was to be deducted for the airline ticket). In July 1987 the recruited 18–year-old Philippina came to Japan. After waiting for days in an apartment in Chiba prefecture, she was brought to Nagoya with another two women. On the second day after beginning work, she was forced into prostitution. Her first customer paid 30,000 yen. She was told that one-third of this fee would be given to her on her return to the Philippines. She could keep only the money given to her as tips and used all of this in her escape to Tokyo.

In the second case, a 19–year-old Thai woman entered Japan with a tourist visa, lured by the offer of a job in a jeweller's shop. On arrival, her passport was confiscated by two Japanese people speaking some rudimentary Thai. She had to share an apartment with thirteen other Thai women, and was compelled to work as a hostess in Tokyo Kabukichō. She was always accompanied (that is, controlled), on her way to work. She was told she must repay an alleged debt of 300,000 yen, which she could do only by taking customers. Her earnings from coerced prostitution were taken by her 'employer' who claimed that her debts were not yet discharged. All of her expenses (food, taxi, health examination, etc.) were added to her 'debts'. She tried several times to escape, without success (KBR, 1990:63–5).

The women are reported to be sold from their home countries by indigenous recruiting agents to Japanese 'promoters', for sums of between 300,000 and one million yen. The mediating promoters are said to bag another 200,000 to 300,000 yen per month from the 'pubs' and 'snackbars' where the women are employed. In order to earn (for their employers) amounts of this order, the women's lives are totally controlled by their employers, who force them into prostitution by exploiting their powerlessness as 'illegals' (Umetani, 1989:92; sources of data not specified). Here one can legitimately speak of a slave-trade.

The official reaction to this state of affairs was a revision of the regulations concerning *kōgyō*-visas which came into force on 1 July 1988 (Tezuka, 1989a:132). The new stipulations apply to employers. The issuing of a licence for the employment of dancers and singers was made dependent on the turnover (measured by the value of beverage tax paid) and the surface area of the establishment (Ishiyama, 1989:82). Support organizations fighting for the human rights of Asian migrant workers fear that the tightening of controls on legal entry by *kōgyō*-visa only increases the powerlessness of women trafficked underground and thereby boosts the profit margin of Yakuza and mediators (KNK, 1988:20). I was told, indeed proudly, by a low-ranking Yakuza, a member of the Yamaguchi-gumi, that in his gang a Portuguese national is active – a symbol of 'internationalization' and a potential bridge to Latin America. His (small) organization, he said, is not a recruiter of foreign labour or women, but he somewhat jestingly added that recently Yakuza were eager to study Spanish and Portuguese in order to recruit people from Latin America. Columbia is infamous not only for its cocaine, but also for its extensive prostitution subculture. At the port of entry women from Columbia can be camouflaged as tourists more easily than can, for example, Thais or Philippinas, who already are the object of a generalized suspicion by the immigration authorities. Yakuza, he said, had long been operating in South America in co-operation with the Colombian syndicates, and had been 'recruiting' and trafficking women for work in Japan (personal information in Osaka, 20 July 1990). Official data on 'exposed' female labour migrants supports the accuracy of this assertion. The number of deported Colombian women, who had mainly been employed as strippers, is indeed higher for the 1980s, when approximately forty to eighty Colombian nationals were expelled every year, the figure for 1987 being thirty-two women, twenty-seven of whom were active in strip-tease shows (Ishiyama, 1989:206ff.).

Loree Pimentel, a Philippine activist for an Osaka-based organization, Asian Friends, for the support and human rights of migrant workers, told me in the summer of 1990 that since conditions for a *kōgyō*-visa were toughened Philippinas increasingly attempted to enter Japan with student-visas (a similar note in Hinago, 1990a:88). Data regarding new entries as *shūgakusei* corroborate this trend: the number of *shūgaku*-visas for Philippine nationals almost doubled from 741 in 1987 to 1,349 in 1988 (Shibuya, 1990:231). These facts are symptomatic of side-effects of the new statutory regulations. The effects of enforcement of the revised law are neutralized by displacements, new strategies, more refined evasive manoeuvres and alternative routes of access to Japan.

The focus of interest of authorities and the mass media shifted from female to male migrants following release of the first statistics, which were interpreted as revealing a 'dramatic' rise in male 'illegal' workers, their number exceeding that of female 'exposed' migrants (see, for example, HNK, 1989:39). By this shift of attention, the persisting exploitation and quandary of Asian women in Japan was lost sight of. However, the relegation of Asian women to the status of 'goods' and 'objects' is periodically topical: firstly in the context of AIDS-panics, in which *japayuki* who contract the virus, serve as scapegoats; and secondly in connection with a situation diagnosed as 'lack of brides' (*hanayome busoku*) in rural and peripheral areas of Japan, which leads leading to the 'importation' of Asian candidates for marriage.

AIDS-panics, as a rule, are limited to certain periods and locales, but AIDS, because of its closeness to taboo themes provokes strong reactions. These, through the entrenched and virulent presumption that AIDS is a disease 'imported' from foreign countries (*gaibyō*) are linked with latent xenophobic tendencies. Already in 1984, in Nagano prefecture, a rumour had arisen that one could become infected with venereal diseases by swimming in pools frequented by South East Asian women. This was branded a 'mass hysteria', which led to the rapid spread of the rumour. A massive information campaign by the press confined this phenomenon to a single summer (Ueda, 1987:232–237; more information on AIDS panics from 1986 to the summer of 1987 in Domenig, 1991:510ff.). In periodic media reports, figures concerning the number of HIV-positive people in Japan are usually paired with comments on the 'rapidly rising number' of AIDS-infected foreign Asian women (see, for example, *Asahi shinbun*, 28 November 1990). In particular cases also, an HIV-positive diagnoses of Asian 'prostitutes' are featured in the press (see, for example, *Kanagawa shinbun*, 18 November 1990).[1]

4.1 'Lack of Brides'

Concerning the marriage of South East Asian women to Japanese men, it is claimed that the 'migration goal' of Philippinas, for example, is often to find a wealthy Japanese partner during their activities in the 'services' (Hisada, 1990:72). Since 1987, around thirty applications a day are reported to be lodged in the Japanese Embassy in the Philippines by those who seek a visa as the spouse of a Japanese national (*haigūsha-biza*), and in Manila, specialized marriage-agencies have been set up. Between 1986 and 1988, the number of issued *haigūsha*-visas (spouse visas) is said to have risen roughly by 3,000 a year (Hisada, 1990:76 and 79). This is supported by official statistics. (See Table 4.2. The increase for Philippine nationals is conspicuous, although only new spouse-visas are recorded.)

Tezuka maintains that the pattern of so-called 'international marriages' has reversed since the mid-1980s. Previously, in approximately 70 percent of cases a Japanese woman married an American man. Now, in 60 per cent of these marriages Japanese men wed Asian women (Tezuka, 1989a:71f.). Tezuka remarks on

Table 4.2 New entries with spouse visa ('Old' visa status: 4–1–16–1)

	1982	1984	1986	1988
China	627	825	758	993
Korea	622	728	502	502
USA	452	525	469	441
Philippines	213	268	233	2,009
England	108	98	91	86
Brazil	88	101	84	503
Thailand	70	96	94	213
France	40	42	31	51
Germany (West)	51	51	29	25
Canada	35	30	20	28
Others	440	479	393	597
Total	2,746	3,243	2,704	5,448

NTK, 1990: 64.

the basic trend of those 'international marriages' in regions of Japan dominated by agriculture: the prospective wives are 'in demand' as additional helping hands in family-owned agricultural businesses, or as part-time-workers in small enterprises in the production sector. An increase in divorces will, in the future, reveal the 'inhumane', real face of this 'bride-trade'. Most of these marriages are arranged by go-betweens – quite often with the consent and official assistance of the local administration. To conclude such a 'deal' requires an investment of approximately two million yen (Tezuka, 1989a:105f.; similar sums are cited in Fukuzawa, 1990:60, and in an advertising pamphlet for marriage with a Philippina in Higurashi, 1989:290, and in Satō, 1988:257; the latter is a good introduction in English into the problem and is rich in data). A scandalously brief period separates the first arranged meeting (*miai*) – possibly a group meeting of several pairs of prospective partners – and the wedding. The prospective husbands may have various unfavorable attributes or circumstances (for example, they may be of low-class profession, be from a labour-intensive agricultural household, be middle-aged or elderly, be divorced, or be physically handicapped). Commission fees are high, and pressure is put on the women to adapt to Japanese society (often in extremely conservative social settings). Foreign brides commonly are given Japanese names and, in the end, may find that their function is only to secure the survival of the family by bearing children (Fukuzawa, 1990:60ff.).

Organized group-*miai* (arranged meetings) in the countries of origin of prospective brides are paralleled by the mass-recruitment of 'trainees' (*kenshūsei*) for work in Japan in small factories, who, during this time, are 'examined' by Japanese candidates for marriage (this examination again being mediated by male and female matrimonial agents). In this way, for example, young women were brought from Sri Lanka to Nagano prefecture in order to serve as cheap labour and as a pool of prospective brides (cf. Nozaka, 1990:31).

Even in a book written with optimism and good-will, for example, Higurashi (1989), these women are 'commodified'. The author does not realize his latent chauvinism. In this publication, the foreign marriage-market is described, and Asian brides are extolled, in professional advertising style. At a number of places in the work, sexist, reactionary, and patriarchal values are evinced in the author's comments. For examples, concerning Sri

Lankan women brought to Japan for a *miai*-party, it is noted that it is rather difficult to arrange marriages for them because of their dark skin-colour. On the other hand, they are praised for being chaste and retaining traditional virtues (for example, showing piety towards their parents; Higurashi, 1989:48 and 224). No critique is made of the conditions laid down for prospective Philippina brides: high-school-graduation; knowledge of English; no experience of foreign countries; neither command of Japanese nor working experience in Manila (to exclude prostitutes); middle-class-background; good manners; aged 18 to 25 (particularly able to adapt and quickly grasp Japanese); no chronic illnesses; no veneral disease; no need to send money to relatives back home (cf. Higurashi, 1989:179f.).

The expectations of the prospective husband and prospective wife may be very different. The potential husband (and his family) await a ready-to-help wife, who will take care of the fields, house, children and parents-in-law. The women, on the other hand, often have illusions about the 'rich' Japan, and are often disappointed to find themselves living in a backward rural area instead of a vital and luxurious metropolis. Moreover, the linguistic barrier militates against the formation of real partnerships transcending the merely formal and functional aspects of marriage and (traditional) role ascriptions to women. Entering a marriage of this kind is like 'gambling' (Fukuzawa, 1990:68).[2]

4.2 Fictitious Marriages

The related topic of fictitious marriages, which is also to be found in the mass media, I can touch upon here only through some examples. Again and again, cases of (organized) 'camouflaged marriages' (*gisō kekkon*) are uncovered, and find their way into media crime reports. Since a marriage with a Japanese national permits one to take any sort of gainful employment, foreign 'hostesses' in Japan may be persuaded to undergo mock-marriage. They have to pay high commissions to the professional agents (called *yobiya* in the argot) who often recruit them in their countries of origin and transfer them to Japan with a 'visa as a spouse of a Japanese national'. In a spectacular case, a former official of the

Immigration Control Bureau received two million yen from Korean 'hostesses' for a pseudo-marriage. The Japanese involved received one million yen for offering their family register in which the women are recorded.

For the press, only trends which can be dramatized – aggravations, increases, augmentations or worsening tendencies, and the like – are of real news value. Its comments therefore inevitably state that perpetrations of this kind are on the rise and staged with increasing deftness (*Tōkyō shinbun*, 8 August 1990). In a popular magazine this topic made giant headlines (4 x 17 cm for six characters: *gisō kekkon kyūzō* – 'rapid increase in dummy-marriages') and was reported loudly. In the metropolitan area alone, around 200 'hostesses' are alleged to be married on paper only, and organized gangsters have entered the mock-marriage business. Operating according to the principle of labour division, around twenty gang members (called *koe kakeya*) are said to be searching for potential Japanese 'partners' (the sums of money involved are the same as mentioned above; cf. *Nikkan supōtsu shinbun*, 12 November 1990). In an investigation concerning a Taiwanese go-between, fictitious marriages between Korean and Taiwanese 'hostesses' and Japanese men are reported (the latter again were paid off with 'compensation' of one million yen). This Taiwanese agent is said to have arranged around 100 mock marriages (*Mainichi shinbun*, 30 November 1990).

There are many reports of this kind. I did not delve into this 'current media event' systematically; however, the above examples may suffice. Here we have a sort of 'criminality' in the shadow of a situation created by a law that strictly limits legal access to gainful employment. 'Legalization' by fictitious marriage, however, only abets the profiteering of brokers and mediators, and doubles the exploitation of women (that is, burdens them with high debts and forces them into *de-facto*-prostitution).

It is thanks to committed journalists and women's organizations that the human rights violations against foreign Asian women in Japan have become well known. However, at the end of the 1980s, the increased 'irregular' immigration of male migrant workers slipped into this discursively-opened forefront. Male 'illegals' began to be perceived as the 'actual' problem and to attract public attention. This was not least because politicians saw themselves challenged to take a clear stand with regard to whether or not a 'regular' guest-worker policy should be implemented to relieve the shortage of labour complained of in some sectors. In this shift of focus, the scandal of continuing sexual exploitation of Asian women became a discursive aside.

5 The Early Stage of a Process of Irregular Migration: The Increase in Male 'Illegal' Workers

Since the middle of the 1980s, the increasing number of 'male *japayuki*' (*japaykui-kun*: see, for example, KKSK, 1989:32) became conspicuous. A frequently quoted indicator of this are yearly figures for the 'uncovered' (or rather, recorded) 'illegals' of the Immigration Control Bureau (*shutsunyūkoku kanrikyoku*, abbreviated as: *nyūkan*). In 1986, 27 per cent of all the 'temporary immigrants' entering Japan were males with tourist visas ('working tourists'), a more than three-fold increase over the previous year. In consequence, 38 per cent of the 11,307 'exposed' illegals in the following year were male (Gonoi, 1989:111). In 1988, males outnumbered females in these figures for the first time (8,929 of the 14,314 detected 'illegals' were male). In 1990, male 'working tourists' exposed or expelled comprised roughly 80 per cent of the 29,884 foreigners gainfully employed without an appropriate visa (the overall rate of increase to the previous year also was around 80 per cent, cf. Hoizumi, 1991:7). These official data are those most often cited in reference to irregular immigration to Japan. They do mirror a 'real trend', typically captioned with such a description as 'enormous increase in male illegals', but nonetheless require interpretation. The present study mostly covers for the discussion up to 1990, so the data available to that year are our primary concern. It was precisely the reversal in gender-pattern which received special attention, for example in the sex-related graphs which were now, for the first time, produced and reproduced. In almost every publication on the subject, one can find graphic illustrations similar to the following (figs 5.1 and 5.2):

These figures are arrived at by aggregating data; they reveal some notable gender-related differences. Female migrants 'established' in the services (that is, victims of trafficking for more than two decades) from 'traditional' countries such as Thailand or the Philippines, still outnumber men from these countries, whereas in the case of Iranians, for example, migration is almost exclusively

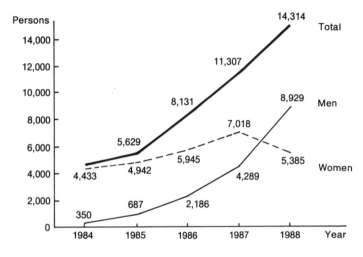

Source: Toshiro, 1989a:101.

Figure 5.1 'Exposed' cases of 'illegal labour offences'

male (data based on estimates of the Immigration Control Bureau, cf. Table 5.1 from *Ampo*, *23*, April (1992), 23).

Although the data appear to substantiate the postulated trend of an increase in the number of male working tourists, I would advise caution in interpreting these figures. Reflecting the control and recording activities of the agencies involved (mainly the Immigration Control Bureau and subordinately the police), they do show that more men than women are registered. This can be read, and typically is read, as showing a real shift in international migration; but may also be the result of a shift in focus. The attention of the agencies of control and of the mass media – both influencing the political discussion (through a process of cyclical and reciprocal reinforcement) – switched to the phenomenon of the existence of male 'illegal' labourers. Attention focuses selectively on male migrant workers, who thereby show up more frequently in the statistics of 'detected illegals'. Other data – for example, number of entries, number of prohibited entries, number of issued visas – are not collated by gender in the publicly released figures. A precise assessment of the effect of public attention therefore is not possible; but the phenomenon nonetheless warrants consideration.

A very similar web of effects can be claimed to influence the

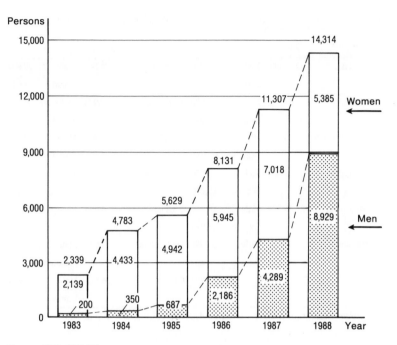

Source: KBR 1990:187.

Figure 5.2 Gender-based distribution of illegal labourers in transition

data specifying nationalities. At the end of the 1980s, the 'rapid rise' in the (recorded) numbers of men from Pakistan and Bangladesh was dramatized – again by reference exclusively to the information on 'uncovered illegals'. Here too it should be noted that this rise could be an artefact caused by the variable of 'visibility' (see Figures 5.3 and 5.4).

Particularly with regard to official crackdowns (elaborated in section 5.1), men from these two countries gain more attention than do, for example, men from China or Korea, due to their distinguishability from Japanese. Analysis of data on entry of Asians corroborates the scepticism expressed above (see Table 5.2). The steep fall in the number of entries of Pakistanis (19,106 in 1988 to 5,938 in 1989) and Bangladeshis (13,994 in 1988 to 2,742 in 1989) and the subsequently low number of entries in 1990 (the effect of the re-imposition of visa-obligations for citizens of those nations) does *not* correlate with a decrease in the number of 'exposed'. The temporary cancellation of visa-exemption (*sashō*

Table 5.1 Estimated numbers of illegal migrants (Nov. 1991)

Nationality	Total			Nationality	Total		
TOTAL	216,399	Male	145,700	Chinese	21,649	Male	16,624
		Female	70,699			Female	5,025
Thai	32,751	Male	13,780	Pakistani	7,923	Male	7,786
		Female	18,971			Female	137
South Korean	30,976	Male	20,469	Bangladeshi	7,807	Male	7,725
		Female	10,507			Female	82
Philippine	29,620	Male	13,850	Taiwanese	5,897	Male	2,790
		Female	15,770			Female	3,107
Malaysian	25,379	Male	18,466	Burmese	3,425	Male	2,712
		Female	6,913			Female	713
Iranian	21,719	Male	21,114	Sri Lankan	2,837	Male	2,618
		Female	605			Female	219
				Others	26,416	Male	17,766
						Female	8,650

Source: Immigration Office, cited in *AMPO*, Vol. 23, No. 4, p. 23.

menjo sochi no ichiji teishi) was explained by the Ministry of Foreign Affairs as being due to the recent 'rapidly rising' incidence of 'misuse' of free-entry provisions for tourists with passports by those whose object was to work 'illegally' (to evidence this, the numbers of 'detected illegals' from these two countries are quoted, that is, politically valorized and given legitimatory currency). In January 1989, legislation was enacted requiring Pakistani and Bangladeshi nationals to obtain visas (see, for example, *Mainichi shinbun*, 27 November 1988).

Moreover, the data released at the end of each year are simply aggregated, and thus obscure certain facts. Firstly, the number of 'detected' irregular migrant workers covers not only those who were 'actively tracked down' by the authorities, but also migrants who have turned themselves in (not necessarily freely) in order that formalities for their departure (or more precisely, their deportation) be instituted. Secondly, increased activity by police and immigration officials led to peak figures for the months of concerted action. These peaks are levelled through aggregation and do not show in the total.

The amendment of the Immigration Control Act came into

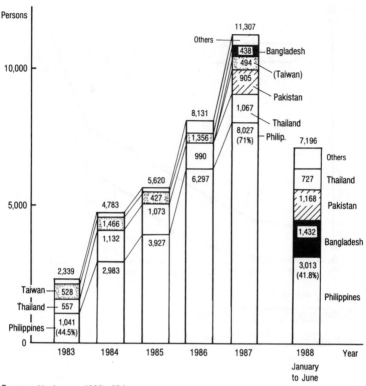

Source: Narizawa, 1990a:234.

Figure 5.3 Changes in the number of 'exposed' cases of illegally working foreigners

force on 1 June 1990 and was equipped with new provisions for punishment (up to three years imprisonment or a fine of two million yen) of employers of 'illegal' workers (the workers themselves were already subject to sanctions prior to the amendment). In the months before enactment of the revised *nyūkanhō*, the legislation was discussed in the media. The Japanese newspapers published in English, in particular, over-emphasized the new sanctions. Movements for the support and human rights of migrants maintained that this emphasis amounted to intentional misinformation and biased propaganda (allegedly steered by the Ministry of Justice). A 'departure panic' (as it was termed by the press) ensued. At first hundreds, then (from the middle of May) thousands, of 'illegals' went to the Immigration Control Bureau in

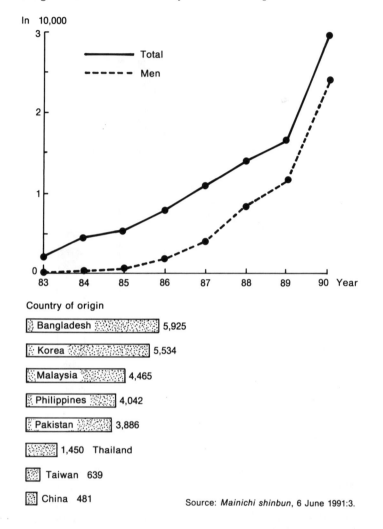

In 10,000

— Total
------ Men

Country of origin

Bangladesh 5,925

Korea 5,534

Malaysia 4,465

Philippines 4,042

Pakistan 3,886

1,450 Thailand

Taiwan 639

China 481

Source: *Mainichi shinbun*, 6 June 1991:3.

Figure 5.4 Further increases in the number of 'exposed' cases of illegal foreign labourers

Tokyo to prepare for their return. On 28 May 1990 alone, 1,500 'illegal' foreigners gave themselves up to the immigration authorities in Tokyo to undergo expulsion procedures (*Asahi shinbun*, 29 May 1990). This was not only because they were afraid that they would be punished from June onwards, but also because many employers of irregular migrant workers, anxious to avoid the new

Table 5.2 New entries from Asia

	1986	1987	1988	1989	1990
Korea	132,604	158,625	270,226	524,072	675,956
Taiwan	279,901	318,122	343,525	449,608	557,631
Philippines	74,594	76,956	73,497	69,567	84,327
China	48,413	56,469	87,264	64,251	74,264
Thailand	28,182	31,163	38,484	44,546	64,313
Malaysia	44,341	38,601	43,726	51,653	54,849
Singapore	33,206	34,981	33,977	36,802	41,910
Hong Kong	31,126	28,749	27,089	29,860	36,481
Iran	15,904	19,818	14,090	16,282	31,289
Indonesia	30,663	23,257	20,197	24,706	30,947
India	17,170	17,805	18,192	17,654	16,724
Pakistan	12,881	11,605	19,106	5,938	4,293
Bangladesh	4,214	5,660	13,994	2,742	2,427

Mainichi shinbun, 25 January 1992: 3.

penalties, dismissed the 'illegals'. The number of 'exposed' illegals for the year 1990 is accordingly high. (It is reported that for the year 1989, 70 per cent of 'detected illegals' sent home were migrants who turned themselves in to the control agencies, *Asahi shinbun*, 23 April 1990.) On 1 June 1990, this departure panic was addressed by the socialist representative Chiba Keiko in the Lower House. The Ministry of Justice – in a way, conceding its 'complicity' – then gave a statement in which it regretted having triggered off a 'departure panic' due to deficient public relations (Hirano, 1990:28). The amendment itself had included a clause stipulating that penalties would not be applied retrospectively to employers who employed 'illegals' before the amendment came into force. Support organizations for migrants issued multilingual information fliers with the aim of informing employers and the 'illegally' employed of this provision. (At this time I wrote an English version for the Osaka-based organization Asian Friends.) Activists claimed that this information campaign actually should have been launched by the Ministry of Justice itself, and that its failure to do so was negligent.

Despite this criticism, the Ministry of Justice initiated a campaign in 1992 which continued its policy. Large advertisements were placed in the *Japan Times* (see, for example, 23 March 1992) which again emphasized the threat of punishment. I include below the full text of one such advertisement, which was labelled 'Official Bulletin: Ministry of Justice', and printed both in English and in

Japanese. It reveals with amazing bluntness the official (Justice-Ministry) attitude. Beside a large photograph showing (what is presumably) the crowded Narita/Tokyo international airport, and under the bold headline, 'Can you spot the illegal worker?' the following text appears:

> A Japanese visa is not an invitation to work illegally.
>
> Japan welcomes more and more visitors every year, a trend we are happy to see. However there is, unhappily, a growing problem: the increasing number of people who come to Japan and work illegally, presenting a potential for social disruption.
>
> For visitors to work in Japan, the correct status of residence is necessary. Violation of the law is cause for deportation, or even criminal punishment. Employers of workers without the correct status or permission to work, or those who refer such visitors for jobs, also face severe legal penalties: up to three years of penal servitude or a fine not exceeding 2,000,000 yen.
>
> Illegal workers are exposed to exploitation by unscrupulous employers. There have been cases where they were forced to work under hard conditions with inadequate insurance coverage for work-related accidents.
>
> Although the question of foreign workers will continue to be studied in depth, preservation of social order is of the essence. So for their own protection, too, it is vital for all of us to prevent visitors working illegally.
>
> If you have any questions, please contact your local Regional Immigration Bureau. (Cited in the Bulletin of the organization Karabao no kai, *Kalabaw, 38*, 20 April 1992, 7–8.)

Noteworthy here are the nervously oversensitive references to a 'potential for social disruption' (*shakai no bunretsu*) and to the necessity for the preservation of social order (*shakai chitsujo no iji*), also the threat of deportation and criminal punishment, and the appeal for the prevention of 'illegal' work – with the expression 'for all of us' (*subete no hitobito*) suggesting a fictive solidarity of the addressees, and with the humane-sounding phrase 'for their own protection' camouflaging its denunciation of illegal workers. Given this over-emphasis on prevention and deterrence, the references to potential exploitation and work-related accidents sound menacing rather than well-intentioned. Moreover, it is implied that 'illegal' workers are a (potential) threat to the whole of society and its stable order. This is a supposition which appears particularly in the context of the debate on 'public (in)security and criminality'. It arouses apprehensions which have no basis in reality and furthers the view that reductionalistically perceives foreign workers only as 'factors' disturbing society. The interest of the Justice Ministry bureaucrats in repression and prevention is plainly revealed here, an approach leading only to intervention, prosecution and virtual criminalization of migrants (who are already labelled 'illegal' in the headlines) before they actually come into conflict with the law.

5.1 Official Crack-downs on 'Illegal' Workers

In the literature and press one finds frequent reports on so-called 'months of concerted action'. These crack-downs on 'illegals' are periodically proclaimed by police and the Immigration Control Bureau. I want to describe these attempts to 'seize' irregular migrants by referring to the reports. The crackdowns in fact are simply interruptions to the *laissez-faire* routine of the agencies of social control, their symbolic function being to declare that effective and sustained measures preventing 'illegal stay and illegal labour' are in place, when in reality the provisions for control are permanently circumvented.

In November 1986, for example, the Immigration authority in Nagoya launched an intensive audit of apartments (*manshon*) rented on a one-month contract-basis and known to be occupied by many Philippine nationals. Thirty-three 'illegal' persons from the Philippines were arrested. At the end of that month, officials also placed telephone booths with international call facilities under surveillance, and took a further nine Philippinos into custody after ordering them to show their passports (Ishiyama, 1989,16f.).

A smaller offensive is reported from Saitama prefecture in November/December 1987. Small firms in the production sector (bookbinderies, foundries, steel mills, vehicle parts manufacturers) were targeted, and more than one hundred 'illegal' workers were apprehended and repatriated (Sawahata, 1989:66–72).

In January 1988, the Prefectural Police Agency in Saitama staged a wide-ranging crack-down. The city of Kawaguchi, famous for the furnaces of its metal foundries, also was a target region, and many Bangladeshi and Pakistani people were arrested. Kawaguchi was well known also for having sought to use 'illegal' migrants to alleviate its labour shortage (cf. Hwang, 1990:15). It is said that an internal instruction of the Prefectural Police Office of Saitama required that every *japayuki-san* and *japayuki-kun* be regarded as 'staying illegally' (Watanabe and Okinawa, 1990:43). This amounts to an order that any such 'strange' foreigners be treated with suspicion and that their activities be kept under control. Relatedly, a police-linked study stated that police officers should become aware of the effectiveness of ex-officio questioning (*shokumu shitsumon*) of suspicious (*fushin*) foreigners. Effective check-ups should be made use of (so advises the police scientist Mishima Tetsu in the May issue of the police magazine *Keisatsu jihō*, with respect also to crimes other than visa offences, quoted in Takahashi, 1990:86f.; a statement such as this is nothing more than an encouragement of stop-and-search procedures against 'illegal' migrant workers).

In May 1988, a 'special month for the exposure of illegal foreign workers' (*gaikokujin fuhō shūrōsha tekihatsu tokubetsu gekkan*) was proclaimed by the Immigration Control Office, during which 1,371 persons were exposed. Of these, 698 were of Bangladeshi, 466 of Pakistani and 148 of Philippine origin. These three nationalities comprised 96 per cent of all apprehended. Ninety-eight per cent (1,346) of the 'detected' were men, roughly 55 per cent of whom were employed in small firms in the production sector and around 15 per cent in the construction business (Mori, 1989:4f.; the above-cited figures are of 'exposures' in Tokyo; altogether 1,870 'illegals' were apprehended throughout the country, these apprehensions being celebrated in press 'success stories', cf. *Hokkaidō shinbun, Asahi shinbun* or *Yomiuri shinbun*, 6 June 1988). The reports on this operation clearly support my thesis of selectivity concerning nationality and gender. During these concerted actions, regions where foreigners live in concentration were sought out and searched. Officials of the Immigration Control Office (sometimes supported by police) broke into 'suspicious' apartments and examined the passports of foreigners brought in.

Another method consisted of posting officials for 'passport control' at stations of the JR (Japan Railways) frequented by foreigners living in the neighbourhood. In the operation reported above, control activities were mounted at 200 strategic points – with a distinct concentration on male workers. Pakistanis and Bangladeshis, by virtue of their appearance are simply more 'eye-catching' and thus more likely to be questioned. (Subsequently, at the start of 1989, it was declared that the visa-exemption for those two nationalities was to be rescinded, because of the spread of 'illegal' work!) The journalist Ishiyama, from whose book the above descriptions and data are obtained quotes a high official of the Immigration Control Bureau as saying after the action: 'We have arrived at the assessment that – had we only the means and personnel – [a complete exposure of all illegals] would be possible'. Ishiyama plausibly speculates that the above action was an experiment to determine how effective concerted, proactive control activities would be (also noting that in a 'case of emergency' claims for increases in budget and staff could be underscored with 'hard facts' – the inflated data of exposures, cf. Ishiyama, 1989:232f.).

In June (Gonoi, 1989:113) and October 1988, a regional (Tokyo and its periphery) and two national campaigns of exposure followed. In October the Immigration Control officials targeted residential areas and small enterprises, and 'detected' 959 'illegals' (over 80 per cent of them male). A new development was the claim that the number of Korean migrants was on the rise (there was a liberalized departure policy for Koreans, many of whom had relatives in Japan), that the regional and occupational dispersion of migrants had increased (*Kanagawa shinbun*, 19 December 1988). In April 1989 in Tokyo and Osaka, a special Immigration Control Bureau taskforce for the exposure of 'illegals' (*tokubetsu tekihatsu kidōhan*) was founded, and special funds from the state budget were made available that year for measures for the exposure of 'illegal' workers and for personnel and infrastructure increases in the Immigration Control Agencies. In the following year, further increases were made (KBR, 1990:129f.). These measures clearly support my earlier assertion that legitimation is procured via repression. It also shows that official policy was for a tougher line to be taken and actions against 'illegal' workers.

From 29 May to 17 June, a further action was initiated under the slogan 'period of [intensified] efforts for exposure of illegal work' (*fuhō shūrō jihan tekihatsu doryoku kikan*). There were crack-downs at 451 locations (enterprises, apartments, etc.), and 2,705 'illegal' foreigners were rounded up. Of these, 749 were Bangladeshi (including only three females), 664 Pakistani (only one woman), 422 Koreans (63 women), 360 were from the Philippines (nearly half of whom – 177 – were women), with the remainder, less than one hundred persons, comprised of Malaysians, Thais, Chinese, Taiwanese, citizens of Hong Kong, Indians, Ghanese and Nigerians. More than a third of those 'exposed' were between 25 and 30 years old. 92.2 per cent of those apprehended were gainfully employed, and 83.6 per cent had exceeded their legally-permitted period of stay (*fuhō zanryū*). Only slightly more than 1 per cent had entered the country illegally (data from Shibuya, 1990:226ff.). Altogether, 3,013 deportations were carried out over a period of three weeks, with this being hailed as 'record breaking' by a newspaper headline in the *Kanagawa shinbun* (21 August 1989). In this newspaper article attention was drawn to the spread of 'illegals' throughout the country (more having been detected in more 'remote' prefectures) and to the increasing diversity with regard to nationality.

Organizations for the human rights of labour migrants describe these control activities as 'hunting down foreign workers' (*gaikokujin rōdōshagari*) and as serving only to make migrants fearful (KNK, 1990:174). However, the staging of this 'prevention theatre' of concerted action also serves to affirm the validity of a norm which is permanently 'endangered' by factual developments.

However, many so-called 'exposed illegal workers' are in fact migrants who have chosen to give themselves up to the authorities (who therefore should be called returning migrants – *kikokusha);* this is especially the case for the increase in 1990 triggered off by the enactment of the amendment of the Immigration Control Act and by the rumours about tough sanctions circulated earlier (cf. KNK, 1990:170ff.). The journalist Ishiyama estimates that around one-third of the 'exposed' actually gave themselves up to the authorities, and that the number of those who gave themselves up to local Immigration Control Bureaus might even surmount that of those actively apprehended. In January 1987, the Ministry of Justice sent an ordinance to all regional Immigration Control Bureaus stating that 'as long as there is no danger of escape' (that is, by those who gave themselves up in order to return to their country of origin) no custody is to be instituted. Thus, those regis-

Table 5.3 Development of number of cases for arraingment of offences against the Immigration Control Acts

		1984	1985	1986	1987	1988	1989
B	illegal entry	513	460	597	542	616	2,349
C	illegal landing	100	123	124	134	149	258
D	illegal activities	357	218	349	372	839	696
E	illegal stay out of this	5,569	6,592	9,215	12,792	15,970	19,105
F	illegally working	(4,426)	(5,411)	(7,782)	(10,935)	(13,475)	(15,912)
G	infringements of penal code, decrees, a.o.	291	260	288	289	280	218
H	illegal labourers	4,783	5,629	8,131	11,307	14,314	16,608
A	Total	6,830	7,653	10,573	14,219	17,854	22,626

HNK, 1990: 44.
A: sum total
B: 'illegal entry' (*fuhō nyūkoku*)
C: 'illegal landing' (*fuhō jōriku*)[1]
D: (wage-related) activities not permitted by visa status (*shikakugai katsudō*)
E: 'illegal' (prolonging of) stay (*fuhō zanryū*)
F: persons illegitimately 'active' (working: *shikakugai katsudō–garami*),
G: infringements of the penal code, decrees a.o. (*keibatsu hōrei ihan tō*),
H: 'illegal workers' (D + F).

tered as 'illegal' could wait in their lodgings for the date of their return flight (this ordinance was a reaction also to the overcrowding of limited detention centres, cf. Ishiyama, 1989:199–201).

5.2 Official Statistics on 'Illegals' in Japan

The Ministry of Justice and, in turn, its subordinate Immigration Control bureaus, publish much more detailed data than those giving merely the number of 'illegal workers'. Figures are provided for all categories of contravention of the regulations of the Immigration Control Acts (Tables 5.3 and 5.4):

Gender-specific developments are also differentiated, and are accentuated by year-to-year comparisons of rates. Rates of increase for men are shown as high – a consequence of the baseline

Table 5.4 Gender-specific distribution of offences in transition

		1984	1985	1986	1987	1988	1989
Total		6,830	7,630	10,573	14,129	17,854	22,626
	M	1,213	1,644	3,325	5,636	10,725	15,201
	F	5,617	6,009	7,248	8,493	7,129	7,425
% portion	M	17.8	21.5	31.4	39.9	60.1	67.2
on total	F	82.2	78.5	68.6	60.1	39.9	32.3
Persons*	M	111	431	1,681	2,311	5,089	4,476
	F	1,951	392	1,239	1,245	−1,364	296
Increase	M	10.1	35.5	102.3	69.5	90.3	41.7
rate*	F	53.2	7.0	20.6	17.2	−16.1	4.2

*increase/decrease in comparison to year before.
M = Male   F = Female
HNK, 1990: 45.

chosen for yearly comparisons. By such comparisons, again, attention is directed to a migration process increasingly 'dominated' by men or to a shift to 'male dominance'.

Authorities are quite conscious of the artifactual character of the rates of increase, but claim that these reflect the 'success' of intensified control (*torishimari no kyōka*) which had become imperative because the problem of illegal work 'constituted a serious situation' exacerbated by the influx of 'pseudo-refugees' from China (*gisō nanmin*) in the summer of 1989 (cf. the official wording in HNK, 1990:44). The high number of 'illegal entries' in 1989 is partly attributed to the Chinese refugees, and resulted in an inflated total which was subsequently dramatized as 'historical record' (HNK, 1990:44). In this official 'balance-sheet', precise information about nationalities is presented. The marked increase in Malaysians (around 90 per cent of them males, a seven-fold rise over the previous year) and Koreans (a three-fold increase over the previous year) is claimed to be a new tendency (HNK, 1990:46). To sensationalize trends of this kind always poses the danger of generating a self-fulfilling prophecy (tougher control and enforcement lead to a rise in recorded infringements). Moreover, year-to-year comparisons of aggregated data are unreliable because of the weight they give to mere contingency. Thus, for example, the increase in the number of Koreans entering Japan in 1989 coincides with the deregulation of South Korean departure procedures following the 1988 Olympics in Seoul.

Another phenomenon perceived as 'a new trend' is the increased diversity of nationality of those entering Japan (as

Table 5.5 The number of persons denied entry

	1983	1984	1985	1986	1987	1988
Pakistan	7	79	153	596	1,355	4,288
Bangladesh	0	24	18	146	707	3,233
Korea	197	68	53	80	133	1,070
Thailand	191	184	343	457	389	996
Malaysia	2	18	7	2	40	394
Philippines	588	633	417	929	1,034	365
China (Taiwan)	277	203	224	402	293	253
Others	115	105	125	139	200	508
Total	1,377	1,314	1,340	2,751	4,151	11,107

KBR, 1990: 185.

inferred from infractions of the *nyūkanhō*, including 'illegal work'). In 1989, persons from thirty-nine countries (including some from Africa and South America) were registered as having violated the Immigration Control Acts. Furthermore, a spread of 'illegal' labourers (from the metropolitan areas to other parts of the country) is noted (HNK, 1990:46). However, both processes are understandable simply as part of the auto-dynamics of a migration cycle.

The data concerning prohibition of entry to Japan further elucidate the connection between high figures and more restrictive control practices. The number of people denied entry rose particularly in the period of intensified political discussion on 'illegal migrants' and markedly from 1987 to 1988 (Table 5.5).

In 1989 entry to Japan was denied to 10,404 persons, a decrease of 703 from the previous year (the decrease is explicable as the result of reimposition of visa duty for Bangladeshi and Pakistani nationals). Entry was denied to 3,906 Koreans (a 3.6–fold increase) and to 2,000 Malaysians (a 5.1–fold increase). The numbers of Pakistani and Bangladeshi nationals decreased 83 per cent (*Hokkaidō shinbun*, 19 March 1990). This decrease occurred despite the fact that greater numbers of Bangladeshis and Pakistanis sought to enter Japan just prior to 15 January 1989 (when visa requirements were reimposed for Bangladeshis and Pakistanis) – with many being denied entry at the airport on the grounds of 'suspicion of pursuing illegal work'. (On 12 January 1989 alone, 200 were refused entry, cf. Umetani, 1989:83f.) This is an indicator of the complex interplay between official intervention and the dynamic adaptive responses of the migrants. From January to August 1990, 12,672 persons were prohibited from entering Japan at Tokyo Narita airport alone, of whom 80 per cent were either of Iranian, Malaysian and Thai nationality. In most cases the reason given was 'suspicion of seeking illegal gainful employment' (Ōiwa, 1991:28). At Osaka airport, a two-fold increase of the number denied entry was recorded in 1990. Seventy per cent of those denied entry were Korean nationals; the rise for Malaysian nationals is also conspicuous (*Asahi shinbun*, 5 November 1990). The high proportion of Koreans is due to the fact that many permanently residing Koreans live in Osaka (*zainichi Kankoku-Chōsenjin* – around 40,000 of whom live in the district of Ikuno alone) and Koreans entering Japan often have the support of networks of relatives. With regard to entry, the earlier-mentioned 'visibility effect' plays a smaller role because nationality becomes evident in passport checks. Nevertheless, the dramatization of increased 'immigration' of certain nationalities and the imputation of the goal of 'illegal' work directs attention toward control (and prohibition of entry) of these people.

I do not deny the explanatory value of the official statistics, but rather advise that they be carefully interpreted since they do not straightforwardly reveal the real developments. After all, they are purely numerical reports of the atheoretical data of the (research) bureaucracy, and must be interpreted in the overall context of Japan's internal policies and those of the migrants' countries of origin, and in the light of the regulations set up administratively and legally. To illustrate and corroborate my conjectures concerning data-producing factors, I shall examine the statistics concerning the most recent immigration, that of Iranian nationals, and the way these statistics were used, although this occurred after the period under study (to 1990) and I can offer only a provisional study of this highly topical issue.

5.3 Excursus on the Use of Statistics

On 26 March 1992, in a morning news report (*mōningu shō*, from 8.30a.m. to 9.30a.m.) on the private channel Asahi-TV, a documentary was launched which had previously been announced in the newspapers under the headline: 'Special report! The true situation concerning the future of illegally-residing Iranians'. Part of the telecast was repeated on the same channel the following Saturday, in the 'golden' time-slot of an evening show recapitulating events of the current week, with comments by 'stars' of popular culture. This time it was announced with the headline: 'In Ueno-park one cannot go cherry blossom-viewing any more!' The motive for these reports was clearly evident: On 15 April 1993, visa-exemption for Iranians was repealed by order of the Ministry of Justice. A bilateral agreement with Iran for the cancellation of visa duty (*sashō menjo sochi*) for nationals of both countries had existed since 1974 (presumably, from an energy-political perspective in the context of the oil-crisis, Iran, though geographically distant, was psychologically 'near', and Japan was one of the few countries Iranians could travel to without applying for a visa). The ending of the Iraq-Iran war (1988) coincides with an increased immigration of Iranians to Japan, and from this time a situation began to evolve that came to be perceived as 'problematic' and which was sensationalized with notorious regularity in the mass media. By at the end of 1990 this new phenomenon had been hitched to such catch-phrases as 'Japan fever' or 'labour migration fever' (*dekasegi netsu*) and thereby semantically transformed in order to fit media interests (cf. the terms used in *Asahi shinbun*, 19 November 1990). The accidental death of a 12–year old Iranian boy (whose whole family was 'illegally' resident in Japan) on the premises of a small firm for the recycling of waste paper led the media to highlight this 'new immigration wave' (see for example, *Nihon keizai shinbun*, or *Yomiuri shinbun*, 11 December 1990). One possible reason for this media interest might have been that Iranian nationals prefer to use highly public places as job-markets, information-exchanges and meeting places: for example, Ueno-park and Harajuku on Sundays, where juveniles wearing wildly styled fashions dance on the street. In Ueno-park, several hundred Iranians gather daily to be recruited for work by fellow Iranians and Japanese labour agents (such scenes provide good news photographs – much better than migrants hiding in their apartments). The implosion of the so-called 'bubble economy' – officially proclaimed at the end of 1991 – and the following slump reduced work opportunities for Iranians. Some began to sleep in Ueno-park (it is said that they 'dislodged' the under-privileged Japanese homeless) and to spend their idle days there, where fellow Iranians would provide them with food.

Journalists immediately coined the term 'Little Teheran' (described and richly illustrated, for example, in Tanaka, 1991; and in English in Colterjohn, 1992). Among the places used for over-night stay by Iranians were 24–hour saunas; later they switched to 24–hour cinemas. This fomented a 'bad mood' in the gutter press. The weekly *Shūkan bunshun*, from 12 March 1992, particularly distinguished itself with heavily discriminatory imputations. In a headline it spoke of a 'big proliferation' (*daizōshoku*, a botanical term!) of Iranians in the Ueno-park, and in the subtitle claimed that, under these circumstances, *hanami* (cherry blossom-viewing) would be impossible. The Iranians were alleged to engage in premeditated cheating, theft of handbags, shoplifting, and extortion from groups of passers-by (the latter described as *katsuage*, a term from Yakuza-argot). Iranians spending their nights in cinemas were said by the article 'to do what they pleased' there. Local residents are quoted, with one claiming that during Ramadan (the Islamic month of fasting) the Iranians became aggressive from fasting during the day and that they held noisy banquets at night. The article closes with an easily remembered slogan, a malicious play on words: *Iranjin wa mō iran!*' (We don't need Iranians any more!). This style of reporting was heavily attacked at a gathering of the Asian Friends and prompted a letter of protest from the International Movement Against all Forms of Discrimination and Racism Japan Committee (cf. Hansabetsu kokusai undō Nihon iinkai, 1992).

An *ad-hoc* polling of eighty-eight Iranians in Harajuku, presented at the regular meeting of the movement for the rights of migrants, Asian Friends, on 26 April 1992 in Osaka, presents the typical picture: almost all of those questioned were between 20 and 29 years of age; most had been in Japan between three months and one year; sixteen said they were victims of skimming-off from wages (*pinhane*); and twenty-seven said they never saw a Yen of their wages for the work they had done. Of those interviewed, 41 declared that they had spent between 500 and 1,000 US dollars for mediation by labour agents (sixteen said they had paid this to Pakistanis). Fourteen spent nights at the apartments of friends and fifteen 'in the open'.

In the meantime, right-wing extremists (*uyoku*, particularly a group named Yūseikai) had driven to the precincts of Ueno and Yoyogi parks in trucks equipped with amplified loudspeakers, and had disturbed the peace with slogans such as 'Foreigners go

Table 5.6 Official entry data of Iranian nationals

Year	Entries	Entries denied
1987	19,818	17
1988	14,090	19
1989	16,282	325
1990	31,289	1,472
1991 (till Nov.)	45,152	7,540

home!' (*gaikokujin kaere*) (eyewitness-report by an activist of the Asian Friends, Mizuno Ashura).

In a report on television, official data on entry to Japan by Iranians were presented in order to illustrate the 'seriousness' of the problem (Table 5.6). Those figures are cumulative for 'illegal' prolongation of stay (exceeding the legal three months) and provide no information as to how many persons were actually visiting Japan briefly. They indicate only that an increased 'immigration' of Iranians had occurred. Of interest is the column on the right. One can see that over the tabulated period the number of persons recorded at entry more than doubled, whilst the number of those denied entry rose more than 440-fold. These figures clearly show the heightened sensitivity of the Immigration Control authorities, and their willingness to suspect Iranians of having travelled to Japan to 'seek illegal gainful employment'. The television report faded in to comments on the new measures cancelling visa freedom from the agencies involved. The Ministry of Foreign Affairs said that in negotiations with Iran it had been agreed that visa freedom was 'misused' for 'illegal' work, making these measures imperative. The Ministry of Justice hoped that the new measures would reduce the number of 'illegal' workers. The National Police Agency was similarly optimistic, saying that it had urged the Ministry of Foreign Affairs for a long time to re-institute visa duty. Taking the same line of police-logic the report then gave as one reason for the cancellation of visa-freedom the fact that 'criminal' occurrences and penal code offences were dramatically on the rise. There was then a fade-in to the following highly-polished table (Table 5.7).

Setting aside the demographic correlation with an increased number of entries (which was fairly pointed to by the journalist Watanabe Noritsugu), one might offer the following interpretation (along the lines of social control theory): the police have an interest in 'solving' the 'Iranian problem', a problem which

Table 5.7 Criminal code offences by Iranians in Japan

Year	Incidents	Apprehensions
1984	36	25
1985	55	41
1986	51	37
1987	101	29
1988	96	37
1989	31	31
1990	131	99
1991	590	561

(because of sensationalized media coverage) cannot be ignored. The police tend to think in terms of repression and legislative measures (see the calls on the Ministry of Foreign Affairs). In order to emphasize their claims and obtain greater leverage to negotiate the 'necessity' of visas, it is sufficient for police to give internal instructions which selectively direct attention toward Iranians and tighten the grip of control (which is rather easy due to the 'conspicuousness' of Iranians frequenting public places). Subsequently, Iranians involved in disturbances and petty incidents (which are re-defined to match penal code designations) are more often criminalized. It is clear, from the data above that only in the last two years has a real increase in recorded suspects (and it is suspects, not 'criminals' that are registered) become evident (previously, only 'natural' fluctuations occurred). The tabulated increase coincides with the increased attention of the mass media and the resultant pressure put on agencies of social control; it statistically shows the increased production of the criminalized (reflections of this kind are contained in the second [main] part of this study). The statistics intended to legitimate the tightening of controls reveal only intensified activities by authorities focussing on Iranians.[2] These selective, concentrated activities lead to statistical reports which can be dramatized and transformed into political coin. The data *produced* by control agencies are then instrumentalized for legitimation of action. The same pattern occurs with respect to migrants of other nationalities. It is noteworthy that always, in the period before a cancellation of visa-exemption for nationals of a certain country actually comes into force, there is a conspicuous rise in the number of nationals of that country who are refused entry to Japan. This is partly an outcome of the 'sensitizing-effect' of control agencies and partly a side-effect of the rush of people from that country who seek to avail themselves of the 'last chance' to enter Japan without bureaucratic hindrance; cf. the 'immigration peak' of Bangladeshi and Pakistani nationals before they were burdened with visa duty (*Asahi shinbun*, 15 January 1989).

The official data so notoriously introduced into the discussion do have a basis in 'reality', but call for interpretation. Moreover, they point to the fact that processes of irregular migration can be no more than directed, deflected and 'steered' by legislative regulations, but not 'totally' prevented.[3]

5.4 Number and Categories of 'Illegals' in Japan

If one is to analyse irregular migrant labour in Japan, one has to take into account the categories laid down in the *nyūkanhō*, and the stipulations with which 'illegals' come into conflict. The following system of classification is common:

(1) By far the largest category of 'illegals' comprises those who enter Japan on tourist visas and engage in paid employment without appropriate 'legal qualification' (a translation of the legal term *shikakugai katsudō*). If their tourist visas expire and they keep working, this is also deemed 'illegal work' (the legal term is *shikakugai katsudō–garami no fuhō zanryū*, usually described by foreigners simply as 'overstaying').

(2) A so-called 'entertainer–' or performance-visa (*kōgyō biza*), as a rule allows the holder to work for six months, for example, as singer or dancer. Holders of these visas are mostly women employed in dubious snackbars and nightclubs as 'hostesses' ('come-on' girls), which is not permitted under the terms of the law, and all too often are forced into prostitution. Often they continue to work after their visas have expired, – for example, so as to be able to continue sending remittances to relatives and dependants in their home countries – thereby becoming 'illegals'.

(3) Students at universities (*ryūgakusei*) or at pre-college level (*shūgakusei*, most of them students of the Japanese language, many of them preparing for university) are allowed to engage in paid work for up to twenty hours a week with the permission of the Ministry of Justice (an application must be made). If they

work longer hours than these, they also come under the category of *shikakugai katsudō*.

(4) A further category of 'illegal' workers is that of the so-called *kenshūsei* (on-the-job trainees or probationers) who engage in work other than permitted by law or fail to receive the legally-prescribed theoretical training to the extent of one-third of their working hours – that is, who are exploited as cheap labour.

(5) Marriage to a Japanese national lifts all restrictions on gainful employment. This sometimes leads to 'sham-marriages' (*gisō kekkon*, which also may be mediated by organized gangsters). It is mostly women who seek (or are persuaded to seek) to acquire legal status for their work in this way.

(6) Any wage-related activity after the expiry of the term specified by a visa is 'illegal'.

(7) Before the amendment of the *nyūkanhō*, *nikkeijin* (descendants of Japanese emigrants to Latin American countries), and relatives of *zainichi*-Koreans with permanent residence in Japan, could enter Japan with a *hōmon biza* (visa for visiting relatives, usually valid for three months without a work permit). Paid work was illegal for holders of these visas while they were in Japan.

It is hard to gauge the number of these contravening the Immigration Control Acts, that is, the number of 'illegals'. The highest estimates in 1990 were between 200,000 and 300,000 (Watanabe, 1990b:168, and Umitani, 1989:84, attempt to categorize irregular migrant labourers). In 1991 estimates were also between 100,000 and 300,000 (*Mainichi shinbun*, 6 July 1991). The figure of 200,000 to 300,000 'illegal' workers is endorsed by Call-Nettowāku, an organization for the protection of the rights of migrants (Tanaka, 1990:34). The figure for 1987 was speculatively put at 70,000, with the estimate rising to 200,000 for 1989 (the source of information remains vague being given as 'according to some people', cf. Mori, 1990:64). In a cautious and detailed study of the Economic Planning Agency, it is estimated that there were 70,000 'illegals', who had exceeded their legally-permitted stay (*fuhō zanryūsha*) as at June 1988, with most of these 'illegal' residents being engaged in 'illegal work' and the actual figure for those working illegally being much higher when the number of students working illegitimately (*shikakugai katsudō*) was taken into account (KKSK, 1989:32). An economist puts the number of 'illegals' at 150,000 (Kuwahara, 1989:125), while the researcher Miyajima gauges their number as between 120,000 and 130,000 (Miyajima, 189:14). An author whose book-jacket description is that of 'immigration specialist', gives the number released by the Ministry of Justice for 1989 as 107,000 'illegals', but adds that, realistically, one should multiply this figure by three, and given that figures for overstay should be treated cumulatively, one might well dare to multiply the officially-admitted number by four or five (Kobayashi, 1990:193).

The Immigration Control Agency itself, in July 1989, put the number of foreigners who had overstayed their visa at 101,171 (Shimada, 1991:120). More recent figures published by the Ministry of Justice and calculated from data on entries and departures, put the number of those exceeding their legally specified period of stay as at 1 May 1991 at 159,828 (80.7 per cent of them held tourist visas or short-term visas). By nationality, this figure included 27,228 Philippine nationals – the highest national representation – followed by 25,848 Koreans, 19,093 Thais, 17,535 Chinese, 14,413 Malaysians and 10,915 Iranians (*Asahi shinbun*, 5 February 1992).

Viewed quantitatively, the migrant worker 'problem' is still a marginal phenomenon (given Japan's total population of approximately 123.8 million people in 1992). Qualitatively, however, it was interpreted as a signal that a 'new' (restrictive) immigration policy was needed. Official data aside, the fluctuations in the estimated figures concerning 'illegals' may again be attributable to the political 'negotiating value' that attaches to them. Activists for the rights of migrants tend to over-estimate numbers (for example, circulating in 1993 estimates of up to 600,000 'illegals') to underscore the 'seriousness' of the 'problem' and put the government under pressure to act in accordance with human rights conventions. Cautious academics, on the other hand, give more moderate figures, as do conservative politicians concerned to prevent criticism of the failure of existing immigration regulations.

In the following sections I will first briefly describe the problems faced by 'illegals'; then I will sketch their social profile and living conditions, in order to outline the initial characteristics of the process of migration to Japan and, eventually, to offer a comparative perspective.

5.4.1 'Tourism for work'

As mentioned, by far the largest category of 'illegal' workers consists of those who enter Japan on a tourist visa or with just a passport and who, after finding a job 'go underground' in order to 'illegally' prolong their stay. Their problematic situation is one of mediated exploitation (through recruitment practices and wage discrimination), legal insecurity (for example, in regard to work-related accidents) and permanent danger of deportation – all of which have grave implications for their well-being.

5.4.1.1 Mediating practices

Most 'illegal' workers have third parties involved at some stage prior to their finding employment, whether at the stage of recruitment in their country of origin, or mediating their passage, or finding them work in Japan. This disadvantages these migrants from the very start, because the high commissions they must pay burden them with debts before they even find paid employment. While the data on these underground activities are not uniform, they do allow the scale and incidence of mediating practices, and their cost and debts of the 'illegals' (and hence the indebtedness of illegals), to be gauged.

Firstly, we should note that the existence of irregular conduits for migration and mediating for the placement of labour in Japan is a direct product of the illegalization of 'unqualified' foreign workers, the more so because no official measures for recruitment of 'guest-workers' exist (except for the professionally qualified sector and for *kenshūsei*).

Mediation can take a number of different patterns. The process was graphically depicted by Umetani in a 'staged model', which shows all of the possible relations and payment arrangements between migration candidates and their go-betweens (Figure 5.5). The journalist, Gonoi, (loosely) distinguishes between 'labour-divided', 'co-operative' and 'direct' recruiting. In the case of 'labour division', migrants are recruited in their home country and collected by labour agents or employers at the airport in Japan. 'Co-operative' recruiting involves indigenous and Japanese agents 'conspiring and planning' together with the migrants, and the agents accompanying migrants to Japan. When, on occasion, direct recruiting is used, Japanese labour agents themselves recruit

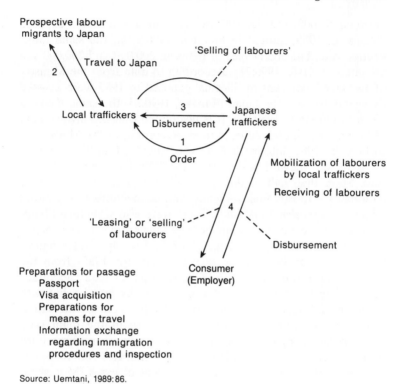

Prospective labour
migrants to Japan

'Selling of labourers'

Travel to Japan

2

Local traffickers ← Japanese
traffickers

3
Disbursement

1
Order

Mobilization of labourers
by local traffickers

Receiving of labourers

'Leasing' or 'selling'
of labourers

4

Disbursement

Preparations for passage
  Passport
  Visa acquisition
  Preparations for
    means for travel
  Information exchange
    regarding immigration
    procedures and inspection

Consumer
(Employer)

Source: Uemtani, 1989:86.

Figure 5.5 'Route to Japan' of unqualified workers

migrant labour in foreign countries. Increasingly, migrant workers who have been successful in Japan recruit their compatriots on their own account. Commissions paid for men are said to be between 250,000 and 300,000 yen, and for women between 400,000 and 500,000 yen. The agents procure the requisite papers (sometimes forged passport and visa), provide 'show money', hotel pamphlets, and so forth, to underscore the tourist motive, and pocket fees paid by migrants and a monthly share of the migrants' wages. According to the Ministry of Justice, up to 90 per cent of 'detected illegals' have found work through the mediation of so-called *burōkā* (from the English broker, for the above cf. Gonoi, 1989:152ff. and 115). Conflicting claims, however, are publicized regarding the incidence of such mediation.

The Immigration Control Agency maintains that brokers are involved in 73.9 per cent of cases, and that commissions are between 50,000 and 100,000 yen (the figures are for 'exposed illegals' in 1989, quoted in Shibuya, 1990:229f.; the same intervention rate, but higher fees of between 200,000 and 300,000 yen are cited in KBR, 1990:71). According to data from the Ministry of Justice 85 per cent of 'illegals' exposed in 1987 were assisted by agents to come to Japan (Tanaka, 1990:35; the same figure is given in Umetani, 1989:82). It is postulated that the involvement of brokers has increased over time. According to the Ministry of Justice, in 1981 intermediaries were involved in 67 per cent of (detected 'illegal') cases, while for 1986 the figure is 88 per cent. More than half of the agents were said to be of Japanese nationality – mostly males – many with connections to organized crime (*bōryokudan kankeisha*). There were also seventeen Philippinas who were married to Japanese nationals and who were active as recruiters (cf. Miyajima, a.o. 1987:9). Closely similar figures (including a 'broker-rate' of 86.9 per cent for 1985) from the official data of the Immigration Control Agency, lead one author to postulate an increased rate of mediation by *burōkā*, but with Japanese nationals comprising only 30.9 per cent of the latter. From this he infers that labour agents are in the main (and increasingly) compatriots of the migrants or persons from third countries. In Japan, professional crime syndicates (*bōryokudan*) are reported to be involved in 14 per cent of cases (Murashita, 1990:115; the same figure is cited for police sources in *Yomiuri shinbun*, 20 June 1988).

The presumption that many Yakuza are active as brokers is made by many publicists, but can hardly be empirically confirmed. Police data indicate a low involvement rate by Yakuza. However, samples are small and sources are restricted to police interrogations of apprehended foreigners, so these data should not be treated as reliable. According to the Police Whitebook, one-third (or eighty-six) of those questioned, but thirty-six (or more than half) of the women, were assisted by go-betweens in their travel to Japan of whom seventy-three were 'foreigners' and twenty-two were Japanese (only three of the latter being *bōryokudan kankeisha*, that is, Yakuza, cf. Keisatsuchō, 1990:20; what here looks to be a mistake in addition, turns out to be the result of multiple answers, as is indicated by the police study on which the above figures are based: see Suzuki, A. O., 1990b:60). Once in Japan, migrants seem to be more dependent upon mediating agents, and the share of Japanese agents rises. More than 50 per cent of migrants, and for women more than 60 per cent, were found jobs by agents. However, the proportion of Yakuza among agents is put at a low 2.8 per cent. In only one-tenth (approximately) of recorded cases was the same recruiting agent involved in both the sending country and in Japan (Suzuki A. O., 1990b:63). Nonetheless, the Police Whitebook notes that Yakuza are conspicuously involved in the luring and mediating of foreign female migrants and that this is one of the sources of income for Yakuza-syndicates (illustrated with case-studies in Keisatsuchō, 1990:49ff.). Thus we find 'The Yakuza and sexual slavery' as a chapter title in Kaplan's and Dubro's study of the Yakuza, which, although based on an accurate investigation, is presented with journalistic exaggeration (Kaplan and Dubro, 1986:200–208). They quote extensively from a study of a movement for the protection of victimized Asian women (Ōshima and Francis, 1988:219ff.). The latter offers qualitative evidence in corroboration a high involvement of Yakuza in trafficking of women. Yakuza have become topical in the South-East-Asian media since the 1970s, and have been covered in sensational articles which often draw rash conclusions (for example, an article with the headline: 'Yakuza-invasion of the Philippines'). It is claimed that detected cases of trafficking in women, drugs and weapons are 'innumerable' (on the Philippine press see Nomura, 1987). In an interview with Yamanouchi Yukio, the former lawyer of the largest Yakuza-syndicate, (conducted in his office on 18 October 1989), I was assured by him that the international activities of Yakuza first of all served the 'domestic demand' for the above-mentioned commodities (women here are indeed transformed into 'goods'). Trafficking in women is seen to be profitable, and is 'traditionally' controlled by Yakuza. However, recruiting male migrant workers and acting as agents for them is not seen as being lucrative enough to warrant large-scale Yakuza involvement.

A Japanese 'investigative' journalist estimates that ninety organizations (including Yakuza) were operating in the underground traffic in illegal migrants. Relying on anecdotal evidence, he describes how these agents 'neutralize' (the agents themselves say that they just want to 'assist' Asians and 'help' them to get a job, since jobs are abundant in Japan) (Gonoi, 1989:162f.). Local gangs clearly are active in the recruitment of women. According to one report, in Thailand alone around forty syndicates were primarily occupied in the trafficking of women (*Nihon keizai shinbun*, 3

February 1988; the same information is presented in a special newspaper report, which also documents a close co-operation between indigenous and Japanese mobster organizations, *Tōkyō shinbun*, 8 August 1990). It is also conjectured that there is close co-operation between Thai professional gangsters and Chinese triads (local criminal organizations) in Hong Kong (*Mainichi shinbun*, 5 July 1990). Most of these global 'analyses' of the involvement of organized crime in a modern 'slave trade' are of a speculative character, basing their claims on single exposed cases from which it is not possible to conclusively generalize.

Let us return, from this corrective excursion concerning Yakuza, to the issue of trafficking. Despite variations in the data, we may say that, as a rule, third parties are involved in labour migration. This involvement may differ according to the nation of origin and the degree to which migration is well-established. This supposition is supported by various examples. One author remarks that the labour agent problem is not so virulent for Pakistanis, because they come to Japan via networks of blood-relatives (Yonemoto, 1990:39). Similarly, Komai comments in his evaluation of his poll concerning migrants from the Philippines and Korea, that they could rely on networks of relatives and acquaintances, and so were less dependent on recruiting agents than Latin American migrants, for example, since migration from Latin America is only in its beginnings (however, his postulation of a 'settling-in' tendency – *teichakuka* – which is the result of social ethnic-networks is premature cf. Komai, 1992a:286f. and 291). Migrants of nationalities for which there is a longer history of migration, seek to disentangle themselves from their dependence on Japanese labour agents. Successful migrants take over the mediating business; for example, a Malaysian who has himself worked for a considerable period in Japan became a labour agent recruiting Malaysian and Chinese *shūgakusei*, or short-term visa-holders, for demolition work at night (Nishina, 1991). Without disclosing his sources, Kobayashi reports that 80 per cent of foreign migrant workers come to Japan through *burōkā*, and that 80 per cent of these *burōkā* were themselves foreigners (Kobayashi, 1990:163). We may note that this unsubstantiated conjecture contains the innuendo that the trafficking business is dominated by foreigners (thus exculpating the Japanese).

Making a profit – in the form of commissions – is the main goal of labour agents regardless of nationality. Various figures for these commissions are mooted in the discussion. In the daily press one periodically finds stories of exploitation, which presumably, are among the more drastic cases – these being regarded as more newsworthy. I confine my sketch to two examples.

In one case, a Philippina paid 400,000 yen as commission to her Japanese 'promoter' for a six-month contract in a bar. In addition, the agent pocketed 150,000 yen monthly from her wage. (The monthly amount is 600,000 yen in cases of prostitution!) From her remaining 70,000 yen per month, she had to repay the cost of her falsified passport and her airline ticket. In total around two million yen went to the trafficking agents. In a second case, a Philippino died on a construction site in Japan at the age of 28 due to heart failure. He had come to Japan burdened with debts of approximately 420,000 yen. He had needed this money for the mediator's commission and acquired it through a real estate mortgage. In Japan he received a daily wage of only 5,000 yen for steel construction work, while 10,000 to 15,000 yen per day was skimmed from his actual wage by his recruiting agent (both cases described in Hagio, 1990:56f.).

That migrants have to shoulder such liabilities and make such high initial investments shows that they are not from the poorest segments of their societies of origin. On the other hand, it is clear how inapplicable are such simple calculations as 'one month's work in Japan equals one year's subsistence back home', especially given the high cost of living in Japan. For many migrants, their stay becomes profitable only after several months of work in Japan. Asian migrant workers are therefore under strong pressure to put up with inferior wages and working conditions reminiscent of early capitalism. To return too soon to their home countries would leave them with a net deficit from their labour migration. The earlier mentioned syndicate selling falsified passports alone burdened migrant workers with debts averaging around 400,000 to 500,000 yen (Hagio, Obata and Hamada, 1990:13).

The financial liabilities of migrant workers can only be roughly outlined. Data are difficult to obtain and often inconsistent. A journalist puts the average financial liability for an 'illegal' worker at between 300,000 and 350,000 yen. He provides the illustration of a Philippino construction worker who came to Japan with a liability of 280,000 yen which it took him three months to repay. For accommodation, victuals, working gear and repayment of debts, around 80 per cent of his wages were deducted; only after three months did he receive his first full wage of 30,000 yen. And only after having changed his job (an extensive information network on job opportunities for migrants is said to exist) and having worked for eight months in Japan was he able, for the first time, to send some 200,000 yen to his family back in Negros – an amount said to be enough to support them for eight months to one year (Gonoi, 1989:33–39).

An activist of the organization Karabao no kai notes that almost all Asian migrants come to Japan with debts of between 400,000 and 500,000 yen. They therefore are fearful of early expulsion, since to repay their liabilities on the low income they would earn in their countries of origin would be virtually impossible. So they are willing to endure the withholding of wages and payment of kickbacks, and when injured at work refrain from seeking treatment or compensation except in the most serious cases. Moreover, when migrants do attempt to claim their rights, employers often threaten to call the police (for examples, see Hanada, 1990:101f.)

The above-mentioned police investigation concerning 253 apprehended 'illegals' gives the following picture: 28.3 per cent of the men declared themselves to have no debts, while only 21.7 per cent of the women made this declaration (and 47 per cent of the women abstained from answering the question!). The average was 683,000 yen: but 'only' 315,000 yen for men, compared to 1,166,000 yen for women (disregarding non-respondents and those declaring 'no debts'). Of the males 40 per cent borrowed the money from relatives, friends and acquaintances; on the other hand, women borrowed from labour agents in 55.2 per cent of cases, and from employers in 20.7 per cent of cases – evidence of their greater dependence on go-betweens (data in Suzuki A. O., 1990b:60f.).

This study also shows that, after an average stay of 19.5 months at the time of arrest, an average 940,000 yen of savings and remittances had been made per migrant. Slightly more than one-fifth had been able to save or remit only up to 500,000 yen, and 11.9 per cent were said to have been unable to put any money aside (but more than one-third refrained from answering – indicating an unwillingness to respond and making the 'poll' methodologically questionable: data in Suzuki A. O., 1990b:61 and 64). Savings and remittances point to the frugal life-style of migrant workers in the early stage of their migration, when they have high rates of saving, forego consumption and confine themselves to the lifestyle and standard of living of their country of origin, thereby also neutralizing feelings of deprivation in their new surroundings – those of a highly-developed consumer society.

5.4.1.2 Wage discrimination

The data presented in the police-study do not show that there is wage discrimination against migrant workers because they give only absolute figures, and no comparison with the wages of Japanese nationals working in the same situation. It is correctly noted that no reliable data on wages are available. However, the available data do indicate that, as a rule, income and working conditions for irregular foreign workers are worse than for Japanese employed in the same sector. It is reported that male migrant workers earn only half to one-third of the salary of their Japanese co-workers (cf. Umetani, 1989:90f.). In the day-labourer area of Yokohama, Kotobuki-chō, where some one hundred Philippinos live, they are paid what is termed the 'Manila-price', which is only half of the daily wage Japanese day labourers receive (Genki magajīn henshūbu, 1989:125). A journalist conducted interviews with twenty 'illegals' and discovered that they earned only between 30 per cent to 80 per cent of the wage of their Japanese colleagues performing the same job (Sawahata, 1989:99ff.). In the smallest enterprises in the production sector afflicted by 'personnel dearth', foreign migrants seem to be best-off. Wage discrimination is said to be rare there because employers are pleased to have finally found an additional hand they do not want to lose (KBR, 1990:74). A concerted investigation in March 1988 by the Ministry of Labour revealed that of the forty-three 'illegal' workers who were exposed, eight of the twenty who were paid daily and four of the fifteen who were paid hourly received considerably less than Japanese working under the same conditions (KBR, 1990:73). Other investigations by the Ministry of Labour and the Labour Standards Bureau attached to it revealed that, in 90.9 per cent of cases (according to employers), foreign employees received the same wage as their Japanese counterparts. (This figure, however, includes both the legally and the 'illegally' employed, and legally employed foreign staff are usually paid as well as, or better than Japanese, for their 'non-replaceable skills'). According to another finding, out of 202 'illegals' only roughly half received the same wages as their Japanese counterparts (both findings cited in Mori, 1990:68). Furthermore, one frequently finds in the literature scandalous cases in which wage-differentials are strikingly high (for example, a daily wage of only 4,000 yen for construction work in Chiba prefecture, which is one-third of the daily amount paid to Japanese day labourers; Ishiyama 1989:33). On the whole it can be reasonably concluded that 'illegal' migrant workers receive lower rates of pay and thereby fulfil their functional role on the labour market in line with the intentions of capital.

5.4.1.3 Sectoral shortage of labour

In the debate on foreign labour during the second half of the 1980s, reference is often made to the tense demand situation on the Japanese labour market. I shall shortly quote several opinions on that issue, because foreign migrant workers are absorbed into exactly those segments which are subject to complaints about the most acute lack of personnel. It is said that young Japanese look for work which is 'fun', pleasant and interesting, and that they increasingly eschew manual labour. This implies that the attitude towards work in Japan has significantly changed. The aspiration to perform more 'easy-going' work is an indicator of enhanced material affluence (see, for example, Harada, 1990:58). The value spectrum of Japanese youth is becoming more pluralistic, and finds its expression in the severing of traditional bonds of loyalty to one particular firm and leads to more workplace mobility amongst young entrants into the labour market (cf. Yorimitsu, 1989:7). It is especially the small enterprises in the production and construction sectors which cannot offer the labour conditions craved for (wages, vacation, bonuses, regular weekly working hours). And it does tend to be the case that the smaller the enterprise, the more evident is the labour shortage. The immigration of male migrant workers correlates conspicuously with the rising sectoral demand for labour since 1985. In the construction sector, wage rises since the beginning of the 1980s were few and low, with workplaces already found unattractive being difficult to fill even with junior Japanese staff (data in Umetani, 1989:997–100). The year 1985 (to be precise, 22 September of that year when finance ministers and issuing bank directors of the five largest industrial states [the G5], met in the Hotel Plaza in New York to negotiate a shift in foreign exchange rates, ending up with a revaluation of the yen) is often cited in connection with a vitalization of the internal market and promotion of big construction projects. It is this date which is seen as marking the start of a new economic situation leading to labour shortages (in construction and subcontractor firms), subsequently to the influx of foreign male workers (see, for example, KBR, 1990:100). In construction firms, vehicle parts suppliers and industrial production enterprises, one out of every two small enterprises is said to have complained of chronic labour shortages (Gonoi, 1989:123). Another author claims that 90 per cent of enterprises in the construction sector, food retailing, and production were struck by a dearth in personnel (Kobayashi, 1990:142). It is also noted that the developing tertiary sector of services had labor-shortage problems, as did the agricultural sector (Noda, 1990:254f.). A poll of 2,000 enterprises in Tokyo (the response rate to the mailed question sheets being 42.9 per cent – 857 enterprises) indicated that 65 per cent of enterprises in construction, 53.3 per cent in production, 35.5 per cent in the retail and catering trades, and 42.7 per cent in services, suffered labour shortages. Among the enterprises 'intending or considering employment of foreigners', the predominant motive was 'because of labour shortage' (56.9 per cent, multiple answers possible; see TSRJ, 1989:17 and 21; no distinction was made in this study between by 'legal' and 'illegal' foreign workers).

Although the data are heterogeneous (with the media periodically giving the latest computations), there is consensus about the phenomenon of 'labour shortage'. Dissension largely concerns the means to alleviate this shortage. The president of the Japanese Federation of Employers Associations (Nikkeiren) pleaded for the exhaustion of the unused national potential (quoted in Harada, 1990:55). Another representative of Nikkeiren warned that the present labour shortage should be regarded as a permanent one, and advised that admittance of foreign workers as the solution would be rash, as they would only have to be dismissed in the next recession (Naruse, 1990:25). In a discussion between economists, it was also remarked that the present labour shortage was a structural one, occurring periodically with economic vicissitudes, and would dissolve naturally with the course of time (Chūma A. O., 1990:16). The Small and Medium Enterprises Agency recommended rationalization and employment of women and older persons, because admittance of foreign workers only delayed the modernization of industry (Chūshō kigyōchō, 1990:20–23). The argument that, by employing foreign labour, the necessary amelioration of working conditions would not be stimulated and modernization would be retarded, meaning that existing deficiencies in small enterprises would be preserved, can also be found in the detailed study of the Economic Planning Agency (KKSK, 1989:106). A representative of the Ministry of Labour insisted also that the labour shortage was the result of a mismatch, that is, supply and demand would not meet on the labour market. Therefore, a focussed utilization of existing potential, together with rationalization, labour economizing, amelioration of working conditions and offering of training courses for technicians, were the correct remedial measures to be undertaken (Yoshimen, 1990:47). For the proponents of admission of foreign workers, the labour shortage is seen as a factor produced by the volatility of capitalist economics, but a factor which necessitated admission of foreign workers into Japan (cf. Noda, 1990:265). Anyway, the catchphrases 'labour shortage' and (the more radical) 'bankruptcy due to lack of personnel' (*hitode busoku tōsan*, describing the rise in insolvencies of small enterprises due to the lack of young Japanese hands) play an important role in the debate regarding foreign migrant workers. (However, as I am not an economist, I cannot conclusively assess the 'reality' behind these dashing slogans.)[4]

5.4.1.4 Sectors in which irregular migrant workers are employed

The Ministry of Justice publishes statistics on the types of employment found by irregular migrants. These statistics actually record the types of work performed by 'exposed illegals' and provide a first sketch of their position on the Japanese labour market (Figures 5.6 and 5.7). It is noteworthy that for female migrants the largest category by far is that of 'hostess'. This usually designates work as a 'barmaid' in nightclubs, snackbars and the like. However, the figure for (coerced) prostitution which is concealed under this category may be surmised to be very high. The category 'factory worker' (*kōin*) includes mainly work in small enterprises (*machikōba*), work for subcontractors and work in the metal fabricating industry. Miyajima maintains that most work of male 'illegals' is in metal works, production of machine parts and food processing *machikōba*. *Machikōba* are lacking in junior staff.

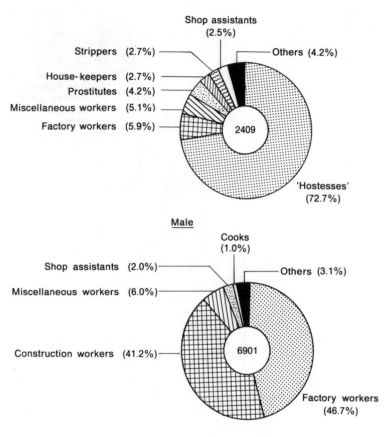

Figure 5.6 Kinds of employment of 'illegal' labourers

Source: Herbert, 1991b:19; from Hōmushō nyūkokukanrikyoku 1989: 39.

Machikōba are very small manufacturing plants, usually in densely populated, mixed urban residence areas. Very often the only worker is the owner and there are no employees. These small enterprises are equipped with outdated machinery, often in contravention of security regulations, and work as suppliers for subcontractor firms (IJUW, 1987:96).

They therefore fall under the classification *san-k* or *san-ki* work – 'three-k' work: *kitanai* (dirty), *kitsui* (laborious) and *kiken*

73

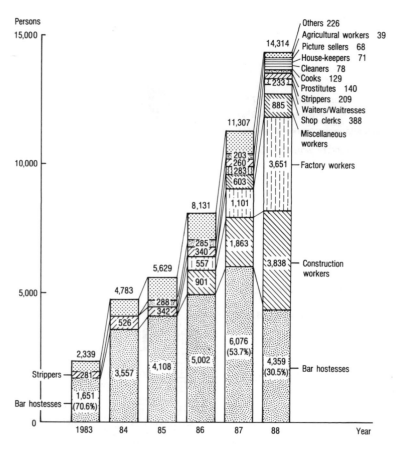

Source: Umetani, 1989:81.

Figure 5.7 Changes in the numbers of labour branches of 'exposed' illegal workers

(dangerous), similar to the English characterization of some work with three 'Ds', as dirty, demanding and dangerous – and this especially is the work sector into which 'illegals' are relegated (Pohl, 1991:23). The journalist Gonoi reports the rather extraordinary case of a Philippino who performed eight different jobs in ten months. These jobs show in an exemplary way which sectors are open to foreign migrant workers. He had worked as a gasoline station hand, in a bookbindery, in a building cleaning firm, in a snackbar, a canteen, a convenience store, on a chicken farm and as a truck driver's assistant (Gonoi, 1987:79). Among foreign migrants workplace mobility seems to be relatively high, due both to dismissals, on the one hand, and to a perennial striving for better working conditions, on the other. The only relevant data known to me are from the police and are hardly generalizable. Of 516 apprehended foreigners suspected of 'illegal' gainful employment after an average stay of 1.8 years, male migrants showed a median job change rate of 1.7 times and female migrants 2.3 times (Keisatsuchō, 1990:23).

A publicist who undertook field research reports on the following: some Pakistanis, Bangladeshis, one Ghanese and one Latin American, all of whom sliced frozen tuna at the fishmarket early in the morning; a Laotian who worked in a cleaning firm; around 500 Filipinos harvesting burdock (*gobō – Arctium lappa*) in Ibaraki prefecture earning a daily wage of 3,000 yen (Japanese housewives received 5,000 yen a day for the same job); some Philippinos working on a chicken farm; and in Saitama prefecture, many foreigners (some as *kenshūsei*, some in Japan partly as 'tourists') employed in foundries (Sawahata, 1989:129–133 and 149f.). Although, as we see, there is increasing diversification and advance of male migrants into services (see KBR, 1990:84), the official statistics seem to be fairly reliable. 'Illegals' are mostly found in bottom-rung jobs in production and construction (male migrants) and in services (female migrants). Chinese *shūgakusei* in Tokyo working as waiters, dish washers, kitchen help, and so forth, also have become a familiar picture, and often their work is legal (that is, when it is less than twenty hours a week). However, a closer examination of this group, as regards nationality and legal status, is not feasible, so the number of males working in services is liable to be underestimated. Generally though, it is so-called 'unqualified work' (*tanjun rōdō*) which is performed by 'illegals', and it was mainly on the assumption that 'migrant workers would be employed in this category that the debate over their admission or exclusion was conducted, despite indications that this categorization was not clear-cut. For example, a distinction between unskilled and semi-skilled work is difficult to make in the construction industry. Therefore, one should rather speak – adopting a classification of the ILO – of elementary occupation (KKSK, 1989:96). In the following section I shall examine migrant work in the construction sector more closely.

5.4.1.5 Foreign workers in day-labourer areas (*yoseba*)

For several reasons, I want to take a detailed excursion into the subject of foreign migrants in day labourer work. Firstly, up to 90 per cent of this work (most of it obtained for workers by labour agents) is in construction, where access to day labour is relatively easy. Secondly, day labourers constitute a class fraction of Japanese society which highlights the 'foreigner question' in many ways. In it one finds a disproportionate number of workers from ethnic and other minorities which are discriminated against in Japan. These include *zainichi*-Koreans and Taiwanese, peripheral groups such as those in Okinawa and those of *buraku*-origin – descendants of a 'caste' excluded from the Edo-period class order, ethnically Japanese, a quasi-pariah class – and also persons with criminal records and workers who are physically disabled (cf. Aoki, 1983:11). These groups show some latent sympathy with marginalized foreign migrants. However, foreign workers come into direct competition with the resident day labourers, and are seen by the latter as a threat to their jobs, a situation which engenders open discrimination. Thus, while the most active movements for the human rights of Asian migrant workers (for example, the organizations Asian Friends in Kamagasaki/Osaka and Karabao no kai in Kotobuki/Yokohama) have originated in *yoseba*, they are also the *loci* of the most militant labour union opposition to the admission of foreign labour. Moreover, nowhere else are the exploitation and the structurally produced problems of migrant workers (viewed as an under-class) more clearly evident. Their legal status as foreigners merely sharpens the focus. We should note also that Japanese day labourers too have to put up with the three traditional 'work evils' (*rōdō san aku*): *pinhane* (skimming-off from wages), *chingin fubarai* (withholding of wages) and *rōsai momikeshi* (concealment of work-related accidents) (see KNK, 1990:285).

I have gained direct insight into the life of day labourers through an extended period of field research (see Herbert, 1992). I can confirm the observations to be found in the literature. Possibly the most detailed study of foreign workers in *yoseba* is that of Aoki (1990, which was brought to my attention by Professor Martin Kaneko); it too is based on participant observation and interviews with experts (representatives of civil movements for migrants, and labour unionists), my own first-hand experience, and the information I have obtained both from activists of the Asian

Friends and from day labourers, corroborate the account given by Aoki.

The new labour migration from South East Asian countries into Japanese day-labourer sectors is perceived as genuine *kokusaika* ('internationalization') and fits with the trend of a global increase in migration processes. At the same time, it can be seen as homologous to the internal migration to *yoseba* in Japan. In the 1960s and 1970s, especially, rationalization, abandoning of pits, industrial re-structuring, decrease in labour-intensive methods in the agrarian sector due to mechanization, and so forth, led to periodic increases in the number of men out of work thus supplying labour for *yoseba*. Owing to the boom in construction, within a few years (by the end of the 1980s) around 7,000 Japanese 'newcomers' had migrated to Kamagasaki (Koyanagi, 1989a:135). The favourable situation for contract labour also gave foreign migrants the chance to 'offer' their labour and engage (temporarily) in labour relations.

The term *yoseba* (deriving from *yoseatsumeru* (gather) and *ba* (place) originally designated only the hiring and gathering place for day-labourers. *Yoseba* have existed since the Edo period, during which people migrating to big cities in the process of urbanization were 'recruited' by force (cf. Kamakyōtō and San'ya gentōin, 1974:153f.). The largest *yoseba* (in diminishing order of size: Kamagasaki in Osaka, San'ya in Tokyo and Kotobuki in Yokohama; Sasajima in Nagoya has a somewhat different structure and will be excluded here) are at the same time residential areas and centres of social life of day-labourers. Here labourers can lodge in 'flop houses' ('pensions', nowadays often euphemistically called 'business hotels') after paying cash in advance (in the sociolect these lodgings are named *doya*, transposing the syllables of *yado* (lodging); the big *yoseba* are also called *doyamachi*, *machi* denoting 'quarter', or 'town'). In Kamagasaki, almost every second *doya* is a 'business hotel', providing many conveniences (satellite-TV, refrigerator, air conditioning, and so forth, and if required, a Western bed) but also charging fairly high prices (around 2,000 to 3,000 yen per night). Old wooden *doya* are gradually being torn down, but cost only between 330 and 390 yen per night (Nakajima, 1990:115). This results in a polarization of *yoseba*-workers into those who earn enough in order to afford the new life style in *doyamachi* and those who are older, feeble, ill, or otherwise disabled and increasingly dependent on welfare – (provided that they are officially registered as day labourers holding a 'handbook' (*shiro techō*)). The number of *techō*-holders in *doyamachi*, how-ever, has drastically decreased (cf. Koyanagi 1990:63f.) and some have to sleep in the open (*aokan*, in the sociolect). Many day labourers experience a cycle of day-labourer work and homeless-ness, the latter often tending to become permanent after a time (see Aoki, 1984:3). These developments fill many *hiyatoi* (day labourers) with apprehension concerning their future, and they are a major concern of the official labour union organizing temporary workers (information from an informal interview with the sec-retary of Zenkōwan in Kamagasaki on 18 December 1990). The average age of day labourers in Kamagasaki is around fifty-one years, a factor that should not be under-estimated in connection with xenophobic reactions against the vigorous, young, foreign migrants.

Approximately nine-tenths of the jobs offered in *yoseba* are in the construction sector. A distinction is made between *genkin*-work (cash work), that is, day work or casual work and *shutchō* (which literally means 'business trip'). The latter implies a 'con-tract', and the working period usually lasts between five days and a month. Contracted workers lodge in *hanba* (shacks) provided by construction firms which also provide catered food; expenses are deducted from wages (Kamakyōtō and San'ya gentōin, 1974:200). Around 80 per cent of the *genkin*-workers are *dokata* (navvies), whose work is excavation and simple construction. The remaining fifth comprises 'skilled craftspeople' (such as scaffold-ers, steel workers, carpenters, construction-machine operators, and so forth). These craftspeople enjoy higher prestige and receive approximately one-third more in daily earnings than *dokata*, with some earning twice as much. They are the main clientele of expens-ive 'business hotels', where they ostentatiously spend their nights. Foreign migrant workers are normally relegated to the lowest rung of the strictly stratified *yoseba* society, and work as auxiliary hands, which does not require Japanese-language skills. Work is mastered on the job through observation and imitation; instructions are often transferred via body-language. A minority of Philippinos work as *daiku* (carpenters) in Kotobuki. In Kamagasaki at the end of 1990, increasingly more Chinese *shūgakusei* were engaged in *zairyōage* (transporting and heaving materials) and in cleaning up jobs after construction ended (information from one of my most important day-labourer informants, Nakajima Fumio).

5.4.1.6 Foreigners in the three largest *yoseba*

5.4.1.6.1 Kamagasaki

In Kamagasaki, the proportion of Koreans, many of whom are second or third-generation residents (*zainichi*), is especially high. The first generation of this ethnic minority came to Japan as forced labourers during the colonial period and the Second World War. ('Forced' here does not necessarily imply that physical violence was used against them; however, there was considerable physical abuse, and there was structural, or 'indirect' coercion to migrate after their homeland was ransacked by foreign domination). Nowadays, many Koreans operate independently in catering, small trade and entertainment businesses. In construction, Koreans are employers as well as employees. Employers often manage small sub-sub-contracting firms (*magouke*), which are at the bottom of the hierarchy of the construction sector. Often the construction firm boss (*oyakata*) personally works on construction sites. This situation is due also to the fact that Koreans not holding Japanese citizenship legally are not permitted to enter directly into contracts (*motouke*), and so must act as sub-contractors (*shitauke*, and below them *magouke*). Korean day-labourers prefer to be employed directly in *hanba* through their relatives' connections (Aoki, 1990:91). Among the labour agents (*tehaishi*) – according to Yamada Minoru, chairman of the leftist day-labourer union, Kamanīchirō – up to 80 per cent were *zainichi*-Koreans (informal interview, 2 December 1990).

'Newly immigrating' (*rainichi*) Korean workers usually enter Japan with tourist visas or visas entitling them to visit relatives (an estimated 40,000 *zainichi*-Koreans live in the 'Korean town' of Osaka, Ikuno, alone). One estimate of the number of *rainichi*-Koreans working in Osaka is as high as 10,000. Many are employed as factory workers or as helpers in the service sector (NKK, 1989:4). Recruiting takes several forms: some *oyakata* (*zainichi*-Koreans) whose construction enterprises are short of labour, personally travel to Korea to *directly* recruit potential hands. Alternatively, they may *indirectly* recruit workers by delegating the mediating business to Korean or Japanese labour agents (Aoki, 1990:98). Few *rainichi*-Koreans lodge in *doya* in Kamagasaki, because it is considered too expensive. They either find accommodation with relatives or rent small apartments in cheap, old wooden buildings, and seek work at the *yoseba* every morning.

There is, incidentally, also an increasing number of Japanese day labourers who rent cheap apartments on the outskirts of Kamagasaki, and commute to the *yoseba* for work (in similar fashion to the daily commuting of salaried personnel to their offices).

Concerning the reactions of Japanese day labourers to Asian migrants, I cite the respective impressions of Mizuno Ashura, a leading activist of Asian Friends. In January 1989 he convened a 'study meeting' addressing the question of foreign workers, in which approximately one hundred day labourers participated. Mr Mizuno tried to arouse sympathy and understanding for the migrants by pointing out that they were 'colleagues', sharing a similar fate, and who had drifted to the *yoseba* in order to escape a destitution and unemployment in their home country – much as had many Japanese *yoseba*-workers. The reactions of the audience were ambivalent. They feared losing their jobs and wanted to protect their own interests, especially as Korean workers were paid at cheaper rates, and it was thought at that time of seasonal job shortage (rainy season, winter, and some months into the new budgetary year) that *oyakata* would give employment preference to the cheap, young and healthy *rainichi*-Koreans. As long as the economy was thriving, the problem would not become virulent, but the future was full of uncertainties. Another string of reactions related to the (class-solidarity) argument that in their common misfortune they should fight together with foreign compatriots for equal wages for equal work (cf. Koyanagi, 1989b). In the summer of the following year, the mood at a similar meeting was distinctly more in favour of foreigners. Most of the attending day labourers had the experience of working together with migrants at construction sites and they knew of their dilemma through direct contact. A day labourer recounted his experiences to me as follows: 'Work on the site has become real interesting. Now I know what "hammer" means in Chinese and Korean. Sometimes we communicate just by gestures, but it is big fun.' The effect of close and personal contact 'reduces social distance and feelings of foreignness and therefore discriminatory intentions' (Kremer and Spangenberg, 1980:112) – a fact becoming repeatedly evident through opinion polls addressing the attitude of the German populace to guest workers.

Upon my return to Japan the situation had again changed. In 1991 graffiti smeared on walls or scribbled into the lacquer of discarded cars read: 'Foreigners go home!' (*gaikokujin kaere!*).

This is attributable to the recession which set in at the end of 1991, hitting Kamagasaki with its full force and drastically decreasing the number of jobs available. On 26 April 1992, I was confronted with a similar reaction. Walking down the main street (called 'Ginza' by the *yoseba*-workers in allusion to the famous shopping street in Tokyo) to the centre of Kamagasaki, a day labourer repeatedly grumbled, clearly audibly to me: *'ore wa komattoru noni, gaijin wa kochi de nani shit'orunya'* (Osaka dialect: 'What does a fore-igner here, where I have troubles').[5]

Labour unions issue cautious to negative statements. Their main argument against foreign migrant workers is that they force down wages and cause loss of jobs for Japanese labourers. They maintain that priority for jobs should be secured for the indigenous labour force (cf. Genki magajīn henshūbu, 1989:125). Much more vehement were the reactions of labour unions in Kotobuki, the *yoseba* of Yokohama, which distinguishes itself by the fact that, in contrast to the situation in Kamagasaki – its foreign migrants live in *doya*.

5.4.1.6.2 Kotobuki

Kotobuki had not yet undergone extensive architectural moderniz-ation. Most of the *doya* are built from wood and are reasonably priced (since one night costs between 800 yen and 1,500 yen, foreigners can afford lodge in them). Many flophouses are owned or managed by *zainichi*-Koreans who, by virtue of their experience, have some sympathy with foreigners. As in Kamagasaki, many Korean migrant labourers come to Yokohama relying on their relatives (*oyakata* or *doya*-owners; around 450 *rainichi*-Koreans are said to live in Kotobuki). As it is a seaport town, traditionally work in the dockyards is available for day labourers. Kotobuki is well known to many Philippino sailors, who at some time may have docked in Yokohama. Through the information of these seamen, many Philippino workers came to the *yoseba* of Yoko-hama. Around 150 live there, some of them together with their infants and wives (Philippinas staying in Japan either with 'enter-tainer-visas' or 'illegally'; Aoki, 1990:95f.). This is rather extra-ordinary, because nowadays *yoseba* are predominantly inhabited by single men (although quite a few have left their families behind or are divorced). Philippinos without dependants usually rent rooms in *doya* in small groups in order to save money. For example, Paul, twenty-three years old, had been in Japan for over one year. He still had debts to his *rekurūtā* (agent) and said that he is in constant fear of being detected by the Immigration Control Authorities. José, forty years of age, had been in Japan for several years, and he too had outstanding debts. At first he had worked in a *hanba* in Chiba prefecture. He was promised a daily wage of 4,500 yen (less than half of what Japanese day labourers were paid), but the money was never given to him. He left the *hanba* without 'authorization'. Via many other *hanba*, he finally came to Kotobuki (both cases are recounted in Ishiyama, 1989:46–52). (The 'one-sided' resignation is a 'soft' form of protest widely practised by Japanese day labourers when they are not content with the working and living conditions in a *hanba*. In their sociolect this is called *tonko* – 'desertion' from the workplace. However, while Japanese temporary workers can claim their wages for work already done by seeking the intervention of labour unions and the public employment security office, this option is avoided by migrant workers out of fear of exposure and detention.)

There are construction sites where Philippinos are named simply by letters of the alphabet. In the list of labourers they are often recorded under common Japanese names such as Suzuki or Saitō, to give the impression that they are indigenous workers. One Philippino misses his left ring-finger, which was pinched off while he was working at a scaffold. Owing to his 'illegal status' he did not file for compensation through labour insurance. In Kotobuki, Philippinos are called the derogatory name '*pinkō*' by labour agents (the *pin* seems to stand for the Philippines; the addition *kō* is found in several other belittling or demeaning names, such as in the term for police, *porikō, pori* being a phonetic abbreviation of the Japanese for 'police'; it is found also in the grossly discriminatory term for Koreans (sometimes also for Chinese) *chonkō*, the *chon* supposedly alluding to the language; for a list of derogatory names for Asian foreigners, see Obata, 1990a:109). As well as Philippinos, a lesser number of Thai, Pakistani and Chinese workers also live in *yoseba*. A journalist even met a Columbian who come to Yokohama several times as a sailor and is now active there as *yoseba*-worker (Sawahata on Kotobuki, 1989:61–64).

Foreign workers and Japanese day labourers living in the same community sometimes come into conflict with each other. Arguments and disputes are common, and when alcohol is consumed sometimes escalate into fights. It is becoming more common for *doya*-owners to refuse to accommodate Philippinos, giving as their

reason that they are too loud (noise being an inevitable consequence of several people sharing limited space and spending their
leisure time together as the Philippino workers tend to do, whereas
most Japanese day labourers lodge in single rooms and take to
the street or public houses to 'hang out' or drink). Sometimes
anonymous callers ask police to take steps against foreigners. The
migrants themselves try to behave as inconspicuously as possible;
they shun going out, and live in constant fear of the authorities
(KNK, 1988:8f.).

In Kotobuki, the organization Karabao no kai is very active. It
fights against wage discrimination, since the daily wages of foreign
workers are usually between 1,000 and 5,000 yen less than
Japanese workers are paid. *Oyakata* justify this with arguments
about foreigners' work performance and command of the language
being poor (KNK, 1988:6f.). Labour unions are conservative, and
on occasion utterly xenophobic. In May 1987, the construction
workers union, Zenken sōren, issued an appeal for the prevention
of employment of 'illegal' workers on construction sites with the
reasoning:

(1) They had insufficient knowledge of Japanese to
     understand instructions, which led to accidents.
(2) Their presence would engender new discrimination.[6]
(3) Foreigners pushed down the wages of Japanese labourers
     and labour conditions would deteriorate (KNK,
     1988:41).

The labour union Zenkōwan distributed a pamphlet in March
1990 which advised: 'If a labourer with a different (*kawatta*, also
'uncommon, peculiar') hair colour crops up, one should report
this to the bureau', which called for the formation of *tekihatsu
patorōru* (exposure patrols). Early in 1989, a group of nine Philippinos was arrested by the police for overstaying or not carrying
their identity documents. All were subsequently indicted and
repatriated. A group of lawyers established by Karabao no kai
maintains that the apprehension was made in an attempt to investigate the labour agent operating behind the scenes. The technique
used by police is known as *bekken taiho* (securing persons for the
investigation of law violations other than stated in the writ of
attachment). The labour agent, however, got off with a summary

procedure and, when measured against profits, a 'painless' fine of 200,000 yen (KNK, 1990:268–70).

In Kotobuki too, day labourers show ambivalent reactions. Older labourers in particular express their concerns about being replaced and losing their jobs. Drunken workers insult foreigners, graffiti appear on toilet walls and other eruptions of feeling occur. On the other hand, sweating and working together is conducive to a feeling of solidarity as 'workmates' (KNK, 1990:287f.), a consciousness which also glosses over the latent structure and hierarchy of discrimination against minorities in *yoseba* – the more so, because day labourers first of all, regardless of ethnic or other origin, define themselves as *nakama* (colleagues; cf. Aoki, 1983:14).

5.4.1.6.3 San'ya

In San'ya, students, mostly Chinese, work as day labourers. Day-to-day necessities (and sometimes high school fees) can set in motion a cycle in which the students, fatigued, overworked, and under time pressure from their double burden of studies plus work, begin to concentrate their interests mainly on working. An estimated one hundred Chinese students come to San'ya every morning to find work for the day. They do not live in the *yoseba*. Many Japanese schools are located within close proximity of San'ya (Aoki, 1990:95). Many *shūgakusei* also sell their labour in the genuine *yoseba*, Takadanobaba, in Tokyo, which serves exclusively for the recruitment of potential workers. It offers Chinese students the opportunity to quickly earn a relatively large amount of money. However, they do suffer wage discrimination (earning around 8,000 yen daily compared to around 10,000 yen paid daily to Japanese day labourers; Gurūpu Akakabu, 1989:17). But the daily wage at this gathering place is also about 1,000 yen lower for Japanese labourers than in *doyamachi*. Experienced foreign migrants, whose information networks have become closer-knit the longer their stay, drift from Takadanobaba to San'ya. According to Aoki, around one hundred foreign workers (Chinese and Malaysians) find work in Takadanobaba every day. They live concentrated in cheap, old wooden houses in the neighbourhood. In addition, many migrant workers, independently of the *yoseba*, work as day labourers in printing shops, foundries, tanneries, carriers, or at the fish market in Tokyo and its environs (Aoki, 1990:95).

5.4.1.6.4. Eki tehai

Eki tehai designates recruitment practices by which *tehaishi* assemble potential workers at large (terminal) stations (for example, in Osaka: Tennōji, Kyōbashi, Umeda, Nanba, in Tokyo: Shinjuku or Ueno) and usually send them directly to *hanba*. Drastic under-payment is common (half of the daily wages of *yoseba*), and if wages are embezzled, workers cannot contact the *eki tehaishi* who operate outside Kamagasaki, because they are not registered officially in the public labour security office, as are, for instance, construction firms delegating *tehaishi* to Kamagasaki (up to four-fifths of *tehaishi* are indirectly and 'officially' registered; interview with Yamada Minoru). Recently, foreign migrant workers have been recruited by *eki tehaishi* and perform the same jobs as Japanese *yoseba*-workers, but for appallingly lower wages (Aoki, 1990:95).

5.4.1.6.5. Evaluation

The figures relevant to the problem of foreign workers in Japanese day-labourer sectors would suggest that they are not dramatic; qualitatively, however, they are of considerable significance. The everyday exploitation – which is the same for Japanese day-labourers – is more clearly evident in *yoseba* than anywhere else. Due to their 'weak' illegal status, foreign day-labourers cannot articulate and claim their rights. Wage discrimination, wage embezzlement, skimming-off from wages, and unpaid overtime are all seen by unions organizing day-labourers as functional aspects of a (foreign) disposable reserve army. These labour law violations by which foreigners are victimized have a direct relation to the migrants' own illegalized status. On the other hand, many day labourers, who fear a worsening of their already insecure position in the labour market as the result of the presence of young, physically-fit foreigners, react xenophobically. Social closeness and empathy through the shared destiny of a life in *yoseba* can dismantle discriminatory attitudes, but can revert to an apprehension of menace in times of recession. The displacement of Japanese day labourers by foreign workers, however, is not yet likely (according to Umetani, 1989:101). The presence of foreign migrant workers in *yoseba* has an important 'enlightening potential'. They are living 'indicators' of the strongly-segmented Japanese labour market, pointing to structural problems in the Japanese economic and social fabric.

5.4.1.7 Social profile of 'illegal' migrant workers

If one puts together the jigsaw puzzle of data concerning age, family status and education, a somewhat shadowy, but reproducible picture of typical labour migrants at the early stage of migration emerges: it is young, mostly single and – measured by the standards of their country of origin – relatively well-educated people who determine the dynamics of the migration process at its onset.

With regard to age structure, data on 'apprehended illegals' from the Immigration Control authorities are available. They show that up to one-third of male migrants are concentrated in the age group of twenty-five to twenty-nine years, white female migrants are, on average, younger (HNK, 1989:40, see Figure 5.8).

These findings are underscored by the police-linked study of Suzuki A.O. (1990a:49). Of the 516 persons classified as 'illegal workers', (including both male and female migrants) roughly one-third are between twenty-five and twenty-nine years of age. The average age is 28.9 years for women and 29.8 years for men. Slightly less than one-third of the arrested 'illegals' are married and around one-fourth declared that they have children (Suzuki A.O., 1990b:57).

The median period of school attendance is 9.8 years (men 10.6 years; women 7.6 years; cf. Suzuki A.O., 1990b:58). In developing or threshhold countries, where most of the migrant workers come from, this is a relatively good educational level. Tezuka claims that 80 per cent of foreigner workers enter Japan with an extra-

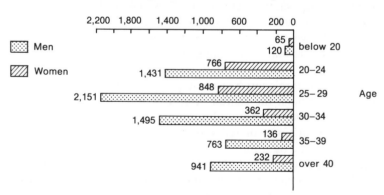

Source: Herbert, 1991b:10.

Figure 5.8 Number of 'illegal' labourers

ordinary high level of education, citing an inquiry initiated by him among 18,500 enterprises (Tezuka, 1991:53). After a personal meeting I obtained his survey, which revealed that only 6,455 of those enterprises responded (that is, roughly 40 per cent), and that only around 30 to 60 per cent of their workers (with some regional differences) could definitely be classified as 'illegal' (Tezuka, A.O., 1992:3–66; Tezuka, 1992a). Accordingly, his results are skewed in the direction of high education. According to his poll, 54.4 per cent of the foreign workers (both 'legal and illegal') were between twenty and thirty years of age, and one-third were graduates from universities (Tezuka, 1990:18). One might suppose that these figures show that there is a creaming-off effect (that is, young, highly educated, physically and psychologically healthy people are more likely to emigrate), but this must remain conjectural due to a lack of studies for contrast. Also inconclusive is a survey in which narrative interviews were conducted with 115 (almost exclusively 'illegal') migrant workers, because of the absence of methodological or statistical controls (this, however, is reflected upon in GRJCK, 1992). But this study has the merit of being the only Japanese study (known to me) which examines in depth the subjective view of migrants. It was made under the guidance of Professor Komai Hiroshi and with the assistance of his students of sociology. Yet it remains open how far the unstructured interviews were methodologically controlled. It is conceded, after all, that contact with 'illegals' would be beset with difficulties. Several interview attempts failed due to 'escape' reactions of the people asked to answer questions. This illustrates the cautiousness, and fear of persecution and expulsion of 'illegal' migrants (cf. GRJK, 1992:74). The case studies (of various lengths) reveal that a certain 'confession catalogue' led the conversations (case-study reports centre on such biographical data as age, education, family status, wage and labour conditions, incidence of discrimination, accident or illness, route to Japan, length of stay, visa-status, future prospects, amount and regularity of remittances, migration goals and reasons, interactional network in Japan, and contact with relatives). Some contain rash interpretations of the interviewer (for example, the supposition that Japanese food is a serious problems for Philippine workers, based on the observation of a Philippino cooking his own lunch, which led the interviewer to conclude that Japanese food did not appeal to Philippinos, GRJCK, 1992:76). This fact, together with the catalogue of questions asked, indicates that opinion was mobilized along the lines of the leading interests of the interviewers. The study notes that a large proportion of Pakistani and Bangladeshi workers had a high educational level (university graduation), whereas Latin American migrants, on the contrary, mostly had only middle-school graduation (after twelve years of schooling) or had been to school only for the period that was compulsory. On the labour market, however, the latter occupy better positions. Therefore, there is among migrants a hierarchy in inverse proportion to educational capital (Komai, 1992a:289).

The emigration of labour – not always an advantage for the sending countries – is sometimes characterised by the catchphrases 'brain drain' (in the case of skilled workers) and 'brawn drain' (in the case of unskilled labourers). The only positive economic benefits to the sending countries are the remittances, which sometimes are an important source of foreign currency. A certain selectivity of immigration to Japan is conceivable. It is characteristic of the profile of poly-annual migrants or workers moving to foreign countries with short-term and clear-cut goals (remittances, savings for a 'new', often independent life home, acquisition of commodities or consumer goods). Savings quotas are high and aspirations at first are oriented toward the standard of living of the country of origin (the typical phases of a migration process are described in Böhning, 1984:81ff.). Selectivity effects of migrations were a long-time 'monomania' in migration sociology (almost everything, from personality-type or character to social background of those who migrate, was investigated in a 'perpetrator-centred fashion' – to the neglect of the macro-social perspective, which would have brought structural determinants to light). Yet the results show

> that the criteria as regards selectivity of migrations even for one and the same region can fluctuate considerably . . . Generally one can state for a wide range of regions of the present world that mainly the younger age groups from rural areas migrate to metropolises or cities in general, with all the consequences this sort of selectivity has (Albrecht, 1972:177ff.).

The migrant populace concentrated in large urban peripheries, itself oftentimes becomes an origin for international mobility. Examining the structural position of migrants in Japanese society and the social profile of potential immigrants, one can (with all proper caution) note analogies with the (Western) European region. Immigration to Japan, first of all, is determined by its irregularity (by the 'illegality', or more precisely the 'illegalization' of labour migrants). This ascription of 'illegality' pre-structures activities of go-betweens and conduits, and those in turn mediate exploitation and positions on the labour market.

5.4.1.8 *Arbeitsstrich* ('Street walking' for work) – comparison of the situation in Western Europe and Japan

While comparisons of the immigration situation in Japan with that of Western European repeatedly refer to the position of guest-workers in Germany, the origins of the immigration 'staged' by the Federal Republic of Germany, and the legal status of its guest-workers and their increasingly peculiar position as *de facto*-immigrants, are clearly very different from the situation in Japan. Considerably closer parallels can be found, however, in the recent 'immigration wave' which followed the so-called 'opening of borders' of former Eastern-bloc countries, and in the emergence of a 'black' labour market in Austria, aptly termed *'Arbeitsstrich'* (prostitution – 'street walking' – for work). Below, I cite several passages from the work of the sociologist Konrad Hofer, which strikingly evoke the living conditions of 'illegal' workers in Japan. As the structural positions of 'illegals' in Austria and Japan are homologous, the similarities between the situations of labour migrants in the two countries are particularly close.

Hofer in the tradition of interactionist sociology, used a qualitative approach, striving for understanding, and inquiring into the meaning which members of sub-cultures give their way of life. He started also from the assumption that socio-political and economic differentials between countries and regions were engine driving migration. He pretended to be a Rumanian of German origin so as to enter more directly into the scene and to investigate the *Lebenswelt* of working tourists. He surveyed Polish immigrant workers,

> who with an officially recorded share of employees of less than one per cent (roughly 12,000) quantitatively represent an insignificant number, but qualitatively leave rough tracks on

the Austrian labour market tracing out the situation for future working tourists coming to Austria (Hofer, 1992:10).

The fact that these workers were from a country geographically so near and so accessible is the main difference between their situation and that of 'illegals' in Japan. Thus, for example, Poles can renew their visas by a quick return to their homeland or by travelling to neighbouring Hungary or Czechoslovakia, returning immediately to Austria without gross financial losses, whereas migrants in Japan, owing to the high cost of air fares, are usually forced to 'submerge' into 'illegal stay'.

Most of the Polish migrant workers had to find work on the black market. Their living and working conditions are only understood when compared with their wretched situation back home. Their earnings allowed them to purchase consumer and electronic goods scarcely available in Poland. This, according to Hofer, was the decisive motive for migration. The description of the situation of a Polish worker in Vienna could also apply to a Pakistani in Tokyo: 'He lodged in cramped rooms, lives in permanent fear of a police-raid and work assignments can dry out from one day to the other' (Hofer, 1992:23). Hofer distinguishes between two types of working tourists. The younger type ('the single type') comes to Austria to fulfil his or her consumption aspirations as quickly as possible and has a higher propensity to emigrate. He rejects the Polish life-style and is oriented towards the 'West' (and sometimes targets further countries for emigration). Older migrants ('the family-type'), on the other hand, come to Vienna to earn money which they will purposefully invest back home (cf. Hofer, 1992:152f.). According to Hofer, it is typical of every migratory movement that 'always, if people decide to leave their home country to try their luck in foreign countries . . . those "fortune-hunters" are prone to depict their experiences abroad in a light as favourable as possible' (Hofer, 1992:35).

Many of the Poles work in the construction sector. Most of their employers are sub-contractors. They have to rely on getting jobs on the street and from private labour agents:

> costs are high, the results, however, oftentimes not
> satisfactory . . . Polish migrants who have been in Vienna
> longer often try to sell their knowledge concerning work
> opportunities to newly-arrived migrants. The tariffs for these

valuable hints range between 1,000 and 3,000 Schillings, depending on how attractive the work place is . . . Labour agents are indeed often reckless and make their money with migrants from Poland (Hofer, 1992:45 and 47f.).

Hofer reports on housing and wage conditions. With regard to lodgings it is found that 'illegals', as a rule, live together in groups in cramped, small rooms in old apartments. They behave as inconspicuously as possible so as not to provoke undesired attention. Their wages are far below standard wages. In the worst case of exploitation, female Polish textile workers earned only ten Schillings per hour. To earn an (almost) adequate income, Poles often endure enormously long working hours (including weekends). They must always be cautious at their workplaces:

The illegality of this work situation became apparent to me from several peculiarities of conduct. For instance, workers basically avoid any contact with other workers on construction sites. They do not draw attention to themselves by loud talking, but rather by their noiseless behaviour. Never do they yell for material or tools as is common among indigenous bricklayers. Often those illicit worker-groups try to give the appearance of legal workers of a firm by wearing white bricklayer gear. Their isolation on construction sites is conspicuous when viewed against other employees. It is only partly founded in the linguistic barrier. To a larger extent, it results from the fear of provoking attention and thereby making more likely a raid, which could mean the premature end of their stay in Vienna (Hofer, 1992:128).

I can confirm that these observations apply also to the condition of 'illegal' workers in Japan – although here I can cite only particular incidents of which I have first-hand knowledge. In the summer of 1989, I worked as a helping hand for *tobi* (scaffolders) and met a worker who was an example of a genuine 'working tourist' – something rather rare in Japan. At the time I described his case as follows:

The work itself is easy to learn, just tote the scaffold parts and put them together. Nobody gives explanations. I watch and do the same as the others. Often the men use hand signals, so the job can easily be done by foreigners even with no command of the Japanese language. One of the *tobi* points to a man, sitting quietly aside smoking, who has already caught my eye: 'He is a foreigner too'. The man, to me indistinguishable from the Japanese, asks in poor English where I come from. There is the predictable confusion of Austria and Australia, country of his dreams, so I explain again: not kangaroos but Mozart and Vienna. His name is Jang and he is from Pusan, South Korea.

He is delighted that I know Pusan is a big seaport. At first he speaks little, but after I give him some juice and a cigarette, he opens up. In reasonable Japanese, he tells me that he has a wife and two children going to elementary school but he has no relatives in Japan and feels lonely. He comes to Japan periodically, on a tourist visa, so he is working illegally. When his residence permit expires after fifteen days, he returns home, waits for the prescribed time to re-enter Japan and then comes back. In Korea there is no work. The profits he makes on his yen earnings far outweigh even the risk of being deported with a one-year ban on re-entering Japan (Herbert, 1989a:4).[7]

It was not least in response to the expansion of the black labour market, that the Austrian government – employing measures similar to those taken in Japanese – introduced restrictions, suspending free entry to the country. At the time, Austria was the only capitalist country to which Poles had free access; it was therefore highly attractive.

This free passenger traffic abruptly changed on 6 September 1990. Before the coming into force of this measure immigration to Austria swelled once more ... Those Poles who had a satisfactory illicit job and wanted to stay could with little difficulty purchase an 'entry stamp' before 6 September for 1,000 Schillings in cash. Others declined this expenditure and hoped not to be detected by police. Thus I know immigrants of the 'single' type who stayed in Vienna for months without a visa. They managed to survive the dangerous period of one year until the repeal of visa-regulations ... The visa obligation partly led to seclusion. The 'established' could remain, the 'failures' willy-nilly had to return. However, to be a member of the circle of 'established' meant to suffer under incredibly low wages and bad housing conditions (Hofer, 1992: 155ff.).

Hofer, with reason, talks of circumstances 'returning us to the conditions of early capitalism' (Hofer, 1992:155ff.). Exactly those conditions characterize the segments of the labour market that migrant workers in Japan end up in. In particular, it is their 'illegality' which relegates them to the function of a proletarian reserve army and makes them especially vulnerable to crude exploitation and infringements of their human rights. If one defines their position in terms only of the criterion 'foreigner', comparisons drawn between their situation and that of guest-workers in Austria and Germany will be deficient. In Japan, comparisons of this kind are usually made retrospectively, depicting the 'social consequences'; for example, it is claimed that the education of the second generation, the increase in unemployment and the integration of migrants into society have given rise to tensions in Germany, and the same type of problems would spread in Japan with a legalization of Asian workers. This is legitimate only to a very limited extent, and is heavily burdened with political interest. However, to characterize the present situation of foreign migrants in Japan, in terms both of the criterion 'illegal' and a comparison with the Austrian black labour market (*Arbeitsstrich*) would be much more fruitful. (It must be noted though that the emergence of the *Arbeitsstrich* in Austria could not at that time have been known in Japan.)

5.4.1.9 Housing conditions

Five to seven foreign migrant workers living together in a crowded room is regarded as the normal for newly-arrived immigrants. They prepare meals together and avoid going out unnecessarily in order not to provoke complaints (and subsequent action by authorities). They live under constant stress and fear of detection (Gonoi, 1989:75). Since they live in regional concentrations, their living conditions are viewed with anxiety as 'slum formation' (KBR, 1990:77) or as incipient 'ghetto-formation' (Yashima, 1989:26). In a newspaper article these concerns may be expressed using the terms 'slumification' (*suramuka*) and 'ghettoization'. Conflicts between Japanese and foreign residents of particular neighbourhoods are said to be on the rise, with there being some risk that they could escalate sufficiently to endanger public security (*Yomiuri shinbun*, 20 June 1988). The interrelations between concentrations of 'strangers' in certain areas and insecurity (criminality) are a universal topic – a topic prompted by the published hypotheses of the police, and born of their prevention ideology.

However, this style of communal living is a phenomenon that can be observed internationally during processes of immigration. It has diverse causes. First of all, it arises from the informal information conduits among foreigners over which knowledge about lodging opportunities is transferred. Further, the 'influx of labour migrants into certain urban areas is not the cause, but the consequence of the agglomeration of bad housing, which is deserted by the indigenous population and not in demand' (Wimmer, 1986b:296). According to a Japanese police investigation of 253 apprehended 'illegal' migrant workers, more than two-thirds of them lived in *apāto* or *manshon* (meaning small rented apartments), 68.4 per cent had fellow lodgers (on average almost three!) who, in the main, were their compatriots (Suzuko, A.O., 1990b:61f.).

At the same time, the segregated concentrations of foreigners are indicative of objective discrimination, which in Japan is here mostly imputed to dealers in real estate. According to one real estate businessman, with the increased numbers of foreign workers the problems associated with renting lodgings to foreigners include late payment of rent, rooms left in a filthy condition, and contracts which, although negotiated with one migrant, were abused by the tenant who would sub-let to others, so that in no time five or six would be packed like 'sardines' in the room, generating permanent conflicts. Thus many real estate firms decided not to serve foreign clientele. One of the dealers plainly expressed his prejudices: he was afraid, but his fear was different (!), he said, from that of other Japanese, because 'among those [foreigners] there are violent folks, capable of any crime, they are like released lions...' (Hatada, 1990:132f.). Interviews with twenty real estate dealers yielded three reasons for the exclusion of foreigners: they were boisterous, ill-smelling, and their number would increase through sub-letting to additional tenants (Obata, 1990b:121). We may note, incidentally, that being dirty and noisy are part of the 'international inventory of stereotypes' of strangers (regardless of nationality). 'Form and content of xenophobic discourse are rather constant . . . Central topics such as criminality, filth and fear of unemployment dominate. And even the applied linguistic forms are similar' (Wodak, 1991:17). It is because many landlords refuse (Asian) foreigners, that they are compelled – through lack of alternatives – to live concentrated where they are finally accepted. Thus, for example, because in Yokohama only a few tenement houses will accept Philippinos, they become highly concentrated in those lodgings, with up to a hundred Philippine nationals per tenement house (Ishiyama, 1989:15). In Saitama prefecture, there are tenement houses originally constructed for Japanese inland migrants (*dekasegi*-workers) from the Tōhoku region. Today, not only are Pakistani and Bangladeshi workers accommodated in these houses, but they have also taken over the functional role of the inland migrants on the labour market (Hagio, Obata and Hamada, 1990:26).

A further reason for the crowded communal living is one of simple economics. The internationally-infamous high rents and cost of living of Japan's large urban areas force the thrifty labour migrants to share the burden of rent with others. A Bangladeshi sadly notes that many Asian migrant workers miscalculate the immense living costs in Japan. In December 1985, two Bangladeshi workers moved into a tenement house which the owner had originally wanted to renovate. In the following year, twenty-one, and by November 1987, forty-eight registered Bangladeshi nationals were lodging there (with 70 per cent of them holding tourist visas; Sawahata, 1989:81 and 84). In order to save money, Chinese *shūgakusei* are reputed to acquire furnishings, radios, television sets, refrigerators, and so forth, for their apartments from garbage dumps. It is part of their everyday knowledge that 'in Japan everything is thrown away in perfectly functioning condition' (Sawahata, 1989:58 and Gonoi, 1989:97).

Also part of the web of factors leading to these enclaves is the fact that they perform another important function, serving the migrants as places for mutual help and information exchange (noted for instance in Miyazawa, 1989:86f.).

Inter-ethnic contacts in ethnic 'enclaves' . . . in the beginning of the stay defuse excessive tensions of disorientation . . . The occupation of badly-furnished areas initially complies with the modest requirements for lodging and infrastructure and the low inclination and ability to pay higher rents. Moving into an ethnically-homogeneous area – particularly in the initial stage – is an important opportunity for adaptation to the new surroundings for adaptation which is low in anomie (Esser, 1980:95 and 154).

In Western Europe, the housing situation of immigrants is perceived as 'one of the most striking features of their social position'. It is further remarked that others who move into cheap, old flats are indigenous low-wage earners, older people, the chronically ill, and similar social groups who form the lower working class. 'Ghettoes are constituted more on class lines than simply according to race or nationality' (cf. Castles and Kosack, 1985:314ff.).

The notoriously uttered apprehensions with regard to an increasing concentration of foreigners (such as foreign infiltration, slum-formation, ghettoization, heightened aggressiveness) obfuscate the problem of general infrastructural deficits in particular areas. They deflect from the disadvantages of lower social classes altogether ... Foreigners create their spaces of familiarity, which can be the basis for national, ethnic, and cultural unions. But first of all, they should provide protection from marginalization and discrimination and, therefore, are rather the outcome of a defensive attitude (Müller, 1985:58 and 60).

The dwelling concentration, although partly viewed as disadvantageous to the actors, also has positive functions, providing them with a subcultural and communicative infrastructure and basis for life, enhancing their feeling of security ('a part of their homeland abroad', Bade, 1983:89). Analogously, a Japanese study characterizes ethnic networks and concentrated communities as 'home or asylum' in the foreign country, formed according to regions of origin and lineage relationships and promoting community solidarity on the basis of work through information exchange and mutual help (cf. GRJCK, 1992:98f.).

Nonetheless, as a consequence of individual mobility 'social isolation' emerges. Because, for migrants, the acceptance into new informal groups is especially difficult, they are more 'anomic' than non-mobile persons (Albrecht, 1972:231f.). A quarter of the male 'illegals' interrogated by police stated that they felt isolated and lonely (29 per cent of the women) and more than a third gave lack of linguistic skills as the biggest handicap of life in Japan (the figure was 23.2 per cent for the questioned female migrants; Suzuki A.O., 1990b:65). A journalist writes of Pakistanis, who try to relieve their feelings of loneliness by making frequent telephone calls back home. The large sums involved were already part of their budget calculations (Yonemoto, 1990:36). But a much more significant psychological stress is the constant fear of authorities or of being reported to them by members of the public. Conspicuousness is avoided, and leisure time is often spent in the migrants' own dwellings. This 'U-boat lifestyle' is often described by journalists who have observed 'illegals' in their usual surroundings, for example, by Hwang, 1990:20, Aikawa, 1987:35, Yonemoto, 1990:45, and Gonoi, 1990:14f. The latter, with an undertone of alarm – albeit well-intentioned – illustrates his account with such dramatic examples as those of suicides and a Thai schizophrenic, and with data such as that while in 1988 there were only twenty-four foreign clients in a public psychiatric clinic, by 1990 the number had reached fifty-four. (See also Shimokawa, 1991:162, who immediately – and unduly – concludes that neurotic illnesses among migrants are on the rise. Interpretation of the figures, however, should take into account the higher foreign population, and the spread of information concerning the accessibility of therapy).

5.4.1.10 Legal status of 'illegals'

Foreign migrant workers live with constant psychological stress and fear of authorities which are products of their 'illegalization'. This 'illegality' generates a 'situation of total absence of rights' (Karabao no kai, 1988:5). A migrant worker's claim on an employer (for rights for example, in a case of wage embezzlement) is often answered with the threat of denunciation to Immigration Control Agencies or the police (with practical experiences from the work of an organization for the protection of the rights of labour migrants: Hanada, 1990). The situation of foreign workers remains precarious even if they turn to official agencies. If they seek the intervention of public labour offices or the Labour Standards Bureau, those authorities are directed by an ordinance (published in Karabao no kai, 1988:75–77) of 26 January 1988 to notify the Immigration Control Bureau of any cases of 'illegal' stay. Deportation formalities are then instituted. Thus, for 'illegals', it is impossible without risk to seek support from labour-related authorities. Whereas agencies under the Ministry of Labour must rigidly enforce that ordinance, the Ministry of Justice issued a suspension of this reporting obligation to the Consultation Offices for the Human Rights of Foreign Workers (*gaikokujin no jinken sōdansho*) established on 16 August 1988. Thus, when foreign (even 'illegal') workers seek the counsel of this agency regarding wage problems, forced prostitution, and so forth, this is dealt with confidentially and notification of the Immigration Control Bureau is permitted only with the consent of the client (Umetani, 1989:93). This measure has been hailed by a discussion panel as being 'epoch-making' (I A.O., 1990:23f.). The strenuous efforts of organizations for the protection of the rights of migrant workers have led Labour Offices also to loosen their reporting practices, so in that, since the enactment of the amendment of the *nyūkanhō*, the Immigration Control Bureau is not inevitably notified of 'illegal' overstayers (Hanada, 1990:108). In October 1990, the Ministry of Labour released an internal instruction according to which, when investigating infractions of labour-related laws (for example, after workplace accidents), it can refrain from reporting even in cases of foreigners staying 'illegally' (although in practice this does not always happen, cf. Furuya, 1991:70f.).

In principle, it holds true that every labour-law-related regulation (such as those contained in the Labour Standard Acts – *rōdō kijunhō*) applies to any employee, regardless of nationality or legal status. 'Illegal' stay is, after all, just an infringement of administrative law, and does not legitimate the exclusion from labour law-related protective measures: *rōdōsha hogohō*). All of the violations of human rights reported in the mass media are offences punishable under existing labour laws. This applies to wage deductions (including those made under the subterfuge that the money was previously lent to the employee by the employer; that is, settlement of outstanding debts via wage deductions is prohibited) as well as to infractions of the minimum wage law and the Law for Safety and Hygiene in the Workplace and to violations of the prohibition against the mediation of employment against payment. According to findings of the Immigration Control Bureau, in 1986 there were 636, and in 1987 there were 492 cases of non-payment of wages (*chingin fubarai*) to foreign workers (Tezuka, 1989a:138; these, of course, are only the cases which came to the attention of authorities; presumably, very many more cases go unreported).

Even the labourer's compensation insurance, which is compulsory for private enterprises to take out, can be taken out and claimed upon retroactively for 'illegal' workers in cases in which their employers had failed to insure them. In 1987 there were twenty-eight such cases, which presumably involved 'illegal' foreigners; nine of the twenty-eight foreigners were Pakistanis, seven were from the Philippines, four were Taiwanese and four were Bangladeshis (*Asahi shinbun*, 19 June 1988; for a concise treatise on labour law-related questions, see Nishitani, 1990). In 1988, seventy-one labour accidents involving 'illegal' migrants were recorded. The case is mentioned of a Pakistani who lost his right arm through a workplace accident while he held a tourist visa, and who reportedly received a disability pension following deportation (*Yomiuri shinbun*, 29 March 1990). In 1989, the number of known workplace accidents suffered by 'illegal' workers was eighty-nine (Hatade, 1991:29). Because foreign male migrant workers are employed in the most accident-prone sectors (construction, industrial production), industrial accidents (*rōdō saigai*) often occur – not least because safety measures are not actively promoted or understood, owing to the difficulty of communication. It is quite common for employers to dismiss foreigners with a severance payment following accidents (Tezuka, 1989a:138; Higashizawa, 1991:47). These employers fear trouble with authorities (for example, an inspection by the Labour Standards Bureau which would reveal their deficient safety measures) or a raising of their premiums for worker accident insurance rate because of the frequency of accidents. Most of the accidents involving 'illegals' happen in the metal-fabrication sector (with press machines) and on construction sites; it is said that foreigners in these industries seldom receive instructions regarding safety regulations or procedures (Tenmyō, 1991:21 and 25). In the forty-two cases of industrial accident handled by organizations for the protection of the rights of migrant workers in 1990, violations of the Law on Safety and Occupational Health in the Work Place (*rōdō anzen eisei hō*) and of the Labour Standard Acts were involved. This indicates also that ('illegal') foreigners work for small enterprises which have become unattractive because of their bad working conditions (hence their labour shortage) and whose deficient safety measures endanger foreign and Japanese workers alike (Furuya, 1991:67).

Negotiations in claims for compensation following industrial accidents occupy much of the time of movements for the protection of migrant workers. Through their adamant interventions, several precedents were set. For instance, a Philippino whose legs were severed by a concrete slab which fell on him at work and who will suffer life-long disabilities (paralysis, incontinence), was deemed eligible to receive monthly compensation even after his return to the Philippines in a wheel-chair (Watanabe, 1990c; Furuya, 1991:73). In cases of less serious injury or illness, labour migrants fear losing their jobs or being reported to authorities if they seek treatment. Many of them therefore keep working even when injured or sick. Only in cases of acute emergency and serious injury do they consult the Labour Standards Bureau or organizations fighting for the rights of migrants. Multi-stage, subcontractual relations (characteristic especially of the construction business) often make negotiations difficult and cumbersome, because responsibilities are unclear, or negligence is denied by the employer, burdening the accident victim with the *onus probandi*). Sometimes sub-contracting firms cannot be traced (Kagoshima, 1990 in a description of the intervention process and 'collective bargaining' of an organization for the protection of the rights of migrant workers after a Philippino broke his leg).

In principle – irrespective of the nationality of workers and regardless of their legal status – far-reaching legal protection of workers is afforded by existing Japanese labour regulations, and a certain equality of foreign workers with Japanese workers does exist except with regard to entitlement to livelihood assistance – *seikatsu hogo* – or employment insurance – *koyō hoken* – against loss of job; see Takafuji, 1990:10ff, for a list of fifteen social welfare regulations and for the dates of their first application to foreigners). Nevertheless, in the debate on irregular migrant workers, lawyers, intellectuals and professors of international law called for Japan to ratify several ILO (International Labour Organization) conventions, including conventions 97 (Migrations for Employment Convention, rev. 1949), 111 (Discrimination [Employment and Occupation] Convention, 1958) and 143 (Migrant Workers [Supplementary Provisions] Convention, 1975). These conventions prescribe legal equality of migrant workers with indigenous workers and proscribe discrimination (see, for example, Onizuka, 1988:73 or Miyajima, 1989:84).

The legal reality for Asian migrant workers, however, remains dismal. Because of the fear of expulsion, lack of knowledge of the law, lack of social capital (contacts with professionals such as lawyers) and the extent of their dependence on employer and work place (for example, due to the pressure to settle debts), their ability to avail themselves of the protection of the law is negligible. Committed journalists report that up to 1990 there were only twenty cases in which the Labour Standards Acts were applied to migrant workers. The Labour Standards Bureau often informed the Immigration Control authorities about foreign workers who were staying 'illegally', but hardly ever took the initiative in calling in Labour authorities in cases of unpaid wages or wage embezzlement (Obata, Hagio and Hamada, 1990:12; the origin of the figure of only twenty cases up to 1990 remains obscure – as it often does in journalistic sources). In this context, it is also lamented that while 'months of concerted action' are regularly staged to expose 'illegals', no similar steps are taken to expose violations of labour regulations or to investigate the victimization of 'illegals'. Thus prosecution of the victims of exploitation takes precedence over prosecution of the perpetrators (Tanaka, 1988:24f.). Lawyers working on issues of human rights, and civil movements for the legal protection of foreign migrant workers, try to offer relief and secure a place for migrants with grievances to receive counsel and active assistance in dealing with the law.

5.4.1.11 Organizations for the protection of the rights of migrant workers

I offer here an impressionistic account – with citations of relevant literature – of the operations of a movement for the support of migrant workers. From July 1989 to December 1990, and again from April 1992, I have regularly participated in the activities of an organization based in the day-labourer area of Osaka, Kamagasaki, and attended all of their regular meetings (*teireikai*). The movement was officially founded in June 1988 under the title 'Ajia kara no dekasegi rōdōsha o sasaeru kai' (Asian Friends) by roughly 200 participants. The events immediately occasioning its foundation were news reports on the deaths of Asian migrant workers in traffic accidents (four Thais in September 1986 in Mie prefecture and three Philippinos in November of the same year in Chiba prefecture). The initiative came from the Protestant Reverend Koyanagi Nobuaki, the Jesuit Susukida Noboru, and the former activist in the 1968 student movement, now making his living as a day labourer, Mizuno Ashura (presently secretary-general of the Asian Friends). They were able to draw upon experience of the traditional support work of Christian churches for *zainichi*-Koreans in the day-labourer quarter. The relatively well-organized network of Christian denominations engaged in the protection of exploited Asian women could also be called upon (cf. Mizuno, 1990). Sisters and priests of various religious organizations periodically attend the *teireikai* and take care of cases of forced prostitution and, of late, increasingly problematic cases regarding the birth of children of migrants, affiliation orders, marriage and divorce questions and so forth – these latter being indicators of increasing maturity of the process of female migration to Japan, and auguries of second-generation problems.

Asian Friends has around one hundred registered members. Approximately twenty can be considered activists who consistently attend meetings and work hard for the movement. Language-skills working groups were formed for Chinese, Korean, Thai and Philippine nationals. Emergency cases are dealt with and monthly reports on recent developments are given. A planned telephone counselling service for migrant workers failed due to shortage of volunteers who could attend the telephone of Asian Friends during the regular hours assigned. Thus telephone calls are answered by whoever happens to be in the office at the time, which sometimes leads to unnecessary delays in assistance, or to the failure of assistance owing to language difficulties – despite the good will of those involved. The organization printed small leaflets and labels the size of a visiting-card in several languages (Japanese, English, Thai, Tagalog, Korean, Chinese). These are distributed at various events, in churches, and at migrants' work places in order to provide them with addresses of people they can consult confidentially in pressing situations. According to Nakajima Fumio, a Catholic day labourer, some of the calls concern industrial-relations matters, such as conflict over unpaid wages and sudden illegitimate dismissals, others pertain to residency matters to do with visas, return procedures after overstaying and such like. More rarely calls are about injuries, sickness or problems regarding payment after treatment; but surprisingly often, inquiries are from unemployed migrants seeking work, who seem to mistake Asian Friends for a labour agency – this is the case for more than half of the calls received!

The activity profile of an organization based in Nagoya, which was founded in July 1987 under the name 'Arusu no kai' (Zainichi Ajia rōdōsha to tomo ni ikiru kai – Asian Labourers Solidarity), is very similar. In its first eleven months of operation it logged 330 cases of counselling, that is, on average approximately one case a day. (Sadly, victimised women comprised a larger proportion of cases than had been found by Asian Friends.) Of these cases, seventy-three concerned relationship problems (marriage etc.), sixty-five concerned distress regarding accommodation, forty-one were inquiries by 'illegal' overstayers wondering whether to turn themselves in to the Immigration Control authorities, thirty-three related to breaches of labour contracts or unpaid wages, twenty-one were cases of forced prostitution, nineteen were consultations regarding visa extension and passport troubles, nineteen concerned medical care, eighteen were of victims of violence, sixteen were requests for support after escape from conditions of coerced prostitution, ten were requests for introduction to employers, nine were reports of missing persons, and thirteen were of various 'other' grievances (118 cases recorded from July to December 1987 and 219 from January to June 1988: Wada, 1990:185).

Another solidarity movement under 'spiritual patronage' (its most active member is the priest Watanabe Hidetoshi) was officially established on 17 May 1987 under the name 'Karabao no kai'. It reports a similar profile of problems dealt with: low or unpaid wages, medical treatment, inquiries concerning abortion, facilities for childbirth, education of children, accommodation (sometimes following eviction), Japanese lessons, visits to migrants in detention following arrest because of 'overstay', support to migrants in court and so forth. Most of those seeking counsel are in distress due to problems concerning wages or industrial accidents (KNK, 1988:31–35, with examples).

The organizations circulate monthly newsletters for their members. My host movement has issued its newsletter since July 1988 under the name of the organization, *Asian Friends*. It reports its recent activities, describes successfully solved cases, covers recent developments in the country, announces forthcoming events including those of sister organizations, reports and critically discusses official statements by government agencies, labour unions or trade associations, and so forth, and reprints current newspaper articles (some of them from the Japanese daily press in English). A *teireikai* follows a similar pattern: recent actions are reported on; the groups specializing in certain countries report on their activities; usually there is a special report on relevant issues (sometimes by invited experts – I had the honour to present a lecture on the situation in Germany in the autumn of 1989 and on that in Austria in the spring of 1992); pressing problems are discussed and solutions are sought for them; new publications are reviewed and official statements from ministerial papers such as *Kanpō* or *Kokusai jinryū* are copied and distributed for discussion. Special events are organized to inform the public; these include lectures and discussion panels, to which lawyers and activists from all over Japan are invited. Since 1989 an annual festival known as the 'Asian festival', is held (usually on 5 November, a day proclaimed 'day of migrant workers abroad' by a Philippine migrants' organization) in the park of the church Tamatsukuri in Osaka, providing ethnic food and art (dance, music, theatre) and a charity bazaar. It is attended by migrant workers, Indochinese refugees, foreign students, activists and sympathizers. Every year an annual meeting is held, reviewing activities, with the meeting sometimes being accompanied by lectures (for example, on 1 July 1990 the activist Sakai Kazuko spoke about problems faced by Chinese students and the lawyer Niwa Masao spoke on the new Immigration Control Act). On occasion multi-lingual fliers or pamphlets are written: for example, in protest against the revision of the *nyūkanhō* or, in the late autumn of 1990, concerning the national census (explaining that one can decline to give information, and that one was under no obligation to show one's passport). Occasionally demonstrations are called, such as that on 11 November 1990 in Kyōto and Tokyo against the new Immigration Control Act, during which activists in the forefront of the debate on foreign workers unsuccessfully attempted to lodge a writ of protest at the offices of the Ministry of Justice.

The organizations work in close co-operation with lawyers, who are sensitized to the human rights situation of labour migrants. Labour-law related conflicts can often be settled by activists negotiating directly (sometimes over the telephone) with employers. Threats or hints by employers that workers will be reported to the police or Immigration Control authorities are answered with counter-threats of legal charges. In order to increase bargaining power, the assistance of lawyers is sought, usually leading to out-of-court solutions. The majority of court cases involving migrants, according to the lawyer Yōfu Tomomi, concern 'illegal' stay or infractions of the *nyūkanhō* and petty offences against penal or special laws (for example, in connection with stimulants or property). When cases come to trial, foreign suspects are supported by members of Asian Friends, who attend court hearings and give counsel. They visit suspects in detention, inform them about legal procedure in Japan and the prospect of getting a suspended verdict. In 1990 I attended four court hearings (two infringements of the Immigration Control Act, one indictment on drug misuse, and one case of bogus credit card use by a Nigerian national; all four cases resulted in suspended verdicts and expulsion). What seemed particularly problematic to me, apart from the half-hearted pleading of the ex-officio defence counsel and the non-professional interpretation (the trial of the Nigerian was conducted in English, translated by a Philippina), was the common time span of three to four weeks between the main hearing and the handing down of the verdict – an unduly long period for suspects to have to remain in detention.

The Osaka Bar Association provides several forms of assistance for labour migrants, including symposia, free legal counsel by telephone, and a handbook on the rights of migrant workers (in Japanese: OBK, 1990, also available in English and Tagalog). In December 1990, a group of roughly sixty lawyers calling itself LAFR (Lawyers for Foreign Labourer's Rights), established through the initiative of six attorneys-at-law in Osaka, was formed for the legal support of migrants; it too offers a telephone service on legal issues for foreigners free of charge.

In June 1990, two scientists (Yamamoto Fuyuhiko of Kansai University and Manfred Ringhofer of Osaka Sangyō University A.O.), a number of activists for the rights of *zainichi*-Koreans, and nine lawyers together founded a study and research group on human rights questions relating to foreign residents in Japan (Zainichi gaikokujin no jinken mondai kenkyūkai). Its monthly meetings include lectures and discussions, which strive to illuminate the issues with theoretical insights. (I am myself a member of the group, and reported on my project on 19 December 1990.)

There are also horizontal coalitions of movements for the civil rights of migrants. These unite organizations dealing with special issues (trafficking of women, Philippine migrants, *shūgakusei*, re-migrants from Brazil, Iranians, so-called information centres and so forth). A relatively loose, horizontally structured national 'commission' connecting several dozen organizations and having a certain representative function, is the Ajaijin rōdōsha mondai kondankai (representing, according to Sawahata, 1989:242, around forty organizations). It has published an English-Japanese handbook on the rights of migrant workers (ARMK, 1990; the most important contact addresses for the larger associations for migrant workers are on pp. 200–204). Eleven movements have joined the 'CALL-network' (Ajia no hataraki manabu nakama to rentai suru rōdōshashimin no kai). At the end of 1991 in Kansai, at the suggestion of Asian Friends and in close co-operation with the Bar Association, the RINK (Rights of Immigrants Network in Kansei – Gaikokujin rōdōsha no jinken o mamoru Kansai nettowāku) network was established.

The whole of Japan is covered by a network of movements for migrant workers, which in grassroots-fashion perform important support and awareness functions. It is characteristic of these movements that they function principally through the work of an active 'core' of one to two dozen persons per organization, while a far larger group of perhaps up to one hundred can be mobilized to attend the organization's special events (symposia, festivals, annual meetings), and an unrecorded number of more peripheral sympathizers can be drawn upon for support, for example, at demonstrations or through calls for donations. Thus, while the membership and number of supporters of these movements is small (for example, compared to the numbers involved in the Peace Movement in Germany or anti-racism demonstrations in France), qualitatively, the work of active members is marked by its notorious pertinacity, its almost fanatical doggedness. Moreover, activities remain locally-focused and oriented towards specific problems, with members concentrating on the same issue over a long period of time (characteristic features of Japanese grassroots and civil movements; I thank the political scientist Hartwig Hummel for comment reinforcing my impression in this respect). For a conclusive assessment – after this piecemeal account – of the socio-political impact of support organizations for migrants, it seems to me that the indirect assistance in information gathering for them and the education of the public proves crucial. They are perhaps more significant than such direct relief and help as legal counsel, intervention in cases of work-related law infringement, and support in court. Insights into the (legally and otherwise) precarious situation of migrants are offered to the Japanese public by the press and other media. The movements provide a voice for afflicted migrants, partly compensating for their lack of articulacy. I was told by Nakajima Fumio after my return to Japan in March 1992, that Asian Friends was primarily occupied with meeting demands from journalists for interviews, information etc. Thus the organization is successful in getting its viewpoint across in the media. I would mark this as an important contribution to plurality of opinion. The depiction of the situation of migrant workers 'from the bottom' and from their own perspective, has done much to raise consciousness and sensitize the public regarding their human rights.

5.4.2 Foreign students in Japan

The presence in Japan of foreign students in increasing number has prompted debate. I can provide only a brief sketch of the situation. The debate centres less on university students (*ryūgakusei*, who in 1988, prior to the amendment of the *nyūkanhō*, numbered 29,154, 88.9 per cent coming from Asia, 53.7 per cent being of Chinese and 21 per cent of Korean nationality), than on students studying the Japanese language and vocational students (computers, cosmetics, hairdressing, etc.). In 1988, students in these latter groups (*shūgakusei*) numbered 47,827, and 95 per cent were Asian (most – 74 per cent – being of Chinese nationality: NTK, 1990:37–45 with detailed charts). In the fall of 1984, regulations and formalities for student entry were liberalized. This might have contributed to the entry boom in the following years. This deregulation originates with a much-criticized plan of the Nakasone cabinet (which had also launched a campaign for the 'internationalization' of Japan) according to which, by the year 2000, more than 100,000 foreign students would be educated in Japan. However, more than 80 per cent of the students from mainly Asian developing countries,[8] or newly industrializing countries, finance their studies themselves (*jihi ryūgakusei*) and are dependent on paid employment. Such earnings are possible through special provisions allowing twenty working hours a week. Support by the state through scholarships, etc., remains deficient; see, for example, KBR, 1990:79; Tezuka, 1989a:60. Interestingly, in the same year (1982) that the plan for 100,000 foreign students was announced, the prohibition on gainful employment for students was lifted: Tanaka, 1990b:22. This, then, amounted to a *de facto* requirement that students take care of their own expenses.

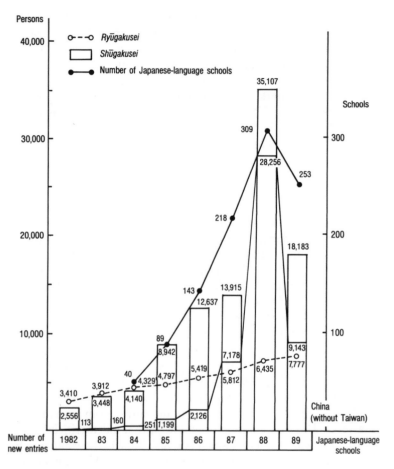

Source: Tanaka, 1990b:23.

Figure 5.9 New entries of foreign students (*ryūgakusei* and *shūgakusei*)
and the number of Japanese-language schools

The move to boost the number of foreign students is praised
enthusiastically as an 'opening measure', however, by a notorious
and inveterate Japan admirer (cf. Vogel, 1989:204).

Figure 5.9 shows figures for newly-arrived foreign students in
relation to the number of language schools officially authorized
to enrol *shūgakusei*. It clearly reflects the booming market which
swiftly led to the foundation of new schools. The fall from 1988
to 1989 is attributable to the tightening of guidelines for accredit-

ation of authorized Japanese language schools by the Ministry of Education (Monbushō), which issued new principles in December 1988. The more stringent requirements for accreditation were a response to various shortcomings and abuses which began increasingly to show up. There were schools established only on paper (aptly dubbed 'ghost-schools' – *yūrei gakkō* – Gurūpu Akakabu, 1989:46; this publication amply describes the deplorable developments outlined below); on commission these bogus schools sold vast numbers of 'warrants of admission' (*nyūgaku kyokasho*) necessary for student entry into Japan. This practice stirred vehement protests overseas, for example, in Shanghai. A new business arose – for the procurement of a guarantor (*hoshōnin*) as demanded by Immigration Control during its investigation prior to the issuing of a visa (*jizen chōsa*). The *jizen chōsa* is often applied for by schools, which provide a guarantor in exchange for commission fees ('market price': 80,000 yen for the application, then 20,000 to 30,000 yen every six months for an extension of the visa). Repeated cases of forged or fictitious documents required for guarantorship were detected – some involving language school managers (cf. Gurūpu Akakabu, 1989:47). The Japanese language schools thought only of their profits, accepted students in numbers far exceeding their staff and placement capacities, offered scant instruction in overcrowded class rooms with unqualified teachers or underpaid, part-time assistants, and sometimes just functioned as labour agencies. The Japanese McDonald's outlet became notorious for establishing two Japanese language schools under its management. Most students of the latter were Malaysians of Chinese origin, and around three-quarters of them worked in the fast-food shops for eight-and-a-half hours per day. It is no wonder that one of these students stated in an interview that he was far too exhausted for language studies. The fastfood chain is accused of simply generating a cheap recruiting pool of labour for its own purposes (Sawahata, 1989:85ff.).

Foreign students (particularly Chinese familiar with Chinese characters used in Japanese writing) have the advantage of being able to obtain work through special magazines advertizing jobs. A poll of 488 foreign students conducted in April and May of 1988 revealed that, of the more than two-thirds who were employed, 56.6 per cent obtained work through recommendation of fellow students, 16.1 per cent via advertizements in the maga-

zine *Arubaito nyūsu* and 8.6 per cent through introduction by their
school (Gonoi, 1989:102; only the three most frequent answers
are given). Since March 1989, the magazine *Arubaito nyūsu* –
actually designed for Japanese students – placed a symbol meaning
'open to *ryū*-and *shūgakusei*' beside advertizements for jobs open
to foreigners as well as Japanese (Harada, 1990:57). This
(potentially) allows independence from profiteering labour agents.
Yet students seem to rely more on their fellow students and
'subcultural conduits of communication', and make little use of
magazine advertizements. However, mediators are obviously
involved initially in the trafficking of *shūgakusei*, offering 'help'
which usually has to be paid for dearly.

Some broker-organizations such as those in Shanghai, recruit
young people and promise them opportunities to make money in
Japan. Travel expenses, admission fees, and outlays for courses,
commissions and such like, on average result in a total debt burden
of between 350,000 and 700,000 yen (according to Gurūpu Akakabu, 1989:67f.; Tezuka, 1989a:67, the agent's fee alone is between
350,000 and 500,000 yen; another publication states that debts
amount to at least 300,000 yen. KBR, 1990:82; these amounts are
the equivalent of between five and twenty years' income in the
migrants' countries of origin, according to a journalist's formula,
designed to impress, in Asano, 1990:162). This debt burden, added
to the high cost of living in Japan – and in some cases to the
additional burden of remittances to the student's home country –
puts students under strong pressure to work. It often leads to paid
employment becoming the focus of the student's life in Japan
(despite any initially serious intentions to study) and to further
neglect of studies. For the extension of a visa, a letter confirming
school attendance is required, which is sometimes purchased for
cash – one stamp attesting presence at lessons costing 1,000 yen
(KBR, 1990:82; Odagiri, 1990:152) – which students again have to
earn – the classic vicious circle. However, to attribute to all foreign
students the intention of coming to Japan to make money would
be unwarranted (for many of them, acquiring language skills is a
precondition for entry to schools offering further studies or to
universities). But realities of life (especially living costs) often
force students to drift into 'illegal work'. Thus the editor of a
newspaper for foreign students counters the stigmatization of all
foreign students as potential 'illegal' workers, noting that there
are those who study earnestly as well as those who are exclusively

work-oriented. However, a clear distinction between those two types is difficult, particularly given the heavy financial burden of study in Japan, which often forces students into (part-time) employment (Zhaò, 1990:32).

The first 'visible' reaction to the difficulties for foreign students in Japan appeared in the fall of 1988. In Shanghai, protest rallies were held in which several hundred would-be foreign students demonstrated daily in front of the Japanese Consul-General's office because they had not received visas despite having completed the necessary formalities and having obtained admission to Japanese-language schools. Altogether, 50,000 'admission permits' (*nyūgaku kyokasho*) had been issued in Japan and as many passports had been issued in Shanghai since Chinese exit regulations had been liberalized in 1986. Of these new passport-holders, however, only 15,000 had received student-visas. From the remainder, there had allegedly been received only 4,700 visa applications (normally filed by Japanese-language schools). The status of the other 30,000–plus cases was unclear. Many students had paid high commission and admission fees for their 'admission permit' (between 200,000 and 300,000 yen according to Gonoi, 1989:85), or had quit their jobs in anticipation of going overseas and were ruined by debt. This led to interventions at the highest diplomatic level. Delegates from the Japanese Foreign, Justice and Education Ministries rushed to Shanghai in order to smooth annoyances. It was revealed that several schools had issued admissions far exceeding their capacities and had even traded (partly bogus) guarantor certificates. In January 1989, twenty-three Japanese language schools were 'disqualified' (*futekikaku*) and closed down. It was objected that only the worst cases were subject to this measure and many more 'unqualified' schools existed. There was also strong criticism of the fact that judgements concerning the adequacy of Japanese schools were made by the Ministry of Justice instead of the Ministry of Education, this being a confusion of competencies (Gurūpu Akakabu, 1989:281–3). Japanese-language schools were already the subject of debate in the mid-1980s, shortly after entry regulations were simplified (October 1984). The first cases of 'pseudo-students' had come to public notice in July 1986. These students had been found jobs by their school. Subsequently, the first newspaper reports of the desolate conditions and deficient language instruction of Japanese-language schools appeared. Japanese-language schools were said to be mostly stock corporations, or to be managed by a single person, and only interested in profiteering. The Ministry of Justice thereupon hastily established an Advisory Body for the Reception of Foreign Students (Gaikokujin shūgakusei ukeire kikan kyōgikai abbreviated as Gaishūkyō) and delegated to it former Justice Ministry officials (so-called *nyūkan*-OBs, from 'old boys'). It was expected that this Gaishūkyō would exercise some control over the authorization of language schools. Its critics, however, objected that it required only the minimum legal standards be met, and that it had merely made entry formalities more flexible. Ultimately it became no more than a lobby for the school managers who did not care about education. At the end of 1988, around 200 Japanese-language schools were organized in the Gaishūkyō and therefore handled roughly 70 per cent of the *shūgakusei* (on the Gaishūkyō see Tanaka, 1990b:22, and Gurūpu Akakabu, 1989:36f.). The schools are estimated to number more than 500 (Gonoi, 1989:70; KBR, 1990:22). Only in May 1989 did the Monbushō (Ministry of Education) found an Association for the Promotion of Instruction of Japanese (Nihongo kyōiku shinkōkai). This time it was ex-Monbushō–officials who were co-opted, and this new Association ought to absorb the Gaishūkyō at some time in the future (KBR, 1990:85).

According to an investigation by the Japanese Consulate in Shanghai, the average age of *shūgaku*-visa applicants was 29.2 years; three-quarters of the applicants had graduated from junior high or high school (nine to twelve years of schooling); many had work experience in small production plants (*kōba*) or bureaus; and many were jobless at the time of inquiry. It was concluded that around 70 per cent of visa applicants went to Japan with the intention of working there (Gurūpu Akakabu, 1989:73f.). Another survey yielded the following aggregated profile: 61 per cent (according to a different survey 58 per cent) of the *shūgakusei* were males; 71 per cent were between twenty-one and thirty years of age; 30.2 per cent were university graduates; and 58 per cent had been salaried personnel in firms before coming to Japan, while 24 per cent were students (Shibuya, 1990:231f.). These data suggest (although one must interpret them cautiously) that *shūgakusei* from China might see an educational stay in Japan as, *inter alia*, an opportunity to achieve upward mobility and gain higher wages. It has been said that six months' earnings in Japan are the equivalent of seven years' income in China (Yashiro, 1989:47). Another estimate is even higher, equating one year's income in Japan with twenty years' income in China (Gonoi, 1989:86). Such estimates convey the imputation that entry of Chinese into Japan as *shūgakusei* was simply a camouflage, paid employment being their primary migration motive (*'shūgaku yori shūrō'*). *Shūgakusei* have come to be lumped with other foreign workers (Tezuka, 1989a:67f.). Alleging that for them 'work takes priority over studies', a journalist maintains that (mainly) Chinese *shūgakusei* took advantage of a loophole in the law to obtain a (quasi) legal stay for work in Japan (Gonoi, 1989:91). In Tokyo, there are only fourteen institutions officially authorized by the Monbushō as Japanese-language schools, yet these are attended by one-tenth of *shūgakusei*, while there are in all throughout Japan around 400 to 500 Japanese-language schools licensed by the Ministry of Justice as 'educational organs'. From this, another author infers that 90 per cent of Japanese language students 'studied' with the actual aim of working in Japan (Kobayashi, 1990:23f.). An empirical survey among 488 students (of whom only 11.2 per cent were entitled to benefit from a scholarship) showed that 67.1 per cent had jobs (more than one-third in the service sector, Gonoi, 1989:101f.). A poll among 285 *shūgakusei* (return quota 62.5 percent) revealed that only 40 per cent of respondents either worked at the time or had worked before. However, more than half of the respondents stated that they faced problems due to high living costs (*Yomiuri shinbun*, 9 October 1989). In a poll of 2,000 students on the Chinese continent and Taiwan, only two-tenths gave as their (manifest) motive for an educational stay abroad 'gainful employment and higher wages' (the abstract, non-committal answer 'for the enhancement of knowledge' was given most often; precise descriptions of the poll design and alternative answer categories are not provided, making it impossible to determine the explanatory value of the survey; the figure above is given in *Asahi shinbun*, 7 April 1990).

However, I doubt that the primary of all *shūgakusei* in Japan is to earn money. It is rather their debt burden, the expensive fees for language courses (on average 30,000 yen to 40,000 yen per month), and the high cost of living, which can be reduced only slightly by economizing (sharing rent for overcrowded rooms in old, wooden lodgings, cooking together, acquiring household gadgets from garbage dumps, etc.), which force students to work. Many have jobs in the service sector (as waiters and dish-washers) for hourly wages of between 600 and 800 yen, or work as construction labourers or hands in *kōba* (KBR, 1990:84ff.). The regulations of the amended *nyūkanhō* permit *ryū-* or *shūgakusei* to work only for four hours a day (or twenty hours a week), and only if a work permit (*shikakugai katsudō kyokasho*) is granted by the local Immigration Control authority (Chūshō kigyōchō, 1990:44f.). This is meant to ensure that employment does not lead to neglect of studies. However, despite this intention, there remains latitude for interpretation, so that work at weekends or holidays is deemed legitimate because no classes are held at these times (Kobayashi, 1990:104). However, even given the generous interpretation of the rules, foreign students can take only part-time work 'on the side' (*arubaito*). This scarcely allows them to make ends meet with the high Japanese living expenses. They are therefore in constant danger of drifting into 'illegal work'. For example, female students, who want to work as waitresses, barmaids or 'hostesses', and who responsibly apply for a work permit – with the reasonable argument that this enables them to make money in a short time and, furthermore, to practise Japanese – are often denied the permit on the grounds that these jobs would contravene 'moral decency'. They then work nevertheless – but 'illegally' (Chō, 1990:30f.).

In advance of enactment of the amendment to the Immigration Control Act, a circular dated 29 March 1990, was sent to local agencies of the Immigration Control Bureau calling for tighter control of visa extension applications, particularly where 'illegal work' is suspected. Within a month, around 2,000 applications of *shūgakusei* had been turned down (sometimes with obscure explanations such as 'too old'; *Mainichi shinbun*, 29 April 1990). This might have been an effect of the sensationalization of 'illegal' gainful employment of foreign students, and a temporary strategy by authorities to bring about *de facto* expulsion of students through refusal of applications for visa extension.

A problem still remains unresolved after the amendment of the *nyūkanhō* was the requirement that the student prove that she or he had a guarantor (*hoshōnin*), when, after all, the guarantor had no more than a moral obligation (!) to take care of the persons guaranteed and to provide expenses in emergencies for their subsistence or return flights (Yamada and Kuroki, 1990:42). In reality, this guarantor system was devoid of function, merely proliferating the shady businesses of go-betweens (KBR, 1990:86). Until June 1988, it was possible for Japanese-language schools and even for 'brokers' to take over the guarantor function. Accumulating cases of forgery of documents and dubious profiteering led to a tightening of rules – it being no accident that this coincided with media sensationalization of 'illegal labour' and the implication that foreign students were in Japan to work illegally (cf. Hirano, 1990:29). From then on, instead of self-declared income taxation forms (*gensen chōshūhyō*, a favourite document for forgery), guarantors had to produce their certificate of paid taxes (*nōzei shōmeisho*) although again declarations of other persons were sometimes fraudulently used. Furthermore, guarantors had to use their registered seal (*jitsuin*) and prove that the seal was authentic (*jitsuin kantei shōmeisho*; Gonoi, 1990:84). With these tightened regulations, increasingly many cases of forgery of the newly-demanded documents (and also of those required for visa extensions) were exposed. This was dramatized by police as an increase in the refinement and wickedness (*akushitsu*) of the perpetrators (Yashima, 1988:19f.; HNK, 1989:40f., – here illustrated with two cases: in one case sixty-five, and in the other 600 identical, lithographically printed forgeries were seized). The press quoted an official of the Ministry of Justice ('Refined forgeries rapidly increased since April') and reported a 'growing trend'. 'Almost every day a falsification was detected' and, since April 1989, in one month fifty forgery cases came to light (*Asahi shinbun*, 6 May 1090). Among those implicated were the (former) manager of a Japanese-language school who flamboyantly sold faked attendance certificates needed for visa extension (*Asahi shinbun*, 5 December 1988), a former official of the Immigration Control Agency who traded in bogus guarantor documents (*Nihon keizai shinbun*, 21 September 1989), organized groups who purchased falsified papers needed for *shūgakusei*-status (*Mainichi shinbun*, 16 July 1989), and a group of Chinese racketeers forging documents (*Yomiuri shinbun*, 3 October 1990).

This brief sample of newspaper reports gives an idea of the sorts of forgery cases that surface in the daily press with some regularity. These cases illustrate the diversity of the illegitimate market burgeoning in the shadow of increasingly restrictive laws. The tightening of regulations produces conditions more favourable to profiteers at the periphery of the Japanese-language school business and, as a side-effect, *produces* petty criminality. These petty offences are acts of 'self-help' with the aim of legitimizing the student's (otherwise 'illegal') existence in Japan – they are a circumvention of the 'state monopoly' in this matter, and an out-come of systematic 'illegalization'.

However, the tightened rules led to a considerable hike in the prices charged for mediating the residency stay in Japan *shūgaku-sei* from the Chinese continent (Asano, 1990:165, according to whom, after the 'Shanghai-protest' a copy of the family register of the guarantor had to be provided as well). Asano remarks that, after the blood-stained crushing of the democracy movement in China (the Tiananmen Square massacre), the entry of Chinese students sharply declined. Professional 'student-traffickers' turned to NIES-countries (Newly Industrializing Economies) such as Malaysia, Singapore and South-Korea to hire would-be students (Asano, 1990:171).

Summarizing, we may note that with regard to *shūgakusei*, traf-ficking, go-between practices and labour in low-wage sectors are attended with problems similar to those found in the case of 'illegal' working tourists. Because of their visa-status, they occupy a grey zone, but can easily end up in the marginality of 'illegitimate work' when their working hours exceed the limit allowed by law. Data from Tokyo, where most of the *shū*– and *ryūgakusei* live, suggest that they are readily made use of as reserve pool of labour for the service sector, in work places and jobs (waiter, dish-washer, kitchen hand, etc.) characterized by high fluctuation (Tezuka, 1992a:18). To successfully combine studies and employment seems to be difficult, and the high financial burden leads to a shift in interest towards pecuniary goals (exacerbated in some cases by the disappointments of deficient instruction), with the concomitant risk of a drift into 'illegality'.

5.4.3 *Kenshūsei* (trainees)

Renewed public discussion concerning *kenshūsei* (on-the-job trainees) was likewise owing, not least, to economic factors. *Ken-shūsei* occupy a marginal position because they are not paid wages, but only 'pocket money' (*kenshū teate*). Their status is not covered by labour laws (such as the Labour Standards Act). Although they are not to be made to work overtime, often they are required to nonetheless (usually without being granted extra allowances). It is even not seen to be illegal for them to receive even very low payment for their work (for example, 2000 yen per day, which is far below minimum wage standards). Their position is similar to that of 'illegally working tourists' with regard to debt burden, labour market position, poor working conditions and reliance on agents and mediators (KBR, 1990:94).

Accurate official data on the number of *kenshūsei* in Japan are available. However, data concerning their living conditions and allowances are fragmentary, having been drawn from reports of individual single cases and strictly limited surveys. In 1988, there were 8,727 persons with *kenshūsei* status resident in Japan. Of these already staying in Japan in 1988, 86.3 per cent were from Asian countries (33 per cent coming from China, 17 per cent from Thailand, 11.5 per cent from the Philippines, and 9.2 per cent from Korea). A 1982 amendment to the *nyūkanhō* established a special residential category (this determining also the kinds of work and activities permitted) for *kenshūsei* (category 4–1–6–2). There was a rapid increase in the number of new entries by *kenshūsei*-visa. In 1988, 23,432 new *kenshūsei* arrived in Japan as compared, for example, with 14,388 in 1986 and 9,973 in 1982. More than 80 per cent of new entries were Asian (in 1988 20.1 per cent were from Thailand, 18.5 per cent from China and 14.3 per cent from Korea; all figures from NTK, 1990:45–47).

The perception of the *kenshūsei*-system as a problem and the consequent debate are not new developments. Public discussion of the issue of foreign labour, and heightened interest of small and middle-sized enterprises in trainees, has rekindled the debate. However, the history of the issue is forgotten or ignored. The *kenshūsei*-policy is discussed as if it were a 'new' form of co-operation and development aid in Asia. Yet lawyers (citing the socio-economist Komai Hiroshi) point out that even in 1950, during the occupation, Pakistani *kenshūsei* were brought to Japan for technical training at the instigation of the US General head-quarters (GHQ). Since then, increased investments and off-shore-production in the Asian region also increased the number of *kenshūsei*, who have completed a training program in Japan (KBR, 1990:88).

Problematic aspects of the *kenshūsei* system have been discussed in the magazine *AMPO*. Ultimately, the system merely served the interests of Japanese capital, and in particular those of Japanese transnational enterprises. Diverse organizations have functioned as vehicles for the introduction of *kenshūsei*. The role of the private Association for Overseas Technical Scholarships (AOTS) was singled out for particular criticism. Between 1959 and 1979,

17,526 trainees (77.6 per cent from Asia) were brought to Japan by this organization for education and training. Interestingly, there is a close correlation between numbers of *kenshūsei* and the amount of Japanese investment in their countries of origin, especially in industrial machine production and the automobile industry. The scheme was designed in order to educate a labour force locally so that production could be moved off-shore into Asian countries. This was attractive mainly because of low labour costs and because it was thought there would be fewer social consequences (for Japan) than would the importation of foreign labour. Scandalously, *kenshūsei* were contractually bound to the firm (which is illegal in Japan) for up to five years, in exchange for a training program of only six months – the cost of which they had to repay. Press reports of these practices led to the first public discussion, which resulted in 1981, in an amendment of the law which came into force on 1 January 1982 (cf. Nishikawa, 1981). Part of this first round of debate was an article in *AMPO* in 1974, denouncing the yearly admission of around 3,000 *kenshūsei* as a 'vehicle for the importation of cheap labour' (Kaji, 1974:48). The low allowances paid for repetitive assembly line production (requiring no special training) were criticized, as was the organization OISCA (Organization for Industrial, Spiritual and Cultural Advancement). The latter was unmasked by the same magazine a decade later as a pseudo-religious, nationalistic-tennoistic association financed by dubious sources (including, *inter alia*, Sasakawa Ryōichi), pursuing dubious goals (education in 'Japanese spirit, diligence and Japanese discipline' which was deemed as the 'key to the Japanese success') and promoting para-military exercises under Japanese nationalistic symbols (cf. Hayashi, 1988; I owe thanks to the development-aid critic and expert, Professor Sumi Kazuo, for pointing out this organization). Nonetheless, OISCA remains one of the corporations officially introducing *kenshūsei* to Japan (but with a total of only 2,385 trainees under its instruction between 1954 and 1986, its role is very small, KKSK, 1989:31).

Recruitment of *kenshūsei* is undertaken either privately by enterprises, or by organizations specializing in *kenshūsei*, or by government agencies (cf. Tezuka, 1989a:126–130). Private enterprises in particular are guilty of simply hiring cheap labour from Asia and providing no decent training in Japan for *kenshūsei*. Accordingly, they are said to have been subject to especially strict examination by the Ministry of Justice (that is, the Immigration

Control Agency). Between 1954 and 1986, 37,921 *kenshūsei* were channelled to Japan privately and 73,575 'officially', that is, 111,496 trainees in all (data from KKSK, 1989:31, including a list of recruiting bodies). Mostly, small and middle-sized enterprises rely on 'semi-official' special bodies for *kenshūsei*. The first (such as OTCA) were established at the beginning of the 1960s (this is noted to by Koyanagi, 1989a:128, who also addresses the 'historical' dimension of the *kenshūsei* program in this article). In 1974, the JICA (Japan International Co-operation Agency, Kokusai Kyōryoku Jigyōdan) was founded. It is financed exclusively from the government budget and takes care of the majority of 'government program trainees' (KBR, 1990:89).

Advisory handbooks for small and middle-sized enterprises suffering labour shortages set out the legal requirements for the hiring of *kenshūsei*. The training site has to comply with minimum standards laid down in the Law on Safety and Hygiene at the Working Place. There must be a minimum of twenty regular employees for each *kenshūsei*; housing should be provided; one-third of working hours must be scheduled for 'practical training' (*jitsumu kenshū*); private health insurance must be taken out for *kenshūsei*; and overtime and night work are not permitted (Chūshō kigyōchō, 1990:38–40). In another publication, the advantages for business are spelled out: since *kenshūsei* come to Japan to 'study' (*benkyō*) they were to be paid only small sums of 'pocket money' – 30,000 yen to 50,000 yen per month; the *kenshūsei*– system is commended (contrary to the intention of the law) as providing a stable supply of labour, and a strategic advantage to small and middle-sized enterprises in their 'struggle for survival' (Kobayashi, 1990:116 and 60).

With the amendment of the *nyūkanhō*, the requirement that there be a ratio of twenty employees to each trainee was dropped, because this had made it practically impossible for small firms to 'employ' *kenshūsei*. By ministerial ordinance, a four-tiered scheme was established which allowed enterprises with less than fifty employees to accept up to three *kenshūsei*, provided only that the firm was a member of either the Union for Workers of Small and Middle-sized Enterprises or the Chamber of Industry and Commerce (*Asahi shinbun* and *Nihon keizai shinbun*, 25 July 1990). Moreover, the Ministry of Labour proposed to establish a central private recruiting agency under joint guidance of all of the ministries involved in order to relieve the labour shortages in small and middle-sized enterprises. After a year of training, the trainee should be permitted to work full-time in euphemistically described *jitsumukeiken katsudō* – activities providing experience in business practice (*Mainichi shinbun*, 8 July 1990). This was in line with recommendations which had been made in December 1988 in the report of a group within the Ministry of Labour researching the question of foreign workers. Also recommended had been the expansion of the *kenshūsei*-system (Yashiro, 1989:66). Such recommendations and measures for expanding the *kenshūsei*-system did however lead to renewed objections that the government would thereby create a back-door for the import-ation of the cheapest possible foreign labour (Herbert, 1991a:221; Tanaka, 1990:36; Komai, 1990:265; Ishida, 1990:29f; and (on the construction sector) Saitō, 1991).

The criticisms outlined above find confirmation particularly in cases in which *kenshūsei* received inadequate training or no train-ing at all and were simply drafted into hard (dirty) labour. In June 1989, following an unannounced inspection (the first such) by the Ministry of Justice, seven enterprises were admonished because they had clearly assigned their *kenshūsei* as 'regular workers' and were instructed henceforth to offer the prescribed training (*Nihon keizai shinbun*, 22 July 1989). In April and June the same year, an inspection of forty enterprises by the Ministry of Justice revealed that twenty-three of them provided no training or edu-cation. In the most extreme cases (seven firms), sixty-eight *kenshū-sei* were denied visa extensions (this was magnified into a 'dramatic' percentage by the press, under the headline: '58 per cent labour under subterfuge "training"' *Kanagawa shinbun*, 14 August 1989). Further cases have come to light in which pro-fessional *kenshūsei*-agents have received high commissions (of between 200,000 and 400,000 yen) for introducing *kenshūsei* to employers. These sums are debited to trainees, thus burdening them with debts (on the mechanisms of exploitation see KBR, 1990:92–95). An illustration of the poor working conditions of *kenshūsei* is provided by a case which received some news cover-age. Eight Philippino *kenshūsei* working in a tyre-producing plant were required to do shift work, including nightshift, on the assembly line. They left the firm collectively, claiming they had been treated as 'slaves' (*Asahi shinbun*, 27 April 1990, 3). Thus the position of *kenshūsei* is a marginal one which allows them to stay legally as *de facto workers* yet does not define them as 'workers', leading to their readily being included in the statistics of 'illegal activities' (*shikakugai katsudō*) in the category 'illegal workers'.

5.4.4 Nikkeijin

Prior to the amendment of the *nyūkanhō*, a further group of potentially 'illegal' labourers was comprised of offspring of Japanese emigrants – mostly from Latin American countries. Until then they could enter Japan for the purpose of 'visiting relatives' on a ninety-day 'visiting visa' (*hōmon biza*, also known as a *yobi-yose-biza* – a visa for inviting relatives). It was not uncommon for holders of such a visa to take employment during their stay – despite this being illegal, some do work exceeding the ninety-day period (see Hinago, 1990b:181). With the amendment of the *nyūkanhō*, they were granted special status as 'residents' (*teijūsha*) which allows them to work unrestrictedly (Chūshō kigyōchō, 1990:91f.), and thus to legally engage in so-called 'unskilled' work (*tanjun rōdō*, Yamada and Kuroki, 1990:19). In 1990 an estimated 20,000 re-migrants worked in Japan. The Ministry of Labour announced the establishment of an official agency for *nikkeijin* from Brazil in order to prevent their exploitation by employers making traffickers and unauthorized wage deductions (*Kanagawa shinbun*, 20 September 1990). In August 1991, the number of *nikkeijin* from Brazil who had re-migrated to Japan for work was reputedly 120,000 (this would amount to 10 per cent of the Japanese community in Brazil!). While initially re-migrants were mainly first-generation Japanese still holding Japanese or double-nationality more recently it is mostly younger and, therefore, well-educated second- and third-generation Japanese who are said to emigrate (cf. Isa, 1991:35). (The descendants of marriages in which just one partner was of Japanese origin are also included in the number of *nikkeijin* living in Brazil.)

As a result of the boom in officially-sanctioned recruiting of *nikkeijin*, and media interest in the life situation of *nikkeijin* in South American countries and their reactions upon return to Japan (an interest which owed something also to the election of Peruvian president Fujimori, a second-generation Japanese immigrant), there developed in Japan a consciousness of its historical experience as an emigration country. Emigration of Japanese to Brazil started in 1908 and, after interruptions caused by the wars, reached a second peak from 1952 onwards. Only with the boosted Japanese economic growth of the 1960s and its increased demand for labour, did emigration lose its attractiveness (emigration is not least a way of exporting social problems, and thus is often officially condoned). According to a statistic of the Ministry of Foreign Affairs in 1986, 69,835 Japanese had emigrated to Brazil since the end of World War II. There are estimated to be approximately 520,000 *nikkeijin* in Brazil when second- and third-generation Japanese immigrants and those who have renounced Japanese nationality are included. According to the same census, there are also 9,353 Japanese living in Paraguay (Sawahata, 1989:208 and 217). The exodus of emigrants was mostly from structurally weak sectors and peripheral regions of Japan. Thus, around 10 per cent of immigrants to Brazil and 80 per cent of the roughly 70,000 Japanese in Peru originate from Okinawa (Ishiyama, 1989:123). In Argentina, the majority of Japanese is also said to have come from Okinawa (Noro, 1987:40). First-generation Japanese emigrants with Japanese citizenship can re-enter Japan without problems and work unrestrictedly. They are to be mainly interested in making remittances and accumulating savings, and often have re-migrated to Japan because of the desolate economic conditions (such as high inflation) in the country to which they emigrated (Sawahata, 1989:206f.).

However, the special treatment of *nikkeijin* drew harsh and vocal criticism. They had been granted resident status because of their 'bloodline' and (Japanese) 'extraction', and this was sharply attacked as an appeal to the racist myth of the 'homogeneous Japanese people' (Karabao no kai jimukyoku, 1990:311f.).[9] 'Where one speaks of distinct "blood" ... positively or negatively, we deal, consciously or unconsciously, at least with a latent tendency towards racism or proto-racism' (Geiss, 1988:30). When issuing visas for *nikkeijin*, authorities are said to be generous, even tacitly ignoring 'illegal' work. An official of the Immigration Control Agency in Naha/Okinawa comments: 'After all, they have Japanese blood' (Ishiyama, 1989:124).

However, *nikkeijin*, who have been socialized into a different overall habitus and many of whom no longer speak Japanese, are exposed to discrimination after returning to Japan, including discrimination with respect to wages, labour conditions, and such like. And like 'working tourists' they are exploited by recruiters and mediators (however, data are available only for particularly 'news-worthy' cases and so are not quite commensurable). The granting of *teijūsha* (resident) status to *nikkeijin* in 1990 may be viewed as a 'second back-door established by the government' as a countermeasure to severe sectoral labour shortages (as critically noted, for example, in Herbert, 1991a:221). The Small and Medium Enterprises Agency warns of too-aggressive recruitment in Latin American countries and calls for local laws concerning the intro- duction of labourers to be respected. Some labour officials and Latin American journalists and diplomats reacted sharply against offensive recruiting, and some of them pointed out favouritism towards *nikkeijin* and attacked the exclusive opportunities for labour migration for them as 'racism' (Chūshō kigyōchō, 1990:91). Nonetheless, Japanese enterprises recruit staff partly through labour agencies and personnel dispatching firms, and, for example, by advertizing in Japanese newspapers in Brazil (a collection of such advertisements can be found in the clipping anthology, KNK, 1990:17, 57–64). Job offers are in such sectors as construction, vehicle parts manufacturing, packaging, welding, printing presses, supermarkets, cleaners and dryers, nursing – all of them character- ized by labour shortages (Hinago, 1990b:173). At the end of 1989, the head of a personnel dispatching firm (Sankyō Kōgyō, regis- tered office in Yokohama) was arrested in Japan for illegally intro- ducing 'unskilled' labour. He had opened a bureau in Sao Paulo and introduced altogether around 4,000 *nikkeijin* from Brazil, Argentina and Paraguay to more than one hundred subcontractors in the automobile industry in Japan. He had illegally appropriated about 40 per cent of their wages (*pinhane*). Four hundred *nikkeijin* worked 'illegally' partly because they were brought to Japan on tourist visas (see for example, *Ryūkyū shinpō*, 1 November 1989; Sawahata, 1989:218ff.; Hinago, 1990b:176f.). This firm had been active on a large scale since the middle of the 1980s (cf. Noro, 1987:39). A similar case was exposed at the same time. The per- sonnel dispatching firm involved (Nisshō Kikō) likewise had intro- duced *nikkeijin* to vehicle parts production plants and deducted about 30 per cent from the wages of the dispatched workers as profits (see for example, *Mainichi shinbun*, 1 November, 1989). In some cases both Japanese and indigenous agents make high profits (sometimes in co-operation with travel agencies) from trafficking *nikkeijin* to Japan, who then live in poor housing and work under poor conditions including long hours of overtime (Hinago, 1990b:175f.).

In the fall of 1990 in Tokyo, a movement was formed for the support of workers from Latin America (Raten Amerika-kei rōdō-sha o shien suru kai; an unexplained 'CATLA' is given as abbreviation of the organization's name). It deals with the most blatant cases of skimming-off from wages, wage-embezzlement, exploitation by traffickers, and work-related accidents (*Ryūkyū shinpō*, 4 September 1990). The re-migration process was already under way in the mid-1980s (Noro, 1987:37). The debate on the journalistically-dubbed '*U-tān*' or '*yūtān*' phenomenon, that is, the returning of former Japanese emigrants, gained momentum with the discussion on the amendment of the *nyūkanhō*. The clipping collection of Karabao no kai (KNK, 1988) since its number 10 issue (September/August 1989) has devoted a chapter of between ten and twenty pages to this phenomenon under the title '*nikkeijin, dekasegi U-tān*' in every subsequent issue. This reflects the increased attention given by the press to re-migrants. Since the amendment was enacted and 'guest-workers' of Japanese descendants from Latin America were 'legalized', official intervention has increased, and has included both introduction of labour by government agencies and arrangements (such as radio programs in Portuguese and education in Japanese) aimed at facilitating re-integration of these migrants into Japanese society. Various problems have emerged, for example, to do with loss of jobs or with the education of children, which I cannot address here. In the fall of 1992, a bilateral agreement was scheduled to be signed between Japan and Brazil (the source of around 80 per cent of the roughly 200,000 *nikkeijin* working in Japan in 1992). Its objectives were to eliminate illegitimate mediating practices (for example, requiring passports to be deposited with the employer or 'broker' in order to 'immobilize' foreign employees – a common practice with female Asian migrants – wage-deductions, and so forth) by the foundation of an 'employment centre' (*koyō sentā*) in Sao Paulo (*Asahi shinbun*, 20 July 1992, 3).

A typical corollary of any (illegal) labour migration process, is the emergence of shady businesses and strategies for arranging 'alternative' avenues of Japan. In Peru a forgery gang was detected which sold bogus passports and documents (for example, certificates of Japanese origin – *koseki shōhon* – and copies from Japanese family registers or registers of descent – *shussei tōroku-sho* for 2,000 dollars so that non-Japanese could work in Japan (*Ryūkyū shinpō*, 20 May 1991).[10]

5.4.5 Interlude: Refugees

Very briefly, I want to consider the 'refugee question' (a good survey in English addressing the legal situation is Kawashima, 1991), because in summer 1989 this led to an emotional 'panic' press coverage adding fuel to the fire of the debate on foreign migrants. The quantitative aspect of this reporting boom can be gauged from the clipping collection of Karabao no kai. That organization added a whole chapter in its May/June-issue 1989 (KNK, 9:75–83), sixty-two pages (!) in its July/August issue (KNK, 10:89–151), forty pages in September/October (KNK, 11:74–114), with coverage shrinking to sixteen pages in November/December (KNK, 12:58–74). Since 1990, the chapter has been of between five and ten pages.

Even after the collapse of the Saigon regime in 1975, Japan was very reluctant to accept Indo-Chinese refugees, offering the reason, *inter alia*, that it had no room to accommodate them in its small and densely-populated islands. (Japan accepted but three Vietnamese refugees in 1978 and two in 1979.) Japan established a modest settlement quota for refugees only after severe criticism and pressure from abroad. The quota was periodically increased, although it remained small in comparison with quotas of other nations (Japan's quotas were: 1,000 refugees for 1980, 5,000 for 1984 and 10,000 since 1985). Up to 31 October 1990, Japan had accepted 14,559 Indo-Chinese asylum seekers, of whom 6,610 subsequently migrated to third countries, 6,946 settled in Japan and 987 were still in refugee camps (Kawashima, 1991:1f.). Efforts to obtain work for those granted asylum, after they had been given instruction in Japanese and vocational training, were made through special employment agencies. These were successful, with work being found for most of them, although however, mainly in the unskilled sector and in small enterprises. According to information from the employment centres, mobility is rather high, with roughly a third of workers changing workplace within a year (Wakaichi, 1988:47f.).

In the summer of 1989, thirty-seven landing of 'boat people' in hopelessly overcrowded boats were made in the south of Japan, with a total number of refugees amounting to 3,497. By contrast, in the so-called 'peak-years' of 1979 to 1982 around 1,000 Indochinese-refugees reached the shores of Japan (Kawashima, 1991:8). Not only their number, but the fact that a large proportion of the asylum seekers were from the Chinese province of Fujien, spurred a media uproar. Almost instantly the suspicion was set afloat that 'economic refugees' were coming to Japan to find ('illegal') work. This resulted in their being labelled 'pseudo-refugees' (*gisō nanmin*). This 'refugee-wave' coincided with the International Conference on Indo-Chinese Refugees convened in Geneva on 13 and 14 June, which resulted in a Declaration and Comprehensive Plan of Action (CPA) to facilitate a solution to the decade-long problem. This plan proposed a 'screening-system' for distinguishing *bona-fide* refugees from 'pseudo-refugees' ('economic refugees'), so that the latter could be repatriated without delay. Implementation of the CPA plan by the Japanese government on 12 September 1989 made it easy for the government to deport around 800 refugees in the same year with the agreement of the Chinese government (Kawashima, 1991:9).

The government's declared intention to deport 'pseudo-refugees' was dubbed an 'over-reaction'. The National Police Agency inaugurated a 'squad for counter measures to pseudo refugees' (*gisō nanmin taisaku-han*), not least in order to investigate the China-Japan trafficking route and expose the main players and traffickers. Escapes of refugees from detention camps prompted large-scale mobilization of police. For example, 6,000 police were mobilized following the escape of thirty asylum seekers who had landed at end of August, with all escapees having been returned to custody by the next day. Some of the refugees carried addresses or telephone numbers of Chinese studying in Japan and just took the first taxi to Tokyo or Osaka. (However, in some cases the taxi drivers simply delivered them to the nearest police station.) The style of press reporting contributed greatly to the fabrication of an image of so-called 'pseudo refugees' as 'criminals' and 'dangerous' foreigners. The organization behind the emigration of 'boat people' from China, was not Mafia-like but was rather an ethnic-regional network of Fujien-Chinese (Kawano, 1990:22f.).

Measured by media criteria, the immigration of refugees was an ideal topic for sensationalization. Large photos of the emaciated refugees crammed into little boats and pictures of crowded reception camps appealed to feelings of sympathy and pity. As they were intermittent the landings of boat people allowed follow-ups and cumulative number games. When the first 'pseudo-refugees' were exposed, the tone could be changed: suddenly it was a 'criminal' scheme to sneak into Japan in the guise of 'refugees' in order to make money. There appeared such headlines as: 'Refugees flooding in', 'Lured by "wealth" ', 'Motive is labour migration' (*dekasegi*). 'Different from former refugees' (*Ryūkyū shinpō*) (see KNK, 10:131), 'Emigration for labour – motive? Broker-intervention as backdrop' (*Ryūkyū shinpō*, 24 August 1989). One headline coined a new label – *dekasegi nanmin* – 'labour migration refugees' (*Hokkaidō shinbun*, 2 September 1989). The reports under these headlines concentrated on the organizers of the flight from Fujien by boat, and postulated the existence of underground 'bosses' giving the topic a further 'criminal touch'. The beginning of the deportation of Chinese refugees, and the results of screening, could then provide a series of 'success-stories'. The focus of the print media henceforth was not the 'poor' Vietnamese, but the danger posed by the thousands of Chinese who potentially could come to Japan for economic reasons. During the time in which this mood was fomented by the media after the fashion of the reporting of the 'Mongolian invasion' (Watanabe, 1990b:173), and a xenophobic campaign against 'pseudo-refugees' was incited, the amendment of the Immigration Control Act was passed quickly and without proper debate. (Watanabe notes how short was the time between its being passed in the Lower House on 18 November and its being passed in the Upper House on 8 December 1989.) Indeed, with metaphors of floods and tidal waves and such expressions as 'incursion of refugees' (*nanmin shūrai*), and *nanmin rasshu*, (alluding to the rush-hour overcrowded trains), an 'hysteria' was evoked which made emotion-free and rational discussion difficult. Moreover, the categories of immigrant, refugee and labour migrant were indiscriminately and negligently confused in the debate (cf. Sakaiya, 1989; Herbert, 1989b). In line with the 'demographic argument', a 'bursting of the dam' was feared if refugee-policies were liberalized – fears analogous to well-known 'economic refugee fears' in Europe. Accordingly a hard-line (repatriation) was enforced. The supposition that, at least in the case of refugees of Chinese descent, asylum seekers had just chosen a subtle way of gaining employment in Japan led to them being added to the category of 'illegal' migrant workers. It also prevented it from being pointed out that many of them, in the repressive climate after the violent crackdown on the democracy movement on Tiananmen Square in early summer of 1989, had a sufficient genuinely politically-motivated reason for seeking refugee-status. With the confusion of categories and a debate under the general title 'illegal labour migrants', with metaphors of invasion, inundation, and so forth, in an already heated atmosphere of discussion, a rigid attitude against foreign immigrants was pandered to and the arguments played into the hands of proponents of a 'closed-door policy'.

5.5 Summary

Empirical surveys and case studies permit one to identify structural homologies between all categories of illegalized (or potentially 'illegal') foreign workers (tourists, *kōgyō*– or *hōmon-biza*-holders, *kenshūsei* and *nikkeijin*). The structural features are preconditioned by 'illegality', while concrete differences (such as involvement rates of traffickers, number of falsified documents, and so forth) are of accidental nature. Generally speaking, they have the hazardous status of always being at risk of becoming victim to multiple exploitation by recruiting and labour agents who pocket high commission fees (sometimes for bogus-documents) and by employers who embezzle or illegally reduce wages. They receive deficient medical treatment, have only limited bargaining power in case of violations of law, and face expulsion at any time. (This holds true for 'illegal migrant workers' internationally; that is, it holds for every society in which 'illegal' labourers are economically active.) Their subordinate position in the labour market has been publicized by the media in Japan since the 1980s. The increase in numbers of 'illegal' male labour migrants generated a vehement discussion at the end of the 1980s, which I shall next describe. As I have already indicated, I see Japan not as 'homogeneously-closed' but as a pluralistically-open society. This theoretical presupposition is exemplified by the variegated spectrum of opinions concerning the 'guest-worker question'.

6 The Debate Concerning a Formal Policy on Guest-Workers

6.1 Main Arguments

Somewhat unorthodoxly – before I go into detail of particular arguments – I shall summarize the various arguments that have been advanced by proponents of a formal policy for admission of guest-workers, and by opponents of such a policy.

Arguments in favour of admission of foreign labour:

- By accepting foreign labour, Japan can promote its internationalization, become better able to accomodate other cultures, and simultaneously help to reduce international tensions ('Internationalization and development-aid argument').
- It can be expected that the internationalization of Japanese society and intense contact with different cultures will have positive effects ('Multi-culture argument').
- As long as the wealth gap exists, the 'illegal' influx is 'inevitable'. It is not to be curbed by repression and control as such measures do not contribute to the solution of the basic problems ('Global structure argument').
- If the question of 'illegal' workers is met with ignorance and indifference their situation will further deteriorate. 'Illegal' migrants will be forced even further underground. This could result in emergence of a social problem, or even an international dispute which would emerge and 'isolate' Japan in Asia ('Reputation argument').
- The enormous sectoral labour shortage cannot be alleviated by Japanese workers ('Labour market policy argument').
- By creating a clear legal framework for acceptance of foreign labourers, the worst exploitation by employers

and labour agents can be obviated ('Human rights argument').

- It is necessary to open the country and liberalize immigration. One should learn from the example of Western Europe and quickly take adequate measures ('Intervention argument').

Arguments against admission of foreign labour:

- Labour conditions will worsen, resulting in a high rate of unemployment and producing a chaos in the Japanese labour market ('Labour market argument').
- Employment at low wages is exploitation. The relegation of foreigners to hard, dirty labour will before long be harshly criticized, and such criticism has the potential to renew international friction ('International reputation argument').
- Crime will inevitably increase ('[In]security argument').
- Labour shortages in some sectors may be relieved by the acceptance of foreigners. However, the arrival of families, the need for provision of education and other services, education etc. and the emergence of slums will result in high social expenditures ('Social costs argument').
- Hasty acceptance of foreigners will cause racist confrontations and arouse prejudices. Thus it is necessary first to 'internationalize' the consciousness of the Japanese public ('Discrimination prevention' – blaming the victim strategy).
- One should bear in mind the experiences of Western Europe with its unemployment problems and social and cultural conflicts ('Failure argument').
- There should be no radical change to Japan's homogeneous society, on which its economic and social development are based ('Conservation argument').
- It is not necessary to accept foreign labour in order to help other countries. One should rather help and support them through developmental aid, creation of local jobs, economic co-operation and investments ('reverse development-aid argument', cf. Gonoi, 1989:166–168; this list of arguments is almost identical to the compilation of

the Immigration Control Agency, cited in Mori 1989:13;
labelling of arguments in brackets by the author W. H.).

These views could possibly be found in all countries with a high
('illegal') immigration quota, with details and emphases varying
according to political-economic situation. In these arguments,
issues regarding migrants are likely to be reduced to single factors
(for example: effects on the labour market; cost; culture enrichment; importation of crime and criminality; and so forth).

6.2 General Reflections on the (Political) Discussion Concerning Migrant workers

Essentially, I want to explore the discourse on foreign labourers
by concentrating on the arguments. But first, I shall offer an
impressionistic sketch of the politicized debate and the interest
groups involved. To precisely analyze the power relations which
figure in this debate would require a more thoroughgoing inquiry
than can be attempted here. Instead I shall focus on the context
of the argument that 'an influx of foreign labour potentially
endangers public security', noticing how the argument fits into a
broader discourse. In order to trace this contextualization, I want
to highlight the contexts of particular arguments and assign these
argument to their champions. By 'arguments' here I shall mean
statements leading – implicitly or explicitly – to a conclusion which
'either buttresses or devalues an existing causal explanation or
creates a cognitive framework for a rational justification by evi-
dencing or defining a state of affairs as problematic. Statements
therefore turn into arguments only when they can be put into
meaningful connection with options for action' (Lau, 1989:394).

It is noteworthy that the government, very early in the process
of agenda-setting (that is, of defining the problem), eagerly
attempted to gain an advantage in the debate and regarding information policy. After all, it makes quite a difference if the
immigrant question is envisaged as ethical, political, economic,
social or otherwise 'problematic' with all its subsequent effects.
'Problem definitions are . . . selective definitions of reality' and

are oftentimes not made explicit, but rather imputed in other statements as a matter of course. In such cases it becomes clear that presentation of problems relies on sedimented patterns of interpretation and valuation of everyday consciousness. As such, they no longer have to be proved or questioned. The 'art' of problem definition consists in structuring discourses so that this affinity with everyday consciousness is strategically utilized so that the possible outcomes lie in the range of one's own interests (Lau, 1989:396f.).

Once the question of foreign workers is defined as 'social problem', and media catch-phrases (such as 'rapid increase of illegal foreign labour', 'social frictions imminent', 'crimes of foreigners on a quick rise') trickle down into 'everyday knowledge', it becomes difficult to tackle this 'problem consensus' rationally. Once 'the problem' is made topical by political parties, ministries, labour unions, civil movements, control agencies and other interest groups, it is set on the agenda for public debate. The media pick it up, fashion it editorially, vary and comment on the 'problem' and reproduce it until the span of public attention is exhausted. The interaction between the participants in the debate, political concerns and the media can be analyzed with respect to feedback effects. For instance, interest groups try to make news by issuing 'sensational' statements, or media reports place the government under pressure to act or to justify its actions.

The government attempted to seize the initiative concerning the question of foreign labour to gain a monopoly over issues of definition. The involved ministries established research groups, project teams and advisory councils, which then went to the public with reports. The Ministry of Justice, for instance, reacted in June 1988 with the establishment of an Association for Immigration Control (Nyūkan kyōkai) and the publication of a periodical (*Kokusai jinryū*). In this magazine, legislative measures and options were discussed and recent statistics published and commented on. The Immigration Control Agency was thereby able to secure an important lead in the distribution of (official) information. On 10 May 1988, the first programmatic draft of an amendment to the Immigration Control Act followed. On 28 March 1989, in a meeting of the cabinet, its final version was agreed upon.

The Ministry of Labour on 12 December 1987, established a

study group on the problem of foreign workers (thereby defining it *as* a problem) (Gaikokujin rōdōsha mondai kenkyūkai), which subsequently published periodical research reports. It made the proposal of the introduction of an 'employment permit' (*koyō kyoka*) for (potential) employers of foreigners. Repeated, internal directives (*tsūtatsu*) were issued to Labour Offices, requiring them to tighten up control and in particular to report 'illegal' stays to the Immigration Control Agency.

The Ministry for Foreign Affairs attracted attention when it pleaded for an expansion of the *kenshūsei*-system in a statement published on 19 May 1989. It demanded that trainees be paid an allowance in accordance with the minimum wage law, thus acknowledging their status as *de facto* 'labour' and permitting their acceptance to be brought under the scope of bilateral agreements.

The Economic Planning Agency publicized a study (KKSK, 1989) in which economic and social 'problems' consequent upon accpetance or non-acceptance of foreign workers were projected into several scenarios. The Ministry of International Industry and Trade also founded a research association to investigate the feasibility of a rotation system for *kenshūsei*.

The government established a co-ordination on the 'problem' of foreign workers (Gaikokujin rōdōsha mondai kankei shōchō renraku kaigi) in order to bring vested ministerial interests into line. On 31 October 1989 (and foreshadowing amendment of the law) the government called a meeting of cabinet members to discuss the 'problem' of foreign workers (Gaikokujin rōdōsha mondai ni kansuru kankei kakuryō kondankai).

As the debate intensified in 1988 and 1989, groups active in the economy also began to make known their interest. Most of the statements by employers' associations (for example, the Chamber of Commerce and Trade in Tokyo and the Japanese Federation of Employers' Assocations) pointed in the direction of a regulated, numerically limited, that is, 'controlled' acceptance of foreign workers. On 19 January 1989 the Kansai keizai dōyūkai (Committee for Economic Development in Kansai) proposed the establishment of a 'dispatching centre' (*haken sentā*) for 'guest-workers'. The National Committee for Economic Development (Keizai dōyūkai) presented a blueprint for reform of the trainee system. According to this blueprint, *kenshūsei* should be paid the same wages as Japanese workers and around 100,000 trainees should find acceptance in Japanese enterprises. On 14

October 1989, the Japanese Central Committee of the National Association for Small and Medium Enterprises (Zennihon chūshō kigyō dantai chūōkai – Chūōkai) demanded an increase in the number of 'guest-workers' at its national assembly. On 20 October, the National Federation of Construction Associations (Nikkenren) issued a similar demand to the government.

At the beginning of 1988, the General Federation of labour Unions Rengō and Sōhyō, made public their (rather restrictive) positions. In 1988 also the National Police Agency established an 'International Department'. A special division for dealing with crimes committed by foreigners (Gaikokujin hanzai o atsukau senmonka) was placed under it.

The principal political parties (LDP, Socialists, Kōmei, Communists) unexpectedly concurred in their cautious view that the question of the acceptance of 'unskilled' workers should be subject to 'further scrutiny'. Regarding 'unqualified' labourers in particular, the Socialists thought that further 'study' of likely consequences for the national labour market was necessary, while the Communists gave warnings concerning exploitation (*Asahi shinbun*, 3 September 1988). However, contrary to what occurred in Austria for example, the 'foreigner problem' was not transformed into an election-policy issue.

As already described, in the summer of 1988 the first organizations for the support of labour migrants were formed, and in February 1989 the Bar Association in Osaka established a window for counselling concerning human rights of foreigners (Gaikokujin no jinken sōdan madoguchi).

This sketch (which is based on Mori, 1990) has been of the main actors and positions in the discussion on migrant workers. Of course, intellectuals and university professors joined in this discourse by publishing their 'expert opinions' and suggestions through renowned publishing houses and magazines, thereby occupying an influential position in the debate. Many can be seen as supporters of the government lines, contributing to its dominance in the formation of public opinion. The most prominent critics of the 'official line' – lawyers, and activists in support movements for labour migrants – gained less publicity however. Many of their views were published in small 'alternative' magazines or by publishers sensitive to social issues (for example, Akashi shoten). But only through the daily press could they become influential in the debate on foreign labour. This most important of the agencies for dissemination of opinion however, revealed itself to be heavily reliant on the information monopoly of control agencies (the Immigration Control Bureau, and the police). Yet press exposure of violations of human rights and of the law drew a different picture, and showed the position of the press to be an ambivalent one. This exposure of the exploitation of foreign workers could be used or could function in contrary ways: either in legitimation of (preventative) penalties for 'illegal' work or as reason for an 'amnesty' or an 'official guest-worker policy' (which would end trafficking and would guarantee basic human rights).

Of course, besides the daily press, magazines and television were also instrumental in topicalizing the subject of foreign workers. As I did not systematically monitor their contributions, I shall provide only a sketchy outline of their position by representing a few examples.

The 'intellectuals' magazines' *Chūō kōron* and *Bungei shunjū* reacted to the phenomenon with several articles. In the former one finds studies by the scientists Nishio and Tezuka (cf. Nishio, 1989b, c; Tezuka, 1988, 1989b). Both authors cite the 'German example' and argue for a cautious, restrictive policy. The conservative journal, *Bungei shunjū*, published a controversial discussion between Nishio, two writers (Sasakura Akira and Fukada Yūsuke), a journalist (Yamaguchi Reiko) and Gō Munechika, a representative of the Tokyo Chamber of Trade and Commerce (and chair of a 'special commission on the problem of foreign workers' within the Chamber) (cf. Gō A.O., 1989). The discussion's subtitle locates this debate against a backdrop image of refugees running ashore in the summer of 1989: 'How to tackle the big problem posed by the "black ships" of the new era?' (*Heisei no kurobune ga tsukitsuketa daimondai o dō suru?*). Here the phrase 'new era' alludes to the first year of the Heisei-period (that is, 1989) which began following the death of Emperor Hirohito, whose era was posthumously named Shōwa. The phrase 'black ships' figuratively alludes to Commodore Perry's four ships (two of them steam frigates) which anchored at Uraga on 8 July 1853, and thus to Perry's mission the following year which forced the opening of Japan after two-and-a-half centuries of self-imposed isolation. The discussion included rehearsals of well-known arguments such as the proposal that the *kenshūsei*-system be expanded (Gō), and contributions on the question of 'economic refugees' – one of the more notable of these being the journalist Yamaguchi's 'regret' (prefaced by an ineffectual mitigating remark) that one of the 'merits' Japan could be proud of, namely its exceptionally good public security (evidenced by the fact that women can walk safely at night on the streets!), could be harmed by 'illegal' workers (cf. Gō A.O., 1989:307; the argument of Nishio too is notorious: for details see Section 6.3 below).

The 'refuguee question' was also the subject of a televised discussion on TV-Asahi, a channel which periodically stages live all-night discussions (under the series title *Asa made nama terebi;* the debate here was telecast on 28 October 1989 and later published as a book, cf. Shibuya, 1990). On 31 December 1989 continuing through to 1 January 1990, the same station, as the third part of a special live program on the occasion of the turn of the year (*'toshikoshi nama terebi supesharu'*) broadcast another debate on the 'foreigner question' during which Nishio avowed his 'true motive' for his opposition to 'guest-workers' the 'preservation of Japanese culture'. The theme of the 'foreign workers problem' in this program indicates clearly the degree to which this question was present in public consciousness and perceived as a 'current issue'. Privately owned television stations – highly commercialized, dependant on advertisements and under pressure of tough competition – took up the question of foreigners quite often. But usually only official statements (such as recent figures on entries and deportations) found their way into the news. Apart from these, coverage was mostly in documentaries under such captions as 'sensations', 'tragedy', 'menace', or the like. For instance, on 15 March 1989 on Mainichi-TV at 22:00, a report was telecast on the growing number of cases of tuberculosis among Asian students, their infection-rate being claimed to be forty times higher than the Japanese average.

Crimes committed by foreigners have high news-value and lead to special reports, for example, that on 25 July 1990 (Mainichi-TV, 19:00) concerning Taiwanese 'Mafia' operations in Shinjuku. Part of a documentary (TV-Ashahi, 14 September 1990, 21:00) in a series in which twenty-four hour police work is 'tracked' by the camera, was announced with 'Rapid increase! Crimes by foreigners' (*gekizō! gaikokujin no hanzai*). Yet the only cases reported in the program were those of a Thai national suspected of prostitution attempting suicide, a British national making a row at a police station after quarrelling with his girlfriend over 1,000 yen, an African who had no idenfication documents and was unable to pay in a 'snack-bar', and a Chinese national whose visa had expired and whom the police 'suspected' was in Japan only for work. Yet following its report of these mostly petty incidents, the documentary's final comment was that 'Because of the many foreigners the face of Ikebukuro [an area of Tokyo] will change'.

Also frequent on television were good-will reports of human rights violations, forced prostitution and so forth. After my return to Japan in spring 1992, the main topics on television relating to foreigners were: *nikkeijin* (for example, Peruvians who acquired a forged family register – reported 19 August 1992 at 18:00 on the local station Kansai-TV); Iranians; and children of illegally-overstaying Asian women (nationality and visa complications).

The semi-public station, NHK, transmitted a documentary (partly about Pakistanis) on 12 May 1989 at 19:30 and a discussion on the following day (19:20) under a title alluding to 'camp formation' (opening-of-the-country faction versus isolationist-faction – see below), with the participation of Nishio Kanji and the writer Ishikawa Yoshimi (who represent contrary positions). It may be remarked here that – presumably in accordance with internal standards of 'balance' – in the casting of participants for debates on Japanese television, intellectuals and public figures are invited who hold divergent positions (for example, Ministry officials and members of the bar). With regard to content, the arguments of course do not differ from those in the print media. However, private channels come close to popular magazines and tabloids, adopting a more sensationalist style, not least because circulation figures and transmission range are the leading editorial interests.

Journalists divided the discussion on foreign labour at the end of the 1980s into 'camps'. The proponents of an acceptance of 'guest-workers' were dubbed the 'opening-of-the-country faction' (*kaikokuha*) and the opponents as the 'closing-of-the-country faction' (*sakokuha*). *The sakoku-kaikoku* debate was described as being 'ideological' (*kannenteki*, Tezuka, 1992b:7), fraught with emotion and predilections, culturalistic and irresponsible (Kuwahara, 1989:126f.). Sometimes a third possible position was identified between these poles and called the 'cautiously-scrutinizing' attitude (this faction was named *shōkyokuha* or *shinchōha*, cf. Tezuka, 1989a:6ff.: KBR, 1990:120f.). Strict assignment of views to each of those 'discussion camps' is not always feasible. In the following I attempt to circumscribe statements (understood as arguments according to the earlier-given definition linking statements with options for action). Demands for liberalization or restriction of the immigration-related laws compete with each other. But on a meta-level, there appears to exist a kind of hidden consensus that some legislative action should be taken any way. This assumption itself is not reflected upon anymore and, as a premise, precedes any division into 'openers' or 'isolationists'. The amendment of the Immigration Control Act (*nyūkanhō*) which came into force on 1 June 1990, can be seen as a result of the discussion. The amendment figures under the notions *kaisei* ('reform') or *kaitei* ('revision'). Looking at its content, I would rather speak of an 'affirmative supplementation', because substantially nothing changed regarding the basics of immigration policy in the post-war era. A marginal deregulation in the sector of 'skilled' workers stands against the long established non-acceptance of 'unskilled' workers, which was just laid down anew. The forced acceptance of *nikkeijin* (under the legal title of *teijūsha*) and *kenshūsei* can thereby be read as a concession to the interest of business executives. The 'penalizing' of employers of 'illegals' and 'illegal' employees is concordant with labour union interests (in the face of a forcing down of wages and an exacerbated segmentation of the labour market). In the following, I describe mainly the debate among intellectuals on foreign labour, picked up the arguments of the introductory summary in detail, and furnish them with proof by examples.

6.3 Arguments for a Restrictive Immigration Policy (*Sakokuha*)

The 'isolationist' position is epitomized by the pronouncements of its champion, Nishio Kanji, Professor of German Cultural History at Denki Tsūshin University. He has repeatedly made kown his views on the issue (for example, Nishio 1989, a, b, c and 1990 a, b; in his 1990b one can get a glimpse of his method of argument in English). Here I shall refer to his book *Rōdō sakoku no susume. Gaikokujin rōdōsha ga Nihon o horobosu* (Recommendation for the closing of the country to labour. Foreign workers ruin Japan – Nishio 1989a. Page references are to this work unless otherwise indicated. It was newly edited and published as a cheap paperback by PHB bunko in 1992). In this book, the basic motives for a restrictive immigration policy appear most plainly (the restrictive position became increasingly connected with Nishio as the debate progressed, resulting in less attention being paid to similar positions advanced by other participants in the discussion). An examination of Nishio's argument is based on an ideologically-tainted fabrication of images of Japanese society.

According to Nishio, Japan is the typical example of successful elimination of lower strata of society and the realization of freedom and equality (4). In Japan no clearly circumscribed classes exist. Every university graduate starts in an enterprise as 'simple worker' (*tanjun rōdōsha*, the euphemistic term for an unskilled, manual labourer – the debate about acceptance or non-acceptance of foreign labour being centred on this group). Contrary to what is common in Western societies, university graduates do not immediately take on leading positions just by virtue of their academic qualification. In Japan everybody begins as 'simple worker'; therefore everybody could become a 'boss' or 'leader'. The notion *tanjun rōdōsha* is used so vaguely in Japan because it was transferred from the Western context, that is, imported from clear-cut class societies (27). In Japan, however, no class of lifelong 'unskilled workers' exists. Nishio uses the example of apprenticeship in a *sushiya (sushi*-shop, *sushi* – vinegared rice and fish). At first the apprentice has to wash the dishes, but later in the apprenticeship there is training and practice in the preparation and presentation of *sushi*, until finally the former apprentice is fully trained and independent. However, were a foreigner to have been employed he or she would have to wash dishes forever, leading to the emergence of a rigid class of 'simple workers'. This class would be perpetuated by second- and third-generation 'dishwashers-only'. Yet the permeability of classes and high mobility in Japanese society are among its vital merits (27f.). In the classless society of Japan (*mukaikyū shakai Nihon*), everything is different from European class societies in which guest-workers just form the lowest fraction of the underclasses. In Japan, however, only importation of foreign labour could lead to a segregated labour market split into two segments (*nijū rōdō shijō*) claims Nishio (30). As his crucial motive for his opposition to acceptance of foreign workers, Nishio states that he wants to avert racist tragedies. When the economy slows and unemployment increases, Pakistanis and Bangladeshis would inevitably be persecuted in Japan. Their lodgings would be attacked and set on fire – as happened frequently in France to people from the Maghreb (39). There are some though who believe attacks on foreigners (such as those reported in France or Germany) would be unlikely to happen in Japan because the Japanese are warmhearted, gentle (*onryō*) and tolerant (58). Here one finds generic descriptions of national character (see p. 57) which are pseudo-metaphysical and unacceptably crude and overgeneralized. In the phrases 'some believe', and 'people believe', we see part of Nishio's 'by-hearsay style'. Thus in a different context he asserts that in France, even in cases of homicide – where the victim is a labour migrant, and the perpetrator is French) the judicial system often allows the perpetrator to be acquitted (and although the sentence is qualified by the term *rashii*, expressing dubiety, the claim is scarcely scientific when empirical evidence is not provided).

In European countries (Nishio here mostly refers to Germany, France and Great Britain, which according to him, are ethnic caste societies in which 'coloured' people occupy the lowest position), new guest-workers were no longer accepted. The European Community could be seen as paradigmatic of this isolationist tendency, because (labour) mobility is possible only within the Community but is not open to 'EC-externals' willing to work. In the same way, the USA would be eager to defend its living space and close its borders (89f., 103 and 110). Japan led the world with its historical experience of a closed country (*sakoku*). In a world which appeared to be becoming introverted and isolationist, a renewed policy of isolation would be sheer 'Loyalty to history', and true to the historic instincts of Japan. Thus this historical guiding principle should be adopted once more for the 'defence' of the country. This should be seen not as imitation of the closures of the USA and Europe to immigration, but as a repetition of Japan's earlier pioneering act (117 and 121). In consequence of its isolation from the beginning of the 17th century to the middle of the 19th century, Japan had acquired a high degree of 'cultural conformity' and had created a highly homogeneous society (*dōshitsu no takai . . . shakai*) which could be proud of its efficiency. This should be seen as Japan's success and 'good fortune'. In a world in which other countries had begun to imitate this policy of isolation, there was no reason to throw away the 'trump card' of 'cultural conformity'. Each people should live in their own 'style', which they need not change (138 and 140f.).

By accepting foreign workers, a country became increasingly dependent on their power. Work ethics and value structures would change so that any unattractive work would, as a matter of course, be relegated to the foreigners (186f.). The Germans, for instance, were dependent on the vigour and 'power' of guest-workers to such a degree that their willingness to work was lessened, as were their procreative power (*seishokuryoku*) and vitality (196). There would hardly be anybody who would deny that proportionately more dependence on the 'power' of guest-workers would emasculate the native-born. The Germans had realized this. Nishio here quotes the 'Heidelberg manifesto', which claims that Germans would become extinct in the 21st century unless, for the preservation of their culture, they produced more offspring and limited the number of foreigners. The negative reactions to this manifesto are seen by Nishio as a consequence of its touching on the taboo topic of racism, which has been regarded as a great evil in postwar Germany (196–198). (The *Heidelberg Manifest* of 17 June 1981 was signed by eight German university lecturers and objected to 'infiltration of the German people by the immigration of millions of foreigners and their families, ... foreign infiltration of our language, our culture and our national essence' (*Volkstum*), demanding 'the return of foreigners to their ancestral home countries' and calling for 'the foundation of a party-politically and ideologically independent alliance with the task of preservation of the German people and its spiritual identity on the basis of its Christian-occidental heritage' (cited in Bade, 1983:112). The Manifesto was fiercely criticized because of its openly fascist vocabulary.)

Nonetheless, Nishio brazenly argues on exactly the same lines when he notes that through the acceptance of foreign labour 'a mentality of dependence on them [the 'guest-workers'] will emerge and, at the same time, have a far-reaching effect on population statistics. Finally, one's own culture and one's own people will be absorbed by this huge and vital power [*seimeiryoku*] and will be lost . . .' (196). An acceptance of foreign labour in Japan would thus be extremely hazardous, because the rate of population growth of ethnic Japanese was in decline and was the world's second lowest after Germany (199). Nishio even invokes the decline of the Roman empire in his argument. This decline was, according to him, the result of the importation of a foreign proletariat (slaves). This led to the decadence-syndrome of decaying social morals, a rise in the number of divorces, increased crime, and the coming into vogue of homosexuality (201).

The demographic argument then turns to the countries surrounding Japan. In these countries there will exist a reserve of superfluous labour of over 100 million persons, constituting a 'menace' to Japan (214 and 216; a similar remark was made by the Immigration Control official Yamazaki, cf, Hanami, A.O., 1989:22; Kuwahara, 1989:170 also views the 'population explosion' in Asia as 'threatening'). Nishio's language becomes even more militant: this latent labour surplus in surrounding countries is overwhelming and goes into hundreds of millions. 'Japan . . . is besieged by crowds of invaders vigilantly poised around it, waiting for a chance to enter Japan' (251). Japan, which because of its inherent power dynamic is the only highly-developed country in Asia, is thus exposed to a critical situation – to an insecurity unequalled in the world. To meet this challenge is therefore a matter of life or death for Japan, a matter of security and 'national defence' (221).

Nishio then assesses possible options, speculating on the outcomes of an offensive immigration policy, a controlled rotation model (the Swiss example) and a rigorous policy of isolation (this chapter also appeared in the intellectuals' magazine *Chūō kōron* – Nishio, 1989b). Ultimately, any 'controlled' acceptance of guestworkers would lead to their settlement, and transform the receiving country into an immigration country incurring high subsequent costs (229). The Swiss 'saisonier' model (which according to Nishio, is closely similar to the sanctions policy of Singapore, where infractions of regulations covering stay were punished by whipping, and where female labour migrants who became pregnant were deported) was inhumane, degraded human beings as tools and, therefore, was not feasible. But Switzerland is an exceptional country anyway – not even a member of the United Nations, and its 'national character' is *'spröde'* – Nishio gives the German original, which means 'inflexible, reserved'. It is a super police-state in which foreigners are under total control (234). Moreover, rotation of foreign workers would in the long run result in their immigration, necessitating costly integration measures. The only remaining option for the preservation of one's own culture and history is implementation of a defensive closed-door policy (266).

It is not my intention here to refute every one of Nishio's arguments. His polemic, his rhetoric, the proto-racist undertones of his arguments (for example, the typical racist potency-fear in talking of the higher fecundity of immigrants), his simplistic ascriptions of national character, are so obvious as to make comment (almost) unnecessary. His *Leitinteresse* is clear from the start, this being to exclude foreign workers from Japan, and he shapes his 'theories' accordingly. He needs justification for his view and provides it by dichotomous, black-and-white, exaggerated and distorted images of both European societies and Japanese society. His image of the latter is manufactured in line with positive self-representation and the construction of an 'us/them' discourse. Only the negative aspects of European guest-worker policies are presented. Nishio's argument strategy thereby shows several characteristics of 'prejudiced discourse' (cf. Wodak and Matouschek, 1993, esp. 239f.).

In the image he traces of Japanese society Nishio presents his premises: Japan to him is an egalitarian, equal opportunity offering, homogenous and classless society which would be shaken to its foundations (the foundations fabricated by Nishio) and turn into an ethnic caste society. Less dogmatic, but along the same lines, are the statements of Yamazaki Tetsuo, a high official of the Minister of Justice commenting on the amendment of the Immigration Control Act. Using various sociologisms ('homogeneous society' (*dōshitsu shakai*), '90 per cent middle-class', 'fair' (*kōsei*), 'classless and vocationally non-discriminatory'; Yamazaki, 1991:139 and 148)[1] he presents an 'homogenized' image of Japanese society. In another publication one can find the *Nihon-jinron*-term – which was obviously shunned here: Japan is described as a country with minuscule minority problems because it is inhabited by an 'homogenous people' (*tan'itsu minzoku*), cf. the economist Hanami in Hanami A.O., 1989:14). That these assertions are reductionist fictions, with all of the attributes of myth, and relying for their plausibility on the contrast with an equally abstracted counterpole (formerly China, today 'the West'), has been repeatedly shown (for example, by Mouer and Sugimoto, 1986; Dale, 1986:92 also points to the fact that talk of 'homogeneity' is nothing less than the post-war euphemism for 'racial purity').[2] According to Yamazaki, during its period of massive economic growth Japan, unlike European countries could, by its own efforts and without making itself dependent of foreign labour make its industry and economy highly efficient and highly productive, and such as it would be proud of in a world wide comparison. In the future, further endeavours in the direction of rationalization, automation, labour saving and structural reform should be promoted, and Japan's own internal labour potential should be used to the full (for example, by raising the age for qualifying for an aged pension from sixty to sixty-five in a greying society). Acceptance of foreign labour should be only a last resort, as it would lead to foreigners being assigned only dirty work, and would generate a structure of discrimination, which for both foreigners and Japanese would be an 'unhappy' situation (Yamazaki, 1991:148f.). Nishio radicalizes this, maintaining that by 'procuring minorities' Japan would become responsible for the ethnic conflicts which would result – as they did in France, where one could speak of downright 'religious and racial wars' (Nishio, 1990a: 186ff.).[3] Nishio also believes that Germany had lost the 'high-tech war' just because, instead of instituting a technological revolution, it had imported 'cheap' foreign labour; that is, the importation of foreign labour paralyzed efforts for structural reforms (this is claimed to be a *teisetsu*, an established theory, by Nishio, 1990a:190).

Nishio's stock of arguments is not yet exhausted. Almost every statement made in favour of guest-workers he picks up and turns to his own purposes. Particularly fiercely attacked are exponents of a 'cultural argument' (*bunkaron*). The expectation that through a clash of peoples with different cultural heritages an enrichment and 'renewal' of Japan would occur, would not be satisfied. Before any such 'renewal' could occur, disaster would have befallen Japan, and the result of the cultural innovation would be merely disparagement, ignorance, indifference and discrimination (132). Intellectuals who advocate the introduction of 'guest-workers' as in to European states so that Japan can meet its 'obligations' as a highly industrialized state and not to be 'isolated' in the world, are diagnosed by Nishio as having a 'Western-humanist complex' (142). He cites the economist Koike Kazuo an exception among intellectuals – as one 'who perceives the world realistically' – for his having deemed as nonsense the idea that acceptance of labour, from developing countries could aid them economically. Recruitment of foreign labourers would only worsen labour conditions in Japan and boost unemployment, depriving indigenous unskilled workers of jobs (144f.). Journalists, according to Nishio, liked to assume an attitude of 'raised consciousness', contrasting the 'ugly' rich Japan with poor Asian countries, and allowing this perspective to distort their view of justice at home. In this way, they intermingled politics and morals and – because they could not even make this distinction – revealed their psychological infantilism and lack of mental training (152). Many Japanese intellectuals, in Nishio's view, are self-deceiving idealists suffering under 'compunctions' and prone to 'giving the people some beautiful edification'. He refers to professors Ōnuma and Miyajima, and remarks that he respects their engagement with minorities and their human rights. However, he cannot understand why both professors sympathized with the acceptance of foreign workers. In so doing they did not consider Japan's 'security', but instead advocated the importing of conflicts into Japan. Nishio then rhetorically asks whether to prevent the development of new minority-problems (by non-acceptance of 'guest-workers') would not be the decision 'adults' would take (158).

Totally defamed by Nishio is the writer and critic (*hyōronka*) Ishikawa Yoshimi, who has repeatedly championed a policy of acceptance and advances arguments of 'multi-culturalism'. That is, he maintains that, by accepting foreigners from diverse countries of origin, Japanese society would undergo a cultural vitalization. Ishikawa in his youth spent several years in the USA as an 'illegal' worker (for example, as a strawberry-picker in California) and after his return to Japan took up university studies and began to publish books. Nishio comments that those with a 'simple' (*soboku*) horizon of experiences would also be simply naive mentally. The acceptance or non-acceptance of foreign labour is a comprehensive problem encompassing politics, diplomacy, economy, education, and so forth, which would be beyond the grasp of Ishikawa (161f.).

In this regard, Nishio cites the following comment Ishikawa made in the magazine *Voice* in February 1988:

> When many foreigners live [in Japan] public security will
> doubtlessly deteriorate. Or we will be on guard in fear that
> it may deteriorate. But does this sort of thrill not belong to
> any country in which *human beings* live? Should we not
> produce a situation of this kind in Japan that resembles a
> balloon that will be deflated by a little push. If this is so, I
> believe that we should, as a strategy, let *human beings* we call
> foreigners come [into the country] (quoted in Nishio, p. 161,
> emphasis his).

Nishio condemns the proposition of this sort as destructive and warns that it would more easily be taken up by young people than conservative propositions. Ishikawa regards the acceptance of foreigners, with its resultant increase in crime and destruction of Japan's one-dimensional society as 'strategy', but had no perspective to offer thereafter. This would be neither strategy nor anything else, but simply 'irresponsible' (161). What is noteworthy here is that, in this argument (for and against 'guest-workers') neither disputant questions the assumption that, by introducing foreigners, public security will deteriorate and crime will increase. This shows how deeply in everyday understanding and unquestioned assumption this presupposition (or prejudice) had sedimented.

This is enough to convey Nishio's position. In the spectrum of discussion, his polemic is the most vehement and his conclusions are the most radical. He argues that adroitly and is an erudite sophist. He can count on public sympathy with his nationalism and regard to the sovereign power of Japan (for instance, in refusing to tolerate American influence on public opinion in Japan, Nishio, 1989c:148f.). Only Nishio goes to such extremes in arguing that the question of foreign labour is one of the 'survival or non-survival of Japanese culture' (154) – proof of his ultra-conservatism. His 'culturally' centered position, however, is essentially reactive, and is curiously dependent on the contrary arguments counter-position of proponents of the acceptance of 'guest-workers' (who welcome a more multicultural Japan) since the latter too *presuppose* that Japanese culture is 'uniform and mono-cultural' and that this has been a source of social harmony. The arguments grouped around Nishio's central thesis are found in the views of other opponents of foreign labour, and to some extent also in those of cautious proponents of a regulated introduction of 'guest-workers'.

6.4 The position of the cautious (*shinchōha*)

Opinions expressed by labour unions range from strict opposition to a policy of admitting 'guest-workers' (for example, the construction labour unionist Katō Tadayoshi, 1990:83, who is 'in principle opposed'), to acknowledgement of the 'need to further examine the question carefully' (*shinchō ni kentō subeki* – as the labour union's federation, Sōhyō, put it in this favourite phrase of politicians, in *Ōhara shakai mondai kenkyūsho zasshi*, 376/3:57). Utmost caution is admonished concerning importation of 'cheap labour' by an official of the labour union's federation, Rengō (Katō Toshiyuki, 1990:79). These positions are shaped by the interests of 'cartels for the sale of labour' (labour unions) which fear the efforts of cheap imports and wish to prevent worsening of labour conditions. Similar arguments can be found in all the cited articles, although varying slightly in nuance. The construction labour unionist further believes that, in the already accident-prone construction sector, the introduction of foreigners would cause an increase in the number of work-related accidents because of their lack of linguistic skills (Katō Tadayoshi, 1990:83). Journalists also note that (almost) all labour unions in Japan seek to restrict foreign labour because of apprehension regarding unemployment (see for example, Ishiyama, 1989:68, and Gonoi, 1989:119). Because the wages of 'illegal' workers could be the first to be forced down, harsh sanctions against this group are demanded (Sōhyō in *Ōhara shakai mondai kenkyūsho zasshi*, 376/3:58 and Katō Tadayoshi, 1990:84). Thus the labour unions are clearly in favour of the line of the Ministry of Labour, which in May 1988 had already inaugurated a 'discussion group for the examination and study of the problem [!] of foreign workers' (Gaikokujin rōdōsha mondai no chōsa kentō no tame no kondankai). It assembled functionaries of Sōhyō, Rengō, Nikkeiren, Chūōkai, scientists (for example, Koike Kazuo, Hanami Tadashi, Miyajima Takashi), business executives, and the correspondent of the Süddeutsche Zeitung, Gebhard Hielscher, as well as 'observers' from the National Police Agency and Ministries of Labour and Justice (Yoshimen, 1988:61f.). This can be seen as a broadly-designed 'consensus-finding action' in the advance of the planned amendment of the Immigration Control Law. The group came to the conclusion that, due to the far-reaching influences an acceptance of (unskilled) foreign workers would exert on the Japanese economy (deleterious effects on unemployment, the labour market and labour conditions) and on Japanese society, admission of 'unqualified' foreigners would not be desirable, and effective measures to prevent 'illegal' employment should be taken also (Yoshimen, 1988:62f. cf. the interim report of this study group: Rōdōshō 1990).

The conjectured bad effects on employment, security, wages and labour conditions are implications of the trivialized theorems advanced by many Japanese economists. Tezuka points to the fact that the Japanese labour market already shows a dual structure, the result of insecure labour relations, such as those involved in part-time, seasonal, or dispatched labour. As is seen in European countries and there 'coolly analyzed by almost all scientists' foreign workers would be channelled into these extremely insecure segments only as a 'buffer for labour market vacillations'. This would lead to a further deterioration of labour conditions and an exacerbated segmentation (Tezuka, 1989a:110–115). Tezuka had early introduced the 'experience of Germany' into the debate and had extensively commented on these (placing emphasis on integration problems and failed repatriation measures), concluding that introduction of foreign labour to Japan would be unacceptable (Tezuka, 1988:284). (The apprehension expressed concerning competition for work, lowering of wages, and labour market segmentation is slightly different in Kuwahara, 1989:148 and 154f.). In a statement by the Ministry of Labour in 1988 (fully reprinted in KBR, 1988:62–75), it is maintained (in a similar tone) that the introduction of foreign labour had 'bad effects' on unemployment and labour conditions. Thus efficient control (*kontorōru*) was imperative. It is added that the deterioration of labour conditions could at the same time negatively affect the international image of Japan (KBR, 1988:21). (however, the fear of damage to Japan's reputation abroad is merely a reversed nationalism appealing to 'shame' and national morale, cf. Huisken, 1987:29.)

The argument concerning worsening labour conditions is often linked with another which claims that *'Unterschichtung'* (boosting of the lower strata) will retard modernization, paralyze technological innovation, and forestall rationalization and structural reform because all are made unnecessary by the importation of a cheap foreign labour force (as is emphatically argued by Komai, 1990:263f.; see also Kuwahara, 1989:156, and Rōdōshō, 1990:219). The implied corollary is that rationalization and structural amelioration in (small) industry, together with improvement of labour conditions, were the correct 'recipe' for ending the sectoral labour shortage (see, for example, Kuwahara, 1989:161, who maintains that otherwise small enterprises which had long ago lost their competitive edge would be preserved). Furthermore, it is held that the labour potential of peripheral regions, older people and women could be drawn upon by more attractively organized work places, which would alleviate the dearth of personnel without producing the far-reaching subsequent problems which would result from a rash acceptance of foreigners (Yoshimen in a discussion panel, in Hanami A.O., 1989:18; and Ōta Fusae, an official of the Ministry of International Trade and Industry, in Hanami, A.O., 1989:19). A further alternative to a 'guest-worker policy' – which would not change the basic structure regarding labour migration and migration would only be detrimental to the sending countries – would be the boosting of development aid and technology transfer. In this way, places of work and education could be created in Asian countries. This proposal is often intertwined with the demand for an expansion of the *kenshūsei*-model (see, for example, Yoshimen, 1988:65; Ōta in Hanami A.O., 1989:27; Komai, 1990:269; Yamazaki, A.O., 1991:144).

In academic discussion, those who take the 'cautious' line advert to the 'example' of Europe (usually Germany and France). On the other hand, this is held up as an example of a foundered immigration policy (*shippai no rei* – 'example of failure' – see, for example, Kuwahara, 1989:158; cf. Miyajima, 1989:46, who criticizes the lopsided utilization of 'Western' experiences). On the other hand, commentators point to the consequences and 'problems' of integrating 'guest-workers', which would make high social costs inevitable (for example, KKSK 1989:84; Kuwahara, 1989:164f. Rōdōshō, 1990:215; but cf. Miyajima, 1989:11f., who argues against a cost calculation, stressing the 'immaterial', cultural impetus given by foreigners). Exactly because the acceptance of 'guest-workers' is a 'problem' which will affect the overall future of society and not only the economy, it is imperative that a careful examination be given to the question (for example, Yamazaki, 1991:144). It would be necessary to create a public consensus, and this implies that it would be premature at present to admit 'unskilled' foreign labourers. Moreover, before such admission were allowed, it would be necessary to prepare its social basis (education, housing, medical care, social guarantees, and so forth) as well as its psychological basis through education for tolerance and understanding of peoples with different values, and this provides a further reason for deferring acceptance of guest workers (Yamazaki, 1991:149f., speaks of an 'internationalization of hearts' – *kokoro no kokusaika* – a pathetic formula which also depends on the premise that the island-state of Japan, with its homogeneous people, has up to now hardly been confronted by identity problems of foreigners; see also Sōhyō in similar vein, in *Ōhara shakai mondai kenkyū zasshi*, 376;3:56). Finally, since the foreign labour question would be a matter of national interest (*kokueki;* Kuwahara, 1989:163; Hanami, 1989:182f.), adequate control and regulation of immigration would be indispensable (Yamazaki, 1991:143).

As I will show later in more detail in the context of an analysis of the so-called problem of guest-workers as one of overall societal impacts, a strategic locus is implicitly determined for the insecurity argument: because society as a whole is claimed to be affected, public security will also be affected. The effect commonly postulated is 'endangerment' of law and order.

6.5 Some Agruments for the Legalization of Irregular Workers

Almost no one from the so-called 'opening of the country faction' advocates an uncontrolled or unrestricted 'opening'. Rather, there is a certain 'consensus' that, were labour migrants admitted, legislative regulations and conditions would be needed to control length of stay, number of 'guest-workers' and equity for Japanese employees.

The legalization of labour migration, including migration of 'unskilled' workers from Third World countries', is supported by movements for the rights of Asian migrant workers (KBR, 1988:18). They propose that a special status of stay be granted – in the manner of an 'amnesty' – to those already working 'illegally' in the country. Within the existing legal framework this could be done by granting them 'resident status' (*teijūsha*). This would also remove the cause of human rights violations (Karabao no kai jimukyoku, 1990:315ff.). Their argument runs as follows: Foreign workers stigmatized as 'illegal' are notoriously exposed to pre-modern exploitation and infringements of their human rights. However, it would be rash to demand an immediate 'general amnesty'. The 'minimal' solution would be to grant a special residence permit to victimized foreign workers following exposure of labour-law violations, so that they can claim their rights. Thus the focus of attention would shift from a one-sided concentration on immigration control to the rights of migrants giving migrant workers the same legal protection enjoyed by Japanese (Nishitani, 1990:134; likewise the economist Mori, 1990:27). I was personally told by one of the most agile activists of the movement Asian friends, the Reverend Koyanagi Nobuaki, that the primary aim of his organization would not be official guest-work recruitment, but to obtain urgently needed legal protection for the thousands of 'illegals' already staying in Japan.

Some of the views of opponents of admission of foreign labour – already petrified into 'self-evidence' and hardly questioned – are nonetheless sharply criticized by proponents of legal acceptance of labour migrants. It is often argued that if the Japanese policy of restricting entry of foreigners is seen as analogous to recent German policies – just because the same trend became visible -, this would be nothing other than 'deceit'; while Japan at all times has maintained a restrictive, isolationist policy, Germany has legally admitted 'too many' guest-worker workers since the 1960s. Therefore, the problems of the two countries differ both quantitatively and qualitatively. To speak of 'failure' of guest-worker policy, would be to overlook the fact that the situation of guest-workers in Germany, by virtue of legal safeguards and efforts to eliminate discrimination, is unlike that of 'illegals' in Japan. The notion 'failure' more aptly describes the continuing discrimination against minorities (Koreans, Okinawans, people of *hisabetsu buraku*-origin, Ainu) in Japan (KBR, 1988:22). Labour emigration from Asian countries is the consequence of Japan's economic neo-colonialism and of transnational companies which have exploited raw Asian material and labour. The people thereby 'deprived' come to Japan to regain by labour migration the portion of which they have been 'robbed' (KBR, 1988:17). (This kind of argument both simplifies the issues and is moralistic).

The view that only if foreign labour were introduced would there be labour problems is also criticized as being contrary to fact. Japan has long had dual-structured economy and a proletarian underclass employed at the bottom of an already segmented labour market. Guest-workers entered a labour market which was already split, and were not its cause (KBR, 1988:25). The argument that admission of foreign workers provoke discrimination is reversed in the same way: discrimination against Korean, Chinese and Taiwanese nationals has long existed, and it is the neglect of this problem which had resulted in discrimination against more recently arrived foreigners. The problem is not that acceptance of 'new' foreigners would be 'premature', but rather that anti-discrimination measures regarding 'old' foreigners were 'belated' (Karabao no kai jimukyoku, 1990:321).

In Japan in the 1960s, an offically-sanctioned and promoted re-structuring of the economy occurred. This created a surplus of indigenous workers (for example, from the primary sector and from coal mines which were abandoned as they became unprofitable). In the short-term this made the admission of foreign labour unnecessary. However, further rationalization and change within labour markets enlarged the unskilled sector (and increased demand for those prepared to work in jobs described as 'dangerous, dirty and laborious'). This situation, continuing to the present, makes the acceptance of labour migrants absolutely necessary (KBR, 1988:23f.). The government line, re-affirmed in the amendment of the Immigration Control Law, that foreign labour not be allowed into Japan is refuted by the reality of 200,000 to 300,000 'illegal' workers already present in Japan. This fact indicates that immigration of migrant workers cannot be curbed as long as global economic disparities exist, although even a 'legalization' would lead to the continued existence of an 'illegal' sector (Karabao no kai jimukyoku, 1990:307f. and 323).

The pet argument of proponents of the acceptance of 'guest-workers' is the – loosely labelled *'Multi-Kulti'* (multi-culturalism) in Germany – that foreigners from other cultures and with dif-ferent values bring about an enrichment and stimulation of society and culture. Thus, for instance, the intellectual Ōnuma maintains that 'internationalization' (*kokusaika*) should not be reduced to 'Westernization'. It rather signfies the reciprocal acceptance of various cultures and personalities. In order to change the structure of the 'Japanese soul' and Japanese life-style, a gradual accept-ance of foreigners would be necessary (see the discussion in Miyajima A.O., 1987:20). Japan to date, under the illusion of a homogenous people, had denied cultural identity to its own minor-ities. The admission of foreigners would at last provide an opportunity to dismantle discrimination and to learn to perceive and respect other cultures. In Japan, it is 'Western' culture which is primarily associated with '(foreign) culture'. Contact with people from Asia and the Third World would provide the opportunity for contact with their cultures and smooth the way for a multi-ethnic society in Japan (KBR, 1988:26). A liberalized immigration policy for an Asian labour force (!) would as 'a cultural phenomenon yield interesting results' (Kashigiwa, 1990:31). In order to fundamentally alter Japan's deep-rooted xenophobic, discriminatory consciousness, and its attitudes towards Asia, a soft restructuring of Japanese society into a pluralistic society tolerating various cultures would be desirable (Tanaka, 1990:37). The influx of foreign migrants constituted an opportunity to arouse more understanding for minority groups and generate a society richer in variety and permeability, able to absorb divergent value systems. Thus the 'problem' of labour migrants due to these cultural aspects transcended the plain of labour and economy (Ishiyama, 1989:241). To break down isolationism and the 'myths of uniqueness' of Japan, Ōmae Ken'ichi pleads for the introduction of ten million foreign workers. Thereby 'broad-mindedness' and tolerance and, as a consequence, internal internationalization and world acceptance of Japan would be increased (Ōmae, 1990:48). (In all of these statements – and clearly in the last – pedagogic imperatives and moralistic overtones are clearly evident. Even here ideas of 'profit and utility' for the immigration country – migrants as cultural enrichment factors – are to be found, although the proponents of immigration reproach politicians and economic interest groups in particular because their style of discussion is dominated by a 'utility-calculus', cf. Miyajima, 1989:11f.).

I wish now to follow this outline of the debate concerning acceptance or non-acceptance of 'unskilled' foreign labourers with a brief account of some opinon polls on this question, from which it was concluded that a 'consensus' among the public had not yet been reached.

6.6 Opinion polls

If one examines demoscopic surveys, one finds a consistent polarization regarding acceptance of labour migrants. To the question of whether the government should loosen, tighten or leave unchanged the present restrictions concerning foreign labour, 42 per cent answered in favour of deregulation, 32.3 per cent favoured tightening up and 12.8 per cent endorsed the status quo (13 per cent 'did not know'). Further 39.4 per cent considered the present phenomenon of migrants entering on a tourist visa and working 'illegally' as 'not good', and 45.4 per cent considered it as 'not good, but inevitable' (15.2 per cent 'did not know'). 51.9 per cent supported a limited acceptance circumscribed by clear conditions for 'unskilled workers', while 24.2 per cent agreed with the maintenance of the present course of not admitting 'unqualified' workers into the Japanese labour market (with 23.8 per cent who 'did not know'). 37 per cent were in favour of the rigid practice of deportation of 'illegals' under the coercive power of the state. There is also a punitive demand in regard to employers of 'illegal' employees, with 43 per cent opting for a stiffening of sanctions via new legislative measures, 29.8 per cent backing the existing legal situation, 8.2 per cent holding sanctioning to be unnecessary, and 18.6 per cent giving no answer (poll by the Prime Minister's Office, NSDKK. 1989:141 and 156). One year later, respondents were asked whether they would approve or oppose the admittance of Asian 'unskilled' labour migrants: 14 per cent were unconditionally approving, 31 per cent 'rather in favour', 13 per cent opposed and 35 per cent 'rather against' such a measure. A different formulation of the question, this time asking in which field Japan should advance its 'internationalization', resulted in 27.3 per cent supporting (the fairly abstract opinion) 'international co-operation' (active contributions to the 'international community' in the spheres of politics, economy, science, and so forth). The concrete option of 'internationalizing society' through the introduction of foreign labour was supported by only 11 per cent, while 25 per cent voted for 'economic measures' (opening of the market and economic structural reforms), and 17.4 per cent wished for changes in the cultural sphere and 7.6 per cent favoured changed in the intellectual sphere.

Inquiry about people's actual contacts with foreigners (*gaikokujin* – this category including also 'legal, qualified' foreigners from Western countries) reveals that only 4.8 per cent have regular contact with foreigners; 16.6 per cent 'from time to time have the opportunity for a chat', 16.4 per cent 'encounter foreigners at their place of work or in the neighbourhood, but do not communicate with them', 48.7 per cent 'see foreigners on the street' and 14.3 per cent 'almost never see foreigners' (NSDKK, 1990: 120, 347 and 485). This indicates that actual contact with foreigners is largely limited to the visual. A latent reservedness regarding 'association' with foreigners can more readily be inferred from a poll commissioned by the police. In this survey, interviews were conducted with 1,600 inhabitants of eight (unspecified) regions, in which foreign workers (the majority presumably 'illegals') are concentrated: 68.1 per cent stated to that they had either heard of or seen foreigners engaging in 'unskilled' labour (or possibly doing so) in the precincts of their residence. These respondents were asked about the nature of the association. Only 10.5 pe cent declared that they kept company with foreigners or greeted them. Further questioning of those 'having contacts' revealed that for 72.2 per cent this consisted of a short greeting on the street. Reciprocal visiting or an advisory relationship was the answer given by only 14.2 per cent (13 per cent briefly 'chat' on the street, 0.6 per cent abstain from giving information). Only 1.5 per cent of all the respondents had such 'real' contacts with foreigners as visiting and giving advice. When asked whether they would consider getting in touch with foreigners 'by way of opportunity' in the future, of those having no contact with foreigners, up to 33 per cent said they would 'not consider this' and 44 per cent 'did not really take such a thing into consideration'. This meant that 74 per cent had an antipathetic attitude towards association with foreigners (the relevant terms always is *tsukiai*). Reasons given were 'troublesomeness or possible complications' (45 per cent) and lack of confidence in one's own competence in foreign languages (25.4 per cent; 13.6 per cent abstained from answering) (cf. Keisatsuchō, 1990: 27–29).

A poll conducted by the newspaper *Asahi* resulted in a similarly dichotomous picture: 81 per cent of respondents said they had heard or seen something about 'unskilled' foreign labourers; 56 per cent were in favour of an admittance under specified conditions, while one third favoured continued non-acceptance and 11 per cent did not know or refrained from answering; 45 per cent supported 'legalization' of foreign labour, while 34 per cent endorsed strict enforcement of existing laws and 16 per cent believed one should, except in cases of serious abuse of the laws, 'generously shut one's eyes', and 5 per cent were undecided. Altogether, the two camps were clearly demarked, with a more liberal attitude among younger and educated persons (cf. *Asahi shinbun*, 6 September 1989:9) – in this context of questioning, probably an internationally reproducible and constant factor. A vindicating indicator for the relative importance of education is to be found in the results of a differently-designed questionnaire (from a poll by the Tokyo Chamber of Industry and Commerce in May 1988; the following accounts is in accordance with my source but corroborative evidence is not available). When asked whether, for Japanese society, a more firmly enforced admittance of 'guestworkers' than at present was 'necessary' (*hitsuyō*), more than three quarters of the thirty-five polled university professors, 66.7 per cent of the eighteen polled journalists and researchers, and seven of seventeen labour unionists (41.2 per cent) saw such a 'necessity' (TRK, 1988:73).

Similar results emerged in a poll by *Mainichi shinbun* in January 1990. The proponents of admission for foreign labour (17 per cent in favour, 34 per cent 'rather in favour') comprise 51 per cent and the opponents 44 per cent of respondents. In comparison with the previous year's poll, a slight increase of proponents was recorded, especially among employers of whom one out of four were in favour of admission (*Mainichi shinbun*, 5 February 1990). Looking at tendencies over the course of time in comparable surveys (by the Prime Minster's Office) regarding immigration regulations, in 1961 15 per cent, in 1980 10.3 per cent and in 1988 17.8 per cent favoured deregulation of admission and facilitation of formal procedures. In 1961, 19 per cent, in 1980 42.4 per cent and in 1988 34.6 per cent wanted a tightening of regulations and formalities. (Abstention rates were 51 per cent (!) in 1961,[4] 21.1 per cent in 1980, and only 14.6 per cent in 1988) (cf. Yorimitsu, 1989:21). The decrease in 'indifference' and absence of an opinion indicates that the question was increasingly perceived as something personally 'tangible', that is, as demanding a statement. A linear increase is shown in the percentages of those favouring a stiffening of requirements for admission. This can be interpreted as a side-effect of media coverage focused on 'illegal' workers. Those who favoured the tightening of restrictions might have expected such measures to redress the 'social problem of illegals' (which was defined as such by politicians and the media in the first place).

With respect to their sampling design, the polls of the Prime Minister's Office and those of the daily newspapers, are carefully and amply modelled that the usually advisable scepticism or resevation is not called for. However, the formulation of the questions was heavily influenced by the *zeitgeist* of the current debate. This holds true particularly for the directly demanded responses concering an 'opening or closing of the country' and for the investigation into attitude regarding legislative measures (and how far these would be 'legitimate'). The surveys by the Prime Minister's Office in particular, repeatedly include complex questions on liberalizing or stiffening legal restrictions. Here suspicion of 'legitimation' via opinion polls can scarcely be subdued.

Industrialists are to a striking degree in favour of admittance of foreign labour. Relevant polls consistently indicate a high degree of willingness to alleviate the existing labour shortage with foreign labour. I want to refer to some selected examples. The Tokyo Citizens' Bank (Tokyo-tomin ginkō) mailed 1,057 questionnairs to manager customers in June 1989, and obtained 513 responses. Almost 80 per cent of entrepreneurs in small and middle-sized enterprises bemoaned a shortage of labour, 17.7 per cent were in favour of a liberalization and 59.1 per cent advocated a conditional (*jōkentsuki*) introduction of foreign workers; that is, three out of four in this group of employers supported a policy of expanded admission. The reason given most often (66 per cent of multiple answer options) was 'shortage of personnel' (*Kanagawa shinbun*, 21 July 1989). A national poll of a thousand medium-sized core enterprises (*chūken kigyō*) conducted by an insurance company (Daijō Seimei) revealed that more than seven-tenths of entrepreneurs favoured acceptance while only 11.8 per cent were against it (with 10.7 per cent who 'do not know'). Sixty per cent of respondents reported a demand for labour (*Asahi shinbun*, 6 September 1990). The Tokyo Bureau for Labour and Economy (Tokyo rōdō keizaikyoku) on 12 June 1990 published a differently fashioned poll, in which small and middle-sized enterprises (with more than ten but less than 300 employees) were surveyed; 5,200 questionnaires were mailed to a random sample of firms (return figure: 2,080). According to the results, 10.7 per cent of the enterprises already employed foreigners (whether legally or 'illegally' is not specified). One out of every four firms which had not yet employed foreigners showed willingness ('*yatoitai*') to do so (*Nihon keizai shinbun*, 13 July 1990).

The industrialists' highly positive attitude towards introduction of foreign labour reflects the fact that economic organizations in the discussion were the interest groups pulling most weight in favour of an admittance of foreign labour. A demand issued by the Osaka Chamber of Trade and Industry made big headlines in May 1990; in this it was said that even unskilled labourers should be able to obtain permanent resident status, and that they should be introduced to Japan through 'recruiting centres' with

their number determined through bilateral agreements. Furthermore, present 'illegals' should be granted a special permit to stay
for one year. This was possibly the most 'radical' advocacy of an
official guest-worker policy. Similarly positive, but more hesitant
expressions of interests also came in from other organizations.
Kanzai keizai dōyūkai had already in January 1989 championed a
gradual introduction of 'guest-workers' through 'dispatching
centres'. The latter would have to shoulder the responsibility for
housing and re-migration. The national Keizai dōyūkai opted
for expansion of the *kenshūsei* system. The Federation for
Economy in Kansai (Kansai keizai rengōkai) in April 1990
endorsed an 'inevitable' admittance of foreign workers with residence limited to three years and work restricted to particular areas
and vocational fields. Only the Kansai Managers' Association
(Kansai keieisha kyōkai) was unreservedly in favour of maintaining the status quo (*Nihon keizai shinbun*, 25 May 1990:10).

In summary, it is evident that views (reflecting the *sakoku-
kaikoku* polarization) concerning an opening or closing of the
country, when directly asked for, show a markedly 'split' profile
of opinion, with a slight, but not significant majority favouring
accpetance of foreign workers. When views regarding (stiffened)
legislative measures are investigated, a good third of those polled
adopt a rigid attitude. The willingness to admit foreigners
decreased when alternatives are offfered (for example, 'international co-operation') and there is very little real readiness to
(intimately) associate with foreigners. The interests of industry are
reflected in an over-proportionally high willingness to endorse a
guest-worker admittance policy.

It is clear that the polarized opinion profile 'officially' serves as
legtimation for a 'further, careful investigation' into the question.
In effect, this means nothing more than adherence to the existing
policy concerning 'unskilled' foreign labour. Thus a commentary
on the amendment of the Immigration Control Acts states that
this amendment was decided upon after thorough deliberation
and consideration of the views of all interest groups. A residence-
category for 'unskilled' labour was not created, with the Parliament justifying this (in an additional resolution) with the reason
that public discussion in Japan on 'unqualified' foreign workers
was characterized by divergent and multifarious views. An exhaus-
tive, adequate and cumulative investigation (*jūbun na kentō*) into
the question, taking various opinions into consideration, was to

be undertaken (thus it was put by a high official of the Ministry of Justice, Yamazaki, 1991:145). The amendment to the Immigration Control Act can be seen as a condensate of the debate of 'new' legal provisions for foreign workers, which was strongly determined by the power of definition of ministerial bureaucrats. In the following, I shall enumerate the main points of the amendment.

6.7 Revision of the Immigration Control Act

The law in question has the long-winded title *shutsunyūkoku kanri oyobi nanmin nintei-hō* (abbreviated: *nyūkanhō*) which literally means 'Departure and Entry Control and Refugee Recognitions Act'. The 'affirmative amendment', fiercely debated at the end of 1989, passed through the Lower House on 17 November 1989 (with approval of all influential parties – LDP, Socialists, Kōmei and Democratic-Socialist Party – but without the support of the Communists). The main aims of the amendment reputedly were:

(1)   To provide a detailed specification of 'residence titles' (*zairyū shikaku* – literally, 'residence qualifications') which were reclassifed from eighteen to twenty-eight categories.
(2)   To establish sanctionary regulations applying to employers and traffickers of 'illegal' labour.
(3)   To accelerate immigration formalities (the checking of documents and details) by specifying immigration control requirements in further detail (*Nihon keizai shinbun*, 18 November 1989).

As an additional, and important, fourth measure, it was made possible for foreign workers to obtain a 'labour permit certificate' (*shūrō shikaku shōmeisho*) (see, for example, Yashiro, 1989:67 and Chūshō kigyōchō, 1990:12).

Similar declarations can be found in publications of the Ministry of Justice. These refer to the increased number of entries of foreigners and to the rise in the number of 'specialists' economically active in Japan in various professional sectors as requiring an adequate legislative response. The issue of 'illegal' workers, with

Foreign Workers and Law Enforcement in Japan

its far-reaching social implications, is labelled a 'grave problem'
which makes 'harsh countermeasures' imperative (Sakanaka,
1989:18). The 'problem of illegal's is declared to be a main triggering factor for the apparently 'panicky' law revision. The precise
description of the activities lawful for each residence title, and the
designation of residence titles by name (for example, *ryūgaku* –
studies, *keiei* – management) instead of by the former numeric
combinations are regarded as important reforms. It should thus
be clear at a glance (and clear also to potential employers) into
which residence category the holder of a residence title falls, and
hence the scope of the holder's permitted activity (cf. Sakanaka,
1989:19: the law as promulgated, and detailed descriptions published of activities corresponding to the various residence
categories, in the official organ of the Ministry of Justice, *Kanpō*
54, 24 May 190:74–7; these were publicly issued by the then Justice
Minister, Hasegawa Shin). Abstracting from the various details,
European and an Anglo-American immigration-law models could
be constructed with the former focused on residence and labour
permission, that is, having 'residence control' as its primary
concern, while the latter, analogously to the Japanese model,
focuses on 'immigration control' (since the residence title granted
upon entry to Japan automatically determines what type of work
and activities (for example, studies, mission, trade, and so forth)
are legally permitted (Yashiro, 1989:35f.).

The vital point is that the amendment introduced no residence
title for 'unqualified work' (*tanjun rōdō*), work which could be
'performed without special techniques, skills or know-how'
(Sakanaka, 1989:19). The measures for the prevention of 'illegal'
work are exhaustively described by the bureaucrat Sakanaka, who
maintains that 'efforts to expose foreigners who engage in illegal
labour are necessary, and particularly so for strict control of enterprises who employ them or let them work, or otherwise aid and
abet illegal work' (Sakanaka, 1989:22). Stiff penalties for
employing or introducing illegal labour and for 'professional'
activities 'furthering illegal labour' (*fuhō shūrō jochō–zai*), these
penalties including up to three years' imprisonment, and fines of
up to two million yen. (These penalties do not yet apply retroactively to 'illegal' labour relations entered upon before the law
came into force on 1 June 1990.) In this way, a 'deterrent effect
against illegal work was hoped for and, moreover, an effective
instrument was created by means of which one could proceed

against "vicious" criminal acts (*akushitsu hanzai kōi*) perpetrated in connection with illegal work and becoming public recently' (Sakanaka, 1989:23). Here is evident the 'prevention-optimism' of a professional jurist and bureaucrat, whose comprehension of the law is mainly one of repressive orientation. Journalists and concerned members of the bar have berated just this kind of attitude. They considered that, with a policy concentrated on sanctions and repression, the already-occuring human rights violations and existing mechanisms of exploitation would only become more subtle and refined and be pushed further underground. 'Relatively good-will' employers, out of fear of punishment, would cease to employ foreigners, who then would definitely become the victims of profit-oriented exploiters (xf. KBR, 1990:15 and 141; Shakai bunka hōritsu sentā, 1989:12f.; Ishiyama, A.O. 1989:222). Since I have repeatedly referred to various elements of the new legal situation, I refrain from reiterating these points here.

In summary, it can be contended that the 'revision' was not substantial; on the contrary, the criminalization of 'irregular' labour, and emphasis on repressive measures (even if they are actually used only in 'vicious' (*akushitsu*) and professional cases – as I have been personally informed by the lawyer Yōfu Tomomi) entrenched and facilitated the disciplining of 'illegal' foreigners by means of the penal code. The second part of this study addresses this thesis.

7 Migrant Workers and Criminality

7.1 Preliminary Remarks

This study deals mainly with issues concerning the 'criminality' of foreigners in Japan in the context of the debate on foreign labour. However, this enterprise poses something of a dilemma. Speaking of the 'criminality of foreigners' carries the risk firstly of overemphasising the status of being foreign, and secondly of assuming that criminality of foreigners is of a special or peculiar type. Ethnocentric pre-suppositions can easily enter such a study, obscuring the view of structural features of society at large. The status 'foreigner' is just one attribute that pre-structures position in society and possible living conditions. First of all, therefore, the explanatory potential of general criminological theories must be fully exploited in order not to blur perception of the general social texture by concentrating on foreignness. However, the stigmata 'illegal' and 'foreigner' overshadow the whole existence of those so-labelled, and where foreigners are linked with illegality there is risk of a dual degradation: as a foreigner and as a criminal. This situation, of course, must not be misunderstood or neglected.

The topic of criminality of foreigners, besides being dealt with as a distinctive aspect of a social problem (foreigners being pre-defined and prejudged as a problem group), is in danger of being dramatized, on the one hand, or diminished (by good-will) and underestimated on the other. Both positions are oftentimes connected with (socio)political demands and contaminated by leading interests and biased perceptions. It is not the intention of this study to furnish empirical proof regarding the criminality of foreigners, be it low or high. Given available data, this cannot be attempted anyway. Moreover – according to a sophistical argument – 'empirical statistical "counter-evidence", first of all, is the affirmation of racism' (Huisken, 1987:142). Here one would attempt to demonstrate that foreigners are actually quite 'normal' and not particularly criminal. I rather want to locate the strategic position of the notion of 'deteriorating public safety due to the influx of ("illegal") foreign labour to Japan'. Moreover, the combined effects of the activities of relatively autonomous fields (the general public, mass media, police and judiciary) have to be illuminated. These effects converge, and condense the phenomenon of 'criminality of foreigners' into a 'development'. This development is manifested in statistical, media 'realities', and in actual reality. The interaction to be elucidated here subsequently has effects of reciprocal confirmation and reinforcement, which can be viewed as a feedback process. This process is not necessarily set in motion consciously. Nevertheless, it coincides with a result that is interpreted and discussed as a crime wave. I shall examine the genesis and ideological utilization of such a phase of criminalization.

7.2 The Discussion Regarding Criminality of Guest-workers in Austria and Germany

First of all, a short excursion into the criminological research on the criminality of guest-workers should help to delineate a theoretical framework for dealing with the Japanese situation. My perfunctory survey cannot claim to be representative. I shall rely on work already done, citing exemplary insights, and can provide only a sketch of the various theory-models.

> A look into the development of the discipline of criminology shows that the theme criminality of foreigners has marked booms which are in conspicuous relation to changes in strategy of policy on foreigners ... The topic 'delinquency of foreigners' comes under debate when national labour market limits, employment and immigration policies are once again controversial (Pilgram, 1986:349)

That is, ' "criminology concerning foreigners" always flourishes in specific political contexts. Formulation of questions and results of the discipline are to be accepted with critical caution in the light of this fact' (Pilgram, 1984:17).

Initially in the formulation of a policy of employment of foreign workers, discussion was of problems which could emerge from an eventual conflict of culture. The focus of debate then shifted markedly when recruitment ended and bans were imposed on entries in 1973; debate now concerned the integration and marginalization of guest-workers, and problems of the second generation. This change is linked with a distinct 'progression of theories' and a change in paradigms. In the following review we must not lose sight of the overall social, political and economic climate.

7.2.1 The culture conflict model

The first criminological interpretive model of interpretation applied to the criminality of foreigners in Germany was the theory of culture conflict. This theory had been developed against the specific societal backdrop of the USA in the 1920s (which included a general feeling of crisis and restrictions on immigration). Recourse to the sociological reflections of Sellin allowed the ideology-imbued Nazi-criminology to be passed over. But reception of Sellin in Germany was cursory and 'overlooked the ethnocentric premise that a relatively low rate of criminality of isolated, homogeneous, so-to-speak "undisturbed" developing societies would rise as a consequence of immigration'; it also ignored Sellin's own further developments of the theory (Pilgram, 1984:18f.). In a textbook outlining various theories of deviance, it is stated that 'from the clash between different cultures ... one can incur explanations for the emergence of deviant conduct' (Lamnek, 1990:143). The author brings this view close to theories on subculture. Both theoretical attempts have sociological character and 'invoke subcultural or culture-conflicting constellations which can be grasped socio-structurally' (Lamnek, 1990:143 and 145). This perspective does not concentrate on conflicts between immigrants and residents and is more adequate in view of the heterogeneity of the receiving culture. In the host country, an immigrant is forced to adopt conflicting roles (Albrecht, 1972:240, in reference to Sellin. Albrecht also attempts to validate the concept of culture conflict with respect to second-generation immigrants.).

By incorporation of the findings of traditional cultural anthropology, it [the hypothesis of culture conflict] then concludes that groups of the populace with culturally-specific

and marked formations of basic personality are more likely
to be forced to criminal conduct if they – as in the case of
migration from an agrarian to an industrial society – are
confronted with a dominant value structure contrary to their
prior rules of conduct (Richter, 1981:264).

However, in Germany the hypothesis of culture conflict is
accepted (if at all) only partially and in connection with certain
offences (for example, violent acts arising from a different code
of honour, illegal gambling which is not proscribed in the home
countries of the migrants and so forth). But even in this reduced
form, the hypothesis has been subject to grave objections. It cannot
explain why the majority of immigrants abstain from criminal
conduct and why first-generation immigrants show a lower rate of
criminality than residents of the host country (given the theory's
assumption that they would suffer the worst stress and the most
severe value conflicts). It further ignores intra-cultural conflicts in
a pluralistic society (Richter, 1981:265). The lower crime rate of
first-generation immigrants can possibly be explained by the fact
that they retreat into their own interpretive models (for example,
in regard to status hierarchy) and this can lead to a neutralization
of potential conflicts. 'The cultural autonomy could make exceptionally unusual situations more bearable which, without this
background, actually could end up in depressions and aggressions'
(Pilgram, 1984:27). The concept of culture conflict was used almost
exclusively for explanations of criminality in situations of apparently inter-cultural conflict, and came under stricture. The critique
can be summed up as follows: *'The concept of "culture conflict"
is too vague for a precise analysis and explanation of the relations
between deviant and criminal conduct'* (emphasis in Trotha,
1985:290).

'The eclipse of the culture conflicts paradigm in the German
literature on the criminality of foreigners has been readily
apparent since Kaiser (1971). In later works on the topic, the
concept figures almost exclusively as example for poor theory'
(Pilgram, 1984:23). In a recent edition of his *Kriminologie*, Kaiser
notes in conclusion:

> *There is no indication that cultural conflict would enhance in
> the area of criminal law norms* ... Individual cases of
> criminality motivated by cultural specifics do not run counter

to that. Even frequent pointers of guest-workers' lack of command of the language and to the different morals and customs in their countries of origin cannot obscure the fact that a *majority of potential culture conflicts are solved by means other than criminality* (emphasis in Kaiser, 1989:358).

Kaiser also makes the important remark that, even where particular offences are over-represented, it is not the otherness of being a foreigner which is of primary importance, but rather the fact that the integration of foreigners is mainly into the subculture of lower classes. In this substratum, use of violence for 'conflict resolution' is in certain cases more acceptable (for example, in the affirmation of 'honour', reputation, or virility). Therefore, the frequency of occurrences of assault and battery can be seen as an expression of a preferred subcultural mode of conflict management (cf. Kaiser, 1989:360). If one changes perspective, infractions come to fore which 'rather point to a particular *sensitivity and vulnerability, and to the strategies of prosecution of the German host culture.* One thinks, for instance, of the proportion of foreigners involved in gambling, and of course of the handling of the Foreigners' Law' (emphasis in Kaiser, 1989:364). This remark glances sidelong at the labelling approach, whose relevance I will examine later. If one looks to society at large it can be seen that 'a "culture conflict" results . . . out of the incapability of our society to discard the category of "foreignness" with all the concomitant restrictions (for example, of social chances of the persons concerned)' (Hamburger, Seus and Wolter, 1981:15).

7.2.2 The thesis of 'social deprivation'

This theory attempts to explain the criminality of foreigners on the basis of the socio-structural chances of their participation in society. The thesis tries to challenge the culture conflict model stressing the 'social deprivation' of foreigners. This refers to the opportunities for the second generation of foreign workers. 'The general conditions and those in the family for socialization, as well as the lack of opportunities for education, profession and future, engender for young foreigners an "institutionalized outsider role" ' (Albrecht and Pfeiffer, 1979:9). Albrecht and Pfeiffer, in the quantitative part of their study which is differentiated according to age-groups, find an excessive over-representation of foreign juveniles and young adults in some criminal statistics. They connect these findings with the social deprivation of foreigners. Rather than culture conflict,

> socio-structural moments and mechanisms, thus access to economic, professional, scholastic and other opportunities, together with identity problems owing to socialization-specifics, 'can claim to be of much greater weight than factors, which can be comprehended as pure culture conflict in the sense of a clash between incompatible regulations of conduct (Albrecht and Pfeiffer, 1979:53, citing Sack).

'The positive resonance this survey found right after its publication shows that the hypothesis of social deprivation is now the dominant approach in interpretation [of the criminality of foreigners] in the Federal Republic' (Richter, 1981:264). However, the representativeness of the study was called in question. Moreover, multiple recording was ignored in the data interpretation. The presented figures on crime rates therefore seem a quite dubious basis for the hypothesis. Crime involvement (when looked at according to age, offences, regions, and so forth) is inconsistent and scattered – a fact which is obscured by the overall rates, and which scarcely supports the general thesis (cf. Richter, 1981:268f.). Another considerable objection is that the data for comparison are presented in abstraction from social strata.

> The assumption is well-founded that only a small percentage of Germans belong to the same social stratum as the foreign resident population in the FRG. This restricted circle of natives [that is, the small percentage in the same socio-economic position as foreigners] presumably accounts for a disproportionately high share of criminalized. The over-representation in crime rates of foreigners in relation to all Germans, therefore, is hardly sensational (Pilgram, 1984:25).

Mansel published a study informed by the social control theory. He cites data concerning prosecution and, particularly, conviction statistics, rather than the figures recorded by police. He then shows that the surveyed Turks and Italians 'show a significantly lower criminal involvement than the German control group, that is, persons who live in a comparable social environment' (Mansel,

1986:310 and 314). This means that the proportion of indictments in all offence groups is lower for foreigners than for Germans, and

> that police (supported by the higher inclination of the indigenous public to report foreigners):
>
> (a) criminalize the offspring of guest-workers more often after private troubles.
> (b) launch investigations against young foreigners even in petty occurrences.
> (c) are more likely to suspect them due to generalized suspicion and, therefore, institute investigations into trivial offences and criminally-irrelevant actions and more often file complaints (Mansel, 1986:323f.).

7.2.3 The theory of anomie and other etiological fragments

Close to the concept of social deprivation is to the theory of anomie as a model for explanation of the criminality of second-generation foreigners. As was classically formulated, this theory holds that 'Aberrant conduct . . . may be viewed as a symptom of dissociation between culturally-defined aspirations and socially structured avenues by which those goals can be reached' (Merton, 1968:289). Killias propounds a strain theory that might account for the over-representation of immigrant youths in criminal statistics. One is to proceed from the values and attitudes among immigrants and their position within the host country's social structure. The anomic strain results from a high level of aspiration of the immigrants' second generation and a lack of resources to achieve consumption goals by legitimate means. Crime may be just one of several possible outcomes of this disparity. Crime rates seem to be related to the degree of integration and the labour market situation. Killias also quotes an array of studies showing that 'immigrant youths may not disproportionately engage in delinquency compared to native-born juveniles from similar socio-economic backgrounds' (cf. Killias, 1989:20f.). Another author, Gebauer, writing in the police-linked journal *Kriminalistik*, discards the most conventional attempts to explain the criminality of foreigners. He sees the theory of anomie as a 'suggestive frame of reference' (Gebauer, 1981b:83). He points to the disadvantages immigrants face in education, jobs the real estate market and so on. According to Gebauer, one can infer 'an explanation of the strong over-involvement in crime of the second generation by consulting the theory of anomie and considering the socio-structural disadvantages which show up in multifarious ways' (Gebauer, 1981b:86). Immigrants develop their own levels of aspiration which result in the substitution of general, culturally-accepted success-goals by more easily accessible, prestigious consumption goals.

> Particularly the discrepancy between consumptive goals and available means could have effects on the crimes against property. An exaggerated masculinity-cult on the other hand, could be instrumental in explaining offences of violence and against persons which do come to notice abundantly (Gebauer, 1981b:84).

In this article, violent crimes are also explained 'conventionally' by subcultural characteristics. Peer-group pressure and incidents specific to socialization (for example, authoritarian, punitive education-style) are invoked as being factors conducive to aggression (Gebauer, 1981b:85f.). This should make violent crimes understandable. Here we are on classic, 'etiological' terrain. Joining this inquiry into causes of criminality, Wolter (who also subscribes to the labelling approach) attempts to comprehend certain forms of criminality in terms of the notion of 'deviance characterized by anomie'. This type of delinquency is grounded in the conviction of immigrant youths that their aspirations are legitimate. They try to secure a way of life that is considered desirable or is misleadingly depicted by the mass media as attainable. He differentiates the situation of anomie by remarking that foreign youths with a life perspective centred on the host country show a sort of deviance typical for juveniles. In adapting to what is seen as adequate in the host country they develop aspirations which are *situation-linked* and mostly materialistic (emphasis in Wolter, 1984:272). The immigrant youths recognize the barriers to their mobility as due to socio-structural reasons, recognise their under-privileged position, but refuse to be subordinate and develop their own legitimations for their (deviant) conduct. They react to the label 'foreigner' in the manner of Goffman's account of stigma-management. However, they interpret objective disadvantages in terms of those theories on discrimination and generalized xenophobia which emphasize the daily experiences of actors. Hereby the factual socio-structural matrix of power relations is obscured (cf. Wolter, 1984:275 and 278).

It tends to be the case that

> in the analysis, etiological factors such as social deprivation, diffusion of identity as a consequence of bi-cultural and broken socialization, lack of competence in action, and deviance as a mode of reaction against discrimination and stigmatization of guest-workers and their descendants, are in the foreground of reflections ... The results of the inquiries, however, do not furnish an homogeneous picture (Mansel, 1985:170).

In an extensive, qualitative study (Hamburger, Seus and Wolter, 1981) an attempt is made to account for etiological factors as well as factors pertaining to the theory of social control (density and frequency of control, structural differences in power, stigmatized status). Subsequently, a theory of cumulation of these factors is outlined. This is not a 'pure' labelling approach, thus it attempts to take its insights into consideration. The authors typify a 'singular-spontaneous' deviance and an 'anomic-consolidated' deviance; the latter could also be described as contra-cultural. The first type is said to be quite typical for juveniles and is characterized by a lack of professional competence and acts oriented around immediate needs and action. Offenders of the anomic type have a repertoire of neutralization and legitimation techniques at their disposal. They also operate with more planning and high materialistic goals. Deviant conduct is interpreted by them as a form of 'coping with life'.

> Delinquency is not a problem specific to foreigners. But as regards foreign juveniles, the mentioned structural features cumulate. The patterns of interpretation specified in connection with being foreign consolidate only in the process of deviance consolidation and as effects of control procedures. In the type of acts characterized by anomie – whether exemplifying consolidated deviance or subcultural retreat – the status 'foreigner', which was first repudiated as being a negatively-valued imputation, is now subjectively realized (and accepted) (Hamburger, Seus and Wolter, 1981:175).

The authors also address another element informed by social control theory: foreign juveniles 'burdened with leisure' who loiter around such niches of the metropolitan life sphere as discos, cinemas, game centres, and public parks or fast-food restaurants, that is, mostly in places highly 'public'. These hang-outs offer a challenging appeal for action and place a strain for consumption on youths. The behaviours of 'hanging-out' and 'action and stimulus seeking' also have to be seen in connection with the unattractiveness of the family and peer-group orientation (Hamburger, Seus and Wolter, 1981:93). The places in which foreign youths prefer to spend their free time have also been called 'de-central ghettos.'

> Through occasional confrontations with German juveniles, the risk gets higher that they [foreign youths] are criminalized more often. Fighting in the vicinity of the de-central ghettos is inevitable. When the police are called in, these conflicts, in the most cases, end with charges against the foreigners (Bielefeld and Kreissl, 1983:87).

'As regards control procedures, one has to proceed from the assumption that foreign juveniles are under higher "density" of prosecution, particularly so in places easily surveyed by police'. This can lead to situations of permanent control, even if the initiating offence was of a trivial nature (cf. Hamburger, Seus and Wolter, 1981:146). With these reflections in mind, I want to introduce a further theoretical approach to aberrant conduct (of foreigners).

7.2.4 The social control paradigm and the labelling approach

'Neglect of the, in recent years dominant, "labelling approach" to foreigners can be ascribed to a misled helper-syndrome of criminologists with their predilection for problems' (Wolter, 1984:266). The diverse concepts branded 'labelling theory' are 'not etiologically oriented. They do not search for causes prior to the emergence of deviant behaviour, but *understand deviance as process of imputation of the attribute deviance to certain forms of conduct in a setting of interaction*' (emphasis in Lamnek, 1990:217). Of paramount importance to the theory, therefore, is the societal reaction to aberrant conduct and the 'grasp' of agencies of social control. This is perceived as a process, 'an escalating interplay performed by stigmatization and deviance. It results in the adaptation of one's self image to definitions from outside and leads to the acceptance of a deviant role', which is, as a rule, staged in a subculture (Pfeiffer and Scheerer, 1979:49f.). The agencies of control, therefore, are strongly implicated in the 'production of criminals'. A certain selection takes place in this process. Stigma is the key metaphor of the concept. The stigma 'criminal' entails reduction of opportunities for conforming action, deprivation of social opportunities, and formation of an identity fixed to the ascriptions 'deviant', 'delinquent', 'criminal' imputed by others, and, ultimately, this stigma consolidates the newly-accepted role.

This theory can claim high plausibility, particularly regarding recidivism and 'criminal careers'. In Germany this approach was 'radicalized' and integrated in a highly sophisticated theory by Fritz Sack. He discards any inquiry into causes and highlights the aspect of power in society. The distribution of criminality is seen to be determined by class-structure. The labelling approach itself had a remarkable career undergoing differentiating and further development. However, Sack deplored the fact that 'labelling theory . . . was simply pocketed and reduced "etiologically" ' (Sack, 1988:16; for a presentation of the theory, see for example Lamnek, 1990:216–236; for a cogent critique on the labelling approach, see Goode, 1993).

The labelling approach attempts to abandon the focus on the individual perpetrator characteristic in 'traditional' criminology. Crucial points are the negotiating and imposing of norms, the enforcement activities of institutions of social control and the societal handling of 'deviance' and 'criminality'. From this perspective, the process of criminalization is only one part of the whole story of powerlessness and being de-privileged.

> Low class members . . . as persons lacking competence in
> action, again and again prove to be 'more criminal' in
> comparison with members of the rest of society, because
> in many settings of interaction (particularly those which are
> pre-shaped by institutions) they have reduced opportunities to
> carry through their points (Bohnsack and Schütze, 1973:273).

This lack of competence in negotiating a non-deviant identity can be seen to be valid for foreigners (especially 'illegal' ones). They face dual stigmatization as 'foreigner' and as 'suspect' and this situation is exacerbated by linguistic problems. From a social-control perspective, it can be observed that this is to the detriment of foreigners. They already are confronted with a higher density of control and a certain publicity of their 'crimes'. 'For reasons of a strong "sensitivity" of the German public for potentially criminizable deeds of foreign youths and for reasons of a police behaviour prone to prevention, they get into the criminal statistics of the police more often via a high quota of arrests' (Wolter, 1984:266). Stereotyped prejudices, feelings of being menaced, the imputation of a 'criminal energy' to foreigners, and the implicit criminalization of foreigners in media talk of a 'social time bomb', lead to a situation of permanent suspicion and readiness to call for the police, and constant control. The stigma 'foreigners', not least, serves the construction of scapegoats, canalizing 'downwards' potential frustration and aggression. It also serves as an instrument of domination through the withholding of opportunities for social, economic and political participation (cf. Wolter, 1984:269 and 271). Kaiser too points in his textbook to the harsher strategies of control of foreigners along the lines sketched above (also cf. Kaiser, 1989:346). Richter also attempts to comprehend the delinquency of foreigners in Germany in terms of the labelling approach. In connection with the high involvement of foreign youths in criminal conduct, he concludes that it is more reasonable 'to speak of a process of criminalization owing to the foreigner stigma rather than a criminality generated by culture conflict or social deprivation' (Richter, 1981:274).

Where criminology makes the delinquency of foreigners topical, 'the general predilection of criminology for a "deficit theory" of crime' is characteristic (Pilgram, 1986:350). First it was the traditional 'other' culture, subsequently the lacking of social opportunities, that were perceived as risk factors. The following statement is representative: 'Causes of criminal conduct of foreign youths are, according to our findings, primarily deficits in the areas of school, education, profession, leisure, housing and partly already in the family' (Donner, 1981:140). Diagnoses of this kind are usually paired with negative prognoses and coupled with political demands for more integration and allocation of social opportunities to abolish those deficits and disadvantages. This has to be seen in connection with the overall political climate.

A heavy involvement in crime due to this problematic situation seems to be easily comprehensible and, if not yet observable, it can be gathered from it. Thus the danger of producing the developments apprehended through its prediction is grasped in analysis informed by control theory (cf. Wolter, 1984), but it is not averted. On the contrary, as further defect foreigners are now 'awarded' their stigmatization (Pilgram, 1986:350).

Pilgram draws the conclusion that one has 'to mull over the relations between labour market, control policies and criminality in general and to consider the disciplining and resistance of foreigners as a special case of the effects of social control' (Pilgram, 1986:352). He demonstrates that the practices of criminalization are mirrored in the labour market and in social circumstances and policies concerning them. Certain practices intensify in restrictive phases of the employment of foreigners. Mansel argues similarly, and contends that, in view of the differences in crime rates between the several *Länder* in Germany, 'the more restrictive policies regarding foreigners are, the higher the KBZ [*Kriminalitätsbelastungsziffer* – per capita crime rate for 100,000 of a population] of foreigners' (Mansel, 1985:178). The same author, in a more recent study, shows that the risk of being criminalized in federal states ruled by conservative parties is one-and-a-half times higher than in those ruled by Social Democrats. In respect of infringements of the Foreigners Law, young Turks are convicted as much as five times more often in *Länder* with conservative rule than in those with social democratic domination. Here the connection between policies of criminalization and political aims distinctly comes to the fore. These policies serve as an instrument for disciplining and marginalizing certain minorities so as to reduce the number of foreigners living in the Federal Republic (Mansel, 1990).

7.2.5 The criminal statistics of the police

7.2.5.1 Problems and contents
If one examines empirical findings concerning the criminality of foreigners, one sees that the crime rate of the first generation is lower than that of the indigenous populace. In the second generation, conversely, officially-recorded criminality among foreign

juveniles is higher than that of natives (see Killias, 1989:18, for a general examination of the criminality of immigrants in Europe).

Before I delve into empirical data and their inherent distortions, I want to make several general reflections upon criminal statistics (particularly those of the police). 'If, despite all the scientific critique, the boom in use of criminal statistics continues unabated, this can be read as an indicator of their important legitimatory function' (Albrecht, 1983:18). This especially pertains to questions that preoccupy public discussion. Criminal statistics provided by police again and again are made to serve as 'evidence' for opportune trends. This also holds true for the discourse on foreigners, for example, with regard to the call for integration, which is sometimes seen as the best form of general prevention (see, for example, Berckhauer, 1981). But for the agencies of control themselves and for the framers of criminal policy, the postulation of rising crime rates serves to legitimize demands for more financial resources and staff in the sector 'internal security'. However, offences are recorded in the statistics in a manner which grossly oversimplifies the *Lebenswelt* and abstracts from a very complex state of affairs. Factual findings have to be subsumed under abstraction and 'proper' penal code designations used in a bureaucratic fashion. 'If facts of a case are once assigned to the police by the way of a regular complaint, the police are forced to construct a "case" by means of ritualized and institutionalized "manufacture" – regulatives' (Albrecht and Lamnek, 1979:21). Even more succinctly: 'Criminality is "produced" by society through the utilization of social stereotypes' (Ludwig, 1983:50). 'Criminal statistics from this perspective rather are a record of the activities of the criminalizing agencies than a portrait of the real deviant behaviour in society' (Albrecht, 1983:23).

A scientific school with a special field in criminology has been established under the title of 'criminal statistics': it deals with structures, developments, tendencies in registration, distortion factors of statistical recording and the filtering process from the lodging of a complaint to the verdict. A 'naturalistic' assessment of criminal statistics as a mirror of social reality has thereby been profoundly corrected and there are many researchers who deny any value of criminal statistics (Kerner, 1985:262 and 266). There seems to be consensus on the contention that absolute figures, as tabulated in criminal statistics, are quite meaningless. They gain some expressive value only when they are related to the underlying groups of the populace (cf. Albrecht and Lamnek, 1979:23). It has become international practice to operate with crime involvement figures (*KBZ*), a relative figure for measurement, expressing the number of suspects out of 100,000 persons of a certain group of the population. A way out of a categoric rejection of criminal statistics is shown by Pilgram. According to him, criminal statistics are not to be considered in respect of their precision, but should be read as references to 'the conditions for convergences or divergences of the strategies of criminalization of a number of state agencies and societal groups, [that is,] to conditions for coalitions of interests or interest conflicts concerning the practical employment of criminal and sanctioning norms' (Pilgram, 1982:94). The statistics hereby become the object of scientific research with respect to criminal policy. Criminal statistics can be 'sociologically examined, not be "false", not be imprecise or useless; they are just a part of social reality ("part of the natural world")' (Pilgram, 1982:93 quoting Black).

> One subsequently learns to read criminal statistics not as indicators of criminal conduct, but rather as descriptions of the employment of criminal norms, as information concerning the intervention of state authorities in controversies, and concerning procedures of negotiation regarding right and wrong, and criminal sanctions and corresponding social degradations (versus rehabilitations) (Pilgram, 1982:99).

Most writers on the criminality of immigrants deal with the police statistics less dispassionately. Richter remarks on the willingness to accept the findings of Albrecht and Pfeiffer (1979) appear to be correct. This readiness

> is predicated on the common presupposition that crime involvement figures (*KBZ*) could be coupled with the social deprivation approach. *KBZ* are therefore not comprehended as a mere record of policing activities, as an expressive account of acts recorded by police and thereby transformed into criminalized acts, but – if only the statistics were corrected carefully enough – as descriptions of criminal behaviour (Richter, 1981:270).

176

This 'correction' of police figures and putting police statistics into proper perspective has become an intellectual exercise for critical criminologists. I want to illustrate several 'methods for correction' in order to be able to apply the same methodology to Japanese crime statistics for an assessment of their value. To begin with, I want to deal with the numeric corrections; then I want to discuss several aspects of social control theory (which cannot be transformed into exact calculations).

7.2.5.2 Distorting factors

First of all, it usually is hinted that the criminal statistics of the police distinguish only between Germans and non-Germans. The latter category comprises such diverse groups as tourists, travellers, border-crossing workers, members of armed forces stationed in Germany and their dependants, people staying illegally, and so forth. None of them are registered by population census, and in a collation of crime figures the rate for non-Germans is therefore disproportionately inflated (cf. Mansel, 1985:171). This fact is known in the Japanese discussion and is taken into consideration as a factor explaining the low criminality of first-generation immigrants; but it is always considered together with indications in official data of the conspicuously rising criminal activity of second-generation immigrants which comes to the notice of the police (cf. Tezuka, 1989b:164; Yashima, 1988:15). In the year 1985 in Germany, 7.2 per cent of all suspects were tourists, travellers, and such like, and 14.8 per cent were 'illegals' (Traulsen, 1988:30). In 1986, only 28.3 per cent of the non-German suspects were guest-workers (Kaiser, 1989:356).[1] An isolated view of absolute figures here is misleading, because the increase of foreigners residing in Germany has to be taken into account (data in Eichinger, 1982:603). Concerning data on later stages of law enforcement procedure obtained from court statistics, it is also noted: 'Thus it cannot be denied that looking into the absolute frequency of legal occurrences, young foreigners do emerge disproportionately often in the verdict statistics, but this is to be seen solely in connection with their rising share of the population' (Mansel, 1985:178).

Multiple counting which results from the separate recording of each suspected offence by a suspected multiple offender can also lead to grave misjudgments (Mansel, 1985:171). 'Defying presumption to the contrary, there are fewer repeat violators among foreigners than among Germans. Since "real" offender counting has been introduced nationally, this problem no longer plays any role' (Traulsen, 1988:33).

It is further mentioned in the literature that there are wide disparities in the structure of populace. The foreign population has a different structure, in terms of age and gender, from that of the more 'balanced' native population. In some collations of recorded crime figures for the overall German populace, children up to fourteen years old (a group not disposed to criminality) are included, which conveys a distorted picture (moreover, birthrates differ too; see, for example, Chaidov, 1984:356). At any rate, in comparison with the German population, foreigners have a lower proportion of women and a higher share in the age-group from eighteen to fifty-year-old persons (Villmow, 1985:128). Hence they are over-represented in the 'criminally active' segments (particularly, young males). A simple collation of the foreign minority with German society at large is not conclusive and burdens foreigners with relatively more 'crimes' than is actually the case.

The phenomenon exposed by 'criminal geography' – that in 'big cities certain offences are recorded ten times more often than in rural areas' (Kaiser, 1989:187) – is relevant for the proportion of foreigners involved in criminal acts. Foreigners, to a higher degree than Germans, live in large towns with more than 100,000 inhabitants (this distortion factor can be differentiated by offences, cf. Traulsen, 1988:32f.; the same point is made in a critical remark on the study of Albrecht and Pfeiffer which was conducted in big towns: Gebauer, 1981a:7). Furthermore, the higher mobility of the foreign minority has to be taken into account. If it is not, reference figures are distorted and statistical artefacts result (Eichinger, 1982:604).

A further distortion results from immigrants' different position in society. Guest-workers are mostly member of the sociologically-constructed 'lower classes'. Even if one omits considerations drawn from the controversy over the validity of 'production factors of crime', it is clear that in any society members of the lower strata are criminalized to a higher degree. This class-linked, over-representation cannot easily be quantified. Mansel assumes that the crime rate of German juveniles should be multiplied by a weighting factor of 1.8 when it is compared with that of foreign youths, in order to construct an adequate control group (Mansel, 1986:314; in other publications Mansel reduces this factor to 1.593

and 1.5 without giving sufficient explanation; cf. the critical remarks in Traulsen, 1988:32 and Killias, 1989:20).

7.2.5.3 Strategies of control and selectivity

An important, but not computable factor adding to the burden of foreigners is seen in the syndrome of tighter social control, higher sensitivity and proneness to report incidents on the part of the native population, and the selectivity and generalized, 'methodic suspicion' of agencies of social control (Feest, 1973); all of which is fed by stereotypical imputations of a 'criminal potential' to foreigners and prejudices of the middle-class. 'It is predominantly assumed that the criminality of foreigners is subject to more intense attention, [and] that informal control, but official prose-cution pressure as well, are more pronounced than in regard to the German populace' (Villmow, 1985:130). It is once again noteworthy that the criminal statistics of the police tabulate only suspects who, in accordance to the presumption of innocence, are not 'criminals'. These statistics therefore are merely an expressive illustration of incrimination by suspicion. Increase in efficiency of police work is expressed by the increased production of delin-quents. Hereby statistics are infrequently overloaded with 'cases' having no legal or judicial consequences. This is even more the case when police are put under legitimation constraints or when police have internal and budget allocation reasons. Then segmen-tally boosted crime figures are wished for. The prosecution practices and structural problems and adversities outlined above were taken into consideration mainly by the labelling approach and models inspired by social control theory. Registered crimi-nality is not a product of chance. Even such attributes as, for example, 'social class', 'deficient socialization', 'social disinte-gration', all favourite themes of traditional criminology obsessed by etiology, and 'which all together correlate statistically signifi-cantly with the independent variable criminality measured by official data, point to regularities of the visible surface structure of criminality produced by strategies of selectivity' (Sack, 1985:393).

The first gatekeeper of criminal procedure is the reporting public, who thus determine the threshold of selectivity. Lodgement of a complaint leads to a decision not only as to 'whether, but whether formally or informally recording should take place, . . . the first strategically-important decision in the process of selective prosecution is taken here' (Heinz, 1985:28). To a vast extent the

179

reporting behaviour determines registered, thus 'visible' criminality (and conversely the structure and dimensions of the dark field).[2] This is true particularly for offences which come to the attention of the police through a complaint. The police then respond reactively. By contrast, the frequency of detection of offences exposed by control and surveillance (for example, narcotic or drug-related offences, and infractions of traffic-laws) is determined by proactive action and intensity of policing. The rate of lodgement of complaints varies considerably by offence, as does the rate of their placement on record by police. In Germany, offences against property are far more often reported to police than offences against persons (for reporting behaviour cf. Heinz, 1985). Blankenburg reveals, in a study on shoplifting, that 'the inclination to report foreigners is much higher and independent of the seriousness of offence .... Likewise in the next instance a German can more likely count on being let off with a warning than a foreigner' (Blankenburg, 1973:141). In a Swiss inquiry into violent offences Killias comes to somewhat different conclusions. He states that 'victims of violent offences lodge a complaint independently of the nationality of the perpetrator' (Killias, 1988:162).[3] The statistically low significance of the important variable for reporting behaviour, 'acquaintance between victim and offender', did not conceal discrimination against foreigners. If one takes stock of 'data such as those presented here, no conclusive answer can be given to the question of whether and to what extent racial or national-cultural minorities in the ambit of social control are exposed to discriminating practices' (Killias, 1988:164). Concluding, Killias declares his implicit theoretical position: 'The explanation of deviant conduct among immigrants might, in the long run, be more fruitful than investigation into processes of selectivity' (Killias, 1988:164). A contrary conclusion is drawn in a qualitatively-designed study which was predicated on intensive face-to-face interviews with criminalized foreign juveniles:

> As long as living conditions specific to foreigners exist and foreigner-specific modes of procedure in the area of control structures, symbolized in the possibility of expulsion, can be proven, we have to plead for full honesty on part of the organs of control that foreigners, after all, are not treated equally and plead for the disclosing of the particular mechanism

of selectivity concerning foreigners (Hamburger, Seus and Wolter, 1981:183).

Selectivity occurs step-by-step from the filing or not of a complaint (the latter constituting the dark field – offences/offenders remaining unknown to the police), to treatment by police (recording or not), to the taking of legal action (indictment) or not, which can lead to a verdict of guilty or not. Police suspicion (as set down in their protocols) remains highly contentious until the end of this process. 'Constituent facts' are negotiated, and often at court the original (police) definitions of offences are mitigated, altered or reduced to lesser offences. In an extensive survey of court practices concerning foreigners for the year 1978, it was shown that, in regard to the specification of an offence, in 70 per cent of cases the legal designation in the police report and in the court decision were the same. However,

> regarding the offences of rape (26.1 per cent), robbery (21.6 per cent) and assault (33 per cent), the court of law, above average, assumed a less serious offence than did police . . . . Prosecutors . . . declared that, in cases of 'inaccuracies' with respect to differing offence specifications, there were no differences recognizable between Germans and foreigners (Donner, 1981:120).

Similarly, Killias cautiously notes in a survey of the literature on the criminality of immigrants:

> The absence of discrimination at, say, the prosecutorial or court level may or may not conceal differential treatment by the police. The available evidence does not allow us to rule out, at least for the time being, the possibility of differential treatment overall – that is, when all stages of the criminal procedure are taken together (Killias, 1989:17).

Most of the studies on differential treatment concentrate on discriminatory practices at the prosecutorial stage (arrangement or dropping of charges) and on the sentencing practices of courts of law.

For Austria, it is observed that

in sum total the risk of being sentenced for foreigners at the district court in Vienna is not higher than for natives accused, and that sanctions against them (measured by the portion of custodial sentences) are not stiffer than against Austrian nationals. However, as victims of a law violation, foreigners obviously experience selective treatment in the way that they more often have to count on no judicial sanctioning consequences against transgressors charged by them and when they file a complaint (Hanak, Pilgram and Stangl, 1984:50).[4]

In general, discrimination of the judiciary cannot be ascertained. But there is differential treatment with regard to means for securing a trial, pre-trial detention). Foreigners face a higher risk of being held in custody on remand for incidents of trivial nature; they remain longer and more often in confinement, but get 'milder' sentences (Hanak, Pilgram and Stangl, 1984:63). The same holds true for Germany: 'Foreigners are locked up *considerably longer* in prison on remand, 54.3 per cent for more than eight months' (emphasis in Bosetsky, Borschert and Helm, 1981:220). Questioning of juvenile court assistants resulted frequently in statements that pre-trial detention is more likely to be visited on foreigners. Regarding sentencing it is said that in the area of petty offences reaction to foreign suspects is harsher. In cases of more serious perpetrations, particularly where it is crucial to prevent expulsion, a milder sentence is often chosen (Albrecht, Pfeiffer and Zapka, 1978). 'It may be that foreign minority group offenders are considered to be bad risks because of the likelihood of their returning to their home country before trial takes place' (Albrecht, 1993:96). In France also it is suggested that time spent in police lock-ups and in pre-trial detention seems to be extended in cases of minority offenders. 'Research from the USA does support these findings, which generally lead to the conclusion that the input to the criminal justice system seems to reflect fairly impartial decision-making' (Albrecht, 1993:96).

In Austria recently, after the so-called 'opening of the borders to former Eastern-bloc countries', an intensifying of pre-trial detention practices concerning foreigners was evident. Increases of recorded infringements by 'other foreigners' (non-guest-workers) are conspicuous and can be attributed to a selective attentiveness on the part of the reporting public and police. A 'risk of escape' (that is, of immigrants fleeing to their home country) can easily be constructed given that permanent residence in Austria is naturally non-existent in case of foreign travellers. Offences are also transformed into 'professional crimes' (even in cases of petty shoplifting), and this leads to disproportionately frequent imposition of pre-trial detention on foreigners, instead of more informal procedures (in Vienna every fourteenth suspect was put into prison on remand, but every fifth foreign suspect had to face this measure; cf. Morawetz and Stangl, 1991:11). This is pertinent to the new public 'climate', which is described (in part) as anxious/ aggressive, nationalistic and xenophobic. The increase in complaints is seen to be a 'control-policy by retail trade enterprises which, for reasons of prevention, resort to criminal law to enforce this policy against persons not familiar with the capitalistic way of presenting goods' (Morawetz and Stangl, 1991:14; similar motives can be assumed to be behind the high reporting rate of shoplifting and larceny committed by foreigners in Japan).

7.2.6 Summary

In summary of the above and of my 'excerpt collection', it can be stated that the criminality of guest-workers is controversial. According to the basic theoretical position, the criminality of foreigners is analyzed from an offender-centred or interactionist perspective which considers societal reaction and processes of definition and control. The results must be interpreted in a particular context of utilization. This context might sometimes shape the findings through a corresponding *Leitinteresse*. Be it a demand for more restrictions on immigration, or for the integration of *de facto*-immigrants or for the abolition of the discriminatory legal status 'foreigner', it always operates selectively with the results of criminological analysis, and cites them legitimatorily. Marked booms of the topic are triggered by political and economic constellations mostly contrived as crises situations. I shall examine the important role of the mass media in this connection in my account of the Japanese situation. The preoccupation with criminal statistics released by police obscures the background processes of data generation, which correlate with strategies of (criminal) policy. All the attempts to come to grips with and explain the criminality of immigrants in Germany and Austria must be judged only partially valid. What seems to me the most fruitful approach is one which avoids isolation of the phenomenon of 'guest-workers delin-quency' by highlighting the overall political and societal conditions which constitute this 'delinquency' in the first place. From this 'birds-eye-view', the criminality of foreign workers (particularly the 'quantity' surfacing statistically) can be seen as just one element of an encompassing strategy for handling strangers, the de-privileged, socially marginalized and labour market reservists.

The concept of culture conflict in its popular version was subject to devastating critique. It can be read as the first (and a now obsolete) attempt to deal with the 'strangeness' of guest-workers categorically. Here achievements of adaptation on the part of the mostly young and dynamic migrant workers were lost sight of. The 'other' culture served as backdrop for the comprehension of 'deviant' conduct. By the stress on this 'otherness', the status of being foreign is fixed and perpetuated through denial of integra-tion, which is now pathetically called for (in a manner sometimes sounding like a threat of coercion). In the thesis of social depri-vation, exactly those life opportunities withheld are detected as 'criminogenetic deficits' and described as societally structured and produced 'anomic situation' of the second generation. In social control theory, 'foreignness' and its social correlate (assignment of subordinate positions and membership of the working class) are identified as status positions that can be utilized in accordance with the economic situation through general and special (that is, criminal) policies (for example, promotion of measures for repatriation – or in other words, exportation of the jobless – restrictions on family reunification programs, exclusion from the labour market measuring giving priority to German nationals, and so forth). Increasingly the 'stigma' of foreigner is accepted by those (of the second generation) so-labelled, who re-interpret their objective situation of being de-privileged in terms of xenophobia. The rebellious and enlightening aspect of criminality, which points to socio-structural disadvantages is thereby concealed. Foreignness is also the vantage point for the labelling approach which sees foreignness as an element of focussed attention. Through constant suspicion and tightening of the net of social control, this figures as one factor in the production of inflated figures of the criminal-ized. None of the theories completely escapes the vicious circle of comprehending the criminality of foreigners as something peculiar to them. A 'total decategorization of the notion of criminality of foreigners' (Hamburger, Seus and Wolter, 1981:183, emphasized there) remains a mere program as long as foreigners legally and politically remain 'aliens'. I have to face this same dilemma when approaching the Japanese situation.

In doing this, I want to examine 'explanations' for the delinquency of foreigners only when they turn up in the literature. The concept of culture conflict, as well as considerations informed by anomie theory and piecemeal control-theoretical fragments, all play a role here. The topicalizing of migrant criminality is steeped in the whole (political) discussion on 'illegal' migrant labour, which produced the climate in which crimes of foreigners could be sensationalized. Subscribing to the social control paradigm, which can claim high plausibility owing to its intrinsic logic, I want to demonstrate that the crime statistics are a result of this atmosphere: a product of the willingness and co-operativeness of the reporting behaviour of a public sensitized by a manipulative and exaggerated press coverage, of reactive and proactive policing and of intensified prosecution and harsh sentencing. The production of a crime wave, therefore, is a complex interaction between mass media, the public, law enforcement agencies and the judiciary, as well as general and special crime policies. None of these factors is effective when isolated, but together they initiate a feedback-process with reciprocal reinforcement effects (working almost synergetically in the Japanese case). This is not the result of a consciously-staged and concerted action to criminalize foreign workers, but rather a mechanism developing its own dynamic. This does not furnish an explanation for the criminality of migrant workers, but it does explain the crime panic and the high figures recorded in police statistics, which are subsequently read as 'verification' of the fear of crime setting in motion the whole merry-go-round of denouncement to police, tighter control, rising crime figures, distorted press reports, preventative penalizing, and so forth.

7.2.7 On the comparability of the situation in Western Europe and Japan

The above excursion should accompany our further inquiry as an ever-present theoretical matrix and backdrop. The transfer to Japan of theories developed in Germany and Austria accounting for the criminality of guest-workers has to be made with care and caution – the more so because, in particular, the formal-legal status of foreigners differs. Both Austria and Germany implemented their 'official' guest-worker policies through bilateral agreements. In Japan we find the initial stage of an 'irregular' labour migration which proceeds differently, both quantitatively and qualitatively. In Austria

> the original intention of a boosted admission of foreign labour was the elimination of short-term labour bottlenecks by the employment of foreign target workers, a labour force which wants to earn money as quickly as possible to return to their home country again (Biffl, 1986:33).

This short-term perspective coupled with clear acquisition goals might be found to be that of 'illegal' migrant workers in Japan. On the 'objective' side, it has to be noted that Austria tried to ensure that guest-workers would have equal status in regard to labour laws and, to a certain degree, social security, through bilateral agreements on recruitment (in 1962 with Spain, 1964 with Turkey and 1966 with Yugoslavia). However, in the course of time foreign workers were assigned a complementary function on the labour market and, despite low economic performance after the recession, they could be laid off only in limited numbers. This led to immigration in the traditional sense.

> In the year 1981, roughly 291,000 foreigners were counted, one-third more than in 1971. Their proportion in the whole population therefore increased to 4 per cent. Nevertheless, the foreigner density in Austria, in comparison with its neighbour states, still remains low (FRG, 1980, 7.5 per cent; Switzerland, 1980, 14 per cent) (Biffl, 1986:36).

In Germany too a recruitment 'offensive' was pursued, making it a *de facto*-immigration country despite political opposition to this.

> From the first year of full employment, 1960, to the crisis-induced 'end of recruitment' in 1973, the foreign population gainfully employed in the Federal Republic increased from approximately 280,000 to roughly 2.6 million. The immigration strain originated in the economic development gap between the Federal Republic and the countries lagging

furthest behind economically, particularly those in transition from agrarian to industrial societies, and in the attractiveness of highly-developed industrial nations. The progressive internationalization of the labour market in the Federal Republic, however, was not primarily the outcome of a free unfolding of the causal relationship between socio-economic push and pull-factors resulting from the development-gap.

Rather decisive, was the growing demand for labour in the Federal Republic since the beginning of the 1960s and the focused, contractually-agreed recruitment of a work force in foreign countries. . . . After the recruitment agreements concluded with Italy in 1955, with Spain and Greece in 1960, agreements with Turkey, Portugal, Tunisia and (in 1968) with Yugoslavia followed. . . . The buffer function of the employment of foreigners according to economic conditions in the transitions between boom and slump was not only the result of the supply-demand tension in the international labour market, but of the intertwining of these freely operating forces with the steering instrumentation of national labour-market policy (Bade, 1983:67f. and 78f.).

The migration theory implied in these remarks is considered to be valid also in Japan. Economic disparities between Japan and surrounding South East Asian countries, as well as a massive, sectoral shortage of labour in Japan and enormous differences in wages and income between Japan and the countries of origin of migrant labour, make labour migration, even when labelled 'illegal' and incurring the risk of expulsion, profitable for both the employer and the employed. Unofficial recruitment conduits and illegal status, however, oftentimes lead to exploitation of Asian workers and exacerbate their inferior position in society and their *Lebenswelt*. Quantitatively, the number of cases of 'irregular' migration to Japan in comparison with that to Western European countries is not great. The highest estimates of the number of 'illegal' workers in Japan puts it between 250,000 and 300,000, while the Japanese population is roughly 123 million (cf. Watanabe, 1990b:168). The vehement debate over 'illegal' labourers in Japan nevertheless is reminiscent in several respects, of the discourse on guest-workers in Germany and Austria in the 1960s. Proceeding from the assumption of a basic comparability of industrialized states, I offer comparative reflections and inevitably follow the track laid by the discourse in Japan – one should beware of being trapped by exclusive study of Japanese sources – the discourse in Japan frequently refers to the situation in Western Europe in an oversimplified fashion. The antagonistic poles of the Japanese debate [on the situation in Western Europe] may be labelled the moral (human rights-ethical) and the cautionary (which implicitly is equally moral, as both are implicitly political). The moral attitude points to the higher security of guest-workers in Germany, for example, in consequence of labour-related laws, and demands the same for migrant workers in Japan and an amnesty for 'illegals' (as, for example, is practised periodically in France). The cautionary faction, on the contrary, hints at subsequent social problems (unemployment, integration of the second generation, racist violence, criminality, and so forth) and opposes Western-style admission of 'guest-workers'. In comparisons of this sort, however, one should not overlook the fact – which appears most markedly in the treatment of 'the stranger' and of minorities – that problematic constellations exist which can be found in *every* society (for example, the phenomenon of xenophobia). A coupling of political consequences with moralizing finger-pointing at other societies can obscure the fact that *homologous* problems exist in one's own society and cloud one's vision of 'other' societies by extolling only their 'positive' sides in order to create a 'beautiful' example for a moral lecture. Japan can serve as *one example* of the universal societal handling of foreigners, and comparisons should be drawn without over-generalizations and judgemental comparisons of whole countries (for example, 'In Germany everything is better/worse').

Provided that relevant socio-structural universals exist for highly-developed industrial countries, many theoretical conceptions, particularly those of power-control theory (besides pure mathematical-statistical considerations), may be transferred from one national setting to another. This is the case with criminality of foreigners as debated in Japan (provided one takes certain differences into account). These remarks contain a preliminary decision of great theoretical importance and which runs counter to preoccupations with Japan as 'completely different', or as requiring some obscure 'specifically Japanese intuition' to be understood.[5] The debate in Japan too is characterized by a plurality of opinions, and various models are proposed for approaching the subject, Japan. Against the mainstream of

harmony-models, Japanese society may be comprehended as basically conflict-oriented. Japan has a long 'emic tradition' of conflicts
and of schools of thought conceptualizing society as fundamentally
conflict-determined (cf. Mouer and Sugimoto, 1986:64–69). Over-
estimating the divergence of the Japanese society from other
highly-industrialized societies leads one to mistakingly claim that
the whole Japanese model could be given in terms of 'holistic-
monocausal', reductionist and culturalist explanations (that is, of
uniqueness).[6] Here one operates with single key metaphors, for
example, 'vertical society', or *amae* ('dependence', or according
to the psychologist Balint, passive object-love), which are then
projected onto the *whole* Japanese social fabric (cf. the remarks
in Pörtner and Schaede, 1990:410f.). To declare that only a 'pure
Japanese' (dogmatic-emic) insider-perspective is legitimate pre-
empts any attempt at comparison, while preventing any application of 'Western' theory to Japan, and leading to the *Aporie* of
a total cultural relativism. Concepts of this kind have long been
recognised as an ideology, under the title *Nihonjinron* ('discussions
on the Japanese'), and have been devalued in their explanatory
potential. 'In complex societies like Japan, the "indigenous"
version of how that world is perceived is often deeply coloured
by ideological interests' (Dale, 1986:7). But this holds equally
for 'the other side'. Under the catchwords, or nowadays rather
invectives, 'eurocentrism' or 'orientalism', the scientific 'imperialism' of conceptual occupation of phenomena of other cultures
has been sufficiently criticized. Nevertheless, in a (scientific)
approach to a different culture and society, one needs categories
and cognitive models. 'The alternative to "classical" eurocentrism
can not be the renunciation of those categories any more than can
the solution be the simple exchange of our system of unreflected
categories by another, for instance, a Japanese one' (Hijiya-Kirschnereit, 1988:209f.). A way out of this dilemma can probably be
found by a hermeneutically-imbued approach, which is particularly
relevant when meaning and understanding are called. 'Seeing
one's way into an unfamiliar culture is possible only to an extent
of a successful translation between it and our own culture'
(Habermas, 1985:264). Understanding always occurs through one's
own knowledge which, as anticipation, flows into the things to be
understood and can be corrected from there. If this circularity and
one's own ever-present horizon are brought in through reflection
(eurocentrism made conscious as a pre-condition of the possibility

of undistorted perception, cf. Hijiya-Kirschnereit, 1988:210), a 'valid translation' of societal and cultural (in this case, Japanese) phenomena is feasible. I therefore want to hint at some pointers to Japanese 'self-exoticizing' (for example, when structural universals are declared to be peculiarly Japanese). But I also want to address differences as such and retain them. By lining up the above quotations, I wanted to indicate that I am aware of the problems of an approach to Japan with theoretical instruments developed in the USA and Europe. The debate concerned with these questions, and reflections based on the theory of cognition or science in Japanese studies, still seem rudimentary to me and preoccupied with a dual defence (against the reproach of eurocentrism and against Japanese myths of uniqueness). I will point to divergences as well as convergences between the Western European and the Japanese situation, without determining a general dominance of one of these two structures. With respect to various segments of society, this may appear differently according to each case. Whenever it seems heuristically fruitful and adequate to the matter in hand, I shall employ 'Western' as well as Japanese categories, and assess their grasp and 'translatability'.

7.3 Attempts to Explain the Criminality of Foreigners in Japan

If one searches for theoretical reflections in the literature dealing with labour migration and the criminality of foreigners in Japan, one can hardly find a consistent and detailed theory of immigrant criminality. There are some attempts to 'explain' crimes by foreigners, but these 'explanations' are merely asides or annotations. Usually the authors point to the position of foreign workers in society, their *Lebenswelt* and living conditions. They often link their claims, according to their point of view, with political demands for restriction and control of immigration, expulsion of 'illegals', amendment of their legal status or legal redress, and so forth. I seek to bring order to the presented concepts and 'explanations' by grouping them according to their implicit theories of crime.

Culture conflict is mentioned very often, but is not analyzed theoretically; rather it is regarded with apprehension and alarm, for example, in the editorial of the *Yomiuri shinbun* 10 August 1990:

> Foreign workers are not only people who produce things or give services. They live in Japanese society, are human beings who come into contact with Japanese and the Japanese culture. When people with different cultures, languages and customs live together in the same society, troubles [*momegoto*] will occur. Sometimes this generates crimes. How to face these social frictions [*masatsu*] is one of the big questions concerning the problem of foreign labour.

Potential conflicts and social problems which accompany immigration of 'illegal' workers, are often described apprehensively in very general terms: 'Influences are not only exerted on the domestic labour market, but there are multiple influences on the life of the people. The problem of law and order is one of them' (*Yomiuri shinbun*, 10 August 1990). In a study by the police, foreign labourers are assessed as an economic liability. The aspect of costs should be thoroughly scrutinized in the debate on admission or non-admission: admission of foreign labour would result in serious expenses because of ensuing social problems, particularly with respect to public safety and requisite counter-measures (Sasaki, 1990: 19).

I traced the implicit assumption of potential cultural conflicts when I tried to locate the context of the argument over the (presumed) worsening of public safety due to the influx of foreigners (see 6.3). Nishio Kanji argues vehemently for this assumption, maintaining that, in the long run, the problem of foreign labour has to be dealt with as a 'defence of culture'. However, he operates within a very narrow definition of 'culture'. Culture to him means the 'spirit' (*seishin*) of the Japanese, who diligently produce by hand those things which are the basis of Japanese technology; this basis is deemed to be in danger of being destroyed by foreign workers (Nishio, 1989a: 226). Nishio propounds a host of ethnocentric generalizations of this kind, which I have already examined in my discussion of the '*sakoku* faction' (opponents of admission of 'guest-workers').

The situation in Germany is often cited. In a summary of the 1990 *White Paper on the Police* (see also Keisatsuchō, 1990: 52–9, especially p. 59, where there is an identical passage) the following claims are presented as a 'common' explanation for deviant behaviour of guest workers in Germany:

> The trigger for deviant behaviour and crimes is the experience
> of stress. This stress results from antagonism between the
> culture of the mother-country and that of the immigration
> state – a culture different from that of the foreign minority.
> It amounts to a clash between norms and values. Foreign
> inhabitants are 'deprived' of the living conditions Germans
> enjoy. This becomes clear in regard to high unemployment
> rates, dearth of adequate housing, and lack of adequate
> education in schools and professional training.
>
> In the process of socialisation of juveniles the internalisation
> of a solid corpus of values and norms is impeded; they are
> therefore prone to committing crimes (Sasaki, 1990: 13).

Here there is no critique of the concepts of culture conflict and social deprivation exacerbated by deficits in socialization. Similarly, in descriptions of the situation of immigrants in France, the validity of the culture conflict theory is plainly accepted. The different culture, religion and customs of the mainly Northern African workers are seen as the cause of conflicts with the French (Keisatsuchō 1990: 61). In another study, the concept of culture conflict is treated with more reservation: 'This theory [of culture conflict] seems not to be plausible' (Yashima, 1989: 15). This evaluation is inferred from differences between the crime rate of foreigners and the (lower) crime rate of the first generation of immigrants, who actually should face and 'digest' the most intensive 'culture conflict'. Nevertheless, the author warns, referring to developments in Western Europe, where there is considerable influx of immigrants, critical problems of 'public safety' could occur, these including: the emergence of ghettos and slums; high unemployment rates in times of economic recession, particularly in the segment of 'dirty labour'; social friction due to different languages, religions and customs, which could lead to 'foreigners-go-home-movements' and violence; lack of identity of the offspring of immigrants, and social handicaps, which will lead to deviance and crime (cf. Yashima, 1989: 9f.).

A further study by the police also asserts, in reference to the 'experiences in Germany and other Western European countries', that the concentration of guest-workers in parts of towns engenders the 'emergence of slums' (*suramuka*) as a hotbed for crime. This segregated habitation results from the inability of the guest-workers to assimilate (*dōka suru*). In metropolitan Japan also, regions were emerging in which foreigners were concentrated. This fact is coupled with the demand for extensive measures to comprehend the 'reality of crime' and to prevent it. The setting up of a 'Committee for the Promotion of Counter-measures against Foreigners of the Saitama Prefecture Police' is heralded as a praiseworthy example (Mishima 1988: 99). Here one can see the pointing to geographical 'breeding areas' of crime directly linked with the mobilization of police resources to fight and control it. It is also implicitly imputed that foreigners living in regional concentrations had a high potential for delinquency. Further, theoretical treatment of the criminality of foreigners is not undertaken in this article. The 'danger' of the emergence of ghettos of foreigners, who prefer to lodge in cheap, old and wooden houses, is also stressed elsewhere (cf. Yashima, 1989: 26).

In a police inquiry, foreign suspects were questioned about the motives for their misdemeanours or infringements of the law. The questions reflect the implicitly guiding theories of crime. Seven hundred and fifty-seven suspects were interviewed (those who came into contact with the police only because of violation of the Immigration Control Act were not questioned as to their 'inducement'). Almost 40 per cent of the offences were against property; only some 3 per cent were crimes of violence. (The sample for these percentages was all 949 suspects, including those infringing only the Immigration Control Act. This results in a distorted proportion; cf. Suzuki, 1990a: 51). The motives inquired into were 'some other sort of advantage' (43.7 per cent), destitution, 'want, need' (13.7 per cent), other (11 per cent), playing, curiosity, thrill (8.9 per cent). This reveals a non-cooperative attitude towards answering and suggests that the motives covered by the response alternatives may have been constructions of the authors of the questionnaire. Classified by type of offence, the answers give the same picture, except that, in the case of felonies, emotional motives were given more often (anger, heat of passion: up to 37 per cent). The inquiry was conducted with a questionnaire, which was more detailed for those in custody (346 of the sample) than for those not in detention. A survey of this sort undertaken by the police is, of course, highly questionable as to methodology.

The context of questioning much resembles the situation of interrogation with its asymmetry of power. Thus only manifest motives and answers which fit into the categories provided by the police are elicited. Directly asking for motives does not elicit reliable answers because only rationalizations and not the 'true' motives are given. For this reason, opinion polls addressing political issues no longer use this kind of questioning (personal communication by Professor Paul Kevenhörster). The assumption that 'destitution or want' leads to crimes against property hints at the living conditions of 'illegal' migrant workers. They are analyzed in the second part of the study (Suzuki, 1990b).

Living conditions of 'illegals' are blamed for their taking to illegitimate means in particular cases. For instance, a Chinese student, ailing from acute pneumonia and living on water and bread for three days, took a rucksack out of a car because he hoped to find food in it. He was indicted for theft at the district court of Tokyo (Ōnuki, 1990a: 95). Another lawyer describes the case of a Philippino who worked as a construction labourer. He received only half the wage of Japanese labourers and got into a predicament that led him to steal (Onizuka, 1988: 71). The lawyer Ōnuki, who is very concerned with the question of delinquency of foreigners, postulated two patterns of crimes as outcomes of the living conditions of foreign 'illegals': *seikatsu konkyūgata* (destitution-type) and *jiriki kyūsaigata* (self-help-type). In an illustration of the first type, he cites the above-mentioned 'rucksack-thief'. The latter type, in which justice is taken into the offender's own hands, can be seen in several cases where labour migrants attempted to reclaim their money by robbing or stealing from the labour agents who took their cash for their 'services' (Ōnuki 1990c: 256f.). These constructs are quite speculative. One could try to adapt and 'translate' them into the theoretical terms of the concept of anomie. Many migrant labourers come under heavy pressure to 'make money' in Japan. Most of them come burdened with considerable debts (borrowing money for the airline ticket, kickbacks to mediators, expenses for passport, visa etc.). In Japan they are further exploited. Expenditure for subsistence and repayment of loans impede their reaching the goals of their migration (remittances to relatives, saving for a 'new' life back home). In addition to wage discrimination, migrants face previously unknown deprivations due to the contact with a highly-materialistic and developed consumer society, where possessions such as colour televisions, radio-recorders, cameras, cars, etc., are a matter of course and are deemed 'indispensable' (cf. Böhning, 1984: 80). The experience of being underprivileged and discriminated against, together with disillusionment of their migration dreams, could exert an 'anomic strain'. This strain causes migrants to cope with life deviantly or to take to illegitimate means for achievement. It makes crimes against property, and up to certain point, robbery or violence (in 'retaliation' against employers or labour agents who are felt to have wronged the migrants), understandable. Crimes of violence often occur against the backdrop of troubles connected with working conditions (costly fees for mediators, embezzlement of wages, deduction from wages). Often labour agents are victimized (illustrated with examples in Kobayashi, 1990: 44f.). Another author blames 'stress' for migrants' victimization of their fellow countrymen. Stress results from their 'illegal' status (migrants fear being too conspicuous and avoid public appearance, which forces them to spend their free time together in often very crowded dwellings) and from the pressure to work hard in order to repay their debts (Kawano, 1989: 26). In an editorial of *Tōkyō shinbun*, 8 August 1990, prejudice and discrimination are held to be responsible for the isolation and destitution of foreign workers. This situation is branded as criminogenic.

Most of the theoretical reflections on these matters remain fragmentary, but their elements can be classified under either the culture conflict thesis, the concept of anomie, or the labelling approach (where authors use terms in isolation, and not within a broader theoretical horizon). Almost all of the studies dealing with the delinquency of foreigners concentrate on police statistics, on the characteristics of single cases, and on problems relating to judicial procedure in court and to discriminatory practices of the judiciary. The latter surveys contain reflections on social control. I shall present first the criminal statistics and show how they are received by the mass media. Then I shall criticize their contents using methods which were developed in the discourse on the subject in Germany, describing the factors involved in the production of crime figures through application of the social-control theory.

7.4 Criminal Statistics Released by the Police and Their Reception in the Mass Media

> Despite a somewhat sluggish routine of reporting, alteration, acceleration and enhancement, special reports turn up mostly on the occasion of discussions of unusual developments or 'jumping' developments in crime. . . . In sum, particular changes, and especially increases in criminality, 'crime-waves', and other disasters of higher news-value and leverage in political debate, are reported (Pilgram, 1982: 96).

In Japan, *The White Paper on the Police* is published every year, and besides describing the overall situation of crime, it always focuses on one issue in a 'special report'. These special reports reflect the 'boom' of themes and point to dramatic developments and the necessity of policing and counter-measures to curb 'new' criminal tendencies.

The 1987 *White Paper* was subtitled 'Activities of the police in reaction to the advancing internationalization'. It stressed the necessity for international co-operation, described the victimization of foreigners living in Japan, and assessed public safety. Cases were then presented. These were of types said to be on the rise: Japanese perpetrators fleeing to foreign countries; importing of illegal stimulants and weapons; and, for the first time, a special chapter was devoted to the 'crimes' of *rainichi gaikokujin* (foreigners coming to Japan). This category includes all short-term foreign visitors and excludes *zainichi gaikokujin*, that is, foreign residents, most of whom are of Korean or Taiwanese origin. The latter are second- and third-generation descendants of those brought to Japan in the 1930s and 1940s as forced labour. The category also excludes members of the US army stationed in Japan and their dependents, those who have been granted asylum, and those with permission to reside in Japan permanently (cf. Keisatsu-chō, 1987: 6). The alleged increase of suspects and apprehended *rainichi gaikokujin* was illustrated using a ten-year comparison. According to the absolute figures given, there was a 5.9–fold increase in penal code infractions (actually the figures were for suspects) and a 4.7–fold increase of apprehended suspects (Keisatsuchō, 1987: 24). The maintenance of public safety 'at a leading level among free, developed countries' was declared to be the continuing objective of the police (Keisatsuchō, 1987: 5 and 6).

The 1990 *White Paper on the Police*, published in August 1990, bore the subtitle: 'Special report: rapid increase of foreign workers and the reaction of the police'. This strategically-placed special report occupied almost one-fifth of the text and was published shortly after the amendment to the Immigration Control Act came into force (1 June 1990). The media echo was prompt. All of the prominent daily newspapers gullibly accepted the statements of the police and turned them into effective headlines. Only a few editorials attempted to present a more detailed view of the police figures and warned against jumping to hasty conclusions. Banner headlines read: 'White Paper on the Police. Rapid increase in numbers of illegal male workers: murder, robbery and violent crimes at a peak!' (*Asahi shinbun*, 8 August 1990, Osaka edition); 'Organizations exploiting "illegal labour". Special report on the problem of male workers in the *White Paper on the Police*' (*Mainichi shinbun*, 8 August 1990); 'Rapid increase in illegal labour, crimes of foreigners' (*Asahi shinbun*, 7 August 1990); 'Sudden increase: Crimes by foreigners [increase] seven-fold over ten years!' (*Tokyo shinbun*, 7 August 1990, evening edition); 'Counter-measures to crimes involving foreigners. Brutality of crimes conspicuously rises' (*Yomiuri shinbun*, 7 August 1990). Again, I emphasize that the figures publicized by the police provide information only on their own activities, for example, the successful application of the label 'suspect' to foreign persons. In the following, I want to point to several matters which cast doubt upon the value of these data, and place them in their correct perspective. The rapid media response is revealed as rash and thoughtless.

The term *rainichi gaikokujin*, in the context of this political discussion, functions to suggest that 'illegal' migrant labourers are indicated. The police obviously fabricated this category to build a comprehensive picture of the crime situation concerning ('illegal') foreigners and thereby construct a 'social reality'. But *rainichi gaikokujin* subsumes tourists, foreigners staying briefly (for example, on business), and so-called 'hit-and-run-offenders'. The latter are identified as members of organized criminal gangs coming to Japan for 'professional' reasons. They are deemed to operate for a short time on an extensive scale ('hit') and to immediately return ('run') to their home country (the term alludes to the analogous behaviour of a batter in baseball). The *White Paper* gives three examples: a Philippino burglary gang; a Nigerian fraud group, whose object was to acquire goods by misuse of credit cards; and a Pakistani gang of larcenists (Keisatsuchō, 1987: 26). A police study contends that the operations of such professionals are changing from 'travel-type' to 'target-type', that is, a 'Japan defenseless against international crime' becomes the prime target of international mobster organizations. Moreover, it is claimed that the increase in numbers of long-term foreign residents will lure and spawn international crime of the 'resident-type' (cf. Mishima, 1988: 93). In the case of professional criminals, one has to take into consideration that they are multiple offenders who thus inflate the statistics. This is strikingly illustrated by the following example: A gang of pick-pockets from Seoul came several times to Japan in groups of between three and seven men to do their 'business'. Three suspects were apprehended. According to police they confessed to more than 420 acts of pick-pocketing during three visits. The suspects set themselves a daily goal of ten to fifteen purses and stole them exclusively from handbags of older victims and women (*Asahi shinbun*, 22 November 1990).[7] Thus professional perpetration of offences against property (to continue with this category) in the cited case inflates police statistics on 'crime'. In the matter of the delinquency of foreign labourers, one must strictly distinguish between professional criminals and migrant workers. To attribute all of the offences appearing in the statistics to the latter would be blatantly false. According to the information of a high-ranking police officer, professionally-committed crimes and offences by 'illegal' workers are not registered separately (Gonoi, 1989: 126ff.). In the present (first) stage of migration, migrants come to Japan mainly with the object of staying no longer than a few years. Their motives and interests centre around work, saving, remittances and purchase of consumer goods (cf. Böhning, 1984: 80f.). If the money longed for can be earned only 'illegally', they avoid becoming conspicuous to the authorities or police. Their constant fear of deportation and failure to fulfil the aim of their migration is a powerful motive for them to avoid infringement of the law (mentioned in Ōnuki, 1990c: 253). Looked at cynically, maintenance of the 'illegal' status of foreigner migrants offers the cheapest form of crime control and prevention (that is, given the dubious logic of prevention).

In a previously quoted study by the police, attempts were made to classify 'crimes' (here also it is suspects who are meant, although the study notoriously speaks of *hanzai* – crimes). Three types are formulated:

(1) Offences committed by foreigners who come to Japan with a 'regular' goal for their stay.
(2) Offences of foreigners who come to Japan as 'unskilled and illegal' workers with the goal of earning money – this being an infraction of the Immigration Control Act – and who become prone to other misconduct.
(3) Crimes committed by foreigners who come to Japan to commit crimes (for example, to import drugs or weapons, or to commit robbery and larceny).

Of the 948 surveyed suspects, 516 fitted into the category 'illegal labourers' (Suzuki, 1990a: 48f.) Twelve per cent of the suspects were identified as professional criminals; 4.8 per cent of them allegedly had contacts with organized criminal syndicates; and 6.3 per cent of suspects – although 'amateurs' – were said to have been exploited by organized criminals. Altogether, around 70 per cent of the suspects could be described as non-professional perpetrators (there being also 11 per cent of suspects who refused to answer questions. See Suzuki, 1990a: 54). Even taking into account the previously-expressed reservations in regard to methodology, it can be seen that not all of the offences of so-called *rainichi gaikokujin* are committed by 'illegal' migrant workers. It also has to be taken into account that the proportion of suspects who infringed only the Immigration Control Act is relatively high. The survey registers only 'leading offences' (Suzuki, 1990a: 51), that is, where multiple offences are suspected, only the most serious is registered. Thus it may be assumed that altogether 16.1 per cent of the delinquents (27.6 per cent of male 'illegal' workers) have violated only the Immigration Control Act. Registration by leading offence (that is, one offence per person) avoids multiple enumeration but tends to inflate the categories of more serious offences. For example, an 'illegal' migrant who infringes the Immigration Control Act and also commits a robbery will show up in the statistics solely in the category 'robbery'. Petty crimes are therefore 'absorbed' into more serious offences. This absorption can lead to false assessments of the structure of registered crime. If every offence committed were counted, the percentages (presently 40 per cent against property, and almost 3 per cent violent crimes) could be revised. Offences against property would comprise a larger proportion and the percentage of violent crimes would be smaller. The second part of this inquiry into suspects (Suzuki, 1990b) obviously served as a blueprint for the description of the living conditions of migrant workers in the *White Paper on the Police* (c.f. data in Keisatsuchō, 1990: 15–26). This survey shows that the police do themselves attempt to differentiate and subdivide offences committed by foreigners. With this analysis – while methodologically it is still contestable – it can be shown that not all of the offences should be imputed to 'illegal' foreign migrants.

The data presented in the *White Paper* cover offences which came to the notice of police in one calendar year. Here one can find instances of multiple-registration of suspects. But there is no mention of whether suspects were counted only once or were multiply-registered when credited with more than one infringement. The police unhesitatingly calculate the increase of crime rates by operating with absolute numbers, and by ignoring the demographic correlation with the rising number of foreigners entering Japan. (If they have any validity at all, crime rates are valid only with reference to relevant population numbers.) These dubious rates of increase then turn up in newspaper headlines without their validity being questioned. The figures given are highly arbitrary, and dependant on the year selected as baseline. The simple calculation using the baseline of 510 suspects apprehended in 1979 does yield a seven-fold rise over ten years (3,572 apprehensions in 1989) (Keisatsuchō, 1987: 25 and 1990: 33 and 34). However, if one were to use 1980 figures as the baseline the number of suspects would show only a 4.1–fold increase. Or if one took the five-year period beginning in 1984 (2,340 arrests), the same calculation would result in a much less sensational increase of only one-and-a-half times. But without reference to the growth of the foreign population in Japan and to the rise in the number of entries to Japan, these figures have no meaning anyway. Nonetheless, they were dramatized and led to a clamour by the press, which translated them into the formula 'Crimes [!] committed by foreigners increased seven-fold over ten years'.

Similar reservations are in order with respect to rates of increase and decrease expressed as percentages. Here particularly the baseline figures are highly influential on the results. Small baseline figures generate high relative growth (for example, one gets a 50 per cent increase by the addition of just one offence when the base figure is two, while an absolute increase of fifty offences yields only a 10 per cent increase when the base figure is 500). Calculations from one year to another are risky due to fluctuations. Moreover, it is assumed that criminality is constantly on the increase, which is not the case. This assumption is exemplified in a newspaper article in which it is contended that apprehensions of foreigners rose by 52.2 per cent and the number of arrests by 61.4 per cent from 1987 to 1988 (*Yomiuri shinbun*, 16 August 1989; these same percentages are given by Yashima, 1989: 24). If one examines the recent police data this computation turns out to be rash. The large increase in absolute figures from 1987 to 1988 (from 1,871 apprehended persons to 3,030) is seen to be retrogressive (for 1989 and 1990 the figures are 2,989 and 2,978) despite the rising number of foreigners entering Japan. The fluctuations with regard to suspects are also left out of consideration (figures for 1987 to 1990 are: 1987: 2,567; 1988: 3,906; 1989: 3,572; and 1990: 4,064) (Keisatsuchō, 1991: 97). The higher figures are attributable to the practice of multiple-registration. In the last-cited year the number of multiply-registered suspects increased, while the number of suspected persons decreased in the last two years. This could corroborate the police claim concerning intensified activities of professional criminals, who as a rule are multiple-perpetrators. It could also be the case that more attributions of offences to 'persons unknown' were made by the police, that is, no presumptive perpetrator could be apprehended. In a poor 'analysis', police presented – again without reference to demographic developments – a comparison of crime rates over a period of five years which claimed there was a growth-rate of roughly 102 per cent in cases leading to an apprehension (1982: 1,187 cases, 1987: 2,567 cases). The rate of increase in numbers of arrested foreigners is deemed to be around 80 per cent (cf. *Yomiuri shinbun*, 20 July 1988). Those high rates are also a statistical artefact resulting from the method of calculation and the arbitrary selection of base- and end-year for the calculation. Fluctuations are ignored. In 1981 there were 1,236 officially registered offences (more than in the base-year of the calculation above). Were 1981 taken as base for an analogous calculation, this would undercut the 'menacing' 100 per cent-mark. With respect to fluctuations, the figures for registered suspected infringements of the penal code are: 1984: 2,340; 1985: only 1,725; 1986: 2,537 (Keisatsuchō, 1990: 36).

The preoccupation of police and the press with crime figures and (entirely arbitrary) increase rates (and *only* with increase rates) can be attributed to the fetish for statistics prevalent in Japan (and in Japanese social sciences), to credulity towards 'officially' produced data which are generated without scrutiny, and to a covert *Leitinteresse* of social control agents and their instrumentalization in political debate.

In a newspaper report one may find a 'wild' calculation of percentages in a context that needs interpretation. The article is introduced with the claims that crimes of foreigners are becoming more and more brutal and that the National Police Agency identifies the steep rise in numbers of foreign workers as the background of this development. Therefore, a need for a 'Department for the Foreign Labourers Problem' is projected, and 'counter-measures against the internationalization of crime, are vehemently advanced. At the end of the article the latest police data are quoted: from January to October 1988 there were 3,002 crimes (!) committed by foreigners known to the police, an increase of 50 per cent over that period in the previous year. Diagrams are given, but these manipulate the data for demagogic purposes. The line indicating the number of entries to Japan, which is always included in police data and shows the correlation between the number of foreign arrivals and law infringements, is omitted. The horizontal axis of the graph is shortened so that the lines indicating the rise of offences are extremely steep (*Kanagawa shinbun*, 19 January 1989, cf. Figures 7.1 and 7.2).

There are several striking features to be elucidated. I do not have to stress again that what actually is a 'suspect' is simplified into a 'crime'. The alleged 'enormously increasing number of crimes' is polemically linked to the 'greater need' for 'counter-measures'. This should materialize in the foundation of a new specialized department, which naturally will be in need of personnel and resources. The necessity for these means is legitimized in advance by police leaking semi-official figures to journalists, who readily produce a 'menacing' percentage. But calculations from one year to another, in particular, have little meaning, and rises or declines can scarcely be explained. The present leakage of internal data in precipitant acts of 'information policy' can be read only as an anticipatory legitimation for action ('more criminality requires more control') and a calculation of needs for future funding. The title of the article makes this apparent: 'A

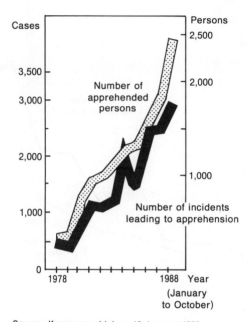

Source: *Kanagawa shinbun*, 19 January 1989.

Figure 7.1 Criminal code offences committed by *rainichi*-foreigners

series of violent crimes involving foreigners [*gaijin*]. National
Police Agency: founding of a division for counter-measures'
(*Kanagawa shinbun*, 19 January 1989).

7.4.1 Further factors in the overloading of the statistics with 'crimes of foreigners'

The police particularly stress the increase in registered violent
crimes (*kyōakuhan* – homicide, robbery, arson, rape). They are
said to rise in number 'year by year' (Keisatsuchō, 1990: 37). A
closer look reveals that this is true only for the period 1987–9;
prior to that (from 1980) there were some large fluctuations. The
increase precisely matches the period in which the number of male
labour migrants began to exceed that of females (their disproportion has been especially conspicuous since 1988, cf. HNK, 1989:
39). Data from the Ministry of Justice and the Immigration Control
Bureau refer to cases of illegal stay or work which have been
'exposed', and these have to be seen in relation to the intensity

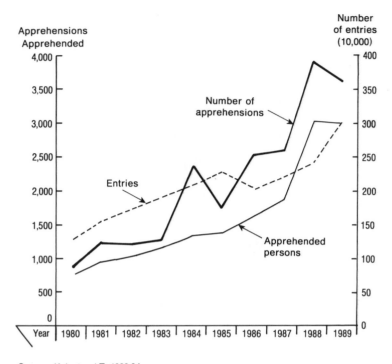

Source: Keisatsuchō, 1990:34.

Figure 7.2 Number of entries of foreigners into Japan and apprehensions of *rainichi*-foreigners on suspicion of criminal code offences (1980–89)

of enforcement and social control activities. The focus has shifted to male workers, and there is a real tendency reflected in the increased registration of male migrants. Violent crime is definitely and overwhelmingly dominated by males (cf. Kürzinger, 1989; for the Japanese situation see Hōmu sōgō kenkyūsho, 1989: 74f.). The registered increase in violent 'crimes' (that is, suspects in cases where there has been violence) has to be seen in this context. Seen thus, it follows the 'natural, demographic' trend and is due to the fact that the absolute number of foreigners entering Japan was swiftly on the rise in the relevant period. The next distorting factor and problematic issue is the process of classifying an offence as a violent one. From his experience as a laywer, Ōnuki Kensuke supposes that, for example, resisting a public officer in the execution of an arrest for shoplifting may readily be manufactured into a 'robbery' (classified according to penal law as *kyōakuhan*). In other cases, the rash classification of offences as violent crimes generates an artificial statistical rise in offences of violence. On the other hand, it can be gathered that Japanese shoplifting offenders may get off with an informal 'solution' after an excuse and by being admonished, whereas non-Japanese, Asian suspects have to face formal procedures and official intervention by police and prosecutor, culminating in judicial proceedings. This results in an over-representation of criminalized foreigners, when compared with Japanese suspects, in the data on petty crime (cf. Ōnuki, 1990c: 255f.). The increase in the registrations of violent crimes is emphasized by the police because other offences show a decline in 1989, despite more foreigners entering Japan. This over-emphasis has the function of maintaining the formula of the steeply rising crime rate of foreigners. Violent crimes are also suitable for reinforcing diffuse anxiety and fear, and for triggering a crime panic.

Additional factors inflating the statistics are the age, gender and occupation-structure of foreign workers. Persons in the younger age-segment predominate. Male 'illegal' labourers are concentrated in the age-group between 25 and 29 years, which comprises about one-third of the total (cf. HNK, 1989: 40). This same segment is the largest in the inquiry on perpetrators in Suzuki (1990a: 49). Both sexes are strongly over-represented in the twenty to thirty-year age range. Of the persons questioned by Suzuki, 75.7 per cent were men; and the proportion of 'exposed illegal' male labourers reached around 80 per cent in 1990 (*Mainichi shinbun*, 6 July 1991). The propensity to come into conflict with the law varies considerably for different demographic groups: in any society young men commit offences most frequently; they are the 'criminally most active' group. A comparison with the total Japanese population would miss its mark.

Migrant workers are over-represented in 'susceptible' occupations, or jobs providing a higher opportunity for illegality. These jobs are subject to more intense attention by the police and involve a higher probability of a person being registered as an offender. Here, too, a comparison with the overall Japanese populace, which shows a different and 'more balanced' professional structure, would be highly distorted. Nearly two-thirds of female migrants are active as so-called 'hostesses', and risk being forced into prostitution. In the so-called 'businesses which may affect public morals'

Table 7.1 *Rainichi*-foreigners arrested, classified by general crime category for committing penal code offences

		1980	1981	1982	1983	1984	1985	1986	1987	1988	1989
Total	A	867	1,236	1,187	1,269	2,340	1,725	2,537	2,567	3,906	3,572
	B	782	963	1,031	1,153	1,301	1,370	1,626	1,871	3,020	2,989
Felonious offences	A	15	28	13	23	19	20	18	33	48	98
	B	14	30	18	34	22	28	20	38	78	94
Violent offences*	A	77	96	79	91	89	95	94	69	92	107
	B	118	139	110	151	139	125	113	121	135	138
Larceny	A	576	814	828	938	1,815	1,198	1,655	1,661	2,689	2,353
	B	501	587	671	693	847	906	1,044	1,177	1,816	1,776
'Intellectual' offences**	A	110	172	128	72	241	193	453	397	243	190
	B	30	49	42	42	59	39	94	62	86	104
Others	A	89	126	139	145	176	219	317	407	834	824
	B	119	167	190	233	234	272	355	473	905	877

*Violent offences = assault and battery etc.
**Intellectual offences = fraud, counterfeit etc.
A = Cases   B = Persons
Herbert, 1990b: 16; following Keisatsuchō, 1990: 36.

(*fūzoku eigyō*), that is, sex services) the opportunity for coming into contact with drugs – for example, stimulants or amphetamines, which are called 'speed' or 'ice' on the world market, and are illegal in Japan under the title *kakuseizai* – is part of everyday life in this subculture. More than 40 per cent of male migrants work in the construction business and more than 45 per cent as industrial workers in small and very small factories (the data for occupational structure were inferred from cases of 'exposed illegals', cf. HNK, 1989: 39). In the day-labourer areas (*yoseba*) where 90 per cent of jobs are in the construction sector, foreign workers are in social surroundings in which violence, for instance, has a different (sub)cultural meaning, and 'archaic' forms of conflict resolution occur. The strategies of arrest and policing priorities lead to higher likelihood of 'illegal' workers being placed in custody in cases of street-fighting or violent transactions. Watanabe Hidetoshi, a priest concerned with Asian labour migrants in Kotobuki, the day labourer quarter of Yokohama, comments: 'When Philippinos and Japanese have troubles, only the Philippinos are arrested, the Japanese can walk [away].' (Cited in Ōnuki, 1990c: 255). Particularly if foreigners are 'overstaying illegally' (*fuhō taizai*), an immediate apprehension *inflagranti crimine* is possible (and likely) according to the stipulations in the Immigration Control Act. Lawyers complain that the warrant-of-arrest principle is totally undermined, and any slightly conspicuous or 'suspicious' foreigner could be taken into custody. This often leads to investigations concerning other offences (a practice which is subject to stricture under the title *bekken taiho*, cf. Ōnuki, 1990b: 44). An over-representation of foreigners criminalized due to factors of occupational class has to be taken into account.

A positive distortion factor could, however, result from the propensity of delinquency among foreigners not to come to the notice of police because the (foreign) victims fear expulsion and loss of jobs and income due to their 'illegal' status (referred to in Yashima, 1989: 26). But this hidden or dark area of crimes by foreigners could be counterbalanced by the inclination of the Japanese population to denounce and inform against foreigners to the police, and by more intensive investigative efforts on the part of control agencies. Thus language, habitus, 'different' appearance, and so forth, provide visible criteria for investigation and subsequent apprehension of foreigners (Albrecht and Pfeiffer, 1979: 22, propose this as valid for the German situation).

Another (but lesser) inflation of the criminal statistics is due to the fact that 'illegal' workers are concentrated in the major urban centres. This geographical factor is relevant to the criminological truism that incidence of crime is generally higher among urban than rural populations.

If one compared the crime rates of foreigners with Japanese, one would have to construct 'correct' control and reference groups. They must be homologous with respect to age, profession, gender-structure, regional dispersion, class, and social surroundings (since these influence frequency of police contacts). I make this remark because concerned lawyers present comparative data in good faith, but ignore the above-mentioned distorting factors. They compare crime-rates per 10,000 for foreigners visiting Japan (*rainichi gaikokujin*), and for Japanese (from the overall population). With proper reference groups the following differences in the crime rates would be even greater. The data presented indicate a significantly lower crime rate for *rainichi gaikokujin*, but they are not really conclusive. If one follows Ōnuki's calculation for the year 1988, there were 11.9 larcenies registered per 10,000 *rainichi gaikokujin*, while the number per 10,000 Japanese is 115.8. The rate for violent crimes is 0.2 for foreigners and to 5.4 for Japanese (the bases for calculation are the numbers of suspects registered in the criminal statistics of the police; cf. Ōnuki, 1990c: 256).

The attorney-at-law, Hidejima, provides analogous data. In 1985 the number of apprehensions per 10,000 Japanese for larceny (23.2 arrests) was 5.8-fold that for foreigners apprehended for the same offence. She compares the numbers of suspects who were formally submitted to the prosecutor (per 10,000 of the whole Japanese population and of foreigners, respectively, with the latter including *zainichi gaikokujin*, which disproportionately augments the rate) and finds that the rate of prosecution for robbery was 0.039 for foreigners and 0.15 for Japanese, and for rape 0.064 for foreigners and 0.14 for Japanese (Hidejima, 1989: 20 and 21). Both calculations can be attributed to well-intentioned action of the bar to refute the allegation that law and order are deteriorating due to the influx of foreign migrant workers. The insufficient basis of comparison, however, makes such attempts mathematically suspect and scarcely reliable. The way the data are treated naively sustains the supposition that they mirror the 'criminal reality', and more value is attributed to the figures than they actually have.

Moreover, the manner in which they have been generated is left out of consideration.

The historical concurrence of the alleged increase of crimes committed by foreigners becoming a theme of police and press, the public discussion of 'illegal' workers viewed as a 'social problem', the mobilization of law-makers to amend the Immigration Control Act, and the rise in numbers of expulsions because of 'illegal' stay and in refusals of applications for admission to the country, constitutes a climate in which statistics on crime have a strategic location which needs to be elucidated. Crime figures acquire an eminent political value. They are cited to underscore the arguments of both proponents and opponents of an official 'guest-worker policy'. The crime statistics therefore must be examined in their context of generation and utilization.

7.5 The Argument Concerning the 'Deterioration of Public Safety' in Japan due to the Influx of Foreign (Illegal) Workers

7.5.1 The argument in the context of the debate on foreign labour

The increase of registered criminalized foreigners and the absolute numbers of infractions are often isolated from their social and demographic context and then translated into generic formulas such as *chian ga akka suru* (public safety deteriorates) or *gaikoku-jin no hanzai ga kyūzō suru* (crimes committed by foreigners rapidly increase). The reference to the criminal statistics of the police showing steep rises in offences spuriously corroborates the every day theory of the high delinquency of foreigners. In the first instance I want to inquire into the periphery of the supposition that there is a risk of more crimes because there are more foreigners, by examining published books dealing with the 'problem' of foreign labour. Then, using data from opinion polls, I shall show how fear of foreigner criminality is quite common. Nor is it a phenomenon peculiar to Japan:

If one makes an observation of the press, and also of pseudo-scientific publications, one can notice over and over again that prejudices against guest-workers are *inter alia* rationalized by the alleged 'fact' that these persons are to a much higher degree criminal than the indigenous. This observation is valid not only for Germany but for nearly all immigration countries of the world (Albrecht, 1979: 232).

Although Japan does not regard itself as an immigration country, there is a close correlation in timing between the emergence of the argument regarding deteriorating public safety and the influx of 'illegal' migrant workers which became 'visible' by virtue of increased media attention and the beginning of political discussion of counter-measures. The argument is proposed by the opponents of admission of guest-workers (mainly into the unskilled sector), and by cautious proponents of admission, and the police. But even 'radical and progressive' proponents of admission of foreign labour uncritically accept the argument and unwittingly abet the position of their opponents. For instance, Ōmae Ken'ichi supported his contention that a proportion of 10 per cent of guest-workers in the overall population would be no problem, by arguing that 'If foreign workers commit crimes and import drugs, if they show conduct not tolerated by the state, one can take rigorous action against them' (Ōmae, 1990: 51). A vigorous repudiation, however, was articulated by the specialist on France, Miyajima Takashi, who holds that the intertwining of the discussions on 'unskilled' labour and on an increase in crimes which endangers public safety amounts to 'racial discrimination'. To speak of 'culture conflict' and 'safety problems' together with 'racial contamination' is a form of socially-accepted discrimination. The pairing of admission of foreign labour with crimes and delinquency in the discourse was stereotypical and hasty, and has been proven to be false in Western European states (Miyajima, 1989: 242 and 53). In a discussion, Miyajima explicitly addressed the journalists present and remarked that the mixing of immigration with crime in argumentation was extremely cheap. Newspaper articles incessantly speak of a future law-and-order problem. Linking immigrants with crime had already turned out to be erroneous in Europe. Considered objectively, this style of discussion is characteristic of ultra-nationalist campaigns in France (Miyajima A. O., 1987: 22), Germany and elsewhere.

In a country described as having 'become one of the safest nations in the world, blessed with a favourable public-safety situation' (Shikita and Tsuchiya, 1990: 2), the argument in question is a particular touchy one, and reactions to it are very sensitive. The above quotation is from a work addressing the development of crime in Japan from a long-term perspective (1926–1988) based on official data. It describes, through extensive comparisons with Western European countries, the advantageous position of Japan regarding public safety. It was written in English, and distributed free to foreign scientific institutions (for example, in Vienna to the Institute for Penal Law and Criminology at the University of Vienna and the Institut für Rechts- und Kriminalsoziologie). In most of the White Papers on Police one finds such statements as: 'Japan has the highest level of public safety among the developed industrial countries' (see for example, Keisatsuchō, 1987: 6). This is then 'verified' by extensive comparisons of international official crime statistics. Comparisons of this nature have to be viewed with reservations, and criminologists range from cautious to negative in their treatment of them: 'A comparison of crime-statistical data on an international level, gathered by agencies of social control of different countries with differing societal arrangements, is meaningless' (Schneider, 1977: 70). The assumption that Japan is a particularly safe country has the consequence that potential menaces to this safety provoke a high degree of sensitivity, which is also brought to bear in considering preventive policies and in judicial proceedings. The argument may be reconstructed as follows: Japan is a harmonious country with low criminality. This harmony recently has been disturbed by foreigners, therefore it must be recovered through stiff verdicts setting precedents for 'general prevention' (see Takahashi, 1989c: 91).

The assumption that 'increasing immigration of foreigners is detrimental to public safety' can be spotted in diverse contexts. Sometimes it is articulated bluntly as above; at other times it is part of expressions of concern regarding 'guest-worker policy'. In the following I shall locate the argument contextually and clarify its function. The economist Umetani states that the question regarding foreign workers is primarily one of the advantages and disadvantages of admission of an unskilled labour force. Above all, he is concerned with 'apprehension in regard to social problems, that is, social tensions and the deterioration of public safety [*chian no akka*]'. Other concerns relate to unemployment and worsening working conditions for Japanese workers. The first point discussed is a social and racial (*jinshuteki*) problem. To offer housing, education, medical care, etc., to foreign workers would inflict a considerable financial burden on the Japanese populace (cf. Umetani, 1989: 94). In the same anthology dealing with views concerning the 'guest-worker problem', the economist Kuwahara Yasuo also hints at the 'importation' of social problems, and at costs once immigration is allowed. With the rising number of foreigners in Japan, the number of crimes, illnesses(!), drugs, etc., they bring with them, or bring about, plainly will rise also (Kuwahara, 1989: 164). The economist Hanami Tadashi presents a long list of problems purportedly arising from immigration, and complements it with the notion that this is not only a problem of labour market policy but a pervasive social problem. General social guarantees, education, insurance, hygiene(!), crime, and law and order were to be considered (Hanami 1989: 186). In the conclusion of this omnibus volume, it is stated that, in view of the population explosion in Asia and the national policy in some countries of exporting labour, and for 'the prevention of an inflow of criminals' (*hanzaisha no ryûnyû bôshi*), the promulgation of diverse restrictions on immigration was necessary (Kuwahara, 1989: 204).

In a broad theoretical study of the Economic Planning Agency (Keizai Kikakuchō) several scenarios are delineated – maintenance of the status quo; a policy of isolation; controlled immigration and a policy of integration. These are considered with regard to their possible implications for the Japanese economy, society and international reputation. With regard to the scenario of maintenance of the status quo, it is claimed that 'By virtue of the existence of illegal workers, public safety will deteriorate. Slum-like regions will emerge and the living environment will deteriorate' (KKSK, 1989: 74f.). Then follows a reminder that extensive measures will be necessary, and among the counter-measures enumerated, crime-control of course shows up (KKSK 1989: 113). A document offering guidelines on the legal situation in hiring foreigners makes the claim that the establishment of ethnic enclaves will generate crime (Kobayashi, 1990: 44). In a book on the revised Immigration Control Act, it is mentioned with regard to the admission of 'unskilled' labour that a final conclusion would be premature and that diverse aspects pertaining to public safety had still to be carefully scrutinized (Yamada and Kuroki 1990: 20). Among those who have strong reservations concerning the official admission of guest-workers (called by journalists *shinchōha*, the faction of the prudent) are conservative politicians. They frequently advance the public-safety argument. The head of a Commission for Investigation into the Problem of Foreign Workers of the LDP, Hayashi Yoshirō, asserted in a televised discussion:

> This is not a question of labour force or economy, it is a matter of public safety. I am cautious, because very 'wayward' (*katte na*) people will come to Japan. It would be a nuisance if public safety were to come into disorder. This is a problem of public safety, customs and morals. (Shibuya, 1990: 77).

A comment from a member of the audience of this programme reflects the same opinion: 'If we permit foreign labour, problems will occur, because Japan will be an economic superpower with a chaotic public safety situation' (Shibuya, 1990: 139).

In a report by the Ministry of Justice, one reason given as to why 'unskilled' labourers should not be accepted in Japan is 'the apprehension that the crime rate will inevitably rise' (cited in Mori, 1989: 13). The Ministry of Justice often points to repercussions in society due to cultural differences and to the emergence of a social problem relating to 'unqualified' workers. With regard to the present situation it says that the increase in illegal workers not only leads to erosion of the basis of entry and departure control, that is, the system of residence-titles, but begins to be accompanied by diverse problems concerning public safety, morals, public hygiene, the labour market, foreign relations, and so forth (Yamagami, 1988: 37, 41 and 51). Another high ranking official of the Ministry of Justice points to the importance of a 'rigorous response' (*gensei na taiō*) to the 'problem' of 'illegal' workers, because it not only touches upon law and order and labour conditions in Japan, but is a 'grave problem' which, beginning with the problem of public safety, will have effects on the life of the Japanese people (Sakanaka, 1989: 18 and 24, in the conclusion of his explanations regarding the Amendment of the Immigration Control Act). A representative of the Ministry of Labour asserts that, besides the detrimental effect admission of foreign workers will have on labour conditions, reason for concern is given also by the conflicts which will occur between foreigners and Japanese citizens and by the negative effects admission of foreigners will have on safety, as the experiences of Germany and France show (Yoshimen, 1990: 42).

This selection of citations testifies to the fact that apprehension concerning public safety, and with it the implicit imputation of a criminal potential to foreigners, is often articulated in a broad context of concern regarding 'problems'. This usually takes the form of a warning against uncontrolled immigration, and proposals for various controls, repressions, restrictions, conditions and prohibitions on entry. The foreign (and particularly the 'illegal') population is viewed only as a presumptive 'social problem'. A psychologist working in (criminal) sociology notes with regard to the function of the label 'social problem':

> The adjective 'social' implies that it deals with 'problems' of society (not that somebody or something causes a 'problem' to another), which is on the one hand a belittlement (because it spirits away the struggles involved when something is declared a 'social problem' or not and is dealt with in a certain way or not). On the other hand, it is a dramatization (through pretending that everything disturbing somebody is immediately a danger to a society's existence and to its mode of functioning). The notion, therefore, is first of all not analytical, but moral and political (or immoral and apolitical) (Steinert, 1981: 56).

Nisho Kanji, the most prominent representative of a 'closed-door' policy, argues in a distinctly polemical manner concerning the 'social problems' Japan would incur even with controlled immigration. A restricted 'opening of the country' would pose the problem of selecting the proper workers. If selection were left to the sending country, then for all Japan knew psychopaths or criminals might be dispatched to Japan(!). Were the selection to be made by Japan, a physical and blood examination would be indispensable. Prospective workers should also be investigated to determine whether they have criminal records. A simple intelligence test and a test of the candidate's ability to understand Japanese society should be carried out. Moreover, the period of stay and the number of persons admitted would have to be restricted (Nishio, 1989c: 151). The covert, but nevertheless clear-cut, racism behind these assertions is evident. However, Nishio continues, a controlled rotation of the foreign labour force would not be practicable anyway, because it would unavoidably lead to permanent immigration and high costs for education, housing, medical care, unemployment payments, professional education, old age pensions, public safety, and so on. He therefore pleads for a 'defence of culture and life' (*bunka bōei, seikatsu bōei*), and concludes that Japan – in apprehension of a 'human tidal wave' (*jinteki tsunami*) from neighbouring countries – had only the option of a defensive policy of closed doors (Nishio, 1989c: 146). The metaphor-transfer from the field of military and natural disasters to foreign workers proves that his style is demagogic and intentionally exaggerated. The term *sakoku* (closing the country) is a deliberate allusion to the historic period of the isolation of Japan from roughly 1641 to 1854, in which, except for extremely restricted and controlled contact with foreigners, a policy of isolation was implemented. This notion is also applied by journalists (in the term *sakokuha*) to opponents of admission of foreign labour, and serves as a catchword for the title of one of Nishio's books, *Rōdō sakoku no susume* (Recommendation for closing the country) (cf. Nishio, 1989a). In an article published by the Japanese government in English in the semi-official magazine *Japan Echo*, Nishio airs those same suppositions and concerns. He claims that, with an increase in numbers of foreign workers:

> they would cluster by ethnic groups in neighbourhoods run by local bosses – miniature countries within a country, where the rule of Japanese authorities would not extend. The incidents of killings and other violence that have already occurred among foreigners living in Japan are an omen of worse to come if the gates are opened wider ... they would engage in bitter feuds beyond the ken of the Japanese, causing social order to deteriorate. ... Many people in Japan worry that a rise in the number of foreigners living in this country would lead to an increase in crime, making it impossible for women to walk alone at night.

This, he asserts, would certainly happen, and a sort of 'minority bashing' by the majority would come about. He also maintains that Japan is close to being a classless, egalitarian society, but that with a large number of foreigners,

> Japan's social fabric would suffer damage, and its moral standards would decline ... The presence of many foreigners would in time lead to an increase in the number of people of

mixed race. This would probably be accompanied by the emergence of a sense of crisis in some sections of society, along with the abandonment of traditional values (Nishio, 1990).

This should suffice to demonstrate that Nishio's rhetoric is pathetic, full of moral admonishments, regressive tendencies and racist slurs (in fact, he employs the language and arguments used by Neo-Nazis in Germany). Nishio openly declares his position and exposes himself through his outspokenness. What seems dangerous to me, is the fact that a polemic of this kind, full of rhetoric and warnings regarding social consequences of a guest-worker policy induces a 'sense of crisis' and is an incitement to xenophobia, arousing permanent suspicion of foreigners as a (criminal) danger to society. In short, the definition of foreign workers as a 'social problem' insinuates that a wide range of problems will occur (for example, rising crime rates) affecting the *whole* of society. Their being deemed a 'social problem' also implies that this is a matter to be tackled with counter-measures. The irony of social control lies in the effect that social controllers create what they set out to control (cf. Marx, 1993). The ready labelling of foreigners as a 'social problem' finally serves to legitimize repression and rigid control.

7.5.2 The argument in police-studies

Studies by the police and by kindred bodies present the 'increase in crimes by foreigners' not as conjecture or as an hypothetical scenario, but as an established fact. It is noteworthy that virtually all criminological surveys and research in Japan are undertaken by in-house researchers and police executives of the National Police Agency, not least because of their exclusive access to internal data – a fact to be lamented with regard not only to studies on the police themselves, but also studies in other criminologically relevant areas (cf. Miyazawa, 1990: 36 and 43, where a plea is made for more independence in Japanese criminology 'since in-house researchers of police and other governmental agencies are working under tacit expectations that they will produce positive results').

The police publication with the highest public profile, the *White Paper on the Police* – particularly that of 1990 – repeatedly uses the formulas noted above, which then enter newspaper headlines and articles. As early as its Introduction, the 1990 White Paper points to tendencies perceived as problematic, claiming that 'violent crimes involving foreigners have conspicuously increased' (Keisatsuchō, 1990: 2). In the special report on foreigners this claim is extended: now there is held to be a general rise in crimes committed by foreigners, and it is remarked that a further increase in the influx of foreign workers will lead to continually rising crime rates. Crimes of violence already showed a 'rapid increase' (*kyūzō*) (Keisatsuchō, 1990: 33 and 36). In a police study addressing problems of interpretation during interrogation, it is stated:

In recent years, against the backdrop of a progressing internationalization of society, many foreigners of diverse nationalities have come to Japan and remained. The wave of internationalization has an indisputable and heavy influence on the public safety situation of our country . . . at any rate the rise in crimes committed by so-called *rainichi*-foreigners is conspicuous.

Only on the next page does one find the correct notion 'increase in the number of suspects' instead of 'rise in crimes' (Kitamura and Hayakawa, 1989: 36f.). From the perspective of maintenance of law and order, adequate and efficient counter-measures had to be implemented, because diverse problems with foreigners will worsen, as will the situation of the police, due to the increase of crimes by *rainichi*-foreigners (Kitamura and Hayakawa, 1989: 36f.).

In a further paper, written from a perspective close to that of the police, 'illegal stay' (that is, stay which is longer than the residence-status allows) was criminalized by the term *fuhō zanryū zai*, and it was commented that in this case arrest on the spot was possible. The legal control of entry and stay was deemed to have serious consequences for public safety, and served to protect the national interest (*kokueki no hogo*). The police acted against 'deviant foreigners' (*furyō gaikokujin*), and in any such case should inform the Immigration Control Bureau so that an investigation could be instituted to determine whether there was cause for expulsion (Toshiro, 1989b: 139). With this rigid attitude, the existence of 'illegal' foreigners is criminalized *per se*. As the matter is put in another study: 'Activities outside the range legally defined [*shikakugai katsudō*] and "overstay" are illegal as such [*fuhō na sonzai*]' (Mishima, 1988: 98). In this article the increase in crimes committed by foreigners was repeatedly spoken of as not only a quantitative increase, but as also a trend towards more serious infractions (*akushitsuka*) and greater deviousness (*kōmyōka*). It was claimed that these developments would continue to worsen (Mishima, 1989: 91). These (fictitious and *ad hoc*) prognoses premise a linear increase. However, this is refuted even by recent police data showing a decrease in most offences in 1990 (cf. Keisatsuchō, 1991: 97). Expectations of a constant worsening of the safety situation are aroused, from which the author extrapolates: 'In the future, and against the background of changes due to internationalization, the increase in crimes committed by *rainichi*-foreigners will become the most influential factor in public safety' (Mishima, 1988: 92). Consequently, in the conclusion of this paper a reinforcement of police counter-measures and an intensification of international cooperation in fighting crime are called for (Mishima, 1988: 104).

Next I want to discuss a prognostic study published in 1991, which seems to me paradigmatic in several respects. It is exemplary of the way in which criminal sociology is conducted by researchers of (or close to) the police, and of theory construction in accordance with *Leitinteresse* (predominant interests). The author, Kiyonaga Kenji, a member of The National Research Institute of Police Science, postulates that foreign workers have become indispensable to the Japanese economy. He hints at the acute shortage of labour in small enterprises in the production sector, using the catchphrase 'bankruptcy due to lack of personnel' (*hitode busoku tōsan*), and at the progressive aging of the Japanese population. He evidences this trend with complicated calculations showing that, for every three persons of productive age, one will be of unproductive age by the year 2005 (the proportion in 1985 was 6.7 to 1). On the basis of this calculation he maintains that it will be imperative for Japan to admit between 500,000 and 1.1 million foreign workers to offset an aged society in the year 2005 (Kiyonaga, 1991: 41–45). This is the vantage point for the following prognosis of the crime situation.

In his introduction Kiyonaga says that in Germany and France the 'apprehended situation' has become one of an increase in crime and of victimizations involving foreigners. (Here Kiyonaga, 1991: 36, quotes Nishio Kanji, 1989a, the classic work of an opponent of admission of foreign workers, and not a work of criminological analysis!). By the year 2005, grave effects on the crime situation in Japan are to be feared as a consequence of conflicts between Japanese and foreigners and conflicts among foreigners (*dōkokujin no kattō*) – a popular media-theme. Because of difficulties of mutual cultural understanding, regional conflicts (*chiiki funsō*) may be expected. Two highly questionable scenarios follow: In the first, the trend in increasing 'crime'-figures (from police statistics concerning suspects) is simply prolonged. It is inferred that the number of apprehended foreigners by the year 2005 will be 30,964. The second scenario refers to the 'German experience', and official German police statistics are uncritically accepted, along with the assumption that, in the German situation, foreign suspects were over-represented in the ratio of three to one with German suspects. Simply transferring this assumption of a three-fold over-representation of foreigners to the Japanese situation (without questioning whether it would be valid for Japan) Kiyonaga arrives at a figure for foreign criminals (suspects!) in Japan by the year 2005 of between 8,052 and 17,522 (dependant on the base assumption of the 'necessary' number of foreign labourers, which is also given with the same absurd precision at between 561,174 and 1,123,258). Furthermore, not only the quantity but also the quality of 'crimes' is made into a problem through the citation of police figures concerning (registered) cases of suspects of violent crimes (*kyōakuhan*). He then forecasts that by 2005 – again dependant on how many foreign workers will be required – foreigners will account for one out of every thirty suspects and one out of every seventeen apprehensions for violent crimes in Japan (Kiyonaga, 1991: 45–47). The basis of calculation for both prognoses is provided by the figures given by the police in the 1990 *White Paper*. These statistics are naively misunderstood as a mirror of reality. At the end of his paper Kiyonaga argues that the rise in crimes committed by foreigners constitutes a challenge to criminal sociology, and calls for a new theory. The theory of deviance should be abandoned in favour of one of safety control (*anzen kanriron*), or rather, safety management. Kiyonaga offers an abstract outline of such a theory. The prevention of crime is needed to prevent new sociopathies (*shakai byōriteki mondai*). This last organic metaphor illustrates the implicit assumptions upon which the above 'prognoses' are premised. The increase in foreign workers implies an increase in conflicts and crimes, which are seen as harmful to the 'body' of Japanese society. (Even an 'organic' sociologist such as Durkheim contests the idea that crime should be seen only as pathological, showing that it is instead functional for society; (see for example Durkheim, 1991.) The presumption of an increase in crimes by foreigners is then computed with mathematical precision and 'substantiated' with meaninglessly precise figures. This serves to underscore that the analysis is 'hard' science.

Thus the premises are false, or at least highly contestable: Criminality does not simply rise linearly over time; as a rule there are fluctuations. The first prognosis, therefore, is ahistorical, and, moreover, is based on police data of strictly limited explanatory value. The second prognosis plainly transfers the German situation to Japan without inquiry into the differences in legal status and position of guest-workers in Germany and 'illegal' migrants in Japan. In Germany it was long ago demonstrated that police data provide a distorted picture (cf. 7.2 of the present study), and the 'three-fold over-representation' (in all infringements) of guest-workers fails to differentiate among types of offences, and in any case is not valid for the first generation. Both scenarios seem to me to be the expression of a fetish for numbers and statistics characteristic of a wide range of criminal sociological research in Japan. The figures released by 'authorities' are not questioned but are gullibly accepted and used in mathematical analyses (providing a 'scientific' air). The results are interpreted as 'social reality' and the analyses show no application of the sociological imagination. The whole study is more or less a pseudo-empirical 'proof' of the simple police-logic: more foreigners means importation of crime, hence control and prevention are called for. This prejudice of the police is then projected into the future with a gesture of alarm and buttressed with senseless figures. Circumstances are then prophesied which are not to be expected except as consequences of this very type of argument. The prophesy feeds continuing suspicion and strengthens calls for reinforced 'prevention-measures' – measures which would push more 'crimes' to the statistical surface. This study is therefore nothing more than an anticipatory taxonomy of the details of the author's presumptions that crimes(!) of foreigners will continue to increase and that foreigners are more criminal(!) than Japanese and, hence, require more control.

The publication of a series of articles in the police-scientific magazine *Keisatsugaku ronshū* (Mishima, 1988; Kitamura and Hayakawa, 1988; Toshiro, 1989a, b; Sasaki, 1990) and of reports by the National Institute of Police Science (Suzuki, 1990a, b) in which developments in foreigner 'crime' (again the figures cover only suspected crimes), are dramatized in the way illustrated above, directed police attention to this 'new' phenomenon. The conjuring of a future danger to public safety, which is linked with demands for stricter control, the gathering of more information, and more investigation of 'illegal' labourers and counter-measures against them, focuses interest on those developments. This is the pattern also for other periodic sensationalizing – for example, of juvenile delinquency, drug offences, and organized crime. Public concern with these themes shows marked booms and fluctuations over time, but the police are influenced by these fabrications of 'dangerous tendencies' and translate them into everyday theories which then direct their actions. For instance, it may be supposed that the perception of foreigners is primarily shaped by the general suspicion of 'illegality'. Sociologically this is reflected upon as 'selectivity of police action' or 'selective sanctioning by the police' (cf. Feuerhelm, 1987: 14ff., who convincingly applied those concepts to the way in which police treat the minorities of Sinti and Roma in Germany). Police-work is determined by selective perceptions according to pre-defined suspicions (suspicious neighbourhood, appearance, conduct). This 'methodological suspicion' is then made tangible via control. In the control situation, the power of definition is on the side of the police and is decisive in whether an act is criminalized or not. It is particularly those with low competency in negotiation and little power to appeal (such as members of the lower class, and 'illegal' foreigners) who have a much higher likelihood of being automatically characterized as 'criminal' by the police (see Feest, 1973, especially 170f). Police and mass-media sensationalizing can put the police under pressure to act, that is, to produce more 'criminals' as evidence for their effective work. Stricter repressive action, law enforcement, and crack-downs then result in higher figures of the criminalized. The dynamics of a self-fulfilling prophecy are set into motion: rising crime rates of foreigners are postulated; control and surveillance are intensified; stricter policing and shakedowns result in an increase in registration of offences committed by 'illegals'; this (seemingly) 'verifies' the everyday theory of the high criminality of foreigners; and so it continues. This has to be seen in connection with the allocation of police resources: special new departments for counter-measures against the delinquency of foreigners have been founded. Their *raison d'être*, financial means and staffing have to be negotiated. The increase in successful registrations of foreign suspects serves as legitimation for, and provides leverage to, demands for budget and personnel. Even newspaper articles take this line of argument: 'rising number of crimes committed by foreigners, prevention imperative, Special Commission for Counter-measures on the Foreigner Problem established by prefecture police' (*Yomiuri shinbun* and *Asahi shinbun*, 24 June 1988).

7.6 Fear of Crime and the 'Situation of Constant Suspicion'

Some indicators show that especially Asian foreigners are under 'constant suspicion' by the Japanese populace. Police and officials of the Immigration Control Bureau often get anonymous calls concerning 'suspicious foreigners'. This forces them to act, and shakedowns and apprehensions follow (there are recurrent references to these reactive control activities in the literature: cf. Yamatani, 1989: 204f.; Aikawa, 1987: 33; Gonoi, 1989: 76). For example, six Pakistanis were arrested because of 'overstay' after people in their neighbourhood telephoned the police: 'Foreigners run after our kids. Please investigate!' (*Saitama shinbun*, 24 January 1990). According to the Immigration Control Bureau in Tokyo, they receive 20,000 letters and telephone calls per year denouncing foreigners, and this tendency is rising (Komai, 1993). This indicates that Asian workers are under heavy informal control and are eyed suspiciously by Japanese, especially in areas in which they are concentrated.

7.6.1 Demoscopic findings

Diverse, closed-question polls show that while there is not a 'blind faith' (Ōnuki, 1990c: 253) that more foreigners would mean more crimes, there is prevalent, nonetheless, a fear of foreigners' criminality. This is especially true for respondents who express reservations concerning the admission of guest-workers. Of opponents of admission of foreign labour (44 per cent of the sample), 37 per cent indicated that they thought 'morals will get into disorder and public safety will deteriorate' (poll by the *Mainichi shinbun*, 5

February 1990). To the question 'How do you perceive foreign workers?', 13 per cent of all respondents identified 'disorder of public safety and morals' as their dominant image of foreign labour. An economic-pragmatic image prevails: another poll found that 16 per cent of respondents think of 'obtaining a cheap labour force', and 29 per cent hope for a 'balancing of the labour shortage' (poll by *Asahi shinbun*, 6 November 1989, no multiple answers possible). An opinion poll by the Prime Minister's Office (Sōrifu) with questions of the selective-choice type (only one reply possible) gives a similar picture: The respondents were limited to those who classified the increase in foreigners as 'not good' (48 per cent of total). As reasons for this assessment, 57.6 per cent feared the loss of their job and 15.2 per cent expressed apprehension about deterioration of public safety (NSDKK, 1990: 572). A different formulation of the question asked the opponents of admission or acceptance of foreign labour as at present (that is, those who were opposed to the presence in Japan of Asian 'illegal' migrant workers performing 'unskilled' labour) to give a single reason for their decision: 36 per cent selected as their answer increasing unemployment of Japanese workers, and 29 per cent the disorder of public morals and deteriorating safety (NSDKK, 1990: 485). A poll by the same institution in the previous year indicates a higher fear of crime. A filtering question again divides respondents into those who rate labour of foreigners with a tourist visa as 'not good' (39.4 per cent) and those who see it as 'not good, but unavoidable' (with 15.2 per cent who 'don't know'). The first group was asked the reason for their decision (up to two answers possible). Responses were as follows: because 'Japanese laws are violated': 36.1 per cent; because 'the number of Japanese unemployed will increase': 23.2 per cent; because 'public safety and morals deteriorate': 47.5 per cent; because 'they [the foreign workers with tourist visas] are hired with cheap wages': 20.8 per cent; because 'their human rights are violated via prostitutions, etc., and a hotbed for crime emerges': 48 per cent; because of other reasons: 0.6 per cent; 'don't know': 0.9 per cent (NSDKK, 1989: 141). This distribution of answers evinces a quite rigid 'law and order' attitude among opponents of 'illegal' labour. No trend can be identified, due to the incongruous formulation of questions in the following year. When proponents of labour immigration were asked for the causes of restrictions on the admission of foreigners (multiple replies possible), 60 per cent gave 'corruption of morals and deterioration of public safety' as their reason (the pre-formulated answer in all of the quoted polls is similar: *fūzoku ga midaretari, chian ga waruku nattari suru kara*) (NSDKK, 1989: 157). When one analyses all of the responses, taking into account the mode of polling and the response-options, no general fear of foreigner crime can be identified. But for opponents of admission of foreigners to the labour market, fear of foreigner crime is clearly part of their overall image concerning foreigners. (Crime fear, however, does predominate in the mood towards foreigners in many countries experiencing an 'unexpected' immigration, for example, in Austria after the so-called 'opening of the borders' to former Eastern-bloc countries, cf. Plasser and Ulram, 1991.)

The question as to whether an increasing number of foreigners is detrimental to public safety is tainted by the presumption of the truth of the implicit statement. The Demographic Research Institute of the Welfare Ministry recognized this subtle imputation (which, until then, had remained below the threshold of perception) as 'discrimination', and withdrew several questions from a planned opinion poll. One of the eliminated questions was: 'If the number of foreigners rises, this results in chaos in society and deterioration of public safety' (*shakai ga konran shi chian ga akka suru*) (*Asahi shinbun*, 7 June 1990).

The Police Agency, however, shows no such sensitivity. It commissioned a poll in eight (unnamed) regions designated by the police, in which foreigners were concentrated. The results were published in the *White Paper* and received broad media coverage. The pre-selection of the questions and respondents meant that opinion was *mobilized* rather than authentically articulated. Those interviewed lived in the neighbourhood of foreigners (who engage in 'illegal' labour or 'possibly' do so), and were questioned as to their feelings of 'insecurity'. The suggestive formulation of the question ('Do you feel uneasy or not?') and the categorization of pre-defined response options, disclose more about the intentions of the polling organization (the police) than about the 'real' mood of the polled: 55.9 per cent stated that they feel 'a vague, but undeniable uneasiness' (*bakuzen da ga fuan o kanjite iru*). This diffuse feeling of anxiety is then queried more closely in terms of the answers contrived by the police. As concrete 'content' for this uneasiness, the following options are given: 'emergence of crime' (68.2 per cent); 'walking alone of women at night' (56.1 per cent); unspecified anxiety (37.2 per cent); 'deterioration of sanitary conditions' (35.3 per cent); 'quarrels and disputes among them' (*karera* – obviously meaning the foreigners) (32.5 per cent); fear that an area exclusively inhabited by foreigners could emerge (28 per cent); fear of quarrels and disputes between Japanese and foreigners (20.5 per cent); fear of outbreak of fires (17.8 per cent) (cf. Keisatsuchō, 1990: 31f.). The police comment that calls from inhabitants of the polled areas for stricter policing and patrolling became louder (Keisatsuchō, 1990: 31). In these regions, from January to March 1990, 504 complaints were brought to the notice of the police, most of them concerning noise and dumping of garbage. The police regard this as an indicator of the different customs of foreigners (Keisatsuchō, 1990: 32). However, the volume of these complaints rather indicates a high sensitivity on the part of the Japanese citizens. They obviously feel compelled to have the police brought in to resolve petty conflicts and disturbances, in case foreigners are involved. For the police, the anxiety provoked by their poll itself is then taken as reason for intensification of their patrol activities. The mode of questioning, by making 'feelings of uneasiness' concrete through a catalogue of response options which rather convey police preoccupations than 'real' fears, has the consequence that latent stereotypes of foreigners are reinforced. Those polled are forced to the concrete perception of their 'uneasiness', and feelings of insecurity are made manifest. By virtue of this transfer into consciousness, Japanese citizens are hyper-sensitized, and attention is directed to potential conflicts, resulting in a tightening of the net of informal social control and formal control by more police patrols.

7.6.2 Crime panics

That the vague anxieties quoted above are prone to escalate into a downright crime panic, is illustrated by a case in Saitama prefecture which became infamous under the title 'Saitama-rumour'. In Kawaguchi-city a rumour was set afloat about Asian foreigners who allegedly violated a housewife. After some time the rumour, spreading to parts of Chiba prefecture, acquired regional variants and menacing additions, although police refuted its contents as not sustainable. According to this grapevine, 'an old woman was raped before the eyes of her husband while taking their dog on a walk' and the 'victim became neurotic and committed suicide', or 'the victim was hospitalized', or 'a young girl was assaulted on her way from cram-school (*juku*)', and so forth. In one area a circular bulletin directed attention to 'the frequent occurrence of violence against women by groups of foreigners'. In another town the regular end-of-year crime prevention patrol was scheduled five days earlier, and in one region sixty portable alarm devices were sold in two months – a three-fold increase in sales for the year (cf. *Asahi shinbun*, 28 November 1990; *Saitama shinbun*, 29 November 1990; or *Mainichi shinbun*, 8 December 1990). This ill-willed rumour was not an isolated incident; similar crime panics are reported from other regions. The contents of the rumours are strikingly similar. Regional police authorities always repudiated the rumour – because no charges were brought and they did not want to be accused of deficient prevention activity. In December 1991, it is reported from Tochigi prefecture that a rumour was spread concerning foreigners who forcibly entered a house and violated a woman before the eyes of her family and husband. The woman was said to have committed suicide afterwards. A second version said an old woman was raped by a group of foreigners while taking a walk in a park. The origin of this rumour was Mooka, a town of 61,000 inhabitants, in which *nikkeijin* mainly from Peru had worked in roughly sixty enterprises for three years. They counted for slightly more than 4 per cent of the inhabitants (*Yomiuri shinbun*, 7 December 1991). Similar reports came from the prefectures of Tochigi and Ibaraki, where it was said that 'a group of foreigners raped a woman'. Police investigations found no substance to the rumours (*Yomiuri shinbun*, 13 December 1991). One-and-a-half years later this process of sensationalist stigmatization made Iranian workers with tourist visas subject to the same kind of rumours. The centre of this pernicious gossip was the central line of the Japan Railways (JR-Chūōsen around Koganei, Kokubunji, Tachikawa in Tokyo). The contents of the rumour were remarkably detailed, perhaps to lend it credibility. The main theme remained the same: 'Woman raped by a group of Iranians while going for a walk with her dog' and 'housewife assaulted and violated by Iranians while out jogging' (*Asahi shinbun*, 5 July 1992: 31). In the first version the woman's husband was said to be worried by the dog returning alone and began searching for his wife. He was said to have thought of getting a divorce, because he thought his wife was partly responsible for the rape. The internal contradiction (the husband reputedly lived apart from his wife – so to which home did the dog return?) and the sexist male fantasy of the woman as seductress luring the transgressors into sexual transgression (a common stereotype) remained beneath the threshold of perception.

These examples illustrate an inclination of the Japanese to perceive (Asian) foreigners as potentially dangerous, and a willingness to report disturbances of their everyday routine which they impute to those foreigners so that police will come to the scene. This points to the social location of criminalization, with this tendency condensing in rising crime figures. The ready call for law enforcement and state power, and the police commitment to be present (intensified patrol activities), have a 'prevention-theatrical' character. By this it is signalled to foreigners that discipline is required and that an immediate formal response by authorities at hand. But this is also an expression of the helplessness of the host community in dealing with petty conflicts involving foreigners, and mirrors the conflict-constellation of society at large and the positioning of 'illegal' foreigners within it as a 'social problem'. Willingness to report to police is further stimulated by the subsequent statistical product of a 'rapid increase of crimes committed by foreigners'. The police join in the game of demanding control, by becoming (internally) sensitized to the topical 'problem of foreign delinquency on the rise', and to calls for repressive and preventive counter-measures (Steinert, 1988: 13).

The subsequently sensationalized increase of 'crimes' reported in the statistics of agencies of control are the mathematical condensate of public readiness to report and police readiness to register charges and intensify control. Criminal statistics, therefore, reveal nothing about 'actual criminality' but rather are a 'representation of crime policy':

> 'Crime policy' on this level means willingness to threaten with penalising state power and actual mobilisation of it when conflicts, problems and troubles occur . . . 'Criminality' is an ascriptive, imputed feature, and consists of the announcement of, and actual organized readiness to set into motion, a program aimed at punishment by the state, whenever authorities are informed of incidents of a certain type (Steinert, 1988: 4).

In the selective 'production of criminality' the prosecutor's office and courts of law also participate. In the context of the whole

227

apparatus of social control, the practice of sanctioning (sentencing policy) can be seen as a mechanism to prolong crime waves. In the following, therefore, I want to illuminate problems concerning police custody, investigative and arraigning activities of the prosecutor's office, risks of being formally brought to trial, and sentencing by courts (harshness of sentences, suspension rates). Here the unfavourable position of foreign 'illegal' workers will come to light most clearly. Several empirical studies conducted by attorneys-at-law on problems pertaining to criminal procedure and stiff sanctioning comprehensively, describe the situation of foreigners facing the criminal justice system.

7.7 Interrogation by the Police, and Police Custody

7.7.1 General problems

Problematic constellations in the interaction between apprehended suspects and police officers are structurally embedded in the positions of the actors, and thus are not peculiar to Japan. But the situation can become more critical for foreign 'illegals' and is aggravated through certain aspects of legal procedure characteristic in Japan, as I shall demonstrate later. To begin, though, I want to reflect generally on the situation of interrogation.

The interrogating officers demonstrate their power and create an asymmetric interrelation by depriving the interrogated of status through 'rituals of degradation'. This facilitates the process of 'making' a suspect into a criminal (cf. Girtler, 1980: 73f.). Interrogation by the police is primarily defined by its character of coerced communication in which the 'facts' of the case are to be reconstructed through questioning of the suspect. 'Reality' is thereby constructed so as to fit a category of criminal law. To achieve this interpretation, re-definition and re-typification are required, and it is noteworthy that 'the police officers own exclusively an institutionally-supported power of definition' (Brusten and Malinowski, 1975: 59). Ordinary lay typifications are often transformed into those of the legal regulations binding police.

A comprehensive repertoire of strategies, tactics and techniques of interrogation, superior knowledge of the law, and solidly internalized everyday-theories [*Alltagstheorien*] for justifying and legitimating their way of acting secure for the police in questioning a clear advantage of competence of action against those ... who got caught in their net of prosecution (Brusten and Malinowski, 1975: 64).

'Successful interrogation' (for example, a confession – which amounts to acceptance of the definition of circumstances provided by police) lessens work and raises the quota of solved cases, both of which are called for by internal institution pressure. Interrogation by the police often is to the detriment of the underprivileged, inexperienced and less competent in taking action (Brusten and Malinowski, 1975).

7.7.2 'Substitute prisons' and strategies of interrogation

The police have a strategic advantage in that the site of coerced communication is in their own territory. In Japan, interrogation rooms are installed close to the place of custody of the suspect, thus interrogation and the police lock-up are structurally intertwined. Roughly nine-tenths of apprehended suspects are confined in the 'substitute prison' (*daiyō kangoku*), as places of police custody (*ryūchijō*) are called. According to the Japanese Code of Criminal Procedure, a suspect can be incarcerated there for up to seventy-two hours. Within this prescribed period, the suspect has to be brought before a public prosecutor, who can petition within ten days for a warrant of arrest from an investigating judge if sufficient evidence can be procured. Further reasons for detention include unknown place of residence, sufficient reason for judging that the suspect is suppressing evidence ('danger of collusion'), and sufficient reason for assuming the suspect would abscond and go into hiding ('danger of escape'). The forumulation used in the law, 'sufficient reason' (*sōtō na riyū*), is problematic in its wide range of possible interpretation, and the decision as to detention is mainly left to the discretion of the investigating judge (cf. Aoki, 1979: 83f.). Imprisonment on remand can be prolonged for a further ten days before the defendant is formally indicted (in case of certain offences another extension of five days is possible). But even when the suspect is brought to trial, the police can continue the interrogations in the *daiyō kangoku* if they deem it necessary for their investigation. This leads to many cases of protracted

229

police confinement. The rate of dismissal of petitions for custody has steadily decreased. In 1969, 5 per cent of petitions for detention were dismissed, by 1984 the figure was only 0.4 per cent (NBR, 1988a: 31). Official data on detention in remand show that in 99.9 per cent of cases in which a petition for custody was filed (85.4 per cent of all apprehended persons), the petition was actually granted. Moreover, 99.8 per cent of petitions for extension of detention were successful. While a mere 2.1 per cent of those arrested were detained by police for (only) five days, 61.6 per cent were held for up to ten days and 32.8 per cent of prisoners at the bar were confined for up to twenty days (Hōmusho, 1989: x).

The police-cells for interrogation were established in 1908 by the Prisons Law, which stated that 'places of detention adjacent to police stations may be used as substitutes for prison' (Igarashi, 1986: 212). This measure was introduced as a provisional arrangement, and these temporary makeshift 'prisons' were to be abolished when the shortage of 'ordinary' prisons was alleviated. Their abolition has been called for by Japanese lawyers, but to date no steps in this direction have been made. Presently around 150 detention centres (*kōchisho*) exist in Japan. They are under the administrative authority of the Ministry of Justice and have the capacity to confine 15,000 inmates. However, in 1988 there were 1,253 police detention facilities (eleven more than in 1985). Police jails had a holding capacity of over 16,000 inmates in 1985.

> Estimates by academics suggest that in the years 1985 to 1987 up to 91 per cent of suspects were detained in police cells rather than in detention centres. During 1987, some 42 per cent spent between one and two months in police detention and 12 per cent spend as much as between five and six months in such detention (Amnesty International, 1991: 29).

In this report of the human rights movement, Amnesty International, torture-like methods of 'interrogation' are also described and the lack of legal redress and counsel criticized (Amnesty International, 1991: 18f. and 23ff.). The cells of the police jails (also called 'birdcages') are built on a design close to the 'panoptical' arrangements invented during the European enlightenment for the disciplining of deviants (cf. Foucault, 1977). They are usually arranged in a fan-shaped manner, allowing 24–hour observation by the guards. This places the inmates under heavy psychological pressure (cf. the figure in NBR, 1988b: 3 and 5). The restricted sphere of life of detainees is thereby totally controlled; as is the flow of information to the outside world.[8] Communication and contact with a lawyer are also restricted and often sabotaged, which leads to a total isolation of the arrested defendant (Gotō, 1979: 222f.).

Reputedly, nearly all of the investigating officials and judges at court believe in the dictum: 'a confession is the king of evidence'. Lawyers claim that the detention in police cells is used to extract confessions. The over-estimation of the influence of confessions at court is conspicuous. The figure of 99.8 per cent of verdicts of guilty in Japanese courts of law was 'miraculous' (NBR, 1988a: 31f.). A Japanese jurist strongly criticizes the practice of questioning by the police and contests its legality. Depositions of confessions obtained out of court run counter to the principle of trial.

> Nearly all known false sentences in Japanese criminal justice procedure can be attributed to false confessions made by the accused due to harsh interrogation by the police in the substitute prisons . . . . The resemblance of the situation of the accused in the Japanese procedure of investigation with that of the accused in the German process of inquisition of the 19th century is amazing (Kamiguchi, 1984: 124–125).

Kamiguchi criticizes the prisoner's obligation questioning, the absence of a legal right to have a lawyer present during interrogation, and the legal ability of police to limit contact with attorneys (that is, to actually restrict communication).

One can, therefore, state that the apprehended defendant is placed within

> the sphere of police-power for up to twenty days virtually without legal counsel. This indisputably is conducive to making him confess. A considerable portion of the literature argues against this questioning procedure of the police, which puts the accused at risk of being forced to falsely incriminate himself. Disapproval of this practice is linked with calls for the legal abolition of the substitute prison, and with criticism of the incompatibility of the legal obligation to tolerate an interrogation with the accused's right to remain silent (Kamiguchi, 1988: 113).

The confession-centred investigation is often advanced by police through illegitimate means. The methods used to put the suspect under pressure to confess during interrogation in the 'birdcage' are extensively described in the above-mentioned symposium report of the Japanese Bar Association. Fatiguing, or protracted questioning is one of the standard techniques of the police where sufficient personnel are available. Interrogators can be replaced hourly. A poll of people falsely accused since 1983 showed that they were questioned for fourteen hours a day on average to extort a confession from them (NBR, 1988a: 62). As a rule, the psycho-physical exhaustion is enough to make the suspect confess (Aoki, 1979: 98). Promises such as a lessened penalty or release from detention are classic lures used to obtain a confession. Along with these methods, further strategies may be employed which gradually become rougher and physically more direct. The following strategies have been described. During interrogation, food and beverages are withheld, going to the toilet is forbidden and the suspect is systematically deprived of sleep. The suspect is threatened with being indicted for a more serious offence, or told custody and questioning will be prolonged endlessly if they do not confess. Other threats are that neighbours will be informed that the suspect is a 'criminal', that dependants and relatives will be arrested, that the professional career of the suspect will be damaged due to police interference, and so forth. Bodily methods include: the desk being bashed into the suspect's chest, suspects being pulled by their hair and having their heads pushed on the desk, slapping or punching of the suspect's face and body, the suspect being continually shouted at, suspects being forced to kneel and prostrate themselves (*dogeza*) in 'apology' while their feet and hands are trampled upon, the suspect being hemmed-in by many police officers and called such names as 'criminal', and so on (NBR, 1988a: 65ff.).[9]

The over-emphasis placed on confessions as a 'solid basis' for a verdict of guilty is closely intertwined with the *daiyō–kangoku*-system. The whole problem of Japanese criminal justice procedure comes to light here most clearly (NBR, 1988a: 65f.). The lawyer Aoki contends that the professional profile and internalized 'prejudices' of police and prosecutors lead to their operating with the assumption of guilt. They readily redefine the suspect as a culprit (Aoki, 1979: 102f. and 108f.). A presupposition of the judges is that 'nobody confesses without reason'. Claims of the accused that they are being 'tortured' during interrogation are for this reason often ignored. Submissions by attorneys regarding the illegitimacy of 'confessions' and their lacking the power of evidence (because of their involuntary extraction) are often not admitted. Only the investigating and prosecuting agencies are given credence (Aoki, 1979: 117 and 120). In Japanese judicial proceedings, the protocols of interrogation drawn up and fabricated by police are almost always uncritically accepted as 'exhibits' and 'evidence'. In cases where the accused denies having committed a crime and pleads innocent, it is notorious that contacts with lawyers are denied (OBK, 1991: 151). Courts are criticized for their *chōsho jūshi* (over-stressing of interrogation-protocols composed by police), and for their becoming degraded into *chōsho saiban* ('protocol-court') (Seno, 1989: 10). In view of these criticisms it is urged that, during an investigation, foreign suspects have access to legal counsel as early as possible (see, for example, Okazaki A. O., 1989: 45).

There is constant and vehement criticism of the system of substitute imprisonment in Japan, and of the coercion of suspects to confess through police use of illicit interrogation practices to reach the goal of a successful investigation (conviction by confession) and of the overestimation by courts of confessions as evidence. Police use of force and other illegitimate means of interrogation is not something peculiar to Japan, but is inherent in the structure of criminal proceedings generally. The criticism of the Japanese judiciary comes from lawyers (and is of course also in their own professional interest) and is sometimes connected with 'state moral imperatives'. With regard to human rights, Japan is dubbed an under-developed country (the journalistic catchphrase is *jinken kōshinkoku*, cf., for example, Yabe, 1991 who uses this term several times). This underscores the legitimate aims of critics of the substitute prison system (abolition of police lock-up, free interaction between defendant and attorney, and the right of suspects to have a lawyer present at interrogation). A close examination of the criticized problematic aspects of the Japanese situation (for example, violence of the police) shows that they are universals. However, for structural reasons they can be seen in concentration in Japan, and it can be surmised that the prison regime of the 'birdcages' is harsher than in Western European countries, and that police violence can more easily be hidden by the secretiveness of the interrogation rooms.

Police custody for many foreign 'illegal' workers is a traumatic experience. Cases are reported (both involving Pakistanis who were confined in single cells), of an 'imprisonment neurosis' (Matsunaga, 1990: 139) or 'imprisonment depression' (Ōnuki, 1990a: 93). In this syndrome may be seen such symptoms as communication disorders, unresponsiveness, and faecal incontinence. Longer confinement always involves deprivation (loss of freedom, restrictions of autonomy, deprivation of material and immaterial goods, deprivation of heterosexual relationships, possible danger from fellow-inmates; cf. Ortmann, 1985). In a discussion between lawyers, it was stated that the total control over all activities of prisoners in the 'birdcages' was unbearable (FRSTJB, 1990: 129). The restriction of freedom to act, permanent regimentation, sanctions from above and deprivation of autonomy are, however, general characteristics of what Goffman calls total institutions (cf. Goffman, 1973, especially 43–54). Both Japanese and foreign inmates suffer under these rituals of humiliation. But the situation for foreigners becomes more critical because the institutional regulations are often not explained to them. This enables authorities to verbally degradate and incessantly obtrude on foreign prisoners even in cases of petty infringements (FRSTJB, 1990: 130ff.).

In Germany there has been discussion as to whether foreign prison inmates suffer under an aggravated imprisonment deprivation or not. A qualitative study noted that foreigners, due to their marginal status in the 'pecking-order' of the prison community, are relegated to the bottom of the discrimination hierarchy. Prison subculture is characterized by defamation, aggression, depreciation and the channelling of frustration from top to bottom (cf. Albrecht, Pfeiffer and Zapka, 1978: 282f.). Another study identified racist prejudices against foreigners in prison, for example, in the pervasive use of the pejorative 'Kanake'[10] for foreigners, which is an accepted part of the 'institutional slang' of prisons (Bielefeld and Kreissl, 1983: 90). However, other criminal sociologists contend that, in the prison subculture, discrimination against foreigners is less conspicuous than in society at large, contradicting a general underdog-hypothesis (Bosetzky, Borschert and Helm, 1981: 234 and 236). This holds true, however, only for second-generation foreigners, who have been socialized bi-culturally (and have a circle of German friends) and are linguistically competent.

The only readily available evidence regarding the situation in

Japan concerns individual cases, from which it is conjectured that foreign prisoners do suffer greater deprivation in the *daiyō kangoku*. Lawyers point in particular to the psychological component of total isolation from the outside world as a factor increasing the deprivation suffered by foreign 'birdcage' inmates (cf. OBK, 1991: 51). For example, a Pakistani claimed that he was beaten up by three Japanese inmates (Matsunaga, 1990: 143). As a rule, 'illegal' foreigners do not have the required financial resources and personal connections to arrange for legal counsel. Their networks on the 'outside' are often limited to 'illegal' compatriots, who naturally shun any contact with the prisoner on trial, due to their fear of expulsion. Thus foreign suspects are totally isolated. During visits the use of their mother tongue is often prohibited (Ebashi, 1989: 5). This amounts to a ban on visits from fellow nationals (Yonekura and Ebashi, 1989: 9).

By virtue of international law, foreign prisoners on remand have the right to inform relatives of their whereabouts and to inform the embassy or consulate of their home country. Police in Osaka claim that they hand out information fliers in Japanese and English to suspects and inform the official representatives of the prisoner's home country if the prisoner wishes it. But given prisoners' diverse nationalities, lawyers criticize the provision of information in only two languages as grossly inadequate (OBK, 1991: 31). In one case which came to the attention of a lawyer, a Pakistani was forced by the police to sign a declaration that he would not inform his embassy. His legal right to an attorney was also obstructed by police who cited the high costs of legal representation (Matsunaga, 1990: 147). In the case of an American citizen who was arrested for a drug offence, a member of the U.S. embassy staff was prevented from seeing the prisoner by police who (falsely) said that the suspect did not want to talk to him. The provision of legal counsel was also delayed for a considerable time. The U.S. Embassy later filed an official complaint with the Japanese Ministry of Justice (Yabe, 1991: 18). In such ways the prisoner's contact with the outside world is greatly restricted. Two members of the bar reported a case of violence and intimidation by police against a foreigner and subsequently remarked that, at a crucial stage of criminal justice procedure – investigation and interrogation by police – private legal counsel is virtually unobtainable for foreigners. Police also fail to adequately respect the suspect's right to have the relevant embassy informed (Yonekura and Ikoma, 1989:

7f.). Similar complaints were made in a discussion between concerned lawyers. They described the case of a Pakistani who was
not informed of his right to remain silent. Another foreign suspect
who demanded a lawyer was told this would involve enormous
expenditure. Police prevented any attempt to contact the Bar
Association. In most cases, a suspect's relatives are still in their
own home country. The isolation of prisoners in police custody
facilitated the use of psycho-physical torture with the goal of
extorting confessions from them (Okazaki, 1989: 35f.). The inter-
nationally-guaranteed right to remain silent during questioning
has to be read at the time of arrest. The suspect must also be told
the grounds for arrest. Neither requirement was met in a case in
which nine Philippinos were arrested. Lawyers assume that this
group-arrest was made only because the police wanted to trace
a labour-agent organization and to obtain information for that
investigation (a classic case of *bekken taiho* – apprehension for
reasons other than stated by the police). Protracted periods of
interrogation, insufficient interpretation, menacing gestures and
physical violence on the part of the investigating officers, were
also severely criticized in this discussion (cf. FRSTJB, 1990).

Sometimes serious degradation of prisoners occurs during interrogation by police. A Pakistani was called an idiot (*bakayarō*) and
a pig (*buta*). The latter is a grave insult to a Muslim (Odagiri,
1990: 157). In the case of a Bangladeshi, a police officer pushed
his thumb into the pit behind the suspect's ear while questioning
him. This caused severe pain and the suspect shouted 'Ouch!
Allah!'. The interpreting (!) policeman yelled at him: 'Call me
Allah, I am Allah!' – for a Muslim a grave blasphemy (Matsunaga,
1990: 146). An Afro-American was confronted with a racist stereotype. First of all, he was called an 'American slave', and police
shouted at him that he should confess and sign the protocol. He
refused on the grounds that he could not read the Japanese text.
Subsequently his stomach and genitals were beaten. When he
wanted to go to the bathroom he was prevented from doing so.
A police held a ruler and remarked: 'It is said that Negroes have
big penises. Is that true?' The suspect felt humiliated. A pamphlet
by the Police Academy intended as a guideline for the treatment
of foreign suspects to be used by all investigating officers, was also
full of racist prejudices. In regard to Pakistanis, it read: 'Among
Pakistanis there are many with an (endemic) cutaneous disease.
After arresting and after questioning it is imperative to wash one's

hands. Due to their particular body odour, the interrogation room and detention cells become malodorous . . .' (cited in Yabe, 1991: 21).[11]

The psychologically and physiologically 'insensitive and harsh methods' of the police are exemplified in the attitude expressed by an investigating officer addressing two foreign defendants of a Japanese lawyer: 'You came to Japan to commit a crime [or misdeed – *omaera wa Nihon ni warui koto o shi ni kite iru n da*]. Because people of your kind come here, Japan's [safety] deteriorates' (Okazaki, 1989: 36). Police violence during arrest and interrogation is repeatedly publicized by journalists. An American citizen allegedly was beaten and kicked by three policemen and suffered after-effects of the injuries. However, it is very difficult to successfully claim state compensation because the *onus probandi* is on the plaintiff (the lawyer Ōnuki Kensuke, in Yabe, 1991: 19). Two other jurists tell of a Bangladeshi who complained about police threats and violence. From the remarks of the investigating officers and the brutality of their 'treatment' of the suspect it was inferred that these illicit tactics were used precisely because the accused was a foreigner (Yonekura and Ebashi, 1989: 8).

The experience of imprisonment on remand in the *daiyō kangoku* is described by foreigners as 'frightening'. Many sign a 'deposition of confession' out of exhaustion and resignation. 'I was scared' (a Pakistani, suspected of larceny), 'It was frightful' (a Pakistani, suspected of larceny), 'I just answered the police at random' (a Philippino, suspected of robbery, homicide and arson), 'I was over-fatigued and said to police: "Write what you want" ' – these are some comments made by foreign *daiyō kangoku* inmates. The police in these cases were said to have used various 'conventional' methods also, such as 'calming-coaxing', 'moralizing persuasion', and so on, to obtain confessions (cf. Takahaski, 1989a: 103).

7.7.3 Arresting practices

Foreign suspects, because of their legal status and living conditions, are in a disadvantageous position with regard to arrest. If they have changed domicile often (for example, while lodging in hotels), 'address or residence unknown' can readily be given as reason for detention. 'Danger of flight' (to a foreign country) is also an easily fabricated justification for 'securing' the person in custody. In the case of a Chinese woman who actually was permanently resident in Japan, it was stated: 'The suspect is a foreigner and it is considered that she could flee'. The public prosecutor thus deemed her foreign nationality a sufficient reason for imprisonment on remand (cf. OBK, 1991: 59f.). Bail conditions for foreigners are considerably more costly than for Japanese (OBK, 1991: 58f.); release on bail is therefore not a realistic option for 'illegal' migrants.

Foreigners who stay 'illegally' in Japan can be arrested on the spot by virtue of their illegal residence status. Lawyers object that here the principle of warrant of arrest is totally undercut and loses its function. Police can place any conspicuous or 'suspicious' foreigner in custody if he or she cannot produce a proper visa. Arrest for 'illegal stay' is sometimes made use of so that other presumptive offences may be investigated. This practice, known as *bekken taiho* (arrest for investigation into matters other than given as reason for apprehension), has been criticized by members of the bar for its use with respect both to foreign and to Japanese suspects. For instance, a Thai national was apprehended for 'illegal stay' and questioned in the police lock-up for twenty-three days concerning the trafficking of hashish. Through lack of evidence, the indictment on the alleged drug dealing had to be dropped and the Thai was put on trial for 'illegal stay' only (Ōnuki, 1990b: 44f.). In a district-court sentence in Urawa, the intention behind the use of *bekken taiho* in the case of two foreigners arrested for 'illegal residence' but investigated on suspicion of arson, was branded 'problematic'. The investigations regarding these suspects' illegal stay concluded in three days, while the remaining period of detention was used by police to investigate the suspected arson. The court also noted that it was obvious that, in principle, cases of illegal stay could be dealt with administratively – without need for arraignment and criminal procedure (cf. OBK, 1991: 26f.).

According to the law, at the time of arrest police must inform the arrested person of the reasons for their apprehension. However, if there is a warrant of arrest, its contents often cannot be read or understood by foreign suspects, because no translation is attached. In cases of provisional arrest – when somebody is 'caught in the act' (as may be the case of 'illegal stay') – the reason for apprehension also has to be given. But because of their lack of linguistic competence, foreign suspects often do not sufficiently understand this verbal notification. The situation is the same when they are brought before a police-jurist or an investigating judge. Some cases came to the notice of attorneys in which the defendants did not know the offence they were charged with until the first visit of a lawyer, or even not until after being sentenced (OBK, 1991: 24f.).

7.7.4 The lack of legal counsel for foreign suspects

The assignment of an attorney for 'illegal' foreigners is beset with difficulties, due to their lack of social capital. As a rule, only after arraignment is a public defender (*kokusen bengoshi*) appointed for foreign defendants. According to a poll among members of the bar in Osaka who had worked on cases involving foreign nationals (altogether, eighty-eight cases), sixty-nine attorneys were active as court-appointed lawyers. In only seventeen cases had they worked as privately-assigned legal counsel, and in just ten cases were they appointed (all private legal counsel) before the indictment (OBK, 1991: 8). Commonly 'illegal' foreign suspects have no legal counsel during investigations by the police. The assignment of a (public) defender after arraignment is often too late. In many petty-offence cases, solutions could have been arranged out of court, through suspension of procedure, summary procedure, or fine.

The journalist Takahashi Hidemine often observed 'sloppy' and insufficiently-prepared work by lawyers in cases involving foreigners. He advances the assigned counsel system as a structural reason for this. Cases of foreigners are shunned even by public defenders because they are troublesome, involve difficulties of language (interpretation), and offer only low remuneration. They are therefore often taken by aged and otherwise under-engaged lawyers (cf. Takahaski, 1989b: 104ff.). In Osaka I personally got to know a seventy-nine-year-old lawyer who was hard of hearing and who was actually retired. He was often 'mobilized' in court as public defender, mostly in cases of nationals of the Philippines, thanks to his (low) command of the English language. In one such case, which I followed during the spring of 1990 at the district court Osaka (the indictment of a Philippina for infringement of the Immigration Control Act and Foreigners Registration Law), his questions at the court hearing were almost the same as those of the public prosecutor. Eventually the sentence demanded by the prosecutor was handed down. Niwa Masao, an attorney concerned with the human rights of migrant workers, cynically commented that a (public) defender was a requisite for legally-prescribed due process, and the old lawyer had fulfilled his decorative function (*kazarimono*). The journalist Takahashi notes that it was not rare for court-appointed lawyers to suddenly pop up at the trial without ever having visited their foreign client in custody (Takahashi, 1989a: 104).

7.7.5 'Illegality' as stigma

We should not let those injustices of the criminal justice system in Japan and their encroachments on the human rights of foreign suspects, cause us to lose sight of the fact that these publicized deficiencies in Japanese legal procedure are of general nature and pertain also to Japanese suspects. But in the case of foreigners, the situation is exacerbated and the general problematic situation appears in concentrated form (cf. the lawyers, Seno, 1989: 15, and Okazaki, 1989: 34). If police violence is more common against Asian suspects than against Japanese, this cannot be established through a few known individual cases. It may be assumed, however, that adamant denial of guilt, as in the case of a Pakistani who was slapped in the face by a police officer when he asked for a glass of water, could provoke police violence (Matsunaga, 1990: 147f.). And as far as 'illegal' foreigners are concerned, it may be surmised – and confirmed by a reading of research papers by the police – that pre-definition of foreign suspects as 'violators of the law' (that is, of the Immigration Control Act) shapes and distorts police perception of them.

Here contravention of administrative regulations is assimilated to an offence under the penal code, blurring the assumption of innocence (*in dubio pro reo*) and making it difficult for the accused to negotiate a non-deviant identity. The automatic pre-identification of an apprehended foreign suspect as 'criminal' which dominates police perception is exacerbated by the 'illegal' status of foreign migrants. The term 'illegal' (*fuhō*) attached to the stay and activities of Asian migrant workers becomes a dominant or master status (a stigma) which overshadows their whole existence. The possession of a deviant attribute can be of symbolic value. People automatically impute a wide range of undesirable attributes on the basis of one deviant attribute – here 'illegality' with regard to residence and work (on stigma theories, see Becker, 1973: 29, or Goffman, 1993: 77). 'Illegal existence' (Mishima, 1988: 98) therefore implies connotations suggesting other forms of 'illegal' or criminal activities. Consequently, intellectuals and movements for the human rights of Asian migrants call for the 'de-criminalization' and 'de-categorization' of the notion 'illegal' in connection with work and residence of Asian migrants in Japan. The label 'illegal' laid the foundation for 'pre-modern conditions of exploitation' and infringements of human rights (Nishitani, 1990: 134). This 'illegality' made legal claims and insistence on one's rights precarious and difficult. It was urgent that an amnesty for *undocumented workers* be offered, so as to guarantee their basic rights (Watanabe, 1990a: 153). To be precise, one should speak here of 'illegalization', because the irregular situation could be changed by the stroke of a pen through either amnesty or regularization. Indeed

> the [UN] General Assembly adopted Resolution 3449 (XXX) in 1975, in which it called on the UN system to use, in official documents, the term 'non-documented or irregular migrant workers' to define those workers who illegally or surreptitiously enter another country to obtain work (Böhning, 1984: 268).

Both suggested terms remain imprecise, but have fewer 'criminal' connotations.

> The terminology used here seeks to use neutral words and objectively verifiable notions in place of the value-laden and sometimes downright pejorative terms that dominate the discussion. Not every foreigner looked upon as 'illegal' has committed an unlawful act under public law, nor are unlawful acts necessarily committed clandestinely, and what is done clandestinely need not be illegal (Böhning, 1984: 268).

My own use of the notion 'illegal' has no stigmatizing intention; I employ the term (in quotation marks) because it dominates the Japanese discussion and reflects the current legal situation in Japan.

One factor contingent on being a foreigner, however, brings migrant workers into a position in which their competence in action and negotiating power with agencies of social control are considerably restricted. It is the problem of the language, which accompanies foreign labourers through all stages of legal procedure.

7.7.6 The language barrier

Poor interpretation is continually almost ritually bemoaned by lawyers. Police, attorneys and courts all call for concrete measures to improve the situation. Inadequate interpreting has grave consequences for foreign suspects, particularly at the stage of police investigation. Questioning by police usually 'condenses' in a protocol of interrogation. The protocol is then 'recycled' and cited in court without its reliability being contested. It subsequently serves as 'evidence'. Therefore a reform of the interpretation practices is of utmost priority, especially at the stage of police interrogation (cf. Okazaki, 1990: 48). A lawyer has expressed the suspicion that interrogation protocols are readily drawn up in Japanese by police even when the suspect speaks only limited Japanese (Odagiri, 1990: 48).

Particularly dubious is the role of police officers who act as interpreters and are well-placed to abet the manufacture of 'stories' that will bring investigations to successful conclusions (that, is convictions). Moreover, illicit methods of police interrogation can be covered up (Okazaki, 1989: 39). The qualifications of interpreting police officers are contested. A Pakistani who insisted on his innocence, asserted that he could not understand the 'police-English': even in simple passages of the protocol mistakes of translation abound (Matsunaga, 1990: 140f.). One case, publicized as the 'patrol/petrol mix-up case', became well-known among members of the bar. It is often quoted as a paradigmatic illustration of the police predilection for 'fictive stories'. One of several Pakistani suspects on robbery charges declared that he had to refill gasoline (petrol) into his vehicle's tank and therefore drove to a gasoline station. For that reason he got to the scene (of the crime) too late to have perpetrated the crime. The word 'petrol' obviously was not understood by the interpreting police officer. He noted in the interrogation protocol that the suspect met a police patrol and turned off into a small by-street. That was the reason for the man's delay. This serves as a clear example of police fabricating stories (see, for example, Okazaki, 1980: 38, or Sawa, 1990: 53). The unconscious transformation of 'petrol' into the police term 'patrol' illuminates the categorically preoccupied way of police thinking. Another attorney worked on the case of a Bangladeshi who did not speak English. The police nonetheless manufactured a detailed 'deposition of confession', because they deemed English the 'official language' of the suspect's home country. The deposition contained incorrect statements, even concerning personal data (Ōnuki, 1990b: 45). A Norwegian suspect who received 'interpreting assistance' by a police officer asserted that he could not understand the officer's poor English. Several members of the bar reported in answer to open questions of the poll by the Osaka Bar Association that the mother tongue of the accused is often 'ignored'. For 'reasons of simplicity', questioning is performed in English. Cited were the cases of a German and of a Philippine national, both with low command of English, whose interrogation protocols contained manufactured false statements (OBK, 1991: 33f.).

The hearing of witnesses in court is also fraught with difficulties. Often important witnesses for the defence are not present. This is the case particularly when they, like the accused are in Japan 'illegally', and fail to appear because they fear legal proceedings (that is, for their repatriation). On the other hand, it can happen that fellow nationals of the defendant are over-co-operative with police in giving testimony, in the hope of dodging legal proceedings and expulsion by co-operating with police wishes. If foreign witnesses are deported after they have given testimony they cannot be subpoenaed again, and so examination or verification of the contents of their deposition is hardly possible (Ebashi, 1990: 43). In one case it is reported that police took away the passport of an 'illegal' Philippino witness and took him to the police station with the promise that they would not inform the Immigration Control Bureau if he complied. He was coerced to testify in conformity with the charges brought forward by police, that is, to give evidence against the suspect. The journalist who described this case stated that police always interrogated (foreign) witnesses along the lines of their own preoccupations (a crude generalization which possibly is not true; cf. Takahashi, 1990: 86).

The police legitimize functioning as interpreters with the claim that a certain amount of legal knowledge and 'understanding of interrogation techniques' (!) were requisite to interpret correctly. For that reason, it is deemed important that police officers be trained in use of foreign languages and that police interpreters be recruited (Mishima, 1988: 97). A police-linked study notes that in court it is the judge not the accused, who decides whether there shall be an interpreter or not. Where there are complications (as when an interpreter for a Thai national could not be found), the hearing may be performed in English if the accused speaks and understands this language. This was not 'unlawful'. By analogy from these 'precedents', the authors of the study infer that the same holds true for police investigations (Kitamura and Hayakawa, 1989: 26).

Police data show that English is the predominant language for interrogation of foreigners. The data, from an internal police research project conducted in 1987, indicate that, of 3,745 foreign suspects (all of them *rainichi gaikokujin*), 1,521 were interrogated exclusively in Japanese. Roughly three-quarters of the remaining 2,224 cases were handled by interpreting police officers; only in 25.1 per cent of cases was a civil interpreter commissioned. Analysis according to languages reveals that there is a clear preference for English over the mother tongue of the suspect. English was used for questioning in 67.5 per cent of cases (Kitamura and Hayakawa, 1989: 32). The data, with their marked over-representation of Asian suspects (according to police figures they comprised 82.6 per cent of apprehended foreigners in 1987, cf. Mishima, 1988: 88), lend support to the conclusion that English is used for pragmatic reasons. Lawyers, however, appealing to human rights conventions, claim the suspect has a right to be provided with an interpreter of his or her mother-tongue, free of charge. In the case of 'minority' languages particularly (for example, Tagalog), English is forced upon the suspect. This dependence on police officers who act as interpreters is further increased, especially as internal education in languages is strongly promoted (Seno, 1989: 13f.). Poorly-qualified police officers, interpreting for (or rather, 'against') the suspect in a language (usually English) other than the suspect's mother tongue, and of which the suspect too has a poor command, is indeed a dubious and highly problematic phenomenon. In cases of uncommon languages (for example, Urdu, Bengali, Tagalog) the number of potential interpreters is inadequate. The police data cited above are self-denouncing, and even their attempts at legitimation cannot remove the suspicion that the police question and hear foreign suspects according to what they see as being in the interests of their investigation. For reasons of procedural rationale and police 'success' – orientation (obtaining confessions), the right of suspects to use their mother tongue, and the need to provide neutral interpreters, are widely ignored.

When a civil interpreter is commissioned, the situation does not necessarily improve. First of all, there is the danger that the interpreter readily accepts police pre-definitions of the circumstances (the interrogated suspect is 'criminal' and 'guilty'). Moreover, there is often a considerable disparity of social status between the suspect and the interpreter. This makes mutual understanding difficult because of different class-specific sociolects, and because of psychological differences resulting from social class asymmetry (feelings of superiority and inferiority). These difficulties can serve to make the interpreter an 'accomplice' of the investigating agencies rather than a neutral language-mediator (cf. Seno, 1989: 12). Again the qualifications of interpreters are disputed. Non-professionals such as students, women with Japanese partners, spouses of trade commissioners, or businessmen stationed in Japan, are assigned to interpret, which they do casually and in their spare time. Frequently they do not have sufficient judicial and legal knowledge (of, for example, special legal terms). Interpreting for the police and in court calls for particular precision. Even nuances can be vital to the sentence given. Foreign suspects here are in a precarious position. In one case the police protocol said of a larceny suspect from the Philippines that she had been under correctional guidance (*hodō sareta*) in her childhood. The examination of the attorney revealed that she had merely said that she was picked up and protected by police (*hogo sareta*) when she got lost in the crowd as a child. The connotations of misconduct attaching to the term *hodō* could have insinuated that she had had a delinquent career, which could have led to a more severe sentence (Takahashi, 1989a: 103f.).

A private attorney visiting a suspect in police custody must pay fees for interpreting out of his or her own pocket, or charge them to the defendant. After the trial, the court settles the expenses in a case in which a court-appointed attorney had been engaged to visit the defendant. Suspects have reasons to demand that high expenses do not prevent them from interaction with their lawyers via interpreters (OBK, 1991: 50f.). Language problems, of course, extend into the court. Again, the poor qualifications of court interpreters, the use of other languages than the accused's mother tongue, dual translations (from the mother tongue into English and then into Japanese), and sometimes the circumstance that the same person interprets during all stages of criminal procedure (police interrogation, consultation with the lawyer, prosecutional investigation, and court hearing) all have been criticized. In the last-mentioned circumstance, it is hard for the suspect during legal proceedings to correct or revoke statements made previously (and possibly under pressure) during police interrogation (see OBK, 1991: 39–50). Spectacular blunders of court interpretation are reported; for example, the confusion of 'police' and 'prosecutor' in a case which was to have been negotiated in Tagalog, but which the judge declared was to proceed in English when the 'interpreter' was found insufficiently fluent in Tagalog (Takahashi, 1989a: 102). Written notices (warrant of arrest, cause for detention stated by the investigating judge, indictment) are delivered to foreign suspects, but are not translated into their mother tongue because this is not required by the Japanese Code of Penal Procedure. With regard to the written indictment, district and supreme court decisions in 1990 deemed it 'unnecessary' that a translation into a foreign language be attached. Here, again, lawyers demand expeditious redress and reform (cf. OBK, 1991: 24, 31f. and 60ff.).

The Japanese authorities are aware of all of these language problems and attempt to alleviate them in various ways. The Metropolitan Police Office established an 'interpretation centre' (*tsūyaku sentā*) of police officers who have a command of foreign languages. The police also promote internal language training in 'unusual' idioms (Thai, Urdu, and so forth) (Keisatsuchō, 1990: 70).

Bar Associations endeavour to draw up their own 'lists of interpreters' so as to be independent of court interpreters and so that lawyers can communicate freely with their clients. Moreover, better training and qualifications for interpreters (including instruction in the fundamentals of Japanese criminal procedure) and relief regarding costs are demanded (cf. OBK, 1991: 86f.; and KBR, 1990: 225).

District courts have developed their own resources for interpreting, establishing internal registers of interpreters. At the district court in Tokyo, for instance, roughly fifty interpreters for twenty-one languages are registered. All of them were put onto the list by 'recommendation'. Their fees are said to be low. In 1987 113 cases in need of interpreters were tried at this court; by 1989 the number had grown to 259. It is doubtful whether, in future, the present number of interpreters will suffice (cf. Takahashi, 1989a: 101f.). It moreover remains questionable whether the qualifications of the interpreting personnel are adequate for competence in this sensitive field. The neutrality of interpreters is also a moot point. Members of the bar call for tape-recordings (which could also be referred to in case of appeals) and use of the American model of a 'check system'. A 'checking-interpreter' should act as 'language-solicitor' and be present at court hearings in order to object in case of misinterpretation. The legality and adequacy of police interrogation should also be opened to scrutiny by use of tape recordings (see, for example, Seno, 1989: 12; Okazaki, 1989: 12; Ebashi, 1990: 42, OBK, 1991: 42).

Thus it is recognized that 'interpreting is the most demanding problem in criminal procedure for foreigners' (OBK, 1991: 86) and concrete measures should be taken. The involvement of police in interpreting remains highly dubious, because it is closely linked with police interests and presumptions. Interpreting by police reinforces the structures inherent in coerced communication. The intended 'conversion' of the suspect (in which the suspect is to accept police definitions and sign an incriminatory protocol) is facilitated by subtly transforming the suspect's statements into the vocabulary of criminal law and police jargon. This interlingual communication transmutes the investigated facts of the case and weakens the suspect's negotiating ability. The constructed findings and 'facts', once fixed in an interrogation protocol drawn up by police, accompany the accused as incriminatory evidence into court. There those 'facts' are again subject to interpretation and court requirements. These constellations clearly disadvantage foreign suspects, compounding the 'illegality' of their situation.

7.8 Indictment Rates and Adjudication

It is notable that Japanese court statistics do not use the police category of *rainichi gaikokujin*. A strict collation of police input (suspects and alleged offences) and court output (verdicts and sentences) using official data is not feasible. The statistics on criminal procedure and arraignment classify foreigners as *zainichi gaikokujin*, a category which includes also those permanently residing in Japan. These statistics appear in the *Kensatsu tōkei*

nenpō ('Statistical Annual Report of the Prosecutors Office'),
edited by the Ministry of Justice (which was made accessible to
me by the lawyer Niwa Masao). Selections from these figures are
publicized in the annual *Whitebook on Crime* (*Hanzai hakusho*).
A comparison of those foreigners regarded as 'suspects' by police
and those definitely found guilty was possible only after analysis
of the figures by nationality (the police, at least up to 1990, did
not publish such data). In the following, I rely both on my own
interpretations of the data and on the work of a research group
examining the sentences given to *rainichi*-foreigners, the Gaikokujin no ryōkei mondai kenkyūkai.

7.8.1 Indictment risk and suspension of procedure

A closer look at indictment practices reveals that foreign suspects
have a dramatically higher risk of being indicted than do Japanese
suspects, even in cases of petty offences. The latter cases, known
as *bizai kiso* (indictment on petty law violations) are strongly
criticized by lawyers. Well-known cases are repeatedly cited. A
Chinese studying the Japanese language was caught in the act of
shoplifting (one lipstick). She had no criminal record but was put
on trial after two months of custody. A Philippine student stole
two compact discs in a supermarket. He was also tried after two
months of imprisonment on remand. In both cases, the perpetrators were first-offenders without previous conviction. There
was no effective damage, because the goods were returned on the
spot. Both cases, therefore, were of a sort which can be dealt with
informally (*bizai shobun*: no criminal record, low damages, first
offence). Japanese suspects could have expected not to be
arraigned or charged in similar cases. Another case, in which
extenuating circumstances could have been taken into account, is
also frequently cited: A Chinese student, after suffering a long
period of pneumonia and because he could not work, became
destitute. Hoping to find some food in it, he took a rucksack from
the trunk of a car. This resulted in his indictment (see Yonekura
and Ikoma, 1989: 9; OBK 1991: 65f.; and Ōnuki, 1990a: 92ff.). A
journalist lists some other incidents which could easily have been
handled with summary procedure (fines) without formal criminal
proceedings, but which instead came to arraignment: a Pakistani
who took a knife from his pocket in front of several people, but
made no attempt to intimidate, harm or rob anybody; a Pakistani

who drank two beers without paying and who then attempted to steal a jacket; a case of attempted larceny of three pairs of trousers by a Chinese national; and a Chinese who tried to take a package of *sashimi* (sliced raw fish) without paying for it (Takahashi, 1989: 105).

The Japanese Code of Criminal Procedure follows the principle of discretion; for example, the public prosecutor's office is author-ized to exercise discretion in deciding whether or not to pursue a particular offence through the courts. This is in contrast to the principle of legality which operates, for example, in Germany and Austria, and which obliges the prosecutor's office to bring to trial every offence which comes to its attention. The significance of the principle of discretion for Japan can be seen in the fact that more than three-quarters of proceedings quashed by the prosecutor's office were dismissed on the grounds of discretion (Bindzus and Ishii, 1977: 28). It is held that in cases involving *rainichi gaikokujin*, this 'discretion' is interpreted in a negative way, leading to indict-ment and petitions for custody (*bizai kōryū*, imprisonment for petty offences), at least in the courts of Tokyo and Yokohama. Since 1989, indictments for offences causing damages up to 10,000 yen (in particular, shoplifting by foreigners) have sharply risen (whereas between 1984 and 1987 only three verdicts were passed for such offences; cf. Ōnuki, 1990b: 45f., who also describes the earlier-mentioned standard examples of *bizai kiso* of foreigners). Examples of 'inadequate' arraignments are also found in Osaka. A Korean national (with a tourist visa) who was drunk and lost his way, was put on trial for trespassing. To 'orient' himself, he had climbed onto the roof of a house. The police arrested him and locked him up. Efforts by his lawyer to come to an out-of-court solution were fruitless, and he was indicted and convicted. Another case involved a Philippina (with a tourist visa and no criminal record), who took food worth slightly more than 10,000 yen from a supermarket on a 'spontaneous impulse'. She too was put on trial (OBK 1991: 64f.).

According to information given by police officer Mishima Tetsu with regard to offences against property committed by *rainichi gaikokujin*, in all such cases formal proceedings are instituted by the public prosecutor's office. On the other hand, roughly one-third of all offences against property committed by Japanese were dealt with 'informally' by police and handled as minor offences (*bizai shobun*) according to data for 1985 (offences of juveniles are excluded from calculation; see GNRMK, 1990: 165). A similar statement is made by a prosecutor. He declared, following an appeal by the bar, that all Asian suspects are sent to trial (Ōnuki, 1990a: 94). A journalist citing a lawyer writes that, with regard to *rainichi gaikokujin*, virtually all offences are handed over to the prosecutor and are tried (Matsunaga, 1990: 148). From these statements we may infer that there is a tendency for formal proceedings (usually resulting in court sentences) to be instituted against Asian suspects, even for summary offences. The likelihood of suspects being indicted corroborates this supposition.

Data from Tokyo in 1985 show that for 43 per cent of offences against property, no indictment followed at the district court of Tokyo. For Philippine nationals, only in 38.3 per cent of cases was indictment suspended. British subjects (for the most part Chinese from Hong Kong) were not prosecuted in roughly one-third of cases. However, the rate of prosecution of first-offender *rainichi gaikokujin* (77.3 per cent) is significantly higher than that of Japanese (36.7 per cent). For this reason, we should compare the indictment-rate of foreigners with that of Japanese first offenders, in whose case up to 60 per cent of charges are dealt with without indictment (GNRMK, 1990: 165 and 170). A further double standard, which can only be interpreted as crude discrimination, is revealed by the disparity between the indictment rates for larceny for American and Philippine nationals collated over a period of thirteen years: on average, 14.3 per cent of American nationals compared with 41.7 per cent of Philippine nationals, were sent to trial; indeed in 1984, Americans were tried in only 17.1 per cent of larceny cases, while the rate for Philippine nationals was 71 per cent) (tables in Takahashi, 1989d: 95). Analogous calculations were made by the Bar Association of Osaka about the situation in the Osaka area on the same bases using data from the *Kensatsu tōkei nenpō* covering a period of three years (1987–1989) for offences against property and for assault and battery. It consistently emerges that the rate of suspension of formal procedures for all of those charged (mostly Japanese, and in 1989 around one-fifth with criminal records) is slightly lower than for foreign suspects (except for U.S. nationals) and is significantly lower than for Chinese. But it has to be taken into consideration that the first-offender rate for foreigners is much higher and hence skews the data, inflating the rate for foreigners. While there are large fluctuations in rates for foreigners over the years of calculation (due to low base figures), there is some significance in the decrease in the rates of quashed prosecutions for offences against property committed by *rainichi*-foreigners. This is clearest for Chinese nationals, with the rate decreasing from 62.7 per cent in 1987 to 40.8 per cent in 1989; whereas the rate of stay of prosecution for the total of all charged was 44.5 per cent in 1987 and 44.6 per cent in 1989. This decrease for foreigners correlates with the increasing number of foreigners entering Japan, and with the subsequent characterization of this irregular migration as a 'social problem' (comment in OBK, 1991: 68).

The computed data on Osaka concerning offences against property present the following picture of the rates for suspension of indictment for all of those charged: 44.6 per cent; for first-offenders: 63.5 per cent; for US-nationals: 69.4 per cent; for Koreans (including *zainichi*): 39.6 per cent; for Chinese: 40.8 per cent; for Philippine nationals: 52.1 per cent (OBK, 1991: 66–9). The data presented here cannot be interpreted cogently – not only because possible previous convictions were not considered, but also because the categories are vague. For example, there are very few US nationals staying or working 'illegally' in Japan, whereas it may be assumed that for Philippine nationals the proportion of 'illegals' is much higher. Another flaw in the data is the inclusion of *zainichi* in the computation for Korean nationals. Thus, as is the case with police data, these data cannot be assumed to be representative for charged 'illegal' migrant workers. Moreover, the Bar Association tabulated suspension of indictment (*kiso yūyo*) *in sensu strictu* (*kyōgi*), that is, only for charges backed up by 'reasonable suspicion'. The journalist Takahashi, however, based his calculation on all charges taken up by the prosecutor's office, so that suspension of procedure here is correctly termed *fukiso* – non-indictment (personal information from lawyer Niwa Masao, 22 July 1992). The Bar Associations's findings therefore do not reflect what happened at the level of police action. Japanese suspects are likely to 'get away' without the intervention of the next level of social control (this is accounted a distorting factor, cf. OBK, 1991: 68). Nevertheless, the tables show that Asian suspects are less likely to have proceedings against them quashed.

Lawyers assume a background preoccupation with general prevention. This presumption is often evident in the concluding speeches of prosecutors at court hearings. It also mirrors the presupposition that a tight grasp on Asian suspects is needed in order to maintain public security (OBK, 1991: 69). A collation of the data above lends support to the conclusion that Asian *rainichi-*foreigners in particular are indicted significantly more often than Japanese for the same offences (holding the variable 'criminal record' constant). When one further considers that foreign suspects are more likely to be formally prosecuted for minor offences, and that suspension of prosecution of foreigners is not significantly more likely for petty and casual offences, the picture of a discriminatory judiciary becomes even sharper.

7.8.2 Cases of indictment because of 'illegal overstay'

Besides contraventions of the Penal Code, foreign suspects often run foul of the requirements of the Aliens' Laws statutorily defined in special law (*tokubetsu hōhan*) – the Immigration Control and Refugee Recognition Act (*shutsunyūkoku kanri oyobi nanmin ninteihō*, abbreviated to *nyūkanhō*) and the Aliens' Registration Act (*gaikokujin tōrokuhō*, shortened to *gaitōhō*). Naturally these Aliens' Laws cannot be contravened by Japanese nationals. They do, however, figure in the repressive treatment of foreigners, reinforcing the impression that foreigners are particularly 'criminally inclined'. Even a police-linked study concedes that the most important factor in the increased number of law violations committed by foreigners is 'premeditated, illegal' stay and 'illegal' work (Yashima, 1989: 19). In Osaka, of ninety-seven charges against foreigners brought to trial (presumably including some multiple tabulations) and which were handled by lawyers, fifty-one were contraventions of the Aliens' Acts and only twenty-one were offences against property (OBK, 1991: 7).[12] If one tabulates a national data set by nationality, the following picture emerges. In 1988, out of 397 charges (266 concerning the Penal Code, 131 special law) involving U.S. citizens leading to court intervention, only thirty-five touched upon the Aliens' Acts (and only four were infringements of the *nyūkanhō*). There were 434 charges against Philippine nationals in the same year, only 110 of which were for violations of the Penal Code, while 324 were for contraventions of special law. Of the latter, 264 pertained to the Aliens' Acts (174 to the *nyūkanhō*). The same pattern shows up for Thai nationals: 186 violations altogether, twenty of them pertaining to criminal law and 166 to special law – 120 of the latter being violations of the *nyūkanhō* (data from Hōmusho, 1989:

200f.). Indictments of foreigners for contravention of the Aliens' Acts clearly harm the public image of Asian 'illegal' foreigners. A closer analysis is not possible, because of the vague categories used by the Ministry of Justice to register convictions of foreigners. Korean and Chinese nationals are included in the category of long-term residents (*zainichi*). Moreover, for many nationalities the absolute figures for other offences are too small to allow a conclusive collation. Most of the violations of the Aliens' Acts by Korean and Chinese nationals are 'insubordination', which can be seen from their high proportion of the total, 77.7 per cent of all offences against the Aliens' Acts being committed by Koreans (including 1,265 violations of the *gaitōhō* in 1988).

In December 1989, the amendment of the *nyūkanhō* passed through parliament and was speedily enacted. It came into force on 1 June 1990. The revision can be read as a declaration in response to the debate on 'illegal' foreign labour. It provides no legal status for so-called 'unskilled' or 'unqualified' foreign labour. It does, however, stiffen sanctions and penalties against the activities of labour agents and employers of 'illegals'. Coinciding with the passing of the newly-created law, indictments for contravention of the *nyūkanhō* increased (for example, for 'illegal stay' – *fuhō zanryū* – aptly called 'overstay' by the migrants). Until this time these contraventions were handled as trivial offences (*bizai*) and dealt with by administrative measures (expulsion). Paralleling the tightened grip on foreigners, trials on for Aliens' Law violations increased in number, in order to 'deter' and 'expel' 'illegal' migrants (cf. *Mainichi shinbun*, 17 March 1990).

Usually the public prosecutor's office draws a line at two years overstay when deciding whether to indict or not. There are, however, cases in which, after shorter extensions of a tourist visa, arraignment followed (the case is cited of a Philippine national who 'overstayed' one year and four months). It might be thought that in future every case of overstay will be tried. However, this does not seem feasible administratively. International trends of de-criminalization entail that petty offences of the Penal Code increasingly be handled with administrative regulations. Developments arising from the *nyūkanhō* run counter to these trends.

Indictment for *fuhō zanryū* is easy because evidence is mostly clear. The bill of indictment usually states, in cases of more than two years overstay, that the violation was premeditated and 'of vicious nature' (*akushitsu*). Indictments mainly serve as deterrence and as exemplary punishment (cf. the discussion panel of members of the bar in FRSTJB, 1990: 141–145). It can be said that trials and expulsions are meant to 'visibly' demonstrate the validity of the norms regarding a 'legal' stay. I monitored two court hearings in Osaka during the summer of 1990. Both cases involved Philippine nationals overstaying four years and four-and-a-half years respectively. They were put on trial for violations of the *nyūkanhō* and of the *gaitōhō*. These reputedly were the first trials in Osaka for both contraventions simultaneously. The sentences were rather stiff: one year and one-and-a-half-years imprisonment with hard labour respectively, suspended for three years. This automatically led to the (intended) deportation. In one case (Rita Lopez, alias 'Miki', born 25 November 1969; trial: 26 June 1990; verdict and sentence: 3 July 1990), the accused came to Japan when she was sixteen years of age. She had a forged passport (for which she was heavily indebted to her agents). She confessed to have been engaged in prostitution. She was arrested in the act with a customer by police after an anonymous call. She claimed that it was only when she arrived in Japan that she had realized she was in possession of a 15-day tourist visa. Her mediators promised to procure her a six-month visa and a job as a dancer. She also declared that she was very frightened of her Japanese agents. At the beginning of her stay she had worked as a 'hostess' in Nagano prefecture and was forced into prostitution (as a minor!). She had once tried to escape and had given herself up to the Immigration Control Bureau in Osaka in order to fly back to the Philippines. But she had no money for the ticket and was not immediately repatriated. On the contrary, her labour agent picked her up at the detention centre and again employed her illegally! In this case it is clear that the accused was actually the victim of exploitation by traffickers.

In the second case (Myrna Johnson-Velasquez, trial: 29 May 1990, verdict and sentence: 12 June 1990), the accused had worked for four-and-a-half years on a tourist visa as a 'hostess' in so-called snackbars. She was apprehended after work by police acting on an anonymous tip. She claimed to have sent most of her cash to her family in the Philippines. Despite the obvious victimization of both of the accused by traffickers and agents, and despite their 'illegal labour' (*shikakugai katsudō*), they were indicted only for violations of the Aliens' Act. I discussed the cases with the lawyer Niwa Masao who offered the following interpretation: prosecution of key players and traffickers, and gathering evidence of 'illegal work', is troublesome and difficult. For reasons of discretion, the public prosecutor often decides against legal proceedings in certain cases since with expulsion in sight (for violations of the Aliens' Acts) the court's intentions will be met in any case. The indictment for violations of both Aliens' Laws (contravention of the *gaitōhō* is common for overstayers because most do not register themselves) served to make charges heavier and facilitated the handing down of stiff sentences. In the final judgement decree, the formula of general prevention had popped up. The long detention between trial and judgement functioned as *de facto* penalty (imprisonment). A verdict of guilty meant that the convicted foreigner was prohibited entry to Japan for one year. Critical in both trials were the indictments on violations of both the *nyūkanhō* and the *gaitōhō*, the heavy penalties, and the establishment of precedents with respect to such joint violations. It can be assumed that once such judgements are handed down they will become common practice.

When 'illegal' status is combined with violation of Criminal Law, this can lead to inordinately severe sentences. In the judgement of an appeal by a Thai female, who had been indicted for attempted murder and had received a three-year unconditional custodial sentence, it was noted: 'The accused entered with a tourist visa and, moreover, dared to perpetrate the crime at issue during her illegal period of stay. It has to be stated that her guilt is heavy' (Saitō, 1990: 151). In this case the 'illegal' stay served as vindication for the stiff penalty, that is, it was treated as an aggravating circumstance.

7.8.3 Sentencing practices and suspension rates

Further indicators of discriminatory treatment of foreigners by the Japanese judiciary are their inordinately stiff sentences and low suspension rates. There has been an extensive empirical survey of these. It recorded 700 verdicts for offences against property committed by *rainichi*-foreigners in the period 1985–87, collating them with those for Japanese property offenders. The rate for suspensions of sentence in cases of pickpocketing was 14.9 per cent for Japanese and 9.9 per cent for foreigners (the rates are generally low because 'professionalism' and 'habituality' are often taken into account by the court). For shoplifting the figures are:

62.5 per cent for Japanese and only 23.4 per cent for foreigners (GNRMK, 1990: 165). The discrepancies are even greater for offenders who have no previous arrest or criminal record. Moreover, in such cases indictment for Japanese is unlikely, while non-indictment of *rainichi*-foreigners is the exception. For shoplifting, sentences for Japanese were suspended in 100 per cent of cases, but in only 21.4 per cent for foreigners. In cases of pickpocketing, 88.1 per cent Japanese offenders received conditional sentences, but only 14 per cent of foreigners (Ōnuki, 1989: 16).

A further inquiry conducted by the research group on sentencing classified property offences according to seriousness of offence and whether offences were first- or repeat offences. Once again, verdicts by the district court in Tokyo for property offences are recorded for the period from 1 January 1984 to October 1987. The absolute figures are mostly low, making a simple transformation into percentages only moderately meaningful. Nevertheless, a markedly lower suspension rate for foreigners' sentences can be seen consistently, thus the trend is clear, despite the mostly small samples. As regards petty thefts (of less than 10,000 yen) and attempted thefts, Japanese receive unconditional sentences in 55.1 per cent of cases, while foreigners do so in 91.8 per cent of cases. In cases of first-repeat offenders, all foreigners, but only one-third of Japanese, are given unconditional sentences. In case of multiple repetition of the same offence (up to eleven times has been registered), foreigners, regardless of the value of the property, always receive unconditional sentences for all categories in which these data are given. Even where higher property values are involved, the ratio changes only slightly. For property offences from 500,000 yen up to one million yen the ratio of unconditional sentences is 86.7 per cent for foreigners to 54.5 per cent for Japanese. With regard to severity of sentencing, the findings show that foreigners are given slightly milder sentences (except in the categories of higher property value, where the reverse is the case). The interpretation given for this by attorneys is that foreigners are far more often sentenced unconditionally, and that therefore judges hand down milder sentences in the low property value categories (data in Okazaki, 1989: 44–47). If one computes these data in order to reach the rate of unconditional sentencing for first, or first-repeat property offences under 500,000 yen property value, one finds that unconditional sentences were received by eighty-eight foreigners out of ninety-nine – 88.9 per cent – while an unconditional sentence was received by only one of the ninety-six Japanese accused (out of 222 charged) (OBK, 1991: 74). This despite the dominant legal view in Japan that for up to the third repeat-offence against property, suspension of the sentence is usual. Even after the fourth similar offence suspension is common, while after the fifth suspension is possible when the sentenced offender is under guidance of a probation office. Only after the sixth offence is an unconditional custodial sentence the rule. A drastic example contradicting this legal view is the case of a Chinese who, after theft of three pairs of trousers in the famous Ginza in Tokyo, was arrested by security guards, arraigned and sentenced unconditionally to one year in prison. Several other examples are given of foreigners who committed trivial property offences but were sentenced unconditionally to one year of imprisonment. This starkly contrasts with the case of a Japanese habitual criminal who supported himself through thefts on public transport for over two months. His sentence of one-and-a-half years imprisonment was suspended for three years. The study citing these cases also links the stiff penalizing of foreigners with the general prevention perspective of the prosecution agencies. The study group, however, comments that no such scientific evidence for any such deterrent effect was available (GNRMK, 1990: 164–7).

Severe sentencing is criticized by lawyers in certain other cases, as, for example, in a qualitative survey by the Kantō Bar Association, in which two statements read: 'Judgements on foreigners are extremely stiff' (KBR, 1990: 222). In the previously-described cases of harsh discretionary indictment, sentences also were harsh: ten months imprisonment, suspended for three years for the lipstick-shoplifting; a one-year conditional custodial sentence, suspended for three years for the shoplifting of two compact discs; and ten months imprisonment, conditional on three years suspension, for the theft of the rucksack (see, for example, Yonekura and Ikoma, 1989: 9). According to lawyer Ōnuki, judgements did not take motives and circumstances into due consideration. Ōnuki also sees another double-standard, which he illustrates with (only) three cases: American offenders are not only sent to trial for larceny less frequently than are Asians, but also they are punished less severely. He refers to the case of an American multiple offender who, only after the fifth shoplifting office (while on parole) was sentenced unconditionally to one year of imprisonment. A member of the US Army, during arrest for shoplifting, assaulted a sales person so badly that the clerk had to be hospitalized for twenty days. Nevertheless, his sentence was suspended. In contrast, a Hong Kong Chinese who took an electronic calculator worth 6,000 yen, received an unconditional custodial sentence despite having no criminal record (Ōnuki, 1989: 16f.). A similar collation is presented by a journalist who monitored judgements on foreigners at the district court in Tokyo over a longer period. He describes in detail the fate of a Philippine woman, twenty-one years of age, who had no previous criminal record. She was forced into prostitution by her 'labour agents' in Chiba prefecture. She was practically a prisoner, and was subjected to continual maltreatment. She suffered an extra-uterine pregnancy and underwent a surgical operation. After that she fled to Tokyo, where she ran short of money. She stole the purse of a customer in a supermarket and was arrested at her second attempt. Although her stealing technique was 'primitive' and showed no indication of 'professional pick-pocketing', her deed was defined as 'premeditated, habitual and dexterous'. With the court's argument of the necessity for general prevention underscored by the statement that pick-pocketing by foreigners was on the rise, she was sentenced to one year of imprisonment unconditionally. The journalist comments, referring to the view of an attorney, that Japanese judicial procedure here was formalized and conducted ritually and mechanically. In the bills of indictment there were always pre-formulated phrases to be found. Defence of the accused, and reference to extenuating circumstances were mere formalities and did not bear credence. In contrast, only the different nationality of the accused could explain the following judgement: A U.S. national who was charged with four evidenced cases of burglary was given a custodial sentence of one-and-a-half years, suspended for four years (described in detail in Takahashi, 1989c).

7.8.3.1 The rhetoric of prevention

The argument for prevention plays a crucial role in sentencing practises. The public prosecutor's office is inclined to hastily ascribe 'larceny' as the goal of foreign suspects in coming to Japan, and so labels them as 'criminal' without consideration of their personal backgrounds. That assumption is unjustified. Of the 165 property cases brought to court which were examined by the Gaikokujin no ryōkei mondai kenkyūkai, only in twelve did the parts of the decree stating reasons for judgement or describing factual findings explicitly speak of an organized larceny gang. This shows that only in a minority of proceedings for offences against property, do the accused have a professional criminal background (as evidenced in court). In cases which should have resulted in parole, custodial sentences were given (for example, one year of imprisonment unconditionally for the theft of two colour television sets by a Chinese national with no criminal record). It is alleged that this is so that foreigners with proper visas can be expelled, since according to the *nyūkanhō*, a conditional sentence is not a reason for deportation (cf. GNRMK, 1990: 166, 168 and 170).

With regard to 'illegal' migrants, their (short-term) visas usually have already run out at the time of arrest. For this reason, after pronouncement of the sentence, officials of the Immigration Control Bureau wait for the offender in order to repatriate him or her (even when the sentence is suspended). Often visas run out while trials are underway, or an extension is denied (for example, for 'legal' students of Japanese, who have 'illegally' long working hours). In these cases visas become invalid when (protracted) court hearings are over. This amounts to a *de facto* expulsion of unwelcome foreigners, that is, of those who have come to the attention of police (Hidejima, 1989: 18ff.). It is also noted that custody on remand or custody for functional detention are nothing short of imprisonment; that is, even when sentences are suspended, the punishment has already been carried out through the 'deprivation of liberty' of detention (cf. Yonekura and Ikoma, 1989: 9; Ōnuki, 1990a: 93).

A draconian verdict is 'explained' in the reason given by the court for the judgement. A Malaysian, who was put on trial for 'attempted fraud', was sentenced to ten months imprisonment with hard labour. He had tried to obtain goods using a fake credit card, but had no criminal record in Japan (however, according to private information he did have previous convictions in his home country). His offence was designated as being a 'premeditated, habitual and dexterous crime'. He was told by the judge: 'If a crime like this is not punished, it will bring about in various respects disintegration and chaos in tranquil Japanese society. . . . In recent times, crimes of this kind by foreigners have been increasing and it is desirable that a severe sentence be imposed from the standpoint of general deterrence' (Takahaski, 1989c: 91). The argument behind this opinion can be interpreted hermeneutically as follows: Japan is a harmonious society with a low rate of criminality. This social harmony is being disturbed by foreigners, (whose crime-rate of course is on a steep rise); to prevent an escalation of this situation, stiff and exemplary punishment has to be imposed as a deterrent. The concept of 'general prevention' is particularly controversial (for example, see Albrecht, 1985). The same sentence (ten months imprisonment) was given to a Pakistani who appeared before the court on a charge of attempted robbery. He had tried to steal a woman's handbag at night. The reasons for judgement read:

> Japanese society is proud of the fact that women can walk safely at night on the streets. The offence you committed makes people feel insecure and must be punished severely. Recently, too, offences have increasingly been committed by people staying illegally in this country and a severe punishment is desirable for general prevention (Takahaski, 1989c: 91).

Here the assertion made by the press and police concerning the rising criminality of foreigners is accepted without debate and used in a highly dubious context as reasons for deterrent punishment. Even semi-ideological phrases, such as that about women being able to walk at night unharmed on Japan's streets, are cited. The police 'findings' on increasing criminality of foreigners are not questioned and are remodelled by judges into the rhetoric of *de-facto* policies regarding crime. The alleged menace to society presented by foreigners becomes an unquestioned premise. In the overall calculation of the 'moral game', 'problematic groups' have to be constructed. Judges become moral entrepreneurs and fabricate an 'endangerment of society' by foreigners. This imputation is reflected in their rhetoric of prevention. Ultimately 'general deterrence' justifies every repressive means, although their deterrent effect is entirely doubtful. In a textbook on criminology, it is stated: 'According to the present state of research, no empirical clues are available for the effectiveness of harsher punishment' (Kaiser, 1989: 131). The rhetorics of general prevention in cases of minor offences rather function along with punishment by pre-trial detention while getting rid of undesirable aliens through expulsion after the final verdict – when extension of visa is denied (cf. Ōnuki, 1990b: 46f.).

In summary, it can be stated that the Japanese judiciary follows and extends the line taken by the police. Police play on (and intensify) feelings of insecurity, producing a state of constant suspicion in the public. Attention is selectively focused on Asian foreigners. They are criminalized collectively through the tendency of courts to give Asian foreigners harsher, and more often unconditional sentences than are received by Japanese offenders. The examples given by lawyers may have been selected for the starkness of their illustrations, but empirical surveys corroborate the claim that the general mood in agencies of social control tends to foster a tighter grasp on 'illegal' Asians. Formal arraignment and criminal proceedings are instituted too often. The preventive arguments claiming that further potential foreign perpetrators must be deterred imply that foreigners are latently criminal. The convergence of the over-heated political discussion which peaked at the restrictive amendment of the Immigration Control Act, with the rising numbers of prohibitions of entry and of deportations of (potentially) 'illegal' workers, the boosted production of officially-recorded foreign suspects in the police statistics and the criminalization of their 'illegal stay' through indictment, the lower figures for quashing of prosecution of foreigners and the greater numbers sent to trial for minor offences, the harsh sentencing intended to lead to repatriation of foreign offenders, and the sensationalizing of the situation of foreigners by the media as a 'social problem', indicate that an (unconscious) 'consensual strategy of criminalization' is in operation. This strategy, being the result of a feedback-process with synergetic effects, is also a mirror of the overall societal and political climate. In the creation of this climate, coverage of the 'problem' of 'illegal' foreigners by the mass media plays a crucial role, particularly in regard to public perception and distribution of 'stereotypes of criminality (of foreigners)'. In the following chapter I shall describe the general features of media representation of crimes, and examine them in connection with the topic of foreigner criminality.

8 The Media and Criminality

8.1 General Characteristics Concerning Media-Coverage of Crimes

Since first-hand experiences with criminality, for most of us, remain limited and piecemeal, the mass media hold a quasi-monopoly on information, which enables them to lastingly influence all of the areas of facts, norms and value-knowledge relevant to action. Mass-media stereotypes of deviance, by influencing the reporting behaviour of the public and the discretionary decisions of control agencies, determine the number and nature of offences, and the class distribution of registered criminality, they have, as a backstage agency of social control, a considerable influence on the societal definition of deviance and delinquency. However, in the foreground of reflection here are not the direct impacts of violence depictions on potential perpetrators, but the formation of consciousness in the general public, its reactions to deviance and its selective promotion of criminal carriers (Pfeiffer and Scheerer, 1979:115f.).

These aspects of consciousness formation and shaping of perceptions regarding foreigners' criminality are the focus of this chapter (unlike that of the highly-controversial 'perpetrator-centred' research into the effects of media reporting on crime). To be examined is the way the media cover criminality, what is reported, what is transformed into a theme, and what sort of image of the 'reality of criminality' is defined and created (cf. Kerner and Feltes, 1980:80).

Regardless of the unsatisfying situation in research, observations on the presentation of criminality in the mass media converge: put simply, the basic pattern is, above all, an inclination to sensationalize. Accordingly, the media concentrate on ... violent crimes. Everyday criminality, on the contrary, is hardly of interest. The media everywhere assume the perspective of law enforcement agencies. This condenses also in the over-valuation of the moment of arrest of the accused. The social context is seldom made into a theme. The complex reality is reduced to the simple denominator of 'good' and 'bad' (Jung, 1985:295).

These remarks might well claim to be generally (transnationally) valid. The article just quoted does remark that 'the media' do not form a monolithic block and that, for example, in the print media, serious newspapers attempt a more rational and detailed coverage than do the mass tabloids. Nevertheless, it remains true that distorted perceptions of the patterns of criminality and the image of offenders are rather amplified than corrected. This occurs through media pretensions of access to 'the real facts' and preoccupation with current topics in the media (leading sometimes to hasty, ill-considered concoction of stories) and to the (mis)-assessment of consumer interest – the expectation that the more spectacular the story, the higher will be the demand. This reinforces extant stereotypes rather than destabilizes them.

But at the same time there exists an interaction between the portrayal of criminality in the media and the attitude of the public towards criminality. The irrational relation of society to delinquency is perpetuated ... Even more: reality changes under the influence of mass media. The media suggest, most of all, the omnipresence and threat of serious criminality. It is certain that the felt threat to public safety, if not triggered by media, is at least increased by them (Jung, 1985:296f.).

The latter connection was evidenced by early regional studies. A 1952 paper revealed that, in Colorado, the frequency of crimes reported in the local papers was only slightly related to the actual frequency of offences while the estimations of the public regarding increased crimes correlated closely with the increased number of newspaper crime stories, but had no connection with the factual developments (cited in Becker, 1973:11). A meticulous study by Fishman in the 1970s gave clear proof of the connection between a crime wave (as a kind of social awareness, or, better, crime brought to public consciousness) and a corresponding, or rather initiating, sequence of media reports – 'crime waves as media waves' (Fishman, 1978:533). These follow a certain pattern of production, in which incidents are subsumed under a general title fitting a theme, are sorted and evaluated according to news value and then placed in the media. The decision as to whether something is treated as a serious type of crime or not is thus made on the basis of what is going on inside the newsrooms, not outside them. Moreover, news organizations interact by each responding to the stories and topics of its competitors. They stimulate each other, and obeying the 'consistency rule', disseminate further news on the general theme created. Thereby law enforcement agencies 'collaborate' with the media by dispatching a continuous supply of additional incidents of the required sort – 'crime news is really police news' (Fishman, 1978:538). Once the dynamics of a crime wave are established, politicians and police officials are interviewed who can then lament a desperate financial situation, or under-staffing or lack of public support. The growth of the crime wave is controlled by the amount of 'raw material' provided by official conduits (in particular, the police). When media interest diminishes, the covered crime phenomenon recedes to its 'natural level' (cf. Fishman, 1978). Fishman's (1978) study elucidates the construction of a new phenomenon of criminality, which does not even need a substance in 'reality'. However, because of its 'newness', it precisely meets the criteria of news production. The study further illustrates the extent to which perception of specific (particularly 'new') forms of crime is not possible until it emerges as 'media reality'. The media thereby have a function of focusing and sensitizing public attention. This can escalate into a crime panic, and lead to an increase in reports to the police (of incidents of exactly those types reported as new and increasing) and the mobilization of police resources. All of these factors interact, forming an amplifying feedback-loop.

8.2 Critique of Crime Reporting in Japan

Several analyses of the production conditions of crime reports in Japan are available. In my inquiry, I want to concentrate on the daily press (partly for reasons of verifiability although the theme 'illegal' labourers, and the more spectacular cases of 'crime' involving them, were heavily presented in television news programs and documentaries and in televised debates at the end of the 1980s). This limitation seems to be further justified by the fact that Japan, with 584 newspapers (morning and evening issues published under the same title are counted separately) per 1,000 persons, has the highest circulation rate in the world. The poll on reading habits periodically conducted by NSK (Nihon shinbun kyōkai) showed in 1989 that 76 per cent of those polled 'read newspapers every day' and 19 per cent 'read papers sometimes' and this with an average daily reading time of 40.1 minutes (Yamada, 1990: 13 and 18). Some older survey data (1974) by the NSK revealed that 'social affairs' (including crime), were, next to radio-television programs, the most frequently read items, with 51.3 per cent declaring that they 'always read them', 45.2 per cent that they 'read them occasionally' and only 3.5 per cent that they 'do not read them at all' (Kim, 1981: 19). A survey by the NSK in 1989 showed that 63 per cent of those interviewed assessed newspaper reporting as correct and credible; and 61 per cent (the highest figure) were said to read the newspaper section on 'crime, local, and social affairs' most attentively (cited in Igarashi, 1991: 75). These findings buttress the supposition that, in Japan also, newspapers play an important role in the dissemination of images of criminality.

The 'Japanese' criticism of the way in which crimes presented in the press centres on the following matters: press dependence on the information monopoly of the police; the criteria of news value; the moralistic attitude of the press; and the problematic institution of reporters' clubs. The press' almost total dependence on the police (and the prosecutor's office) for information is referred to repeatedly (see, for example, Yamaguchi, 1990: 102; Igarashi, 1991: 72f.; Katsura, 1990: 39f.). This dependence has various consequences. The resulting reports are almost always furnished with an introductory phrase such as '*shirabe ni yoru to . . .*' according to investigation [by the police], and as far as contents are concerned, reproduce the standpoint of law enforcement agencies. The presumption of innocence is often blurred by the premature branding of the suspect as 'perpetrator', 'criminal', or 'villain'. In moralistic, black-and-white-stereotypes, the victory of good over evil is hailed (*kanzen chōaku* – a term alluding to didactic dramas and a Confucian motto of Meiji historiography and literature; Yamaguchi, 1990: 104). The crucial points of the descriptions given are the underscored peculiarity, otherness or viciousness of the suspect, the mental agonies of victims and the bereaved, the (huge) amount of damage caused, the difficulties police face in investigations, and, finally, their 'victory' in arresting the suspect. Most reports cover the apprehension of the suspect, and this aspect of the case is generally given the most space and most detailed treatment. The handing down of the verdict (if process goes this far) is most commonly registered with only a small notice (Igarashi, 1991: 69f.). This style of reporting focused on the stage of apprehension suggests the case is thereby solved. The contrary views of lawyers are almost never taken into account. This again has to be seen in connection with the exclusive reproduction of information supplied by the police (Katsura, 1990: 39). The manner of reporting on crime is standardized according to particular patterns for various sorts of cases.

The newsworthiness of a crime story (or a sequel) is determined by possession of the following features: 'endangerment' of the public (the conveying of the impression that the news consumer or somebody in their social surroundings could at any time become the victim of an incident of the reported kind); grotesque, bizarre or shocking aspects, provoking responses such as 'unbelievable' or 'atrocious', a relation to a trend of 'recent developments', thereby guaranteeing the story an air of something 'to be continued' and allowing the reader inner comments such as 'once again a crime of this sort' (Yamaguchi, 1990: 99ff.). The contents of a crime story should cover at least factual findings, the methods or 'tricks' of the offender in committing the offence, characteristics of the offender and victim, and the motive for the crime. While inquiring, the reporter is constantly pushed to rush. The 'motive' for the crime is imaginatively concocted and incorporated in the headline as a factual assertion. The final decision regarding heads, subheads, size of article, set-up, layout and 'degree of sensation' are made at the editorial desk. Decisions are taken not according to 'objective' standards, but in view of the quantity of report manuscripts handed in on the day and according to the subjective evaluations of the editor. On days 'low in incidents', a petty offence can be transformed into something 'interesting' and featured in a big way (HKKSKB, 1990: 170f. and 175).

The Japanese institution of journalists' clubs is also seen as being problematic. There reporters obtain exclusive (but selected) information directly from police officials. Their daily interaction with law enforcement agencies automatically colours their view and leads to their adoption of the attitudes and view of the control agencies, which are then reproduced in the media. One should thus correctly speak of media 'police reports' instead of 'crime reports'. The recruiting mechanisms of large papers also mean that young and inexperienced journalists under pressure to adapt at the beginning of their careers are assigned to the *shakaibu* (local news sections) and to the reporters' club of the police for 'crime stories'. The permanent co-operation with the police and the spatial confinement (long waiting hours in the 'club') is designated by the handy notion *satsu mawari* ('rotating around the police', Yamaguchi, 1990: 98, 108 and 111). Similar observations are also reported elsewhere, for example, from Austria. Reports from the field police, or the law courts are

the domain of newcomers to the editor's office, who have to be particularly zealous in learning and adapting . . . and therefore are especially prone to adopting and unchangingly abiding by traditional criteria of coverage. Further, a certain pressure prevails to also cover the 'good stories' of the other papers. Thus a uniformity of crime reporting emerges . . . The professional situation of the crime reporter compels him to co-operate fairly strongly with police and courts . . . at least . . . the perspective of the agencies of control dominates the crime reports (LBIK, 1976:55f.).

The big Japanese newspapers reputedly are 'largely the same in character and therefore almost interchangeable', they have no 'personality' and are 'consonant in coverage and commenting' due to an 'anonymous consensus' (cf. Pohl, 1981: 50f.). Yet, in regard to criminality, and because of their strong competition, each wishes to distinguish itself by publishing exclusive articles (*sukūpu*, from the English scoop, or *tokudane*). Thus it is that, pressed for time and aiming at 'actuality', newspapers publish police 'half-truths' as the whole truth, turning journalists into accomplices of the police and amplifiers of false suspicions in the cases of suspects falsely accused but labelled as 'criminal offenders' (cf. Yamaguchi, 1990: 96 and 103). Or, if a suspect makes a confession, it is highlighted without any questioning of whether undue pressure by the police was behind it or whether the confession was a 'real' one;

267

thus the over-valuing of confessions by the Japanese justice system is mirrored by the media (cf. Igarashi, 1991:71). Moreover, as reporters are often pressured to produce their story as quickly as possible and present it in a consumable, sensational and 'interesting' manner, they often exaggerate, and indulge in pompous 'beat ups' of their stories (HKKSKB, 1990:176f.). Articles on crime are transformed into consumer commodities; that is, they have to be presentable, entertaining and exciting. This is conducive to exaggeration and distortions (Yamaguchi, 1990:105).

Japanese crime coverage is criticized also for the fact that usually the author remains anonymous, whereas the suspect is named. This, particularly in the case of innocence – which is to be presumed until the contrary is proven – is a tarnishing of the suspect's reputation, and a violation of his or her human rights. Moreover, pre-conviction by the mass media exerts influence on the judges who, especially in spectacular cases, show consideration for the press – which itself has directly reproduced the view of the prosecuting agencies (Yamaguchi, 1990: 114, also Igarashi, 1991:76f.).

Taking stock of these critical remarks, it should not be overlooked that they address a general problematic constellation which, due to characteristic Japanese corollaries (for example, hermetic reporters' clubs), simply manifests itself in a certain manner. Of particular interest are the criteria of news value, which determine selection of information. Given also the topicality of the political debate on 'illegal' workers, 'crimes' committed by 'illegal' foreigners acquire high newsworthiness. Neologisms like hit-and-run offender or 'internationalization of crime' situate the politically-popular catchword *kokusaika* (internationalization) in a new but still familiar context. To characterize someone as an 'illegal foreigner' is easy and often gains attention for headlines. This facilitates identification and gestalt perception of a general theme, even if reported offences are quite disparate. By designating the nationality of suspects, nationality is made the dominant character of actors, and a perception-channelling factor for the news consumers.

Not the least of the effects of this is that 'the offence of an individual is always attributed to the collective' (Klee, 1981:32). This is observed for *zainichi*-Koreans whose names are given in media reports of offences, and perpetuates readers' prejudices and discrimination against Koreans (Taguchi, 1984:171). A Pakistani also deplores that, by crime reporters mentioning suspects' nationalities, collective stereotypes are formed, and that this shapes the perception of all Pakistanis staying in Japan – even of those who display no deviant behaviour (Wakaichi, 1988:215). Further, it is remarked that crime reporting is based on dominant values (middle-class preferences), and that stories on societally-marginalized groups (for example, homosexuals, persons with AIDS, the homeless, ... and Asian labourers) especially those reporting (or alleging) crimes, were themselves modelled on common negative clichés, thereby increasing or reinforcing that marginalization (cf. Yamaguchi, 1990:105). The mass media are also said to reinforce the assumption that public safety might decline due to the immigration of Asian workers, and that this occurs mainly because of the unreflective reproduction of police reports in the daily press (see, for example, Matsunaga, 1990:148; Hidejima, 1989:20). Before I try to verify these assertions, I want to cursorily present two analyses of press coverage of guest-workers' criminality in Germany. Several parallels can be drawn with the Japanese situation.

8.3 Analysis of the Coverage of Crimes of Foreigners in the Print Media

The first monograph known to me on the subject[1] examined 3,096 articles on guest-workers from the Nordrhein-Westphalian press, over three periods between May 1966 and August 1969. It was revealed that around one third of coverage of foreign workers in fourteen news organs was dedicated to 'sensational crime stories' (Delgado, 1972:42). Of the reports on crimes committed by guest-workers, 12.5 per cent dealt with homicide, manslaughter and attempted homicide, 16 per cent with aggravated assault and battery, 8 per cent with rape, and 18.2 per cent with larceny (Delgado, 1972:62). These figures grossly distort the relative proportions of these crimes in the total of all actual crimes of guest-workers, overemphasizing grave criminality. 'The surge in foreigners' criminality is repeatedly emphasized and dubbed a great danger' (Delgado, 1972:63).

Existing prejudices regarding 'guest-workers' criminality were nourished by reports on startling violent offences involving foreigners. Statistically they certainly are of no weight, and usually they are no more hideous than similar offences committed by indigenous persons. Nevertheless, they are reported differently and at greater length ... The dangerousness of foreign criminals is underscored by the explicit mention of motives for the offence ... Headlines become considerably more dramatic and usually the nationality of the perpetrator is covererd (Delgado, 1972:64 and 65).

As to techniques of reporting, Delgado further notes:

Most frequently, it seems to the author, the press on 'guest-workers' employs a part-for-the-whole strategy. Matter-of-fact accounts on the conduct of 'guest-workers' are disentangled from their individual characters and declared to be typical of all. This is so because their 'deviant' behaviour (criminality, disorderly conduct, and so forth) is carefully registered and elevated to the status of paradigm for the whole group (Delgado, 1972:113).

Another, much more limited survey (eight daily papers in Berlin from 4 January to 31 March 1980 – altogether 514 articles on foreigners), announced similar results. Concerning contents of articles, two crucial areas were found, namely political altercations and criminality. The former, however, was inflated by a current event. 'Notwithstanding the theme, delinquency dominates with an average portion of 20 per cent' (Heine, 1981:26). If one excludes three newspapers which ran only two stories on crime, the portion of crime coverage in the remaining papers rose to 29 per cent.

A majority of the stories featured crimes like robbery or fighting; however, reports in the area of drug-related delinquency by far prevailed ... The bulk of articles are short news in the form of a 'police report' with headlines of the kind 'Lebanese with heroin nabbed' (Heine, 1981:28).

(The weight given the theme of drug-dealing could be an artefact of the short period of analysis). The author then states – in wording almost identical to that of the first-mentioned study, which is

270

quoted elsewhere in her account – the frequent reports on incidents in the area of delinquency (except for *Neue, TAZ* and *Wahrheit*), by their quantity alone, impute 'a disposition for violence' to foreigners. This becomes even more obvious when one looks into the style of presentation. It differs considerably from the usual crime reporting of offences perpetrated by Germans. Headlines are set-up more 'dramatically' – almost always with inclusion of the nationality of the foreign offender. This aspect is not insignificant in regard to the effect on the reader: In comparable German cases, the description of the offender gives gender, profession, age, and the like, but concerning foreigners it is first of all nationality that counts, that is, a branding [of the suspect] as foreigner . . .' (Heine, 1981:37). Besides the significance of the number of crime reports on guest-workers, the concentration on violence and serious offences is conspicuous, as are the sensational headlines which regularly feature the nationality of the offender.

8.3.1 A profile of crime reporting based on analysis of a Japanese newspaper-clipping compilation

Along the lines of the above-mentioned studies, I made a quantitative analysis of Japanese newspaper articles. I attempted to check such matters as the naming of nationality in the headline, the frequency of reports on serious and heavy criminality, and dependence on police sources. For this analysis I used a newspaper article collection established by the Solidarity Association with Foreign Labour Migrants in Kotobuki (Karabao no kai [KNK], 1988–). This collection has been compiled since 1988 and was available to me from the April/May 1988 issue. In this compilation all press reports pertaining in some way to the labour migration phenomenon were collected and roughly sorted by contents. Besides the big trans-regional papers (*Asahi shinbun, Mainichi shinbun, Nihon keizai shinbun* and *Yomiuri shinbun*) regional newspapers with smaller circulation (for example, *Hokkaidō shinbun, Kanagawa shinbun, Shinano mainichi shinbun, Ryūkyū shinpō* (sporadically), *Tōkyō shinbun* and *Saitama shinbun*) were represented in the compilation. The clipping compilation consists of articles that members of Karabao no kai cut out of newspapers they personally subscribe to; these acticles they then send to the Solidarity Association. Each volume of clippings is centrally compiled at the bureau of Karabao no kai in Yokohama. One therefore cannot assume that the compilation exhaustively documents the newspapers represented in it. Moreover, there are no articles from the *Sankei shinbun*, a newspaper significant for its circulation, its mediocre reporting, and its concentration on economic issues. Given that the goals of the movement are the support of Asian labour migrants and provision of first-hand assistance in labour- or other law-related disputes, it may be conjectured that sometimes the sending in of crime stories was shirked in order not to tarnish the image of foreign migrant workers. However, since the number of articles on 'crimes' committed by foreigners is quite considerable, we may treat that distorting factor as marginal. In addition to giving a quantitative analysis, I will later give a descriptive account of sequels to reports which fabricated a particular image of 'typical crimes of foreigners'.

In a period of thirty-three months (April 1988 to December 1990) the above-mentioned clipping collection includes 309 crime reports (all of them pertaining to penal code violations, suspects were *rainichi*-foreigners on short-term visas either still valid or expired). The registered reports chiefly concerned the stages of suspicion and arrest, and commitment for trial. The main judicial proceedings (court hearings) and verdicts were documented only very rarely. Criminal law violations covered (and the police definitions of them) were: offences of violence (classified by the police into *kyōakuhan* – felonious offences comprising homicide, robbery, arson and rape, and *sobōhan* – violent offences including assault, bodily injury, intimidation and extortion cf. Keisatsuchō, 1990:1); offences against property (*settō* – larceny, *suri* – pickpocketing, *manbiki* – shoplifting); narcotic drug-related offences; *chinōhan* (or 'intellectual' offences, including fraud, embezzlement, and counterfeiting); offences against the Anti-Prostitution-Act (*baishun bōshihō ihan*, included in my analysis only when legal charges were brought forward); and other penal code offences (most of them 'illegal introduction of labour', that is, violations of the Employment Security Act – *shokugyō anteihō* – and evasion of customs – that is, smuggling). I counted separately general 'analyses' of the delinquency of foreigners (with respect to criminal law), but special features on such matters as soaring numbers of suspected prostitution cases involving foreigners, I did not document. In 'spectacular' cases which were picked up by several newspapers, a multiple enumeration resulted because I counted single articles separately. The attention those 'spectacular' cases received in several papers indicates that they were ascribed high news-value.

The analysis yielded the following picture: of 309 crime reports, 152 (49.2 per cent) dealt with violent offences, forty with *chinōhan* (12.9 per cent, most of them pertaining to forging of documents), thirty-three were 'general analyses' (10.7 per cent, for example, editorials, ten of which appeared at the time of publication of the *White Paper on the Police* in August 1990), twenty-four dealt with offences against property (7.8 per cent) and twenty-six with other infractions (8.4 per cent, the majority being 'illegal introduction of work' to foreigners), eighteen articles were run on transgressions of the Anti-Prostitution Act (5.8 per cent) and sixteen on drug offences (5.2 per cent). This shows a marked preponderance of stories on serious criminality, and the concentration of the print media on violent crimes. In 65.7 per cent of the articles (206 articles) the headline gave the nationality of the suspect. In 22 per cent of the crime reports (sixty-eight stories) terms such as 'foreigner', 'illegal foreigner', 'illegal worker', 'illegal labour migrant' or 'South East Asian' or 'Asian' appeared in the headline. In five articles (1.6 per cent) the label *japayuki* appeared.[2] Only 10.7 per cent (thirty-three) of the articles forebore signifying the foreigner-status of the suspect in the headline. (By headline I mean any prominent typeface or size of characters, usually at the head or right-hand side of the story. In the case of long articles, multiple headings are common and I took not only the main head, but also the subheads, into account.) For most of the articles, their 'exotic' news-value – is signalled by a reference to the suspect's non-Japanese status. 'Being foreign' becomes the dominant sign by which attention is attracted to the article's contents.

In 257 crime reports (83.2 per cent) either the phrase *shirabe de wa* ('according to the police investigation') is used or reference is made to law enforcement agencies by naming the investigating police office or the relevant department. This shows that duplication of police information in newspaper articles is common practice, and underscores the assertion that 'crime reports' should actually be read as 'police reports'. In forty (12.9 per cent) of the recorded cases the police raised the suspicion that organized crime was involved or a professional syndicate operating underground. In thirty-five articles (11.3 per cent) reference was made to the rapidly surging delinquency of foreigners. This correlates closely with the number of global analyses, in which this slogan can almost always be found.

Even in cases of victimization (reports on 'illegal trafficking', wage embezzlement, coercion to prostitution or introduction to work as a 'hostess' in a bar, pub or 'snackbar', and 'pseudo-marriage' – *gisō kekkon* – for obtaining legal status), in which predominantly the suspects were of Japanese nationality and the victims foreigners, the nationality of the victim appeared in the headline in 73.3 per cent of cases (143 reports). In 13.85 per cent of reports of victimization (twenty-seven articles) the headlines used such terms as 'foreigner', '(South East) Asian', 'illegal' worker and so forth. Five stories (2.6 per cent) bore the term *japayuki* in their headlines, while 10.3 per cent (twenty stories) made no allusion to the victim's non-Japanese status. (Here again I include subheads together with main heads.) Of the 195 victimization cases, seventy-two (36.9 per cent) concerned 'illegal trafficking or introduction to labour', ninety-seven (49.7 per cent) 'forced prostitution or mediating in the so-called "entertainment industry"', and twenty-six (13.3 per cent) 'bogus marriage'. Stories of foreign victims which touched upon criminal law (homicide, mayhem, larceny) were too few to be statistically significant, but present a similar picture. The style of reporting suggests to the newspaper consumer that foreigners were involved in 'crimes' disproportionately often. The prominence given in headlines to nationality or foreigner-status reinforces this image.

8.4 Report Sequences and Stereotypes of Deviance

8.4.1 Violent 'offender/victim transactions' among foreigners

8.4.1.1 Pakistanis
In the following I want to demonstrate that determinable 'images of offences' of foreigners were created (even specific as to nationalities) by media themes and periodical waves of reporting. The first topic I want to scrutinize is that of 'violent conflicts among Pakistanis'. I shall examine relevant newspaper reports (mostly from the clipping compilation) and comment on the style of reporting.

The first case falling into this category during the period analyzed, occurred on 6 March 1988. Thus, it was accessible to me only via a 'follow-up' report. In that article, one of the victims, who had gone underground, was interviewed concerning the 'real circumstances of the criminal act'. Six Pakistanis (all of them were later apprehended: two were charged with assault and battery, while the rest were brought to trial and expelled for illegal stay) forcibly entered a room rented by four compatriots. They carried knives and iron rods and battered and kicked their victims. The latter were then 'abducted' and 'interrogated' by the instigator of the assault (a Pakistani labour agent). One of the attacked was severely wounded. A group of six of his friends and equipped with sticks went to the house of the labour agent on the same day. A melee again occurred. The reason for this conflict was the refusal of one of the victims to work with two other Pakistanis in a bookbindery at which the above-mentioned 'broker' was employed and to which he had introduced him (*Asahi shinbun*, 13 April 1988). One week later a long article in the same newspaper reported on the lonely death of a Philippina due to malnutrition (a classic good-will victim story). Below there were two notices made prominent by small headlines. The first dealt with the rising number of 'illegally' residing *japayuki* on tourist visas. The second was headed 'Wage-disputes among Asians [*Ajiajin dōshi*] increasing'. In this item a semi-official computation was presented. According to this, there had occurred in Tokyo since January 1987, twenty-three conflicts among Asians which had involved homicide or robbery. The majority of involved persons were said to have entered Japan on tourist visas and to have been illegally employed in manual labour. The article continued:

> Within Tokyo Metropolis recently violent crimes [*kyōaku hanzai*] committed by labour migrants from Asia are on the rise. In particular a new tendency has emerged of disputes among compatriots or foreigners among other foreigners. Some persons who up to now acted only as unskilled labourers in Japan have become labour agents [*tehaishi*] who introduce their colleagues to work. Many examples of wage problems, and such like, occur (*Asahi shinbun*, 20 April 1988).

On 8 May a similarly situated incident happened. The media obviously perceived it as part of the above-mentioned 'trend', and accordingly reported it under clamorous headlines: 'Attack by a group of Pakistanis in Adachi on the apartment of compatriots' (*Asahi shinbun*). 'Labour migrants: Pakistani fellow countrymen: cash robbed, retaliatory assault. Adachi, five arrests' (*Mainichi shinbun*); 'Pakistanis: group attack, Adachi, five arrests. Two compatriots seriously injured' (*Nihon keizai shinbun*); 'More than ten Pakistanis make a raid: two fellow countrymen seriously injured' (*Kanagawa shinbun*) – all headlines are from newspapers of 9 May 1988. Again the metal 'armaments' carried (iron rods) are given prominence in the reports to emphasize the dangerousness of the foreigners. In *Mainichi shinbun* the number of 'attackers' is calculated as 'around fifteen', stressing the 'menace' posed by Pakistanis 'in groups'. The group escaped in six cars but was hunted down by a police patrol alarmed by people from the neighbourhood. Five persons were apprehended.

At the end of May, a background-story to that *shūgeki jiken* – attack incident – was featured. It concerned the police search for the key instigator, who was said to be a kind of 'boss' of the Pakistanis, whom he provided with lodgings and found jobs for. He was also reported to have illegitimately exported more than a hundred used cars, taking advantage of a Pakistani law which exempted from taxation cars already driven by Pakistanis in Japan. In co-operation with Japanese dealers this 'boss' allegedly used the passports of the migrant workers trafficked by him in order to obtain the necessary documents for tax evasion. He was reported to have ordered the 'raid' because those victimized did not follow his instructions. This story, occupying almost one page (and including a photograph of the wanted suspect), again presents an opportunity for recourse to police data to underscore the sub-head that 'crimes of illegal workers are surging'. This is further illustrated with a wholesome calculation to the effect that apprehensions of foreigners in Tokyo had doubled within five years (*Yomiuri shinbun*, 29 May 1988).

In June a success-story was published on an arrest made in the connection with that same *shūgeki jiken* (assault incident). The number of those apprehended thereby rose to eight (*Mainichi shinbun*, 11 June 1988). The *Yomiuri shinbun* in the middle of the same month ran a long story (with a photograph) on the falsification of the passport of one of the suspects in the case. He had been deported six months after the *shūgeki jiken* on grounds of 'illegal stay'. This barred him from re-entry for one year, and the

Immigration Control Bureau had recorded his name on a 'black list'. The Pakistani, however, simply altered some of the letters of his name and slipped through computer check (*Yomiuri shinbun*, 16 June 1988).

In February of the following year, a Pakistani is reported to have deposed for the police-protocol that four of his compatriots had forcibly entered his apartment, threatened him with a knife (he was slightly wounded) and robbed him of cash and jewellery (*Asahi shinbun*, 21 February 1988). The next conflict prompted a series of news items. On 7 March three Pakistanis were assaulted in their lodgings by several men. One person died from knife injuries. The police were said to have suspected that it was a scuffle among Pakistanis (*Asahi shinbun*, 8 March 1989). An influential economic newspaper reported the case with a dramatic headline, its wording invoking associations with already-publicized 'intra-ethnic conflicts': 'Pakistani assaulted [*shūgeki*]. Stabbed to death in Itabashi. Were more than twenty persons involved?' The story proceeding along the lines suggested by the police, further specu-lated that the incident had been a violent argument among two groups of Pakistanis over their prerogatives on trafficking fellow countrymen. The investigations were concentrating on the back-ground connections and the alleged involvement of 'a big crime syndicate' (*Asahi shinbun*, 15 March 1989). Such guesswork, and other reporting on organized criminals, is tinged with a danger-implying undertone. When police had succeeded in apprehending two Pakistanis (six others were still sought) one finds the mislead-ing headline: 'The Itabashi Pakistani murder. Eight compatriots re-arrested.' Only the contents of the report disclose that only two had been apprehended and were in police custody, while six of those allegedly involved were still sought (*Asahi shinbun*, 4 April 1989).

Here again, the headline is manipulated so as to include figures as large as possible. The reports publicized within the span of recollection are made identifiable by naming the venue, and on the one hand reveal the intention to serialize the case, and on the other reflect the editorial ascription of a high news value. The 'success' of the police is also presented in the headlines of two other papers. Only a careful reading of the contents reveals the headlines to be false, and that the real situation was that eight warrants of arrest had been issued but only two suspects apprehen-ded. 'Eight Pakistanis re-arrested for homicide. The Pakistani-murder' (*Mainichi shinbun*, 4 April, 1989), reads one newspaper's headline, while the other reads: 'The Pakistani-murder. Eight fellow countrymen nabbed. The attack [*shūgeki*] on the apartment in Itabashi' (*Nihon keizai shinbun*, 4 April 1989). Noteworthy is the use of the term 'attack' to mark the theme and category, and to arouse associations. The first headline also speaks of murder (*satsujin*), insinuating that the arrested persons were actually murderers contrary to the legal presumption of innocence (*in dubio pro reo* – 'when in doubt, favour the accused'). Of the 'eight perpetrators', only one in fact was convicted by a court of law (to eight years imprisonment). In the rather detailed opinion accompanying the sentence, the prevention of crimes of foreigners is mentioned in the reasoning behind the sentence. But it is also critically noted that government measures against the influx of illegal workers were belated. The newspaper comments: 'The judge referred to the fact that illegally resident Pakistanis form groups which continually produce contention (*kōsō*)' (*Nihon keizai shinbun*, 8 November 1989). Here the interest of the media in 'intra-ethnic conflicts among Pakistanis' is vindicated by the notion that they occurred 'incessantly'. This can also be inferred from another report on the conviction which also quotes a passage from the opinion: 'A crime of this kind exerts grave influences on the local residents, on Japanese society and the maintenance of law and order. Hence it is imperative to tackle it strictly' (*Asahi shinbun*, 8 November 1989). The 'surge of violent crimes among foreigners' invoked by the police and the press thus is used to legitimate harsh sentencing. The selective quotation from the courtroom emphasizes the importance this newspaper attributes to this kind of offence. It further (implicitly) provides a rationale for repeated stories on the topic, announcing that this type of 'societally-detrimental crimes' deserve further attention.

The next occurrence attracting my attention happened on 3 September 1989. According to the story run, the backdrop was a financial argument. One of the suspects was employed by a spicer and was said to have repeatedly manipulated the balance sheets and embezzled money. He was urged to refund the money he gained illegitimately. Enraged, the suspect gathered some of his compatriots, entered the apartment of the shop-owner (a Japanese citizen) and her Pakistani fiancé. They abducted the latter and several other Pakistanis who happened to be present. They confined them for more than twenty hours in a dwelling and employed

violence against them. Newspaper reports came with the following
headlines: 'Fellow-countrymen assaulted and incarcerated. Three
Pakistanis nabbed. Because of financial troubles' (*Mainichi shinbun*, 20 September 1989), 'Five Pakistanis arrested. Confinement
case' (*Asahi shinbun*, 21 September 1989, Saitama-edition), 'Violence against compatriots, confinement. Five Pakistanis arraigned'
(*Saitama shinbun*, 21 September 1989), 'Searched Pakistani apprehended' (*Asahi shinbun*, 15 October 1989, Saitama-edition). In
the latter article the whole incident was once again described in
detail, and six Pakistanis are said to have launched the assault.
This dispute was picked up mainly by local papers, yet by the
reference 'among compatriots' in the title it is designated as an
'intra-ethnic conflict'.

A series *par excellence* appeared at the end of November and
the beginning of December in *Shinano Mainichi shinbun* (a local
newspaper of Nagano prefecture). On two days running a half-
page article was published with photographs (one of the victim,
two of the venue) and a map. The first report, under a big headline,
'Murder among Pakistanis', described the discovery of the corpse
of a twenty-year-old Pakistani, who had been employed in a plas-
tics manufacturing firm. He had lodged in the factory-dwelling
with another seven Pakistanis. The report noted that in the previous year, according to the Immigration Control Office, 19,106
Pakistani had entered Japan, most with short-term visas. It added
that in the districts around Tokyo the number of Pakistanis
working illegally and overstaying their tourist visas was on the
rise (*Shinano Mainichi shinbun*, 22 November 1989). The following
day a second story appeared under the bold headline, 'Suspicion
of illegal labour', and the smaller subhead, 'The murdered Pakistani in Maruko'. A picture showed the removal of the victim's
body. The article focussed on the labour-relationships of the Pakistanis. The employing company stated that it had adopted them
as *kenshūsei* ('trainees') without checking up on their residence
status (*Shinano Mainichi shinbun*, 23 November 1989). On 28
November a third report announced the impending trial of one of
the suspected Pakistanis (with a photograph of the apprehension
on 24 November). This despite the fact that the accused still
denied all allegations and no material evidence (no weapon) was
produced. The report detailed all of the inconsistencies that the
police alleged were contained in the deposition of the suspect. It
also quoted one investigating officer: 'From now on it will get

tough!' (*Shinano Mainichi shinbun*, 28 November 1989). One week later it was reported that the knife had been found and sent to a scientific crime detection department of the prefectural police for identification and examination. According to the statements given at interrogation by another Pakistani an argument had broken out between the 'offender' and victim about a video device (*Shinano Mainichi shinbun*, 5 December 1989). Two days later the newspaper briefly reported that the terms of custody for the suspected Pakistani (who still denied the offence) had been extended (*Shinano Mainichi shinbun*, 7 December 1987). Here the documentation of this series of articles ended. Presumably there was also a report on the apprehension, which was not included in the clipping collection. However, the serialization met perfectly the criteria of news production: a stabbed foreigner, mysterious circumstances, 'illegal' workers, whose number is on the rise (implying that in the future further developments can be expected), and a successful arrest. The developments emerge progressively and are therefore ideal for a series of reports. Each of the five articles bore the headline 'Pakistani murder', thus providing a title for the 'thriller to be continued'.

In July of the following year there was another story on a conflict among Pakistanis which had been 'resolved' in the archaic way, that is, by violence in the district Shinagawa, Tokyo. Again a dispute over finances was said to have been the motive. The newsvalue is indicated by headline: 'Man from Pakistan stabbed on the road, badly wounded. Arrest of his friend, a compatriot' (*Nihon keizai shinbun*, 8 July 1990).

Two months later another incident was transformed into a media event: 'Pakistanis attack fellow countrymen. 1.1 million yen compensation for workers' accident stolen' (headline in *Asahi shinbun*, 13 September 1990); 'Eight Pakistanis steal cash and ring. Sagamihara, four arrests', (*Kanagawa shinbun*, 13 September 1990). Emphasis was given to the attacks having been made by a 'group', and the fate of one of the victims was described. He had lost a finger in an accident on the work-site and had only the day before withdrawn the compensation money from his bank account. This kind of story-telling is employed to arouse pity and underscore the 'heinousness' of the crime.

At the beginning of October, the Police Office leaked the information that they had apprehended three Pakistanis charged with having robbed Pakistanis, Indians and Sri Lankans residing in

Japan. Allegedly they had targeted their victims since August the year before and had stolen a total of roughly nine million yen from them. The main suspect allegedly had organized seventy Pakistanis under him and had 'secured their subsistence' by ordering them to commit robberies (*Asahi shinbun*, 2 October 1990).

The following month an event of reputedly the same kind is reported: 'Foreigners' dormitory attacked, cash robbed. Tochigi. Group of five Pakistani?' (*Nihon keizai shinbun*, 12 November 1990). Four Bangladeshis had been tied up and their money seized – allegedly by five Pakistanis. Thus the suspicion of the police is given immediate prominence in the headline and the article advertizes itself as belonging to the genre 'conflict among foreigners'.

A consistent theme has not yet been clearly delineated. Moreover, the documentation provided by articles from the clipping compilation of the Karabao no kai is incomplete. And as yet no pattern has emerged with respect to region and period of reporting. However, if one examines analogous reports on other nationalities (particularly on Bangladeshis and Chinese) the picture becomes more coherent. What has become obvious so far is that by use of such term as 'compatriots' (*dōkokujin*), 'among Pakistanis' (*Pakisutanjin dōshi*) and 'group attack', and mention of the number of offenders ('eight Pakistani, six foreigners') and type of crime ('robbery', 'stabbed to death', 'murder') a pattern is created where a general theme is: 'Bands of Pakistanis perpetrate violent offences against countrymen'. Any offence which nearly fits this theme is reported as if it fits it precisely. Following this 'consistency rule' ('every crime that can be seen as an instance of the theme, will be seen and reported as such', Fishman, 1978: 537) editors select further news items and subsume them under the theme. Competing newspapers also pick up the stories and make the 'motif' recognizable for the consumer. Every new case, and each use of the consistency rule reestablishes the rule. 'The rule is used to identify the newsworthiness of certain crimes. Reporters and editors will know, for example, that a certain incident is "another one of those crimes..." and not just an incident that can be categorized in a variety of ways' (Fishman, 1978: 537). In the next sub-section I want to follow up the theme of 'intra-ethnic conflicts' by examining media reports of violence among Bangladeshis.

8.4.1.2 Bangladeshis

The first such story available on violence among Bangladeshi is found in an article already cited, where it functions as an illustration accompanying police data on the surge in 'intra-ethnic conflicts'. In March 1988, the corpse of a 32–year-old Bangladeshi was found in his apartment in Shinjuku, Tokyo. His visa had long before expired. The police surmized that he had worked 'illegally' on construction sites. The motive for the murder was reputedly a disagreement over provisions for introduction to labour (*Asahi shinbun*, 20 April 1988). This suspicion was substantiated after the apprehension and arrangement for search of two Bangladeshis. The title in the newspapers suggests that the case thereby be solved and asserts: 'The murder of the Bangladeshi crime of two countrymen. One rearrested, one sought' (*Asahi shinbun*, 26 May 1988). A suggestive tag is added by another paper: 'Murder among *japayuki*. The March-case. One nabbed, one sought' (*Yomiuri shinbun*, 26 May 1988). The article reports that the deceased was engaged in labour-trafficking of migrants from his home country. A dispute over services paid for but not provided had led to the murder (by strangling with an electric cable). The latter detail was probably meant to illustrate how ghastly the crime was. The latter part of the article by reference to the increase in numbers of 'illegal' male labourers (*otoko japayuki*), also mentions the successful detection and apprehension of four 'illegal' Pakistanis and four 'illegal' Bangladeshis in May in Tokyo. Its final paragraph, although it begins with a mitigating comment (albeit reminiscent of the 'unstable, gold-digger' metaphor), ends on an alarming note:

> Although almost all ['illegals'] are serious labourers seeking high wages and therefore oftentimes changing jobs, they do, on the other hand, thereby get into financial troubles. Cases of criminal involvement, and crimes committed by illegal workers, happen as often as every month' (*Yomiuri shinbun*, 26 May 1988).

The reference to the continually rising number of foreign 'illegals' is a frequently employed stylistic device. It connotes that in future much worse (that is, more crime) is to be expected. When the second suspect in this case was arrested, this was reported under a headline mentioning (disparagingly) the suspect's country of origin, and the 'title' of the case (*Bangurajin koroshi*) and using the term 'compatriot' (*Asahin shinbun*, 9 June 1988).

In the same month a victim story was published. The (suspected) origin of the offenders was written into the headline: 'South East Asians? Robbery. Twelve Bangladeshi victimized'. Two 'assaults' are described in detail. In one a group of five men had forcibly entered a rented house occupied by nine Bangladeshis, and in the other six men had forced their way into a house occupied by three Bangladeshis. The victims were wounded with knives and deprived of their passports, wrist-watches and ready money. The offenders, according to the police, were South East Asians (*Asahi shinbun*, 27 June 1988).

But even where the perpetrators are Japanese nationals the newspaper story is made interesting by the nationality of the victim being given. A scuffle among Bangladeshi and Japanese labour agents which resulted in one foreigner being severely injured with an iron bar, in connection with which three Japanese were apprehended on suspicion of mayhem was reported under a headline which read: 'Bangladeshi beaten with iron-rod' (*Asahi shinbun*, 24 December 1988).

Reporting of the homicide of a Bangladeshi is made dramatically more vivid by a detailed precise account of the inflicted stab wound (4.3 cm in width!) (*Mainichi shinbun*, 11 October 1990). An article on the case in another newspaper quotes several people, who on the day of the offence had observed foreigners arguing in the vicinity of the crime. More than ten Bangladeshis are said to have 'gone in and out' of two nearby houses, but to have disappeared after the time of the crime (*Nihon keizai shinbun*, 12 October 1990). Here it is abundantly clear what the journalist (relying on police investigative reports) is driving at. On 10 November, a fellow-lodger of the deceased was arrested on suspicion of homicide. It was alleged that in the course of a dispute with the victim he fetched a kitchen-knife and slashed his compatriot on the street (*Mainichi shinbun*, 27 November 1990)

8.4.1.3 Malaysians and Philippinos

Offences among other nationalities also fit the pattern 'intra-ethnic conflicts', or the more general pattern 'conflicts among foreigners'. On 23 March 1989, a Malaysian died in a hospital in Gunma prefecture from severe cuts and stab-wounds. His passport revealed that he had entered Japan in January of that year on a tourist-visa. He had worked in a meat processing plant. Malaysians employed there were suspected of the crime, and police arrested twenty Malaysian nationals on the spot of grounds of infraction of the Immigration Control Acts and commenced interrogation (*Asahi shinbun*, 14 March 1989). This appears a classic example of 'arrest for a different purpose' (*bekken taiho* – arrest on a separate charge), since the police appear to have taken the workers into custody in order to advance their investigations in the homicide case. During the interrogations suspicion hardened against one of the workers, who had played cards with the victim on the night before the offence and had lost a considerable amount of money. The criminal act is graphically described following the man's arrest: the offender is said to have beaten the sleeping victim several times with a large bottle and to have subsequently robbed him. The headline uses eye-catching verbal signals: 'Arrest of a colleague. Malaysian slain ...' (*Asahi shinbun*, 19 March 1989).

Philippinos too appear in newspaper stories which can be subsumed under the media genre 'violent conflicts'. Four Philippinos were brawling on the street; another Philippino happened to enter the scene and attempted to settle the argument. He was stabbed in his left foot by one of the quarrelling men with a 17 cm long kitchen knife which, according to the article, was carried by the offender. The stabbed man subsequently died of loss of blood (*Kanagawa shinbun*, 3 January 1990). The reported detail of the weapon, and the mention of the Philippino as having carried this weapon, depict him (and other Philippinos) as dangerous.

Before this case had been solved, the corpse of a stabbed Philippino was found in Yokohama on 23 January 1990. This was announced under headline: 'Body of a stabbed foreign man on the road. South East Asians: Fight among friends?' The headline plainly shows that editors orient themselves toward themes, and that the editor here precipitantly fabricated an 'intra-ethnic conflict' in the absence of any evidence for this suspicion. The editors' supposition was based on the statements given to the police by residents of the neighbourhood where the body was found, who stated that a nearby bar was often frequented by 'South East Asian foreigners'. The newspaper story told how, on the evening in question, two groups of these 'South East Asians foreigners' were seen, one drinking beer at the counter, the other dining. The account is dramatized by reference to a 200-meter-long zig-zag trail of blood on the street (*Kanagawa shinbun*, 24 January 1990). Two weeks later a clearly fabricated headline announced that two Philippinos had been nabbed. Actually apprehended were one Philippino and one Japanese national who was married to a Philippino and therefore had contacts with the Philippine community. The motive given for the offence was the deceased man's (alleged) molestation of girlfriends of colleagues of the arrested men, and his unsettled debts. Again it is mentioned that the Philippino suspect had carried a weapon (a knife) on his person (*Kanagawa shinbun*, 6 February 1990). The report appears under a headline which alludes to that of the first-published report 'murder of man on the street'.

In May 1990, an atypical event occurred which can nevertheless be included under the topic 'conflict between foreigners'. A Philippino stabbed a man ('presumably Asian') with a 'weapon' which was obviously worth mentioning (a twenty centimetre-long pair of scissors!). Together with a group of seven or eight men the Asian man had intruded into a factory's dormitory where the Philippino, the victim, lived. They hit the suspect with sticks and the like. The victim of the stabbing is reported to have been a member of the 'attacking group' (*shūgeki gurūpu*) in the past. The police postulated 'disputes' among foreigners as backdrop' (*Mainichi shinbun*, and short notice in *Ryūkyū shinpō*, both 12 May 1990). Not much later four Pakistanis living in the vicinity were apprehended on suspicion of mayhem and trespass. This time the headline for the story expressed much greater confidence as to guilt: 'Pakistanis who attacked Philippino nabbed. Gunma, four persons' (*Mainichi shinbun*, 14 May 1990). The terms used – *shūgeki* and *osou* – carry assocations connecting the above case to precedent cases of intra-ethnic violence' and implying that cases of this kind continue to occur.

In cases of homicide of foreigners, the police (and the press disseminating their conjectures) quickly seem to narrow the circle of potential suspects to foreigners. In a case in which the corpse was a Philippino, who according to post-mortem examinations had been stabbed in the heart with a fruit-knife, the investigating officers assumed that the homicide had been the result of a conflict between comrades (thus the headline: '*Nakama dōshi no tora-buru?*' [Conflict between comrades?], *Yomiuri shinbun*, 31 May 1990), their assumption being the stronger because the victim had not been robbed. The detail concerning the stabbing, and the wording used, again serve to dramatize the report and provide the mental connection to cases already publicized.

8.4.1.4 Chinese

With notorious regularity, conflicts among Chinese nationals are reported also. They commonly involve so-called *shūgakusei* – 'students of the Japanese language' – who quite often engage in 'illegal' work. On 2 January 1989 in Yokohama, an apartment burned down and a body was later found. The surmise that it was the body of a Chinese was instantly fixed into the headline. The small (four-millimetre-high) question-mark beside the large (1.1 by 1.8 cm.) type of the headline scarcely serves to signal any doubt on the matter: 'Corpse of Chinese man in nearby apartment' (*Kanagawa shinbun*, 3 January 1989). The case is seen as being intriguing enough to warrant a sequel. The following day the first findings of the investigations are reported: the deceased actually was a Chinese student. According to the autopsy he had been strangled. The police assumed that this was very likely the outcome of a conflict among Chinese. The corresponding headline as usual referred to the act of violence: 'Chinese student murdered. Arson. Strangulation. Crime committed by acquaintance?' (*Kanagawa shinbun*, 3 February 1989). The latter surmise was adopted by the headline of the following report in order to identify it as a sequel: 'Why was the apartment set on fire at the same time? [Suspicion of] crime committed by acquaintance [*kao mishiri no hankō*] substantiated' (*Kanagawa shinbun*, 3 February 1989). The report meticulously detailed the police investigations. In the apartment in question six Chinese were said to have lodged. More than a hundred Chinese up to that date had been interrogated by police. The arson reportedly remained a mystery. No further report on it is documented in the clipping collection of Karaboa no kai.

In April again more violence among Chinese was recorded. Three Chinese had been attacked with knives in Ikebukuro, Tokyo. The assailants allegedly had been five other Chinese. Two of the victims suffered stab wounds in the back (*Asahi shinbun*, 3 April 1989).

In June a 'holdup' committed allegedly by four Chinese was reported from Yokohama. The victim was a Chinese *shūgakusei* who had been wounded with a knife and deprived of his cash and passport. The headline used terms which had already become a convention, referring to 'compatriots' and a 'band of four' (*dōkokujin? yonin-gumi*). The end of the story includes quotation of a police statement that many crimes committed by Chinese had recently occurred in Tokyo. These Chinese allegedly targeted Chinese *shūgakusei* – who had come to Japan with the intention of working, stealing their cash and passports (which were then sold) (*Asahi shinbun*, 21 June 1989). Not much later one could read in a competing newspaper of a 'band of four' which robbed their Chinese countrymen. The title strikingly resembles that of the first story: 'Robbery by a band of four Chinese in Kawaguchi. Attack on compatriots' (*Mainichi shinbun*, 25 June 1989). On 9 August of the same year, the apprehension of one of the 'holdup' suspects was reported. Police announced to intensify investigations into possible connections to the 'arson-case'. The article again hinted at the frequent occurrence of similar crimes (*Yomiuri shinbun*, 9 August 1989 – two articles, one probably from the evening edition with two photographs of the apprehended suspect and the rhetorical question in the headline: 'Connection to three similar cases?'). At the end of the month the successful arrest of one of the sought accomplices was reported. Those arrested, however, were not charged with any other offences (particularly the setting on fire of the apartment and the robbery of a Chinese student at the beginning of August) (*Yomiuri shinbun*, 31 August 1989).

The again repeated remark that armed attacks on *shūgakusei* were happening over the whole country seemingly served to strengthen reader expectations of a sequel while also legitimating such sequels. As for evidence, on 15 August two cases occured. Both match the constructed pattern and provide material for the continuation of the series of reports. In one of these cases the victim offered resistance and was beaten with an iron rod, but the allegedly Chinese attackers fled after another Chinese student who rushed to the victim's assistance was injured with a knife (*Asahi shinbun*, 16 August 1989). In the other case it was again reported that a 'gang of four' had threatened a Chinese student with a knife and robbed him (*Saitama shinbun*, 17 August 1989). Three suspects in the latter case were apprehended in October and confessed to two robberies. Allegedly they had founded a gang together with three other Chinese (all six of them from Fujien province). They were said to have organized holdups of economically better-off Shanghai-Chinese. They were also charged with further offences. In their depositions the suspects claimed they were in a financial predicament due to the debts they incurred for travel to Japan. They claimed also that because of the high cost of living in Japan they had seen no alternative than to take to robbery in order to meet their financial obligations (*Hokkaidō shinbun*, 9 October 1989). The same motive was given in an elaborate report on another gang in the *Asahi shinbun*. It told of a gang of ten which had operated in groups of three or four men who staged armed attacks (*Asahi shinbun*, 6 October 1989). The group was also charged with the robbery of a credit card from a couple from Shanghai. They allegedly had used it to withdraw 680,000 yen (*Yomiuri shinbun*, and *Mainichi shinbun*, both 20 September 1989). Further newspaper reports covered additional apprehensions and the course taken by the investigation (*Kanagawa shinbun*, 18 November 1989 and 3 December 1989, also *Asahi shinbun*, 3 December 1989). More 'intra-ethnic' conflicts were publicized in the same period. A Chinese student was injured with a knife by his workmate and countryman (*Asahi shinbun*, 3 November 1989); three Chinese were mugged by two other Chinese (*Asahi shinbun*, and *Kanagawa shinbun*, both 5 November 1989), and a Chinese student was severely wounded by a compatriot (*Nihon keizai shinbun*, 11 November 1989).

At the beginning of 1990, one could read of a case which was featured under the title 'troubles among Chinese' (*Chūgokujin dōshi no toraburu*). Five students were charged for confining a fellow-countryman to his apartment, menacing him with a knife, and robbing him. The victim was said to have been a middleman for an 'agent' of *shūgakusei*. The upset suspects had paid high commission fees for documents needed to obtain visas, but the supplied papers had been insufficient and no visas had been issued (*Nihon keizai shinbun*, 27 February 1990).

Soon after this incident a headline appeared following the finding of the corpse of a Chinese; 'Chinese stabbed, died. Fight among friends?' The report speaks of people having witnessed an argument between the victim and three young men on the road. The disappearance of three workmates of the deceased led the police to suspect that they had been the offenders (*Nihon keizai shinbun*, 16 March 1990). A further homicide case in which the victim and the perpetrator were both Chinese was reported in all of its gory detail from the dissection of the corpse to the packing of the remains into more than ten plastic bags and the sending of them to the bottom of a river. This reporting-style was presumably intended to add a bit of horror to the story. The offender confessed, saying that he had killed his fellow-lodger because of a dispute over borrowed money (*Yomiuri shinbun*, 29 June 1990).

At the beginning of September another sequel appeared. A Chinese was stabbed to death in a bar in the Kabukichō area of Shinjuku, Tokyo after an argument with a compatriot. (*Nihon keizai shinbun*, 3 September 1990, with the theme marked in the headline by the term 'among Chinese' – *Chūgokujin dōshi*). Several days later a robbery occurred, the report on which was also tied into the theme by means of repeated employment of the verbal signal 'robbery gang' – *gōtōdan* (*Asahi shinbun*, 7 September 1990). A gang of seven Chinese reportedly had tied and gagged six fellow countrymen and robbed them of credit cards and cash. The arrest of four suspects is noted in large type. The title, the term 'attack' (*shūgeki*) and the subtitle underscores the 'illegal' status of the alleged assailants with the phrase *fuhō shūrōchū* – 'during engagement in illegal labour' (*Asahi shinbun*, 9 October 1990; also reported in *Nihon keizai shinbun*, 9 October 1990).

8.4.1.5 Summary

Under the general press theme 'conflicts between foreign compatriots' two sub-themes are evident. The first, with regard to Pakistanis, concerns disputes over labour trafficking which are 'resolved' by resorting to violence. The second, with regard to Chinese, concerns the formation of 'gangs' which mug their compatriots. Moreover, any criminal incident occurring among foreign nationals seems to be perceived as newsworthy. If one looks into particular stories without sorting them according to nationalities – as they were sorted here for analytical reasons – a tightly woven net of homologous reports emerges. This, *in extremum*, conveys the image that foreigners are unusually often involved in violent intra-national rows. This is consequently asseverated in popular publications such as Nishio Kanji's pleading for a 'closing of the country', where he claims 'murders frequently occur among them [illegal workers]' – *karera dōshi no satsujin mo tahatsu*'. Some pages later he alludes to the surge of crimes among groups of foreigners resulting out of troubles regarding introduction of labour by labour agents (Nishio, 1989a: 239 and 243). A coterminous formulation can be found in the Justice Ministry organ *Kokusai jinryū*, in which the most recent entry-statistics are also regularly publicized. In a report on violations of the Immigration Control Act in 1989, this journal says that the intervention of fellow-countrymen in labour trafficking had led to a marked trend of (violent) disputes among compatriots (HNK, 1990: 45). Here the recurrent media topic 'conflicts among foreigners' sediments into a general imputation which is expeditiously formulated as a trend.

In an already-cited study based on questioning of offenders by police, however, the 'information policy' of the mass media centring on frictions among foreigners, is openly rebutted. Although the sample of violent offences is small (twenty-three victims), viewed from a victimological perspective, it reveals that twelve victims were Japanese, seven were of the same (foreign) nationality as the offender, and four were of a different foreign nationality from that of the offender (Suzuki, 1990a: 53). Nonetheless, the *White Book on the Police* claims that of homicides by foreigners, the proportion in which compatriots were victims was 63.7 per cent, and thus 'relatively high'. But if one looks into the total of recorded 'violent crimes', half of the victims are Japanese (eighty-six persons) and seventy-five (43.6 per cent) are compatriots of the offender (Keisatsuchō, 1990: 38). Two factors have to be taken into consideration here: first, offences defined by police as 'violent' commonly are altered in the course of judicial proceedings. At the stage of prosecution and adjudication they are often 'bargained down', that is, reduced to lesser charges which may then fall out of the category of serious crime (cf. Kaiser, 1989: 387). This explains the gap between the much higher number of 'violent offenders' so designated by police and the number actually convicted of violent offences. This may serve to rebut the polemical remark of Nishio Kanji, who asserts that foreign suspects were quickly expelled without arraignment and court hearing (he explicitly refers to the 'group attack' by Pakistanis, regarding which, out of allegedly twenty people involved, only one was charged with murder and brought to trial, cf. Nishio, 1989: 243f.). Secondly, the 'relatively high' proportion of victims from the same country is hardly surprising. Homicide is a 'relationship-offence'. As criminologists have shown, murders mainly occur within a close social group. This closeness pertains also to class and nationality, where victim and offender

> to a high degree associate with others like themselves . . .
> Hence it follows that homicides do not represent the
> monstrosity they are stereotypically made out to be. Mostly

they are a matter of attempts (very often on the defensive) to resolve a conflict which has escalated spontaneously or after a long relationship. The conflict is rooted less in the personalities of the subsequent perpetrator or victim but rather than interaction itself (Sassen, 1985: 493).

This holds true for problems sometimes negotiated violently among 'illegal' labourers in Japan. It has to be taken into account that their interaction is strongly structured by social opportunities and constraints and is influenced by factors attendant to their living conditions. This is especially the case regarding their opportunities for gainful employment, which are restricted by labour-market and statutory factors. In the unskilled sector, paid employment is accessible to foreign 'unqualified' workers only through 'alternative' channels, due to their 'illegalization'. These conduits entail constellations of potential conflict. The focusing of the press on personal troubles and motives of the offenders, therefore, obscures the overall societal context which constitutes and restricts the *Lebenswelt* of 'illegals'. The emphasis on 'peculiar' *modus operandi*, or accidental, but 'thrilling' details (extravagant weapons, unusual bodily injuries, holding victims prisoner, and so forth) serves as stylistic means of revalorizing the crime stories (something which affects crime reporting on Japanese suspects also). When even police attempt to correct exaggerated media reporting, this can be seen as indicating that the media have indeed succeeded in their goal of (distorted) image-formation.

This image then condenses into panic-instigating statements such as those insistently voiced by Nishio, the militant proponent of a defensive policy against 'guest-workers'. In an interview Nishio alluding to Germany and France, claims that acceptance of guest-workers leads to the emergence of 'states inside the state' (*kokunai kokka*). Not only Muslims, but any groups which import a different culture, religion and historical background into a foreign country were prone to 'enclose themselves with a fence', 'close their minds' and 'engage in internal wars' (*naibu de tōsō o kurihirogeru*); for example, in Japan for two years there had been frequent cases of Pakistanis killing each other (*Pakisutanjin dōshi no koroshiai, to itta jiken ga tahatsu shite iru*). They would make absolutely no contacts to Japanese and settle all their disputes internally. In Japan – however the evidence at present is scarce – the formation of 'states within the state' loomed. With formal admittance of foreign labour a caste-system below the Japanese people would evolve. The hierarchies of this caste-system would lead to appalling internal combats until they achieved stability. As a consequence, Japanese unskilled workers would be ousted (Nishio, 1990a:186 and 187). This rhetoric is a blatantly propagandist and opiniated consequence of Nishio's own agenda. Nonetheless, he can count on (latent) sympathy for his polemic – a sympathy bolstered by the style of media reporting. An official computation by the Ministry of Justice of violations of the Immigration Control Acts claims (as mentioned above) that the trafficking of foreign labourers by labour agents of the same nationality as their clients was a situation fraught with conflict (especially disputes over money) (HNK, 1990:45).

The concentration of the media on 'intra-ethnic conflicts', is on the one hand in keeping with a voyeuristic consumer demand (the more so because no Japanese citizens are directly involved), but on the other hand, it conveys an image of dangerousness, brutality and violence, an image which can easily become the dominant one of 'illegal foreigners' in Japan.

8.4.2 The image of 'robbery committed by foreigners'

A further foreigner-specific offence-image can be inferred from the relative frequency of reports on robbery and burglary involving foreigners. Mostly these offences seem to interest the media because of the way they are perpetrated (which is reconstructed to meet media criteria) this often being characterized by brute force or by the operation of an organized group (or both). I shall begin here by listing such 'robbery stories' by (translated) headline only. I shall comment on only those articles which are particularly notable for their reporting style or emphasis, or for their journalistic ploys.

- 'Robbery of jewels and the like [worth] 200 million yen. Gang of three Chinese? Shopkeeper locked up. Tokyo' (*Hokkaidō shinbun*, 9 July 1988).
- 'Jewellery plunder by Hong Kong people. Four persons searched' (*Asahi shinbun*, 6 August 1988). The same incident as above.
- ' "Bakusetsudan": 22 persons arrested, four searched. Group of Hong Kong nationals', (*Mainichi shinbun*, 13

October 1988). Bakusetsu-gang is an organized syndicate (*baku* – 'forced open, explode', and *setsu* – 'steal'). It reputedly consists of seventy-eight men who specialize in breaking in through walls (of jewellery stores) to seize valuables and a 'group of fifty-six experts' who shoplift in jewellers' shops. The 'wallbreaking group' was charged with twenty-six offences, and the shoplifting-group with seventy-five. All of the main suspects were said to be members of the 'Mafia' in Hong Kong, which had mobilized gang-members to go to Japan. The high value of the stolen goods is referred to.

- 'Gang of three Philippinos steal 400,000 yen, Saitama. Company in Toda' (*Asahi shinbun*, 6 November 1988).
- 'Precious metals [worth] 45 million yen taken. A further group of the Bakusetsudan?' (*Mainichi shinbun*, 12 December 1988).
- Specializing in jewellery stores: [stolen goods valued at] 80 million yen. Three foreigners nabbed' (*Mainichi shinbun*, 15 December 1988).
- 'Member of the "Bakusetsudan" nabbed. Shoplifting in Nagoya; shop-owner captures [offender]' (*Nikkan supōtsu shinbun*, 22 December 1988).
- 'Pickpocketing by band of two Chinese. Arrested in Ueno' (*Nihon keizai shinbun*, 26 December 1988).
- 'Robbery "business-trip" from Hong Kong. Gang of three; one staff member stabbed' (*Hokkaidō shinbun*, 9 January 1989). Noteworthy here is the creation of the concept *shutchō gōtō;* which literally means robbers travelling on business.
- 'The Bakusetsu-gang steals jewels worth 45 million yen Nihonbashi' (source undocumented; KNK, 7, 86).
- 'Pinball larceny gang. Three apprehended jewellery thieves. Robbed the pachinko-machine key' (*Mainichi shinbun*, 18 February 1989). According to police the suspects were 'three foreigners' (one Thai, two Taiwanese). In the environs of Tokyo thefts from pinball-halls are said to have risen and are allegedly to be the work of the same offenders.
- 'Three members of a Korean pickpocket-gang apprehended' (*Mainichi shinbun*, 11 March 1989).
- 'Be on guard in the lobby of Narita airport. Pair of foreign

pickpockets makes frequent appearances' (*Yomiuri shinbun*, 12 May 1989). It is worth mentioning that the suspicion is instantly fixed into the headline with the warning to beware of foreigners (the mildly pejorative term *gaijin* is used). Around twenty (pickpocket cases) are claimed to have occurred.

- 'Ambushed, takings stolen. Group of two South East Asians' (*Nihon keizai shinbun*, 28 May 1989). Emphasis is given to the beating of the victim with an iron rod.
- 'Iron rod? Robbery in broad daylight. Asians? 1.28 million yen seized. Pachinko-parlour worker injured' (*Asahi shinbun*, 28 May 1989). The same case as above, the references to the iron rod and to broad daylight are printed extra bold.
- 'Chinese pickpockets nabbed' (*Yomiuri shinbun*, 17 June 1989).
- 'Robbery by gang of four Chinese in Kawaguchi. Assault on compatriots' (*Mainichi shinbun*, 25 June 1989).
- 'Foreigners commit holdup on the street. High quality wrists watch, etc., robbed. Chiba Noda' (*Mainichi shinbun*, 18 November 1990).
- ' "Japan is a paradise for pickpockets". Confession: more than 420 offences with earnings of 9.7 million yen. Three apprehended Koreans' (*Asahi shinbun*, 22 November 1990).[3]
- 'Three Chinese attempt robbery' (*Kanagawa shinbun*, 28 November 1990).
- 'Rings and the like worth 14 million yen stolen. South East Asian men, shortly after they came to the store' (source undocumented: KNK, 18, 92). Here it is worth remarking that the owner of the jewellery store became aware of the loss of seventy items after two foreigners had entered the shop. He suspected them of taking the valuables. This suspicion is instantly utilized for the headline.

It is evident that most of the offences reported were committed by groups which had committed a series of similar crimes. As has been repeatedly remarked, this affects police statistics (particularly in cases of 'professional multiple crimes') inflating certain categories through multiple registration. Note too that these crimes cannot be imputed to 'illegal' labour migrants. The frequent reports in competing print media of property offences committed by professional gangs influence public reporting behaviour. Shopkeepers sensitized by these reports might become more inclined to report even petty cases to the police, so that even 'spontaneous, harmless' shoplifting will result in police intervention. The prosecuting authorities methodically launch the suspicion that foreign shoplifters have entered Japan with the 'goal' of perpetrating larcenies. This can lead, as I have shown for particular cases, to aggravated charges and unduly harsh punishment.

8.4.3 Reports on foreign 'Mafia' organizations

The surge in professional criminal organizations perceiving Japan as a lucrative target-country is repeatedly underscored in various publications and in statements by the police. Thus one study comments:

Professional criminal gangs, backed presumably by an international crime syndicate, one after another enter economically well-off Japan, which has no power of resistance against international crime. Japan therefore becomes the target of its crimes. These are large-scale, plotted and perpetrated audaciously. They transcend the common experience of the Japanese [*Nihonjin no kankaku o koeta . . . hanzai*]. Offenders immediately escape abroad and repeatedly commit crimes in a hit-and-run fashion' (Mishima, 1988:89).

The style of these suppositions is ideological, given Japan, that a country with a surprisingly well-established (and accepted) organized-crime scene (cf. Herbert, 1992c), can hardly be deemed to lack 'immunity' to international crime. Equally, it is scarcely tenable that the methods of foreign criminals are so extraordinary, or differ so greatly from those of Japanese criminals in similar cases, that they would be 'outside the common experience' of the Japanese. Disregarding the over-generalization and the invocation of the pseudo-metaphysical 'common experience' what is really meant is that 'foreign criminals' are especially brutal, bold and cold-blooded. The alleged contrast here with Japanese criminals reveals subtle, but nonetheless massive, discrimination.

In analyses appearing in the mass media, the 'brutality' and heinousness of the methods of foreign criminals is deplored. This is particularly so in articles tallying offences retrospectively and postulating a future increase in crimes of foreigners in line with further 'internationalization'. Thus we find an article headlined: 'Crimes of foreigners becoming more heinous and rapidly on the rise',[4] Here one can further read that the 'increasing atrociousness of robberies and murders is conspicuous'. In a 'murder case committed by a group of Pakistanis the "roughness" of methods [*arappoi teguchi*] not seen in conventional crimes surprised the investigating authorities'. After listing 'group attacks on foreigners' the article states that police suspected that around seven to eight groups were operating in Tokyo and its environs. Tighter border control is accordingly demanded in the article's conclusion. The re-introduction of visa-obligations for Pakistanis in January of that year is extolled (*Asahi shinbun*, 4 April 1989).

The cipher 'Mafia' hastily serves to characterize foreign groups which come to notice of the police. This is made clear in the title of another article: 'With illegal labour the "Mafia" is budding' (Sugano, 1989). With this contention a direct relation between 'illegal' labour and the 'Mafia' is maintained. This has stereotype-forming effects insofar as the high frequency of reporting on foreigners victimized by trafficking organizations intensifies this image – notwithstanding the fact that the underground conduits themselves are a consequence of legislation which illegalizes foreign manual labour. In the above-cited article the author refers to conflicts among Pakistanis and to police suspicions of the presence in Tokyo of Mafia-like organizations from Taiwan, by police. He then recurs to a Police *Whitebook*, in which it is said that crimes of foreigners had surged eight-fold over the last ten years. He further claims that the situation of the Italian immigrants in North America at the time of the emergence of the Mafia would have been comparable to that of illegal labour migrants in Japan. The problem of illegal labour had to be tackled efficiently for the sake of the country's future, and the evolving 'crime organizations' (or 'Mafia') had to be 'nipped in the bud' (Sugano, 1989:o.S.). This kind of moralistic exhortation and heroic optimism regarding control, policing, prevention and repression, is characteristic of the unimaginative and conservative approach of many Japanese journalists. Such unreflective 'instant criminal sociology', disregarding overall societal mechanisms and scientific findings on the futility of 'prevention' while social conditions remain unchanged

296

(with repression often being counter-productive), is commonly expounded in editorials addressing issues of crime.

In the same newspaper in the previous year in a report on tightened border controls and the planned establishment of an international criminal investigations information centre at Narita airport, Tokyo, the following reductionist causal claim appeared: 'The rapid increase of illegal labour also becomes a hotbed for the growth of crime...' (*Yomiuri shinbun*, 29 November 1988). One month later a competing paper published a global analysis in which similar formulas were repeated. It particular, the rise in offences against property committed by foreign professional gangs in hit-and-run style was sensationalized (*Asahi shinbun*, 24 December 1988). Since then, foreign professional criminals have become a standardized theme.

The Mafia-metaphor is finally vulgarized in the gutter-press. In a special report on hit-and-run offences, descriptions are given of gangs from Hong Kong 'robbing jewellery stores in broad daylight', and of conflicts among Pakistanis allegedly resulting from disputes between rival gangs of the 'Pakistani mafia' over territories. As could be expected, the surge in officially recorded offences committed by foreigners is also dramatized. Almost every journalistic buzz-word associated with the theme appears in the title: 'Foreign robbery gangs operate secretly. Affluent Japan is targeted... rob their illegally staying companions in broad daylight... bold and fearless burglaries of jewellery stores...' (*Nikkan supōtsu shinbun*, 12 October 1990). The precipitant labelling of diverse Pakistani gangs as 'Mafia' is a stylistic trick to arouse feelings of apprehension. Here both topics – that of 'intra-ethnic conflicts' and that of 'robbery stories' – are united under the general description 'Mafia', despite the fact that their offence-structures are totally different. This can be seen as corroboration for the thesis that undifferentiated stereotypical and 'popular' images of offences were manufactured.

The police particularly suspect that certain regions of Japan are targeted by foreign criminal organizations. In Fukuoka three large-scale robberies occurred. In one case the offenders were armed with handguns, and were identified by the victims as 'Asian foreigners'. This led the police to speculate, that 'The city of Fukuoka, situated close to Asia, becomes the target of Asian organized crime gangs'. The article bears a typical headline, which instantly solidifies this conjecture of the police: 'Crimes committed by foreigners occur frequently. Fukuoka becomes the target area for Asian gangster organizations' (*Ryūkyū shinpō* 5 January 1990). After the arrest in September of a Malaysian who was charged with three robberies, the police maintained that seven or eight Malaysians had founded a robbery gang. This is immediately established as a general trend: the crimes of foreigners were on a sudden increase (*kyūzō*) and the perpetration of criminal acts of foreigners in groups is stated to be a new tendency (*gaijin hanzai no shūdanka keikō*). This is put into the main headline: 'Crimes of foreigners become increasingly refined and collective' (*Yomiuri shinbun*, 10 September 1990).

In September 1992, two policemen were injured by shots from the gun of a 'South East Asian' at a stop procedure to establish his identity in the Kabukichō entertainment-area of Shinjuku, Tokyo (see for example, *Asahi shinbun*, 16 September 1992). This led to a gush of magazine reports on foreign organized gangsters, illustrating that once a theme is constructed it can be recycled when a new incident occurs which is perceived as being related to the topic. The reporters employed all of the devices we have noted, quoting police officers as 'authorities' and using police data, but also citing the apprehensions expressed by Japanese Yakuza, who claimed that foreigners (even women) would carry knives, were prone to unpredictable behaviour, and were dangerous. The list of alleged foreign 'Mafia-organizations' operating in Japan is almost as long as the list of the countries of origin of foreigners in Japan. Gangster groups said to be active underground in Japan allegedly come from: Korea, Taiwan, Thailand, Iran, Columbia, Israel, Pakistan, China, Cambodia, Sri Lanka, the Phillipines, Malaysia, Singapore, Turkey, Nigeria, Ghana and South Africa. It is concluded that 'The foreign Mafia-organizations stage their rivalry-fights in the affluent "Land of gold", Zipangu . . . If one leaves that situation to itself, Japan will be dominated by the Mafia before one knows it' (Hirono and Kobayashi, 1992:34). Thus a phenomenon limited to certain districts (foreigners in entertainment areas) is inflated into a danger to the whole country, and every offence perpetrated by more than one foreigner is immediately attributed to a 'Mafia' (a term apt to arouse associations with Chicago-in-the-1930s, but hardly applicable to every form of 'organized' crime, irrespective of degree of organization – which can well be a matter of loose, spontaneously formed groups – and the nationalities involved). Fiction and speculation abound, and are sufficient for fabrication of a good story which may give a 'thrill' to the reader. Of course the situation is predicted to become worse ('only bad news is good news') and clamp-downs are called for and stricter policing invoked. The new police slogan is 'border-less crime', which even appears in the subtitle of the 1992 *White-book* (for a more detailed analysis of this reporting wave in the fall of 1992, cf. Herbert, 1993; for journalistic accounts of 'foreign crime organizations' see, for example, Hirono and Kobayashi, 1992; Kamimura, 1991; Okuda, 1992). Apprehension regarding a worsening of law and order and an increasing 'Americanization' can also be found in a book claiming to be scientific, in which 'internationalization' and the influx of South East Asian migrant workers is quickly linked with a threat to public security (in the book Yamanaka, 1989:218, a work on Yakuza by the self-pro-claimed criminologist). What I wanted to demonstrate in this chap-ter is that the term 'Mafia' is rashly applied, and is a metaphor void of analytical value and apt only to foment anticipatory fears and stigmatization of Asian 'illegal' foreigners as potential 'gang-sters' by shaping (or rather distorting) perceptions of 'illegal' migrants in general.

8.5 Evaluation of the 'Media-Effect' – Concluding Remarks and Central Thesis

There is a dynamic interplay between police regarding a new development in crime and the crime reporting of the daily press. The trend conceived by the authorities is amplified by the media. Periodic recapitulations and general analyses are illustrated with data released by the police, which corroborate the pre-defined tendency (of more crimes committed by foreigners). This style of reporting reinforces in the reader the impression of potential escalation in the future and of further risks to public safety (which, in consequence of the cumulative effects of press reports on the themes of foreigner crime and the 'rapid increase' in foreign labour is already seen as a 'problem'). Semantically, the develop-ment is described as having the character of a process of aggrava-tion with notions such as 'rapid increase', 'growing internationalization of crime', 'crimes of foreigners getting more brutal', 'increasing subtlety', 'foreign criminals show higher degree of organization', being used. The implicit comparison suggests that an acceleration and aggravation can be predicted.

From the middle of the 1980s, and peaking between 1988 and 1990 (particularly after promulgation of the amendment to the Immigration Control and Refugee Recognition Act), 'illegal' workers in Japan were a constant theme in politics and the media. The topicality of their criminality was just one part of the whole discourse concerning 'internationalization', the opening or closing of the labour market, the restriction or liberalization of conditions for entry or residence, and so forth. But in this context the topic was politically and socially opportune. In quantity, the coverage of crimes was not great. But qualitatively, the concentration on crimes of violence by foreigners, the accentuation of their 'illegal' status, and the repeated 'warning' by the media of a link between immigration and crime, had the effect of forming sterotypes, which were contoured especially against the backdrop of the fabrication of a 'social problem'. The daily press rather increased than corrected the suspicion that foreign 'unskilled' labourers were 'illegal' and therefore potentially criminal. In conjunction with an inclination among Japanese to inform the police about activities of foreigners, this has to be viewed as a factor in the production of excessive figures for foreigner crime (this is not to be understood as direct causal relation but rather as an amplifying variable in a complex web of effects).

> In the same way as actions of specialists in institutionalized agencies of control in social intercourse with deviants and perpetrators are directed by everyday theories on delinquency, common people are directed by them in situations of interaction involving processes of informal social control (Stein-Hilbers, 1976:78).

These everyday theories are mostly shaped at second-hand. 'Factual knowledge' in highly differentiated societies is disseminated primarily through the consumption of mass media. This leads to grossly erroneous assessments of the 'reality of crime', with the importance and frequency of felonies being over-estimated, and feelings of menace being exacerbated (cf. Stein-Hilbers, 1976:83 and 79f.), A contributing factor might be, for example, that crimes of violence committed by foreigners are not directly perceived or experienced, but become part of the reality of everyday life through 'anonymous abstractions' and 'typifications' (cf. Berger and Luckmann 1990:36). The 'illegal migrant worker' then figures as a 'type' in the context of the coverage of crime – for example, under the topic 'violent intra-ethnic conflict' which was fabricated by the media in the first place. At least it is self-evident that a conceptualization and 'ability to perceive reality' of the crimes of foreigners is a product of media reporting. A crime wave is 'a kind of social awareness, crime brought to public consciousness' (Fishman, 1978:531). It may be conjectured that the status 'foreigner' becomes a 'significant symbol', which signals that the 'other' acts deviantly (and thereby the role of scape-goat is assigned). The instruments of argumentation function to build up a (fictive) consensus, by which more-rigid laws and more-severe control should be legitimized (cf. Smaus, 1978:193). This function of legitimation embedded in the coverage of crimes also serves the interests and the information policy of the agencies of control. It is the matrix of interaction – whereby the actors reciprocally take each other into consideration – between distribuents (police), agents and multipliers (journalists, editors), and the consumers of criminal reports (who want 'information' and entertainment). Those reports constitute the 'publicized', and therefore perceptible, 'reality' of the delinquency of foreigners. This 'reality' is, as shown before, distorted, and not adequate to permit a rational and unbiased perception of foreign workers. The opinion polls mentioned reveal a latent fear of crimes committed by foreigners. In the political debate these amorphous fears are utilized and put into abstract formulations such as 'the public safety would become precarious with the acceptance of foreign labour'. It is made tactical use of to elucidate the necessity of restrictive measures. The whole social climate favours repression and control, and therefore 'protects' and facilitates the criminalization of the foreign 'illegal' workers. Disciplining 'illegal' labourers via the penal code and indictments for contravention of special law provisions (immigration related laws), a rigid punitive policy (severe sentences, reduced chances of suspension) and the rhetoric of prevention, indicate that a restrictive atmosphere also directs and influences the daily work of legal staff and the judiciary. The 'purveyors' of 'cases' (meaning human beings) who are to be 'treated', are the police and the population, the consistently arraigning prosecutors and the stiffly sanctioning judiciary, who interact in a way that can be interpreted as an unconscious 'consensual strategy of criminalization' of foreign workers. The sole counter-influence is from concerned lawyers and human rights movements. But it can be argued that their influence is weak, and that given the political 'consensus' in favour of non-admission of 'illegal' workers they are relegated to a marginal position. The argument for high criminality of foreign 'illegal' workers is ultimately a factor producing their delinquency, that is, the delinquency that surfaces statistically in worried appeals for intervention to the control agents. In the topsy-turvy conclusion, the statistics are instrumentalized to legitimate a restrictive immigration policy and serve the rationalization of latent xenophobic stereotypes. This 'functionalizing' of the ascription of a 'high criminal potential' to foreigners can be found also in other countries experiencing 'high' and 'unexpected' immigration.

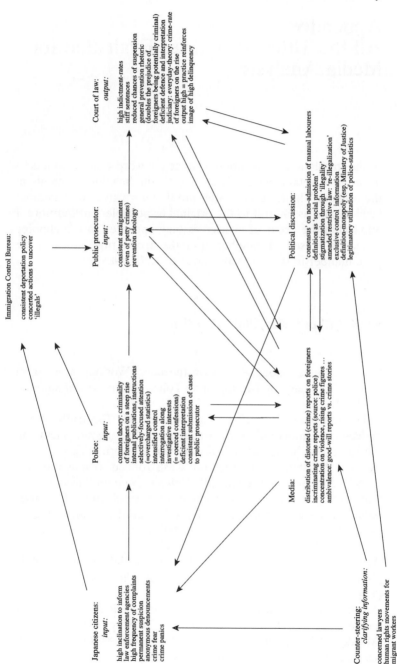

Figure 8.1 Feedback model: how to create a crime wave

303

Appendix
All the Titles of Articles Evaluated for Media Analysis

In the translation I tried not to change the word-order (too much) in order to retain the emphasis put on the headline-elements in the original. The translated titles are therefore given in 'headline-fashion' and as faithful to the original as possible. Furthermore, I duplicated the order of articles as they appeared in the clipping collection I used. A number after the article title indicates the page number in the respective issue of *KNK* 1988–90.

KNK 3 (April/May 1988, 11 articles)

'Wage-disputes among Asians on the rise. "Working away from home". Summary by Metropolitan Police Office', *Asahi shinbun* 20 April (6).

'Migration blues. Report: Foreign workers 11. The truth on the melee-case. Intervention by wage-embezzling agent. Vicky on the run opens his mouth', *Asahi shinbun* 13 April (14).

'Among Pakistani fellow migrant: Cash robbed, revenge attack, Adachi: 5 persons apprehended', *Mainichi shinbun* 9 May (152).

'Pakistani, group attack. Two compatriots severely injured. District Adachi. 5 persons arrested', *Nihon keizai shinbun* 9 May (152).

'More than 10 Pakistani attack. 2 fellow countrymen seriously wounded', *Kanagawa shinbun* 9 May (152).

'With one needle telephone call abroad. Fraudulent use of public phones rampant. Foreign workers', *Mainichi shinbun* 17 May (154).

'Murder among fellow-*japayuki*. The March incident. One person nabbed, one searched', *Yomiuri shinbun* 26 May (155).

'Murder of Bangladeshi offence of 2 compatriots. One arrested, one searched', *Asahi shinbun* 26 May (155).

' "*Japayuki*" carrying hemp. 2 Pakistani nabbed', *Yomiuri shinbun* 31 May (157).
'Principal offender in the group attack case on Pakistani. Illegitimate export of more than 100 used cars. In cooperation with Japanese dealer. Passport-abuse, customs duties evasion', *Yomiuri shinbun* 29 May (158).

KNK 4 (June/July 1988, 16 articles)

'The Pakistani importing hemp committed for trial', *Chiba nippō* 1 June (4).
'Searched compatriot in Bangladeshi-murder arrested', *Asahi shinbun* 9 June (4).
'Foreign women also apprehended for the first time. Streetwalkers, advancing in age conspicuous. Month of prostitution control', *Kanagawa shinbun* 3 June (4).
'Burglary with violence into home of fellow-countrymen: 2 Pakistani arrested', *Mainichi shinbun* 11 June (5).
'Search of date-club. Four Philippinos nabbed' *Chiba nippō* 17 June (8).
'Mistake of Immigration Control, simple re-entry. Expulsed Pakistani. Passport-name misread', *Yomiuri shinbun* 16 June (9).
'Arrest of friend who phoned [the telephone number] 119. Murder of Korean female in Ishikawa', *Asahi shinbun* 29 June (9).
'South-East Asians? Robbery. 12 Bangladeshi victimized. Furukawa', *Ashai shinbun* 27 June (10).
'Band of two Philippinos, waylaid and slashed [pub-owner]. Chiba city: Enraged by admonition', *Chiba nippō* 29 June (12).
'4 *japayuki* arrested for prostitution', *Yomiuri shinbun* 30 June (12).
'Arrest in murder of Korean woman. Incredible: friend who reported [the case]. Relationship since one year. The unnatural circumstances of detection', *Yomiuri shinbun* 29 June (13).
'Slashed by Philippino employees', *Yomiuri shinbun* 29 June (13).
'Jewels etc. 200 million ¥ plunder. Group of 3 Chinese? Shop-owner locked up in store. Tōkyō', *Hokkaidō shinbun* 9 July (21).
'Incidents, accidents involving foreign workers on steep rise. Com-

mission for countermeasures organized by prefecture police',
Yomiuri shinbun 24 June (80).

'Rapid increase in migrant workers from abroad. Prefecture police
establishes commission for countermeasures', *Asahi shinbun* 24
June (80).

'Foreign labour. National Police Agency: analysis and countermeasures. Illegal work: Intervention by organized crime, new income
source. [Emergence of] slums: troubles with residents in the neighbourhood', *Yomiuri shinbun* 20 June (81).

KNK 5 (August/September 1988, 17 articles)

'Laotian refugee: "entry-agent". Introduced 30 Thai to factories.
Committed for trial by prefecture police', *Kanagawa shinbun* 6
August (5).

'Beastly drunk foreigner on wild rampage. Ginza: Trespassing on
hospital and offices', *Asahi shinbun* 6 August (5).

'Jewellery plunder by Hongkong-Chinese. 4 persons searched',
Asahi shinbun 6 August (5).

'Introduces Thai to work, pockets money. Laotian refugee
arrested', *Asahi shinbun* 6 August (6).

'Import of heroin equivalent to 22.1 billion ¥. Historical record of
8.2 kilogram seized. 3 Pakistani carriers apprehended', *Hokkaidō
shinbun* 14 August (9).

'Entry of *japayuki-san* with counterfeit dollars. Five persons
nabbed, "Show-money" for tourist visa', *Yomiuri shinbun* 24
August (12).

'Again comatose condition robbery. Company president robbed
of 900.000¥. Hotel in district Minato', *Mainichi shinbun* 25 August
(12).

'Again robbery after narcotization [*konsui gōtō* = "coma-robbery"] of 900.000¥. Hotel in Takanawa', *Nihon keizai shinbun* 25
August (14).

'Refugee acting as agent for foreigners arrested', *Yomiuri shinbun*
5 September (17).

'Rapid increase in illegal foreign workers. For crime prevention:
department for countermeasures. National Policy Agency: next
year', *Shinano Mainichi shinbun* 5 September (18).

'Due to sudden increase of illegal labour of foreigners. Next year department for countermeasures. National Police Agency' *Hokkaidō shinbun* 5 September (19).

'Slashing after argument. South-East-Asian man. Naka-district', *Kanagawa shinbun* 13 September (19).

'Four Indonesians nabbed for larceny. 2.6 million ¥ at Narita airport', *Asahi shinbun* 17 July (21).

'Cashing of commissions: Laotian arrested: introduction to labour of Thai coming to Japan'. *Asahi shinbun* 17 July (21).

'Prostitution of Taiwanese a.o. [organized]. 5 persons arrested. Two establishments in Shinjuku exposed', *Nihon keizai shinbun* 20 September (24).

'Illegal work of foreigners on steep rise. National Police Agency: department for countermeasures. To be set up next year', *Kanagawa shinbun* 5 September (65).

KNK 6 (October/November 1988, 7 articles)

'22 persons of the "Bakusetsu-gang" apprehended, 4 searched. Group of Hongkong-Chinese', *Mainichi shinbun* 13 October (6).

' "Forgery gang": strongpoint in Hongkong. Malaysians arrested. Several persons acting as converters coming to Japan', *Mainichi shinbun* 17 October (9).

'Philippino painter stabs. Fight in restaurant', *Kanagawa shinbun* 23 October (10).

'Group of 3 Philippinos rob 4 million ¥. Company in Saitama', *Asahi shinbun* 6 November (12).

'Foreign student [manages] prostitution bar' (no newspaper named: 30).

'Enormous profiteering by prostitution bar management. Taiwanese students a.o. arrested, *Nihon keizai shinbun* 28 October (31).

'Foreign students wooed to prostitution snack. Shinjuku. Foreign student? establishment runner nabbed', *Asahi shinbun* 28 October (31).

KNK 7 (December 1988/January 1989/February 1989, 32 articles)

'Robbery of noble metals equivalent to 45 million ¥. A group different from the Bakusetsu-gang?', *Mainichi shinbun* 13 December (10).

'Twist on personnel dispatchment. Hit with an iron rod by Bangladeshi, *Asahi shinbun* 24 December (15).

'Arrangement for the search of a Philippino man. Pubowner murder', *Kanagawa shinbun* 12 January (30).

' "Business-trip"-robbery: from Hongkong. Gang of three, company employee slashed', *Hokkaidō shinbun* 9 January (30).

'Pubowner murder of Adachi. Philippino man turns himself in', *Asahi shinbun* 12 January (31).

'Counterfeit 10.000¥ notes in Utsunomiya. Real estate agents deliver 10 notes. Philippino syndicate involved?', *Nihon keizai shinbun* 14 January (33).

'In succession: Heinous crimes involving foreigners. Towards the new founding of a "department for countermeasures". National Police Agency', *Kanagawa shinbun* 19 January (37).

'Ten-thousand-Yen-note counterfeit case. Asians biggest forgery syndicate behind. Indication by Philippine authorities', *Kanagawa shinbun* 17 January (37).

'Pubowner murder. Philippino main offender arrested. Troubles over relationship with women', *Asahi shinbun* 23 January (40).

'Illegal labour for Pakistani. Broker-organization exposed', *Mainichi shinbun* 17 January (40).

'Again coma-robbery. Company employee plundered of 70.000¥', *Mainichi shinbun* 3 February (45).

'Conciliation of Thai women. 3 persons nabbed, 20 persons under protection', *Nihon keizai shinbun* 2 February (45).

'Thai a.o. prostitution agents arrested', *Mainichi shinbun* 2 February (45).

'3 foreigners arrested. Specialized on jewellery stores: 80 million ¥', *Mainichi shinbun* 15 February (47).

'Again coma-robbery. Women disappears. Hotel in district Bunkyō', *Asahi shinbun* 8 February (49).

'Pinball larcenists gang. The jewellery thieves apprehended. Robbed machine-key', *Mainichi shinbun* 18 February (51).

'Robbery by gang of four: 250.000¥ taken away. Dwelling of Pakistani in Funabashi', *Asahi shinbun* 21 February (52).

'At knife point: "Employ me." Robbery in Sumida', *Mainichi shinbun* 26 February (55).

'Foreign student nabbed for selling fake branded articles', *Mainichi shinbun* 7 December (65).

'Chinese students: band of two commit pickpocketing. Arrested in Ueno', *Nihon keizai shinbun* 26 December (78).

'Pickpocketing by Chinese students in Ameyoko [shopping quarter]', *Asahi shinbun* 26 December (80).

'Killing of Chinese student, arson. Strangled. Crime by acquaintance? Yokohama, district Naka', *Kanagawa shinbun* 4 January (81).

'Jewels equal to 45 million ¥ robbed: the Bakusetsu-gang?' Nihonbashi' (no newspaper named: 86).

'One month after the killing of Chinese student. Why was the apartment set on fire at the same time? [Suspicion] of crime by acquaintance hardens', *Kanagawa shinbun* 3 February (91).

'Water's edge operations against crimes committed by foreigners. "International criminal investigations information center" at entrance by sky. Seven-eight men system. Establishment planned for next year', *Yomiuri shinbun* 29 November (158).

'Penal code infractions most numerous in post-war period. This year: Larcenies and involvement of foreigners increase', *Asahi shinbun* 24 December (159 and 163 = counted only once).

'Thai nabbed. Suspicion of murder of comrade', *Nihon keizai shinbun* (evening edition, no date given: 160).

'The same notes as confiscated in the Philippines? Counterfeit. 10.000 Yen-notes detected in Tōkyō', *Asahi shinbun* 16 December (161).

'Member of the "Bakusetsu-gang" seized. Shoplifting in Nagoya, captured by shop-owner', *Nikkan supōtsu shinbun* 22 December (163).

'Foreign woman? Coma-robbery. 300.000¥ from company president. Asakusa', *Kanagawa shinbun* 12 December (163).

'Philippino stabs liquor-store-owner at robbery', *Nikkan supōtsu shinbun* 4 January (164).

'Counterfeit ten thousand Yen-notes detected. Utsunomiya. Again inflow via Philippine route', *Kanagawa shinbun* 14 January (165).

KNK 8 (March/April 1988, 29 articles)

'Coma-robbery: search for Thai woman and Jordanian. Prefectural police agency', 1 March (no newspaper given: 4).

'Philippine hostess: smuggling of 4 kilo hemp. Two persons nabbed', *Asahi shinbun* 5 March (4).

'Pakistani stabbed to death. Itabashi, intrusion into apartment', *Asahi shinbun* 8 March (5).

'For illegal stay: forged stamps in passports. Two Pakistani arrested', *Asahi shinbun* 10 March (5).

'Malaysian man killed. Takazaki, entry on tourist visa', *Asahi shinbun* 14 March (5 and 8).

'Six Pakistani apprehended. Stabbing to death in Itabashi. In all more than 20 persons involved?, *Asahi shinbun* 15 March (8).

'Arrests in the "coma-robberies": Wanted man and woman. Chase-drama on highway', *Asahi shinbun* 16 March (8).

'Comrade arrested. Malaysian slain. Crime after losing at gambling', *Asahi shinbun* 19 March (8).

3 Chinese attacked with kitchen knife? Ikebukuro, assailants also look like Chinese', *Asahi shinbun* 3 April (20).

'Smuggling of dried cannabis hidden in sole of shoes. Could not walk, carried shoes in their hands: two Thai seamen apprehended', *Asahi shinbun* 8 April (21).

'Getting more heinous: the rapidly increasing crimes committed by foreigners. Several groups in metropolitan area, almost all enter with forged passports,' *Asahi shinbun* 4 April (24 and 134).

'The Pakistani-murder in Itabashi. Eight compatriots re-arrested', *Asahi shinbun* 4 April (24).

'American soldiers violate woman', *Yomiuri shinbun* 17 April (26).

'Thai worker nabbed. Robbery of snackbar in Ayase', *Yomiuri shinbun* 21 April (30).

'For prolongation of stay visa forged. 3 Chinese arrested', *Mainichi shinbun* 6 April (50).

'Renewal of visa "permission seal" forged. 3 Chinese (students) arrested. Big organization behind?', *Yomiuri shinbun* 6 April (51).

'Documents faked: illegal prolongation of stay. Chinese youth nabbed', *Nihon keizai shinbun* 6 April (51).

'Search in "coma-robberies". Thai woman and Jordanian', *Asahi shinbun* 1 March (119).

'Philippina hostess smuggles 4 kilo hashish, 2 persons arrested', *Asahi shinbun* 3 March (120).

'Pakistani attacked and stabbed to death. Group of several South-East Asians?' *Nihon keizai shinbun* 7 March (122).

'Arrests in "coma-robberies": Foreign man and woman in Kanagawa', *Nihon keizai shinbun* 16 March (127).

'Police-cordon on highway. "Coma-robbers" captured', 16 March (no newspaper named).

'Three Koreans of pickpocket-gang nabbed', *Mainichi shinbun* 11 March (127).

'Murder of Pakistani in Itabashi. Eight compatriots apprehended', *Asahi shinbun* 4 April (136).

'Eight persons re-arrested for homicide etc. Pakistani-murder', *Mainichi shinbun* 4 April (136).

'Pakistani-murder: Eight fellow countrymen nabbed. Raid on apartment in Itabashi', *Nihon keizai shinbun* 4 April (136).

' "Coma-robberies": re-arrests', *Nihon keizai shinbun* 5 April (136).

'Again counterfeit "American Treasury cheques". Detected just before cashing. Again international syndicate pulling wires?', *Mainichi shinbun* 11 April (142).

KNK 9 (May/June 1989, 18 articles)

'High profits by dispatching male *japayuki*. Real estate agent a.o. arrested', *Hokkaidō shinbun* 22 April (5).

'Illegitimate acquisition of Japanese passport. Three Koreans arrested', *Mainichi shinbun* 16 May (11).

' "Sells" Thai women to establishments: Malaysian broker arrested', *Nihon keizai shinbun* 19 June (28).

'Illegal entry with forged passports. Chinese students indicted', *Kanagawa shinbun* 10 June (51).

'Burglary with edged tool into apartment of Chinese student. Group of 4 fellow countrymen? 400.000¥ robbed. Search for one person', *Asahi shinbun* 21 June (64).

'Chinese student: Snatched 10 million Yen from woman. "Money for visa prolongation . . ." Nishi Ikebukuro', *Mainichi shinbun* 29 June (68).

'Bogus telephone cards flowing in bulk. Among foreign workers', *Yomiuri shinbun* 1 May (110).
'Be cautious in the lobby of Narita-airport. Group of two foreign pickpockets appears frequently', *Yomiuri shinbun* 12 May (115).
'Under Japanese name fraudulent acquisitions of passports. 4 Koreans nabbed', *Nihon keizai shinbun* 16 May (119).
'Ambush, returns robbed. Group of 2 South-East-Asians', *Nihon keizai shinbun* 18 May (126).
'Iron rod? Robbery in broad daylight. Asians? 1.28 million Yen robbed. Pachinko-hall employee injured', *Asahi shinbun* 28 May (128).
'Murder with knife: Chinese youth nabbed. Fight among biker gangs in Chiba', *Kanagawa shinbun* 31 May (129).
'Midway: firearms brought in? Arrest of members of smuggling gang', *Kanagawa shinbun* 6 June (135).
'Robbery by gang of 4 Chinese in Kawaguchi. Assault on compatriots', *Mainichi shinbun* 25 June (135).
'51 times entry and departure with forged passport. Uses three with Japanese names etc. Korean broker', *Mainichi shinbun* 17 June (137).
'Chinese pickpocket arrested', *Yomiuri shinbun* 17 June (137).
'Prefecture police: Linguistic barrier in internationalization of offences. Languages diversify, interpreters lacking', *Mainichi shinbun* 21 July (141).

KNK 10 (July/August 1989, 18 articles)

'Seal of the minister of Justice forged. Chinese broker apprehended', *Asahi shinbun* 29 July (19).
'Chinese compatriot nabbed. Case of robbery and mayhem on foreign students in Yokohama. One person searched', *Yomiuri shinbun* 9 August (25).
'With illegal labour the "Mafia" is budding', *Yomiuri shinbun* 13 August (25 = Sugano 1989).
'50 million Yen profit with falsified passports. 16 Koreans arrested. Aiding and abetting to illegal stay' (no newspaper named: 32).
'10 million Yen snatched away. Chinese student: "Needed money for visa-prolongation" ', *Yomiuri shinbun* 29 June (40).

'Renewal of residence permission: seal counterfeited. Chinese nabbed. Commissions from students', *Yomiuri shinbun* 29 July (51).

'Case of robbery and mayhem of Chinese student. Ex-student arrested, accomplice searched for. Connection to three similar cases?', *Yomiuri shinbun* 9 August (56).

'Unnatural death of Chinese student', *Yomiuri shinbun* 16 August (59).

'Burglary with violence into room of Chinese student', *Asahi shinbun* 16 August (59).

'Robbery by gang of four of apartment of Chinese student. Slashed with knife, stripped for cash', *Saitama shinbun* 17 August (64).

'Sale of Chinese medicine without license. Foreign students as "purveyors", tie-in with porno-videos', *Kanagawa shinbun* 22 August (65).

'Searched ex-student arrested. Case of robbery with mayhem on Chinese student. Soon deportation. Three apprehended persons,' *Yomiuri shinbun* 31 August (68).

'Police detectives: foreign languages "compulsory subject". From next month: Prefecture police. Preparation for international crimes', (no newspaper named: 158).

'During illegal stay violation of woman. Man with Pakistani nationality arraigned', *Kanagawa shinbun* 18 July (171).

'Robbery by Pakistani', *Yomiuri shinbun (Saitama-ban)* 18 July (171).

'2,000 items robbed from jewellery store. Gang of three south-East-Asians?, Fukuoka', *Asahi shinbun* 12 July (174).

'Verification: crimes committed by foreigners on rapid increase. In ten years sevenfold number of apprehended. Offences getting more heinous, extended over wide area', *Yomiuri shinbun* 16 August (175).

KNK 11 (September/October 1989, 14 articles)

'Assault, confinement of compatriots. Five Pakistani indicted', *Saitama shinbun* 21 September (12).

'Wanted Pakistani arrested', *Asahi shinbun (Saitama-ban)* 15 October (24).

'Chinese students formed burglary gang. Assail persons from Shanghai. Trouble due to repayments of travel expenses', *Hokkaidō shinbun* 10 September (42).

'Robs passports of fellow-students. Police office Kanagawa. Search for Chinese student', *Kanagawa shinbun* 13 October (48).

'Two Chinese searched for inflicting injury. Infiltration by mixing up with "refugees". Prefecture Police Office: arrests', *Hokkaidō shinbun* 14 September (146).

Two further persons searched. Chinese students-robbery gang. 680.000¥ from couple from Shanghai', *Yomiuri shinbun (Saitama-ban)* 20 September (148).

'Compatriots attacked and confined. Three Pakistani apprehended. Motive: monetary troubles', *Mainichi shinbun (Saitama-ban)* 20 September (149).

'Five Pakistani arrested: Confinement case', *Asahi shinbun (Saitama-ban)* 21 September (149).

'Search for 3 robbers from Fujien', *Mainichi shinbun (Saitama-ban)* 20 September (149).

'Attempted departure with faked passport. Two Chinese nabbed in Narita', *Hokkaidō shinbun* 19 September (149).

'Students-robbery group. Fujien-province gang. "Won't be discovered": one case after another. Could not pay back travel expenses due to high prices', *Asahi shinbun* 6 October (150).

' "Robbery gang" targeting fellow countrymen. Even arson and homicide. Life of Chinese "students" is hard', *Kanagawa shinbun* 15 October (152).

'Chinese of jewellery robbery-gang arrested', *Asahi shinbun* 25 October (154).

'Drifting ashore 7. Jipangu in fall '89. Marked increase in crimes, cold judicature', *Mainichi shinbun* 1 October (173).

KNK 12 (November/December 1989, 28 articles)

' "Helped against exhaustion from construction work." Philippinos put to trial for possession of stimulant drugs', *Kanagawa shinbun* 5 November (6).

'Maruko: Murder among Pakistani? Corpse left in company

dormitory. Cuts of the throat. Room-mate disappeared', *Shinano Mainichi shinbun* 22 November (10).

'Suspicion of illegal labour. The murdered Pakistani in Maruko. Tourist-visa expired. Company declares them as trainees', *Shinano Mainichi shinbun* 28 November (11).

'Killing of Pakistani employee. Denying fellow-worker arraigned for prosecution. Police station Maruko: "Two persons at the time of criminal act". Real evidence . . . will be brought forward', *Shinano Mainichi shinbun* 28 November 12).

'Change fraud with Taiwanese coins. Chinese student nabbed', *Nihon keizai shinbun* 4 November (21).

'Stabs fellow-worker, flees. Argument among Chinese fellow students', *Asahi shinbun* 3 November (21).

'Chinese student robbed. Employee dormitory in Yokosuka, *Asahi shinbun* 5 November (21).

'Chinese student slashes fellow student. Dispute on woman', *Nihon keizai shinbun* 11 November (22).

'Robbery and mayhem on Chinese students. Searched colleagues arrested. Police station Taura', *Kanagawa shinbun* 8 November (23).

'Carrying forged? passports. Illegally working Chinese students', *Yomiuri shinbun* 5 November (23).

'Chinese students refine stimulant drugs. Three persons nabbed. 800 million Yen seized', *Mainichi shinbun* 8 December (32).

'Two persons re-arrested, one searched. Robbery-case of Chinese students', *Asahi shinbun* 3 December (32).

' "Mami Rose" goes in hiding in Japan. Osaka Prefecture Police investigates in Philippina-forced prostitution case', *Mainichi shinbun* 4 December (32).

'Investigation after manufacturing report. Ex-policeman of Metropolitan Police Agency. American nabbed in Hashish-case', *Hokkaidō shinbun* 4 December (49).

'Discovered kitchen-knife under full-scale scrutiny. Pakistani-killing', *Shinano Mainichi shinbun* 5 December (117).

'Series bicycle-thefts by foreigners', *Mainichi shinbun* 8 December (117).

'Historical record. 21 kilo heroin equivalent 1.9 million Yen confiscated. Narita-airport. Smuggler from Hongkong? arrested', *Hokkaidō shinbun* 6 December (117).

'Smuggling of highway coupon tickets. Korean student searched.

3.06 million Yen seized at Narita airport', *Asahi shinbun* 8 December (118).

'Detention prolonged. Pakistani-murder', *Shinano Mainichi shinbun* 7 December (118).

'Strangulation of husband wishing to return home. Chinese wife: "Japan is pleasant" ', *Mainichi shinbun* 12 December (118).

'2 Chinese arrested after robbery and confinement. Police office Kagamachi. One searched', *Kanagawa shinbun* 3 December (119).

'Case of aggravated assault by Thai woman. "Sentence stiff". Support group formed: "Respect human rights even during illegal stay" ', *Asahi shinbun* 20 November (120).

'Illicit trafficking of several ten-thousand sleeping pills. Thai woman carrying big amounts', *Asahi shinbun* 7 November (121).

'Philippino stimulant drugs-gang. Eating house foothold: smuggling, use to excess. 13 persons nabbed', *Yomiuri shinbun* 4 November (121).

'Philippino on the run captured. Bonus-robbery in Kōbe', *Yomiuri shinbun* 24 December (122).

'Reservation of punishment for Thai. Linguistic barrier etc. Suspicion of homicide, evidence insufficient', *Mainichi shinbun* 12 December (124).

'Stealing is bad, leaving around too ... Foreign seamen in Yokohama. One bicycle after the other is pilfered. "When sold in South-East-Asia good pocket-money." Symbol of affluent Japan. Three Korean sailors nabbed', *Kanagawa shinbun* 8 December (125).

KNK 13 (January/February 1990, 16 articles)

'Philippino arrested for bodily injury resulting in death. Yokohama. Arbitrator stabbed', *Kanagawa shinbun* 3 January (3).

'Introduced countrymen to work: Pakistani trader indicted', *Saitama shinbun* 27 February (10).

'Conflict among Chinese on documents related to visa. Five apprehensions after abduction of a student', *Nihon keizai shinbun* 27 February (19).

'Arrest of Chinese for passport-forgery. Exquisite [counterfeit] seal impounded. One person searched', *Yomiuri shinbun* 13 January (23).

'Coloration and smuggling of stimulant drugs. Chinese students. Decoloration and refinement to high purity', *Mainichi shinbun* 21 January (23).

'Case of passport-forgery by Chinese students. Again evidence: official seal. Handed it to friend: the suspect, Chen, put to trial, *Yomiuri shinbun (Saitama-ban)* 14 February (31).

'Chinese mother stabs infant to death. Sakai. In Japan since 11 months, could not adapt', *Asahi shinbun* 4 February (42).

'Because of increase in foreigners new estblishment of department for foreigners affairs. Organizational reform of Prefecture police. From April. Priority also for preventative measures', *Asahi shinbun (Saitama-ban)* 26 February (78).

'Payday: Robbery by Pakistani. Company resident a.o. seriously wounded, two arrests', *Asahi shinbun (Saitama-ban)* 31 January (106).

'Robbery with pistol in pinball-hall. 4 million robbed, one person seriously injured. Four, five Asians? Fukuoka', *Hokkaidō shinbun* 4 January (107).

'Crimes committed by foreigners frequently occur. Fukuoka: target of Asian organized gangs', *Ryūkyū shinpō* 5 January (107).

'Chinese arrested for passport-forgery', *Nihon keizai shinbun* 14 January (110).

'Corpse of a stabbed foreign man on the street. South-East-Asian. Fight among colleagues? Yokohama, Naka-district', *Kanagawa shinbun* 24 January (11).

'Re-arrest of room-mate on suspicion of murder of compatriot. Nigerian woman stabbed to death', *Nihon keizai shinbun* 25 January (111).

'Apprehension of Peruvian sailors a.o. Cocaine contraband. Raid of freighter in Yokohama' *Yomiuri shinbun* 8 February (115).

'Two Philippinos nabbed. Murder of man on the road. Confession: premeditated offence', *Kanagawa shinbun* 6 February (116).

KNK 14 (March/April 1990, 5 articles)

'Foreign women forced into prostitution: arrests', *Asahi shinbun* 5 March (36).

'Thai woman murdered', *Asahi shinbun* 29 March (39).

'Contraband of marihuana with international mail. Including foreigners 17 persons apprehended. Twenty kilo seized', *Nihon keizai shinbun (yūkan)* 6 March (78).

'Chinese slashed, dies. Fight among fellow-workers', *Nihon keizai shinbun* 16 March (81).

'Cut up corpse of Thai woman. Apartment in Nagano. Man in company: "Have killed the woman" ', *Mainichi shinbun* 29 March (85).

KNK 15 (May/June 1990, 22 articles)

'Language "wall" in detention house. Crimes of foreigners soaring, interpreters lacking. Lawyers: "Violation of rights" ', *Asahi shinbun* 4 June (6, and 111: computed only once).

'Because of moral offences 192 apprehensions', *Kanagawa shinbun* 5 June (35).

'Arrest for trafficking into prostitution. First implementations of new Immigration Control Acts. Two Philippinas: lure three women from Philippines', *Yomiuri shinbun* 12 June (360).

'Illegal trafficking of some hundred Thai women. Woman: boss a.o., 3 persons nabbed', *Yomiuri shinbun* 13 June (36).

'First implementation of new Immigration Control Acts: Abetting to illegal labour. 3 Philippinas arrested', *Hokkaidō shinbun* 13 June (36).

'Conciliation of more than 1.000 Thai women. 900 million Yen profit in one year. Deceived, brought to Japan, prostitution. Agent residing in Japan arrested. Boss was the woman from the 11th floor, big syndicate in the back. Saitama Prefecture police', *Mainichi shinbun* 13 June (37).

'Exposure of organization for prostitution trafficking of Thai women. Controlled life, huge debts ... "Wealthy life": dark change', *Mainichi shinbun (Saitama-ban)* 14 June (38).

'142 police officers proficient in foreign languages. Internal selection at Osaka Prefecture police. Countermeasure to crimes of foreigners', *Asahi shinbun (Ōsaka-ban)*, 29 June (59).

'Trespassing foreigner stabbed, Gunma', *Ryūkyū shinpō* 12 May (102).

'Pakistani, who attacked Philippinos apprehended. Gunma, four persons', *Mainichi shinbun* 14 May (103).

'Crimes committed by foreigners increase steadily. "Handbook" for court interpreters drawn up', *Yomiuri shinbun* 9 May (103).

'Foreign labourer murdered. In dormitory of painting shop in Gunma. Counter-attack by Philippino', *Mainichi shinbun* 12 May (105).

'Conflict among fellow-workers? Stabbed man: Philippine nationality', *Yomiuri shinbun (Chiba-ban)* 1 June (112).

'South-East-Asian man stabbed to death', *Yomiuri shinbun* 31 May (112).

'Departure with stolen Japanese passport. Chinese, in succession to Canada', *Asahi shinbun* 6 June (112).

'Hid stimulant drugs in shoulder-pad of clothes. 2 Philippine nationals attempted smuggle', *Asahi shinbun (Yokohama-ban)* 9 June (112).

'Sticks sex-establishment-ads in Kita. Columbian nabbed and put to trial. Police station Sonezaki', *Mainichi shinbun* 9 June (113).

'Malaysian carrier arrested. Travellers cheques forgery', *Hokkaidō shinbun* 14 June (114).

'Malaysian arrested, Japanese sought. Counterfeited travellers cheques, task allotment', *Asahi shinbun* 19 June (114).

'Confession: "murder [committed] alone". Complicity of porter investigated', *Yomiuri shinbun (Chiba-ban)* 29 June (116).

'Man attacks female student with edged tool. Stabbed on the street, seriously injured. Sapporo', *Hokkaidō shinbun* 29 June (118).

'Slashed female student dies. Pakistani apprehended. Twist after talk on separation', *Hokkaidō shinbun* 30 June (118).

KNK 16 (July/August 1990, 29 articles)

'Police-Whitebook. Male foreign workers on rapid increase. Homicide, robberies ... heinous crimes: maximum', *Asahi shinbun (Ōsaka-ban)* 8 August (16).

'Robbery by Chinese students. Intrude into office: 3.92 million Yen', *Yomiuri shinbun* 29 August (40).

'For prolongation of stay bogus-marriage. Korean hostesses and two professional criminals nabbed', *Mainichi shinbun* 8 August (56).

'Taiwanese woman arrested for enticement to prostitution', *Kanagawa shinbun* 15 August (56).

'In 10 years almost fourfold rapid increase. "Measures against crimes involving foreigners". Tendency to heinous crimes progresses. Indications by this years Whitebook of Police', *Yomiuri shinbun* 7 August (87).

'Organizations profiting by "illegal labour". Special report on the problem of foreign labour. Police-Whitebook', *Mainichi shinbun* 7 August (88).

'Brazilian migrant workers couple burglarized. Indonesian arrested', *Kanagawa shinbun* 14 June (101).

'Pakistani stabbed on the road, severely wounded. Friend and compatriot apprehended', *Nihon keizai shinbun* 8 July (115).

'Murder of female student: Pakistani sent to court', *Hokkaidō shinbun* 2 July (115).

' "Cheap counterfeit brand goods". Israelia trader indicted', *Kanagawa shinbun* 4 July (115).

'Indonesian nabbed: Migrant workers couple burglarized', *Asahi shinbun* 14 July (117).

'Two chinese captured. Robbery of 45 million Yen. Entry to Japan after premeditating robbery offences', *Asahi shinbun* 16 July (118).

'Leading fellow Chinese woman arrested: Robbery of trading company employee', *Mainichi shinbun* 28 July (118).

'Philippino man and youth apprehended. Murder-case in Deshima, Ibaraki', *Asahi shinbun* 11 July (118).

'Two foreigners rob 12 million Yen. Construction company in Ōta-district', *Nihon keizai shinbun* 26 July (120).

'Sudden increase. Crimes by foreigners sevenfold in ten years. 2.989 persons apprehended, 90% Asians. Language barrier hampering investigations', *Tōkyō shinbun (yūkan)* 7 August (126).

'Illegal labour, crimes by foreigners increase rapidly. Police-Whitebook. Exposed labourers 3.5–fold in five years. Criminal code offenders 7.4–fold [compared with] ten years ago', *Asahi shinbun* 7 August (127).

'The isolation of a lonely youth in a foreign country. The Pakistani, who stabbed student to death. In fear of detection of illegal labour moving from place to place. Wanted to marry and settle down', *Hokkaidō shinbun* 18 August (128).

'Woman confined to room. Korean student arrested', *Yomiuri shinbun* 29 August (128).
'Suspicion on use of counterfeit cheques. Two people from Hongkong in Shinjuku', *Asahi shinbun* 26 August (128).
'Acquainted Korean nabbed. Murder of bar-employee in Shinjuku' *Yomiuri shinbun* 31 August (130).
'198 forged hundred-dollar-notes seized. Several young men using them in Shinjuku', *Asahi shinbun* 22 August (131).
'Search for man with Malaysian nationality. 10 million Yen robbery in Kamata', *Nihon keizai shinbun* 27 August (131).
'Editorial. How to receive working foreigners?', *Mainichi shinbun* 9 August (131).
'An open society and public security', *Asahi shinbun (Ōsaka-ban)* 9 August (141).
'A society, in which foreign workers live', *Tōkyō shinbun* 8 August (142).
'What is the aim of the special report on foreigners', *Hokkaidō shinbun* 11 August (143).
'Increase in foreign labourers and public security', *Yomiuri shinbun* 10 August (144).

KNK 17 (September/October 1990, 33 articles)

'With sham admission illegal stay. Pose as "auditors" of University of Yokohama. Prefecture Police Kanagawa: nine Chinese nabbed', *Yomiuri shinbun* 2 October (17).
'Enrolment forgery gang for National University of Yokohama. At several other universities faked documents too. Two organizations of Chinese. Travel bureau as camouflage', *Yomiuri shinbun* 3 October (19).
'Secret maneuvres of the "Shanghai Mafia". Forgery-case of matriculation at National University of Yokohama. Exposure of companies in the city', *Kanagawa shinbun* 18 October (21).
'Use of faked resident-permits etc. Exposure of 70 Chinese students. Yokohama', *Mainichi shinbun* 18 October (21).
'Disclosure of aiding and abetting to illegal labour. Establishments in Roppongi. Five Philippinas arrested', *Nihon keizai shinbun* 20 September (26).

'Hotel street in Shinjuku: 45 foreign women apprehended. Suspicion on offences against Immigration Control Acts', *Asahi shinbun* 12 September (26).

'Roundup of "prostitution establishments" in the vicinity of Ōgon-chō', *Mainichi shinbun (Yokohama-ban)* 27 September (27).

'Prostitution rampant. Red-light-district Ōgon-chō: Measures for purgation of neighborhood. 40 South-East-Asians exposed. Despite covering-up of establishments rapid increase', *Asahi shinbun* 27 September (27).

'Nine persons arrested, who provides facilities for prostitution', *Asahi shinbun* 5 October (27).

'Exposure of Thai women in Ōgon-chō. International syndicate behind? Nine persons providing rooms arraigned. [From] Thailand – entry with forged passports', *Asahi shinbun* 5 October (28).

'Argument among Chinese, stabbed to death', *Nihon keizai shinbun* 3 September (89).

'Two Chinese youths nabbed. Confess more than hundred thefts', *Yomiuri shinbun* 7 September (89).

'Group of seven? Robbery-gang. Raid rooms of Chinese. Edogawa', *Asahi shinbun* 7 September (89).

'Two Malaysians arrested. Robberies: Bureaus in Shinagawa', *Asahi shinbun* 5 September (89).

'Again 320 counterfeit travellers cheques cashed. Malaysian re-arrested', *Nihon keizai shinbun* 6 September (90).

'Crimes of foreigners get more and more refined and organized. Thai woman carrying four names: Passport, name she calls herself, money transfer, plane-ticket. Cannot be designated for wanted list. Malaysians form full-scale robbery gang', *Yomiuri shinbun* 10 September (91).

'Pakistani fellow-countryman attacked. 1.1 million Yen compensation for workman's accidents robbed', *Asahi shinbun* 13 September (92).

'8 Pakistani rob cash and rings. 4 persons nabbed', *Kanagawa shinbun* 13 September (92).

'New pinball-machine manipulation. South-East-Asian foreigners. Within Prefecture one damage after the other', *Yomiuri shinbun* 13 September (92).

'Two Malaysians re-arrested for robbery. Cash-robbery in Shinagawa', *Mainichi shinbun* 12 September (93).

'Suspicion on series of robberies aimed at compatriots. Pakistani-group arrested', *Asahi shinbun* 2 October (94).

'Suspicion on unlicensed trade and export of used cars. Pakistani apprehended. In 2 years 250 million Yen profit. Saitama Prefecture Police', (no newspaper named: 94).
'Malaysian robbery-gang. "losses at gambling: commit robbery and pay back". Enticement by "wire puller". Man with debts of several millions', *Mainichi shinbun* 29 September (94).
'Chinese student intimidated and robbed. Edogawa: four Chinese arrested', *Nihon keizai shinbun* 9 October (96).
'Suspicion of assault of Chinese compatriots. 6 persons nabbed, sought. While working illegally', *Asahi shinbun* 9 October (96).
'Suspicion on serial burglaries into bureaus in the metropole. 2 foreigners sought', *Asahi shinbun* 8 October (96).
'Nikkan scoop. Foreign robbery-gangs operating in the underground. The Japan overflowing with money is targeted. Honeymoon-trip as pretense for entry. Hit and run (Hongkong) Kukubat (Pakistan). Daringly burglarize jewellery stores in broad daylight. Rob their illegally staying comrades', *Nikkan supōtsu shinbun* 12 October (97).
'Malaysian robbery-gang. Boss internationally arranged for criminal investigation', *Yomiuri shinbun* 8 October (100).
'4 foreigners rob 70.000 Yen. Yokosuka', *Kanagawa shinbun* 17 October (100).
'Bangladeshi stabbed into his right side, dies', *Nihon keizai shinbun* 10 October (100).
'Handgun-contraband from Brazil. Prefecture police nabs dancer. All possible efforts exerted for exposure of route', *Mainichi shinbun* 21 October (100).
'Eleven forged hundred-thousand Yen-notes seized. Import from South-East-Asia', *Kanagawa shinbun* 22 October (101).
' "Migrant pickpockets" ' 3 Koreans arrested. JR-station Ueno', *Nihon keizai shinbun* 23 October (101).

KNK 18 (November/December 1990, 14 articles)

'Malaysians with tourist-visa. Dispatched to construction sites. Broker with Malaysian nationality arrested', *Nihon keizai shinbun* 11 December.
'New way of money laundering? Trafficking of women. As charge

"export" of scrap iron. Warrant of arrest for Thai', *Mainichi shinbun* 1 November (38).

'Visa prolongation with pseudo marriage. Two Chinese arraigned for trial', *Yomiuri shinbun* 2 November (38).

'Organization for introduction to prostitution exposed. 11 Thai sent to court', *Mainichi shinbun (Yokohama-ban)* 16 November (42).

'Again three persons. Prostitution exposed', *Kanagawa shinbun* 11 December (49).

'Two Thai apprehended. 29 kilo hashish in train station locker', *Yomiuri shinbun* 9 November (83).

'390.000¥ robbed by two blacks. Man in Yokosuka', *Kanagawa shinbun* 21 November (84).

'Robbery by foreigners on the street. High-class wristwatch etc. robbed. Chiba, Noda', *Mainichi shinbun* 18 November (84).

'Foreigners dormitory raided, cash robbed. Tochigi. Group of five Pakistani?', *Nihon keizai shinbun* 12 November (85).

' "Japan is paradise for pick-pockets". Confess 420 cases, 9.7 million Yen earned. Three arrested Koreans', *Asahi shinbun* 23 November (87).

'Bangladeshi living together nabbed. Stabbing to death-case in Saitama', *Mainichi shinbun* 27 November (87).

'Three persons from Korea caught in the act of pick-pocketing and arrested. Ueno station', *Mainichi shinbun* 3 December (88).

'Three Chinese attempted larceny. District Minato-Minami', *Kanagawa shinbun* 28 November (88).

'Rings etc. equivalent 14 million Yen stolen. Shortly after South-East-Asian men entered shop' (no newspaper named: 92).

Table Appendix 1 Media Analysis

KNK	3	4	5	6	7	8	9	10	11	12	13	14	15	16	17	18	N	%
A	11	16	17	7	32	29	18	18	14	28	16	5	22	29	33	14	309	12.9
B	–	–	1	1	5	5	5	3	1	1	3	–	2	5	7	1	40	49.2
C	8	9	6	3	16	19	6	10	11	16	8	3	8	11	14	4	152	5.2
D	1	1	1	–	–	3	–	–	–	5	2	1	1	–	–	1	16	7.8
E	1	–	1	–	5	1	3	–	1	3	–	–	1	2	2	4	24	10.7
I	1	3	3	–	3	1	1	3	1	–	2	1	3	10	5	1	33	5.8
P	–	3	1	3	–	–	1	–	–	–	–	–	2	1	3	3	18	8.4
alia	–	–	4	–	3	1	2	2	1	3	1	1	5	–	3	–	26	11.3
F	3	3	3	–	3	–	1	2	1	2	1	1	3	8	3	14	35	83.2
Q	7	11	13	7	29	26	15	15	13	17	15	4	16	22	33	–	257	12.9
QK	1	–	–	2	10	5	2	4	4	2	2	–	2	2	4	10	40	65.7
GI	6	9	7	5	18	22	10	14	13	26	12	3	11	17	20	3	203	22
G2	3	5	6	2	6	2	4	3	–	2	4	2	8	10	8	–	68	1.6
G3	2	1	1	–	·	–	1	–	1	–	–	–	–	–	–	–	5	10.7
G4	–	1	3	–	8	5	3	1	1	–	–	–	3	2	5	1	33	

A = absolute number of articles
B = fraud, embezzlement, counterfeiting etc.
C = felonious and violent crimes
D = 'drugs', narcotic drug-related offences
E = offences against property
U = global analysis of offences against the penal code by foreigners

P = 'prostitution', offences against Anti-Prostitution-Act
a = *alia* (labour trafficking, smuggling etc.)

F = 'formula', indication that 'crimes committed by foreigners are on a steep rise'
Q = source, of the article is explicitly given as police, prosecutor, judiciary
OK = allusion to involvement of Organized Crime
Signification of foreigner-status in the headline by:
G1 = nationality
G2 = foreigner, 'illegal worker', 'foreign student'
G3 = *japayuki*
G4 = no identification as 'offence committed by foreigner'

Notes

2 Phenomenology of the 'Illegal' Labour Migration to Japan

1 If one fragments a social process 'into "factors", into elemental bits, naturally one will then need quite a few of them to account for something, and one never can be sure they all are in.' (Mills 1993:130)

2 Paradoxically, the increase in foreign investment and economic activity (for example, the dispersion of production off-shore) by Japanese enterprises seems to have a catalyzing effect on the push-pull syndrome. This is especially true for the initiation of labour migration, because conventional push-factors such as poverty, over-population or economic stagnation are often virulent before emigration. The uprooting, mobilisation, and 'industrialisation' of the consciousness of the indigenous population – results of intensified activities by Japanese firms – produce a pool of potential labour migrants. It is also remarked that a fair and efficient immigration policy remains impossible, and that statutory measures are counter-productive as long as the immigrants are burdened with the responsibility of international migration while (global) structural pressures are ignored (Sassen, 1991).

3 This is an interesting and sensitive remark: it highlights the danger of focussing on the problems of the immigration country whilst neglecting those of the emigration states. Most immigration studies dealing with a particular country concentrate on the problems caused by the influx of foreign labour into the target country, and lose sight of global inequalities of wealth distribution and power relations, and of the exploitative character of the economic world order.

4 His 'methodological individualism' has been criticized, the objection being that the direction of analysis should be reversed; for example, that those factors in the receiving country should be identified which 'preselectively' call for a certain type of labourer, whose utilitarian-rational or unrealistic-irrational motives are of relative indifference to the system (cf. Wimmer, 1986a:28f.).

3 Some Historical Preliminaries

1 I use the gross 'West' – 'East' contrast commonly found in global discussion of this kind. I cannot examine these empty formulae here. Suffice it to say that, with these generic notions encompassing immensely disparate cultures, and thereby at the same time comprising everything and nothing, the sub- and crypto-cultures of 'West' and 'East' can never be adequately comprehended.

4 Prelude: The *Japayuki* Question

1 Yet, another topic recurring in the mass media is the increase of foreign women 'streetwalking' in entertainment areas in Tōkyō. This is another side-effect of the amendment of the Immigration Control Act with its newly-introduced punishments for employers of 'illegals', many of whom dismissed their foreign 'hostesses' in fear of being sanctioned. The fired women took to the streets, where they openly solicit customers to accompany them to hotels. They are controlled by foreign and Japanese pimps, who are also organized criminals.
2 The sexist language found in this chapter mirrors the sexist reality underlying the practices described.

5 The Early Stage of a Process of Irregular Migration

1 The difference from B is a judicial sophistry: *fuhō nyūkoku* includes all air space (*ryōkū*); To commit *fuhō jōriku* ('illegal') 'setting one's foot on (Japanese) soil' is necessary (information from the lawyer Niwa Masao).
2 Repressive action intensified in 1993. In April of that year, entrance into Yoyogi-kōen, a park in which Iranians often gather, especially on Sundays, was partly closed to the public under the pretext of being for 'replanting rhododendrons'. This was accompanied by a media campaign alleging that Iranians dealt in drugs and manipulated telephone cards in the style of organized criminals. In August 1993, police began to move special units (*kidōtai* – riot police) into the park in order to prevent 'scuffles among Iranians'.

   Periodically police clamp down on persons 'overstaying', and arrest
   them. The whole cycle of focussed attention by the authorities, tighter
   control and, as a consequence, boosted figures, works here in a
   classical fashion.

3 This chapter was partly published in Herbert 1992a.

4 The situation changed following the so-called 'bubble-economy', a
   boom sustained by an inflated real estate market, stockmarket speculation, and other money-games. The imploding of the 'bubble', and
   accompanying recession were officially announced in the fall of 1991.
   Demand for labour sank drastically – see also chapter 5.4.4.

5 The situation has dramatically changed for the worse since 1992. The
   amount of available *genkin*-work dropped to roughly one-third (to
   around 3,000 a day) of that during the economic boom. Even in
   hanba, workers are forced to take 'vacations' (they are told no work
   is available for the day) during which they nevertheless have to pay
   for accommodation etc., even leading to day labourers returning
   from labour-contracts in debt. The number of *techō*-holders dropped
   to a record low. It is estimated that for the first time there were less
   than 15,000 *techō*-owners, comprising less than half of the Kamagasaki population. Many workers are forced to sleep outdoors, dispers-
   ing all over Osaka and constituting a real homeless problem. Around
   1,000 workers daily have to use the free food service (*takidashi*)
   initiated by the union leader Inagaki Hiroshi. This tense situation is
   conducive to hostile reactions against foreigners. But many of them
   are no longer employed by labour agents. (I met several Iranians
   looking for work in the morning, all of whom had been rejected.)
   Tehaishi and *oyakata* tend to accept only workers they personally
   know (called *kaozuke*) and who are healthy and reliable.

6 This argument is a classic example of the 'blaming the victims'
   strategy.

7 Quoted here from the English version published in *Kansai Time Out*,
   No. 156, February 1992, 6–8, under the title: 'One day in the life of
   a day-labourer'.

8 I am well aware that this notion is criticized and that new terms for
   'have' and 'have-not' nations are required. Furthermore, the term
   'developing' implies concepts of modernization and convergence-
   theories that can cogently be contested. Moreover, the term tends to
   assess countries only by their economic performance. Still, I use the
   term because a neutral one has obviously not been agreed upon.
   German leftist scholars seemingly prefer the notion 'countries being
   kept developing', indicating global power imbalances.

9 By instituting a measure of that kind legally, 'race' is constructed,
   and at the same time a sense of imaginary 'Japaneseness' or belonging
   to an ethnically-defined, fictive community is promoted. Immigration

policy, therefore, is conducive to nationalism and 'institutionalized racism'.

10 After the implosion of the so-called 'bubble economy' and lingering low economic performance, the press began to highlight the 'buffer-function' of *nikkeijin*, who were the first victims of the sluggish economy (by being dismissed first). *Nikkeijin* can look for work officially via the central 'Nikkeijin koyō sābisu sentā' in Tōkyō, or through private agencies such as 'Nikkei kōgyō'; losses of jobs surfaced because the number of *nikkeijin* job-seekers rose sharply (cf. for example, *Asahi shinbun*, 23 August 1992:24; 4 October 1992:6; 9 October 1992 *yūkan* 6). It is even alleged that re-employment is determined by 'the thickness of Japanese blood' and that *nikkeijin* from Peru were avoided. (Partly also because 'pseudo-*nikkeijin*' with faked documents from Peru had turned up – this also reveals a deep-rooted quasi-racist obsession with blood-line). It became rather clear that *nikkeijin* served as 'safety-valve' of the labour market (the situation of other 'illegals' might even be more severe; however, they tend to go underground and have no official places to claim work. Thus their plight does not surface this distinctly).

6 The Debate Concerning a Formal Policy on Guest-Workers

1 Neither Nishio nor Yamazaki are sociologists; both, as is characteristic of *Nihonjinron* – engage in 'popular sociology' (Yoshino) or what Pierre Bourdieu would call 'spontaneous sociology'. However, notions such as those mentioned above have a decisive influence on how 'social reality' is perceived and ultimately on this 'reality' itself – (a situation repeatedly analyzed by Bourdieu under the title 'theory effect' (for example Bourdieu, 1992:147ff. or 1990:109ff.) The 'theory-effect' on the 'middle-class society-ideology' in Japan would be worth studying; however, I can only point to the issue here.

2 Cf. also Antoni, 1992:122: 'That Japan in its course of history always has been a country most of all characterized by: stratification and disruption in cultural, social and territorial respects, was ideologically so successfully repressed that the new view of an ethnic, cultural, social, linguistic etc. uniform country could emerge to be the absolute dogma'.

3 Nishio implicitly, and camouflaging the strategy by dubbing the receiving country 'perpetrator', adopts nothing short of the scape-goat-strategy (the presence of foreigners is transformed into the

reason for ethnic conflicts, instead of existing prejudices and discrimination in the host country).

4 According to Bourdieu, refraining from answering is a sociologically significant factor and not just 'apathy' or a subversive attack on democracy; rather, it distinctly correlates with gender, age, educational and economic background and other indicators of one's place in the social 'order', and with the way in which questions are formulated. Moreover, it reveals that problems perceived by 'doxosophs' (pollers, politicians, intellectuals) first exist only for them as such, and sometimes the language used in polls does not appeal to those questioned (or is not quite understood; cf., for example Bourdieu, 1992:208–16).

7 Migrant Workers and Criminality

1 Recent surveys on the situation after the 'opening of the borders' to former Eastern-bloc countries consistently reveal that persons entering from these countries have a much higher risk of being criminalized than guest-workers. In Austria a media campaign started against so-called 'criminal tourists' from Eastern Europe, subsequently leading to selective attention being given to this phenomenon by police and the public, condensing in tighter control and high figures of criminalized foreigners. There was also a tendency to 'exculpate' long-term guest-workers living in Austria (their portion in the percentage of all foreign suspects in latter years is significantly low). Nevertheless, selective policing of foreigners ultimately drove up the number of criminalized guest-workers. Several studies address this 'new' situation, which I cannot describe in detail, but which shows all the characteristics of 'conjuring up a crime wave' (see for example, Morawetz and Stangl, 1991: Dearing, 1993; Pilgram, 1990).

2 'Hidden criminality' or the 'dark figure' (crimes which do not come to the notice of police) are usually called *Dunkelfeld* (dark field) in German criminology.

3 Both Blankenburg's and Killias' findings are pre-shaped by their research design. They focus on just one stage of prosecution (reporting) and one particular offence. This does not provide conclusions pertinent to the overall situation.

4 Although only little research was done in the field of victimology concerning foreign workers, it is noticed that 'there is considerable evidence that minorities are disproportionately affected by victimizing events both in terms of criminal victimization and in terms of

other types of victimization, for example, work-place accidents, economic exploitation and trafficking in women from Third World countries for prostitution' (Albrecht, 1993).

5   In a recent, theoretically well-informed study on *Nihonjinron* it is stated: 'If the attempt at "international understanding" is made through the actively conscious assertion of Japanese uniqueness or through the extreme version of cultural relativism, the unintended consequence of such an "internationalizing" attempt can ironically be the enhancement of cultural nationalism, because it fails to stress the commonality shared by different peoples' (Yoshino, 1992: 180f.).

6   Nevertheless, even usually critical Western scholars sometimes fall into the trap of *Nihonjinron* and give over-generalized and simplisitic 'explanations' of Japanese society. I have demonstrated this in the example of a German 'classic', co-authored by a Japanese scholar, on crime control in Japan (cf. Herbert, 1991c).

7   Ōnuki notes that, of the roughly 9,000 violations of the penal code by foreigners in 1991, around 70 per cent were offences against property. Of those, approximately one-fifth can be attributed to a single professional robbery gang from South Korea (Ōnuki, 1992: 344ff.). The corresponding graph of the statistics, with a steep line indicating the number of offences, of course looks quite dramatic (and can be dramatized). From these uninterpreted figures, the press fabricated an 'historical record' in the formula: 'crimes of foreigners increased tenfold in ten years' (cf. *Yomiuri shinbun*, 14 November 1991).

8   For an account in English of the gruesome conditions in police jails, the overall discipline inflicted on inmates and illicit strategies of questioning, cf. Igarashi (1986).

9   On torture-like methods of interrogation and the manufacturing of confessions by the police see also Igarashi (1986: 201f. and 210f.).

10 This originally meant 'human being' in Polynesian languages. In Germany it is a depreciatory label for foreigners from Southern Europe and particularly from Turkey.

11 The talk of body odour and bad smell belongs to the inventory of 'universal' stereotypes and prejudices against (ethnic) minorities, and can be found almost all over the world.

12 In 1991 roughly two-thirds of court cases needing an interpreter (that is, involving foreigners) were contraventions of the Aliens' Acts, and the lawyer Niwa refutes the police view 'that crimes of foreigners become more brutal and heinous'. A trend of this sort could not be seen at the level of the judiciary (Niwa, 1993: 81).

8 The Media and Criminality

1   There are numerous studies available on reporting of foreigners in the press (although usually they do not concentrate on crime reporting), most of them coming to similar conclusions. They almost unanimously demonstrate that 'news' on foreigners have a negative undertone in accordance with the American saying among journalists: 'Only bad news is good news' (cf. also the bibliography in, Ruhrmann, 1991).

2   *Japayuki* is a somewhat derogatory term actually for labour migrants pursuing prostitution – or as is deplorably common – coerced into doing so, and literally means: (persons) coming to Japan'. It makes allusion to the erstwhile Japanese 'prostitutes abroad' – the *karayuki* of the late 19th and early 20th century. *Kara* here designated not only China, but generally 'foreign countries' (cf. Kurahashi, 1989:19f. on female *japayuki* see Lenz, 1987). The term *japayuki* recently is also employed for male labour migrants; to make the gender plain, often the 'male' suffix *kun* is added, or for female '*japayuki*' the neutral *san* is used.

3   This became highly topical at the end of 1993. The National Police Agency even dispatched officers to South Korea to exchange information with authorities there 'on the sudden increase of pickpocket gangs entering Japan from South Korea' (*The Daily Yomiuri*, 8 December 1993, 2). The article further asserts: 'According to the NPA, the South Korean pickpockets operate in gangs of three to five members each and carry knives and tear-gas sprays, employing a hit-and-run strategy on their targets ... A 1990 crackdown in South Korea on pickpocket gangs led to an increase in pickpocketing in Japan, with 37 South Koreans arrested in 1991 in connection with 644 incidents, and 23 arrested in 1992 in connection with 245 incidents'. The latter figures are due to the inflation of the number of offences committed by *rainichi gaikokujin* (most of them are not 'professional criminals' or multiple offenders, cf. chapter 7.4 of this study).

4   The assertion that crimes committed by foreigners are on the upsurge and become more refined and more heinous has become a ready formula for the police. It is almost like a ritualistic incantation repeated over and over again in publications linked to the police, always in connection with apprehensions that the situation will become worse and control has to be tightened (for a recent example see Morishita, 1992:7ff.). Newspapers thereby just repeat what has become an everyday-theory for the police.

Bibliography

List of Abbreviations

ARMK	Ajiajin rōdōsha mondai kondankai
DIJ	Deutsches Institut für Japanstudien der Philipp-Franz-von-Siebold-Stiftung
FRSTB	Firipinjin rōdōsha shūdan taiho jiken bengodan
GNRMK	Gaikokujin no ryōkei mondai kenkyūkai
GRJCK	Gaikokujin rōdōsha jittai chōsa kenkyūkai
GSK	Gyōzaisei sōgō kenkyūsho
HKKSKB	Hōdō kijun kenkyūkai seiri kisha bunkai
IJUW	Institut für Japanologie der Universität Wien
KBR	Kantō bengoshi rengōkai
KKSK	Keizai kikakuchō sōgō keikakukyoku
KNK	Karabao no kai
LBIK	Ludwig-Boltzmann-Institut für Kriminalsoziologie
NBR	Nihon bengoshi rengōkai
NKK	Nihon kirisuto kyōdan = Nihon kirisuto kyōdan shakai iinkai & Nihon kirisuto kyōdan zainichi-nikkan rentai tokubetsu iinkai
NSDKK	Naikaku sōri daijin kanbō kōhōshitsu
NTK	Nyūkan tōkei kenkyūkai
OBK	Ōsaka bengoshikai
TSK	Tōkyō-to rōdō keizaikyoku
TSRJ	Tōkyō-to Shinagawa rōsei jimusho

Books

For reasons of clarity and to make the bibliography optically more accessible, I listed all the anonymous newspaper articles separately after the books and articles listed alphabetically by author's name.

Aikawa Toshihide (1987) 'Aru "Japayuki-kun" no kyōsei sōkan o megutte', *Kikan Pan* 5, 28–35.
Ajiajin rōdōsha mondai kondankai-ARMK (ed.) (1990) *Ajiajin dekasegi rōdōsha techō. The Asian worker's handbook.* new edn. Tōkyō: Akashi shoten.
Albrecht, Hans Jörg (1985) 'Generalprävention', Kaiser A. O. 1985:132–139.
——(1993) 'Ethnic minorities. Crime and criminal justice in Europe', Frances Heidensohn and Martin Farrell (eds): *Crime in Europe.* London: Routledge, 84–100.
Albrecht, Günter (1972) *Soziologie der geographischen Mobilität. Zugleich ein Beitrag zur Soziologie des sozialen Wandels.* Stuttgart: Enke.
Albrecht, Peter-Alexis (1979) 'Zur Legitimationsfunktion von Jugendkriminalstatistiken. Ein Traktat wider den Mythos von der kriminellen Jugend', Schüler-Springorum 1983:18–31.
Albrecht, Peter-Alexis and Siegfried Lamnek (1979) *Jugendkriminalität im Zerrbild der Statistik. Eine Analyse von Daten und Entwicklungen.* München: Juventa (Juventa-Materialien: M 44).
Albrecht, Peter-Alexis and Christian Pfeiffer (1979) *Die Kriminalisierung junger Ausländer. Befunde und Reaktionen sozialer Kontrollinstanzen.* München: Juventa (Juventa-Materialien: M 39).
Albrecht, Peter-Alexis, Christian Pfeiffer and Klaus Zapka (1978) 'Reaktionen sozialer Kontrollinstanzen auf Kriminalität junger Ausländer in der Bundesrepublik', *Monatsschrift für Kriminologie und Strafrechtsreform* 5, 268–296.
Amnesty International (1991) *Japan. The death penalty and the need for more safeguards against ill-treatment of detainees. Nihon no shikei haishi to hikōkinsha no jinken hoshō.* Tōkyō: Heibonsha.
Antoni, Klaus (1992) 'Tradition und "Traditionalismus" im modernen Japan – ein kulturanthropologischer Versuch', DIJ 1992:105–128.
Aoki Eigorō (1979) *Nihon no keiji saiban.* Tōkyō: Iwanami shoten (Iwanami shinsho 83).
Aoki Hideo (1983) ' "Yoseba" rōdōsha o meguru sabetsu no kōzō.

Ōsaka, Kamagasaki chiiki o butai to shite', *Shakaigaku hyōron* 33/4, 2–19.

——(1984) 'Toshi no hyōryū–tachi. Nojukusha sabetsu no kōzō o megutte', *Soshiorojî* 91/9, 1–25.

——(1990) 'Yoseba to zainichi gaikokujin. Gaikokujin rōdōsha mondai e no sekkin', *Kaihō shakaigaku kenkyū* 4, 88–101.

Asano Kyōhei (1990) 'Ryūgaku burōka wa kinman Nippon to kimagure nyūkan gyōsei no adabana da', Ishii 1990:160–172.

Autorengruppe Ausländerforschung (ed.) (1981) *Zwischen Ghetto und Knast. Jugendliche Ausländer in der Bundesrepublik. Ein Handbuch.* Reinbek bei Hamburg: Rowohlt (rororo aktuell 4737).

Bade, Klaus J. (1983) *Vom Auswanderungsland zum Einwanderungsland? Deutschland 1880–1980.* Berlin: Colloqium-Verl. (Beiträge zur Zeitgeschichte 12).

Bauböck, Rainer (1986a) 'Die zweite Generation am Arbeitsmarkt', Wimmer 1986:331–348.

——(1986b) 'Demographische und soziale Struktur der jugoslawischen und türkischen Wohnbevölkerung in Österreich', Wimmer 1986:181–239.

Becker, Howard S. (1973) *Außenseiter. Zur Soziologie abweichenden Verhaltens.* Transl. by Norbert Schultze. Frankfurt a.M.: S. Fischer (Conditio humana).

Berckhauer, Friedhelm (1981) 'Zur Kriminalität der Ausländer. Eine Herausforderung an die Kriminalprävention', *Kriminalistik* 6, 269–270.

Berger, Peter L. and Thomas Luckmann (1990) *Die gesellschaftliche Konstruktion der Wirklichkeit. Eine Theorie der Wissensoziologie.* Frankfurt a.M.: Fischer [1966] (Sozialwissenschaft Fischer).

Bielefeld, Uli and Reinhard Kreissl (1983) 'Ausländische Jugendliche und Kriminalisierung. Die Bedeutung qualitativer Ergebnisse für die kriminalpolitische Diskussion', Schüler-Springorum 1983:78–95.

Biffl, Gudrun (1986) 'Der Strukturwandel der Ausländerbeschäftigung in Österreich', Wimmer 1986:33–87.

Bindzus, Dieter and Ishii Akira (1977) *Strafvollzug in Japan.* Köln usw.: Heymann (Japanisches Recht 2).

Blankenburg, Erhard (1973) 'Die Selektivität rechtlicher Sanktionen. Eine Untersuchung von Ladendiebstählen', Friedrichs 1973:120–150.

Böhning, W. R. (1984) *Studies in international labour migration.* New York: St. Martin's Pr.

Bohnsack, Ralf and Fritz Schütze (1973) 'Die Selektionsverfahren der Polizei in ihrer Beziehung zur Handlungskompetenz der Tatverdächtigen', *Kriminologisches Journal* 4, 270–290.

Bosetzky, Horst, Jürgen Borschert unter Mitarb. von Siegfried Helm (1981) 'Ausländer in Berliner Haftanstalten', Autorengruppe Ausländerforschung 1981:198–289.

Bourdieu Pierre (1990) *Was heisst sprechen? Die Ökonomie des sprachlichen Tausches. [Ce que parler veut dire]* Wien: Braumüller.

—— (1992) *Rede und Antwort [Choses dites]* Aus dem Französ. von Bernd Schwibs. Frankfurt a.M.: Suhrkamp (edition suhrkamp 1547).

Brusten, Manfred and Peter Malinowski (1975) 'Die Vernehmungsmethoden der Polizei und ihre Funktion für die gesellschaftliche Verteilung des Etiketts "kriminell" ', Manfred Brusten und Jürgen Hohmeier: *Stigmatisierung 2. Zur Produktion gesellschaftlicher Randgruppen.* Neuwied & Darmstadt: Luchterhand (Kritische Texte: Sozialarbeit Sozialpädagogik Soziale Probleme), 57–112.

Castles, Stephen and Godula Kosack (1985) *Immigrant workers and class structure in Western Europe.* 2nd edn Oxford: Oxford UP.

Chaidov, Anthozoe (1984) 'Warum überproportional? Kriminalitätsbelastung junger Ausländer', *Kriminalistik* 7, 355–376.

Chūma Hiroyuki A.O. (1991) 'Rōdō keizaigaku kenkyū no genzai. 1988nen-90nen no gyōseki o tsūjite', *Nihon rōdō kenkyū zasshi* 376/2–3, 2–40.

Chūshō kigyōchō (ed.) (1990) *Chūshō kigyō jigyōsha no tame no gaikokujin rōdōsha mondai Q & A.* Tōkyō: Tsūsan shiryō chōsakai.

Colterjohn, David (1992) 'Iranians find life hard far from home', *The Japan Times Weekly International Edition* 24. February-1. March, 7.

Dale, Peter N. (1986) *The Myth of Japanese uniqueness.* New York: St. Martin's Pr.

Dearing, Albin (1993) 'Der sogenannte Kriminaltourismus. Der Ladendiebstahl und die Öffnung der Ostgrenzen', Arno Pilgram (ed.): *Grenzöffnung, Migration, Kriminalität.* Baden-Baden:

Nomos Verl.-Ges. (Jahrbuch für Rechts- und Kriminalsoziologie 1993).

Delgado Manuel J. (1972) *Die 'Gastarbeiter' in der Presse. Eine inhaltsanalytische Studie*. Opladen: Leske.

Deutsches Institut für Japanstudien der Philipp-Franz-von-Siebold-Stiftung-DIJ (ed.) (1992) *Japanstudien. Jahrbuch des Deutschen Instituts für Japanstudien der Philipp-Franz-von-Siebold-Stiftung. Bd 3*. München: Iudicium.

Domenig, Roland (1991) 'Aids in Japan', Eva Bachmayer, Wolfgang Herbert und Sepp Linhart (eds): *Japan von Aids bis Zen. Referate des Achten Japanologentages vom 26. bis 28. September 1990 in Wien Zweiter Teil*. Wien: Universität Wien, Institut für Japanologie, 506–525.

Donner, Olaf A.O. (1981) 'Straftaten von Ausländern in Berlin', Autorengruppe Ausländerforschung 1981:43–145.

Durkheim, Emile (1993) 'The normal and the pathological', Pontell 1993:63–66 [reprinted from Emile Durkheim: *The rules of sociological method* 1938].

Ebashi Takashi (1990) 'Tachiokureta hōtei tsūyaku seido', *Hōgaku seminā* 35/8, 40–43.

Eichinger, M. (1982) 'Ausländerkriminalität', *Kriminalistik* 11, 603–607.

Esser, Hartmut (1980) *Aspekte der Wanderungssoziologie. Assimilation und Integration von Wanderern, ethnischen Gruppen und Minderheiten. Eine handlungstheoretische Analyse*. Darmstadt & Neuwied: Luchterhand (Soziologische Texte N.F. 119).

Feest, Johannes (1973) 'Die Situation des Verdachts', Friedrichs 1973:151–173.

Feuerhelm, Wolfgang (1987) *Polizei und 'Zigeuner'. Strategien, Handlungsmuster und Alltagstheorien im polizeilichen Umgang mit Sinti und Roma*. Stuttgart: Enke (Copythek).

Firipinjin rōdōsha shūdan taiho jiken bengodan-FRSTJB (1990) ' "Hō" ga ningen o fuminijiru. Firipinjin rōdōsha shūdan taiho jiken bengodan zadankai', KNK 1990:110–162.

Fishman, Mark (1978) 'Crime waves as ideology', *Social problems* 25, 531–543.

Foucault, Michel (1977) *Überwachen und Strafen. Die Geburt des Gefängisses*. Transl. by Walter Seitter. Frankfurt a.M.: Suhrkamp (Suhrkamp-Taschenbücher Wissenschaft 184) [Original: Surveiller et punir. La naissance de la prison. Gallimard 1975].

Friedrichs, Jürgen (1973) *Teilnehmende Beobachtung abweichenden Verhaltens*. Stuttgart: Enke.

Fukuzawa Keiko (1990) 'Nōson no kokusai kekkon no kage ni aru mono', Narizawa 1990a:60–69.

Furuya Sugio (1991) ' "Gaikokujin rōdōsha no rōsai hakusho" ga akiraka ni shita mono', Tenmyō 1991:65–76.

Gaikokujin no ryōkei mondai kenkyūkai-GNRMK (1990) 'Kenshō. Gaikokujin no ryōkei', Narizawa 1990a:164–170.

Gaikokujin rōdōsha jittai chōsa kenkyūkai-GRJCK (1992) 'Gaikokujin rōdōsha jittai chōsa hōkokusho', Tezuka A.O. 1992:70–281.

Gebauer, Michael (1981a) 'Kriminalität der Gastarbeiterkinder, Teil 1: Umfang der kriminellen Belastung', *Kriminalistik* 1, 2–8.

——(1981b) 'Kriminalität der Gastarbeiterkinder, Teil 2: Hintergrund ihrer Lebensbedingungen', *Kriminalistik* 2, 83–86.

Geiss, Imanuel (1988) *Geschichte des Rassismus*. Frankfurt a.M.: Suhrkamp (edition suhrkamp 1530, Neue Historische Bibliothek).

Genki magajīn henshūbu (ed.) (1989) *Kamagasaki sutōri*. Ōsaka: Burēn sentā (Genki magajîn 6).

Girtler, Roland (1980) *Polizei-Alltag. Strategien, Ziele und Strukturen polizeilichen Handelns*. Opladen: Westdeutscher Verl. (Studien zur Sozialwissenschaft 40).

Gō Munechika A.O. (1989) 'Gaikokujin rōdōsha irero oikaese daironsō. Heisei no kurobune ga tsukitsuketa daimondai o dō suru?', *Bungei shunjū* 11, 294–312.

Goffman, Erving (1973) *Asyle. Über die soziale Situation psychiatrischer Patienten und anderer Insassen*. Frankfurt a.M.: Suhrkamp (edition suhrkamp 678).

——(1993) 'Stigma and social identity', Pontell 1993:75–95 [selection from *Stigma: Notes on the management of spoiled identity* 1963].

Gohl, Gerhard (1984) 'Ausländer in Japan', Horst Hammitzsch (ed.): *Japan-Handbuch*. 2nd edn Wiesbaden: Steiner, 330–333.

Gonda Manji (ed.) (1990) *The Japanese press*. Tōkyō: Nihon shinbun kyōkai.

Gonoi Hiroaki (1989) *Dekasegi gaijin zankoku monogatari*. Tōkyō: Eru shuppansha.

Goode, Erich (1993) 'On behalf of the labelling theory', Pontell 1993:96–108 [Reprint from *Social problems* 22 (June 1975), 570–483].

338

Gotō Shōjirō (1979) *Enzai.* Tōkyō: Iwanami shoten (Iwanami shin-sho 81).

Gurūpu Akakabu (ed.) (1989) *Abunai nihongo gakkō. Ajia kara no shūgakusei.* Tōkyō: Shinsensha.

Gyōzaisei sōgō kenkyūsho-GSK (ed.) (1990) *Gaikokujin rōdōsha no jinken.* Tōkyō: Ōtsuki shoten.

Habermas, Jürgen (1985) *Zur Logik der Sozialwissenschaften. Erw. Ausg.* Frankfurt a.M.: Suhrkamp (suhrkamp taschenbuch wissenschaft 517).

Hagio Shin'ya (1990) 'Anyaku suru chūkai gyōsha-tachi', Narizawa 1990a:52–59.

Hagio Shin'ya, Obata Kiyotake and Hamada Akio (1990) 'Gaiko-kujin rōdōsha mondai wa Ajia kara no kōkai shitsumonjō da', Okaniwa 1990:11–27.

Hamburger, Franz, Lydia Seus and Otto Wolter (1981) *Zur Delin-quenz ausländischer Jugendlicher. Bedingungen der Entstehung und Prozesse der Verfestigung.* Wiesbaden: Bundeskriminalamt.

Hanada Katsuya (1990) 'Keisatsu o yobu zo', Karabao no kai 1990:92–109.

Hanak, Gerhard, Arno Pilgram and Wolfgang Stangl (1984) 'Die Strafverfolgung an Ausländern – eine Sekundärauswertung zweier soziologischer Studien zur Rechtsanwendung', *Kriminal-soziologische Bibliografie* 43/44, 42–63.

Hanami Tadashi and Kuwahara Yasuo (eds) (1989) *Asu no rinjin gaikokujin rōdōsha.* Tōkyō: Tōyō keizai shinbunsha.

Hanami Tadashi A.O. (1989) 'Zadankai. Gaikokujin rōdōsha mondai to gaikokujin gyōsei', *Jurisuto* 942/10, 14–33.

Hansabetsu kokusai undō Nihon iinkai (1992) 'Iranjin rōdōsha ni taisuru sabetsu o jochō suru "Shūkan bunshun" (3gatsu 12nichigō) ni kōgi suru!', *IMADR-JC tsūshin* 16 20. April, 7.

Hara Yōnosuke (1990) Ajia chiiki ni okeru kokusai rōdō idō ijū', *Nihon rōdō kenkyū zasshi* 364/16, 1–17.

Harada Shin'ichi (1990) ' "Hito ga tarinai!" 'San-K gyōshū' wa uttaeru', Ishii 1990:49–59.

Hatada Kunio (1990) 'Ōkubo-dōri ni "taminzoku kokka Nihon" no asu ga aru!?', Ishii 1990:130–137.

Hatade Akira (1991) 'Hisai gaikokujin rōdōsha no jinken', Tenmyō 1991:29–43.

Hayashi Masayuki (1988) 'OISCA, initials which spell nationalism. From a classroom in Shizuoka to a paddyfield in Thailand', *AMPO* 19/1, 2–9.

Heine, Elke (1981) 'Ausländer in der veröffentlichen Meinung. Perspektiven einer Integration', Autorengruppe Ausländerforschung 1981:19–40.

Heinz, Wolfgang (1985) 'Anzeigeverhalten der Bevölkerung', Kaiser A.O. 1985:27–32.

Herbert, Ulrich (1986) *Geschichte der Ausländerbeschäftigung in Deutschland 1880–1980. Saisonarbeiter. Zwangsarbeiter. Gastarbeiter.* Berlin und Bonn: Dietz (Dietz Taschenbuch 19).

Herbert, Wolfgang (1989a) 'Japan von unten', *Informationen des akademischen Arbeitskreises Japan* 3, 1–5.

——(1989b) 'Sekai ni tsūyō suru tayō bunka o tsukuru chansu. "Nanmin mondai" o takokunin kara miru', *Hataraku hito* 380 1. November 1989, 2.

——(1991a) 'Motto sekkyokuteki na ukeire o', Tezuka A. O. 1991: 220–222.

——(1991b) *Zur Kriminalisierung ausländischer Arbeiter in Japan.* Tōkyō: Deutsche Gesellschaft für Natur- und Völkerkunde Ostasiens (OAG aktuell 53).

——(1991c) 'Polemische Glossen zum kriminologischen Japanbild bei Miyazawa und Kühne', *Kriminalsoziologische Bibliografie* 72/73, 93–98.

——(1992a) 'Iraner in Tōkyō: Notat zur Verwertungspraxis von Statistiken', *Informationen des Akademischen Arbeitskreises Japan* 1/92, 4–5.

——(1992b) 'Die Tagelöhner–Unruhen im Oktober 1990 und deren struktureller Hintergrund', DIJ 1992:221–253.

——(1992c) 'Yakuza – ausgegrenzte Subkultur oder integrierter Teil der japanischen Gesellschaft?', Ernst Lokowandt (ed.): *Zentrum und Peripherie. Referate des 2. Japanologentages der OAG in Tōkyō: 8/9. Marz 1990.* München: Iudicium, 79–105.

——(1993) 'Ausländische "mafiose" Organisationen in Japan', *Informationen des Akademischen Arbeitskreises Japan* 1/2, 7–10.

Hidejima Yukari (1989) 'Keiji tetsuzuki to shutsunyūkoku kanri to no kankei', *Hō to minshushugi* 242/11, 18–21.

Higashizawa Yasushi (1991) 'Gaikokujin rōdōsha no rōdō saigai to hōteki kyūzai', Tenmyō 1991:45–63.

Higurashi Takanori (1989) ' *"Mura" to "ore" no kokusai kekkongaku.* Tōkyō: Jōhō kikaku shuppan.

Hijiya-Kirschnereit, Irmela (1988) *Das Ende der Exotik. Zur japanischen Kultur und Gesellschaft der Gegenwart.* Frankfurt a.M.: Suhrkamp (edition suhrkamp 1466).

Hinago Akira (1989) 'Japayuki-san no keizaigaku', Ishii 1989: 130–157.

——(1990a) 'Japayuki-san no gyakushū', Ishii 1990:83–91.

——(1990b) 'Kaette kita Nanbei imin', Ishii 1990:173–182.

Hirano Shūichirō (1990) 'Nyūkan gyōsei no hassō. Kaiteihō shikō panikku ga shimeshita mono', *Hōgaku seminâ* 35/8, 26–29.

Hirono Isami and Kobayashi Yasuichirō (1992) 'Kokusai Nippon no anbu o abaku!! Kaigai Mafia "Jipangu konekushon" ', *Sandê Mainichi* 5 January, 30–34.

Hisada Megumi (1990) 'Watashi Nippon no papa-san to kekkon shite happi nē', Ishii 1990:68–82.

Hōdō kijun kenkyūkai seiri kisha bukai-HKKSKB (1990) 'Seiri kisha kara mita hanzai hōdō no osoroshisa', Narizawa 1990b: 169–180.

Hofer, Konrad (1992) *Arbeitsstrich. Unter polnischen Schwarzarbeitern.* Wien: Verlag für Gesellschaftskritik (Aufrisse-Buch 19).

Hoffman-Nowotny, Hans-Joachim (1973) *Soziologie des Fremdarbeiterproblems. Eine theoretische und empirische Analyse am Beispiel der Schweiz.* Stuttgart: Enke.

Hoizumi Junko (1991) 'Ranks of illegal foreign workers growing', *The Japan Times International Edition* 1–7. Juli, 7.

Hōmusho (ed.) (1989) *Dai 114 kensatsu tōkei nenpō.* Tōkyō.

Hōmushō nyūkoku kanrikyoku-HNK (ed.) (1989) 'Heisei gannen kamihanki ni okeru nyūkanhō ihan jiken no gaiyō', *Kokusai jinryū* 12, 38–42.

——(1990) 'Heisei gannen ni okeru nyūkanhō ihan jiken no gaikyō', *Kokusai jinryū* 5, 44–50.

Hōmu sōgō kenkyūsho (ed.) (1989) *Hanzai hakusho. Shōwa no keiji seisaku.* Tōkyō: Ōkurashō.

Huisken, Freerk (1987) *Ausländerfeinde und Ausländerfreunde. Eine Streitschrift gegen den geächteten wie den geachteten Rassismus.* Hamburg: VSA-Verl.

Hwang, Mingi (1990) 'Kyūpora no machi' ningen kōsaten monogatari', Ishii 1990:10–29.

I, Sangho A.O. (1990) 'Zadankai. Gaikokujin rōdōsha mondai no genten to yukue. Gaikokujin to no kyōsei o motomete', Narizawa 1990a:2–28.

Igarashi Futaba (1986) 'Forced to confess', Gavan McCormack and Yoshio Sugimoto (eds): *Democracy in contemporary Japan.* New York & London: M. E. Sharpe, 195–214.

——(1991) 'Sōsa hōdō. Tsukurarekata, tsukawarekata', *Sekai* 2, 67–77.

Institut für Japanologie der Universität (IJUW) (1987) *Sachlexikon. Das japanische Unternehmen. Ein Leitfaden für Wissenschaft und Praxis.* Wien: Literas.

Isa Kyōko (1991) 'Burajiru no Nikkeijin. Nihon ni sō–dekasegi imin mura wa kōhai', *AERA* 13. August 1991, 30–35.

Ishida Noriko (1990) 'Fuhō shūrō to jinken shingai', *GSK* 1990:23–32.

Ishii Shinji (ed.) (1989) *Japayuki-san monogatari.* 10. Aufl. Tōkyō: JICC (Bessatsu Takarajima 54).

——(1990) *Nihon ga taminzoku kokka ni naru hi.* Tōkyō: JICC (Bessatsu Takarajima 106).

Ishitobi Jin (1990) 'Hanaoka jiken kara mita gaikokujin rōdōsha mondai', Okaniwa 1990:61–63.

Ishiyama Eiichirō (1989) *Firipin dekasegi rōdōsha. Yume o oi Nihon ni ikite.* Tōkyō: Jakushoku shobō.

Iwao Mitsuyo (1990) ' "Fuhō" to "sei" o seowasarete', Okaniwa 1990:64–68.

Jung, Heike (1985) 'Massenmedien und Kriminalität', Kaiser A.O. 1985:294–299.

Kagoshima Masaaki (1990) 'Okizari ni sareta keganin', KNK 1990:42–61.

Kaiser, Günther (1989) *Kriminologie. Eine Einführung in die Grundlagen.* 8. neubearb. u. erg. Aufl. Heidelberg: C. F. Müller Jurist. Verl. (UTB für Wissenschaft: Uni-Taschenbücher 594).

Kaiser, Günther A.O. (eds) (1985) *Kleines kriminologisches Wörterbuch.* 2. völlig neubearb. und erw. Aufl. Heidelberg: C. F. Müller Jurist. Verl. (UTB für Wissenschaft: Uni-Taschenbücher 1274).

Kaji Etsuko (1974) 'Japan's new slave trade. Foreign workers in Japan', *AMPO* 6/2, 48–52.

Kaji Etsuko and Jean Inglis (1974) 'Sisters against slavery: a look at anti-prostitution movements in Japan', *AMPO* 6/2, 19–23.

Kamakyōtō and San'ya gentōin (eds) (1974) *Yararetara yarikaese!* Tōkyō: Tahata shoten.

Kamiguchi Yutaka (1984) 'Zulässigkeit der polizeilichen Vernehmung des inhaftierten Beschuldigten in Japan', *Zeitschrift für die gesamte Strafrechtswissenschaft* 96/1, 109–125.

Kamimura Yoshio (1991) 'Mafia no jōriku. Nihon shijō o kuiwakeru gaikokujin yakuza. Mājan tobaku wa Taiwan, mayaku wa Koronbia, sagi wa Naijeria', *AERA* 10 December, 63.

Kantō bengoshikai rengōkai-KBR (ed.) (1990) *Gaikokujin rōdōsha no shūrō to jinken.* Tōkyō: Akashi shoten.

Kaplan, David E. and Alec Dubro (1986) *Yakuza. The explosive account of Japan's criminal underworld.* Reading, Mass. etc: Addison-Wesley.

Karabao no kai (Kotobuki gaikokujin dekasegi rōdōsha to rentai suru kai)-KNK (ed.) (1988) *Gaikokujin rōdōsha no gōhōka ni mukete.* Tōkyō: Shinchiheisha (Hataraku nakama no bukkuretto 9).

——(1988–) *Gaikokujin dekasegi rōdōsha. Shinbun kirinukichō.* 3. Yokohama: Karabao no kai.

——(1990) *Nakama ja nai ka gaikokujin rōdōsha. Torikumi no genba kara.* Tōkyō: Akashi shoten.

Karabao no kai jimukyoku (1990) 'Gaikokujin rōdōsha no "gōhōka" ni mukete', KBR 1990:307–328.

Karthaus-Tanaka, Nobuko (1990) *The problem of foreign workers in Japan.* Rijks Universiteit Leiden: Center for Japanese and Korean Studies.

Kashigiwa Hiroshi (1990) 'Dete iku Nihon no kokusaika', Okaniwa 1990:30–31.

Katō Tadayoshi (1990) 'Zenken sōren no gaikokujin rōdōsha seisaku', *Ōhara shakai mondai kenkyūsho zasshi* 379–380/6–7, 80–87.

Katō Toshiyuki (1990) ' "Rengō" no gaikokujin rōdōsha mondai ni taisuru kangaekata', *Ōhara shakai mondai kenkyū zasshi* 379–380/6–7, 74–79.

Katsura Atsuhiro (1990) 'Sōsa jōhō izon no shuzai, hōdō kara dappi to bengoshi no sekimu', Narizawa 1990b:38–47.

Kawano Shunji (1989) 'Shuzai o tōshite mita gaikokujin no jinken', *Hō to minshushugi* 242/11, 22–26.

Kawashima Yoshio (1991) 'Japanese laws and practices on Indo-Chinese refugees', *Ōsaka University Law Review* 38/2, 1–12.

Keisatsuchō (ed.) (1987) *Keisatsu hakusho. Kokusaika no shinten ni taiō suru keisatsu katsudō.* Tōkyō: Ōkurashō.

——(1990) *Keisatsu hakusho. Tokushū – gaikokujin rōdōsha no kyūzō to keisatsu no taiō.* Tōkyō: Ōkurashō.

Keizai kikakuchō sōgō keikakuchō–KKSK (ed.) (1989) *Gaikokujin rōdōsha to keizai shakai no shinro.* Tōkyō: Ōkurashō.

Kerner, Hans-Jürgen (1985) 'Kriminalstatistik', Kaiser A.O. 1985: 260–267.

Kerner, Hans-Jürgen and Thomas Feltes (1980) 'Medien, Kriminalitätsbild und Öffentlichkeit. Einsichten und Probleme am Beispiel einer Analyse von Tageszeitungen', Helmut Kury (ed.): *Strafvollzug und Öffentlichkeit.* Freiburg i.Br.: Rombach (rombach hochschul paperback 98), 73–112.

Killias, Martin (1988) 'Diskriminierendes Verhalten von Opfern gegenüber Ausländern? Neue Aspekte der Ausländerkriminalität aufgrund von Daten der schweizerischen Opferbefragung', *Monatsschrift für Kriminologie und Strafrechtsreform* 3, 156–165.

——(1989) 'Criminality among second-generation immigrants in Western Europe: a review of the evidence', *Criminal Justice Review* 14/1, 13–41.

Kim, Young C. (1981) *Japanese journalists and their world.* Charlottesville: Univ. Pr. of Virginia.

Kiyonaga Kenji (1991) 'Gaikokujin rōdōsha to anzenron. Hanzai bōshiron ni okeru shiza kumikae e no hitotsu no teian', *Hanzai shakaigaku kenkyū* 16, 36–55.

Klee, Ernst (1981) 'Gastarbeiter als Subproletariat', Ernst Klee (ed.): *Gastarbeiter. Analysen und Berichte.* Frankfurt a.M.: Suhrkamp (edition suhrkamp 539), 25–35.

Kobayashi Hideyuki (1990) *Kō sureba yatoeru gaikokujin rōdōsha. Chūshō kigyō no hitode busoku ni kotaeru hon.* Tōkyō: Asuka shuppansha (Asuka-Business hitode busoku kaishō shirîzu).

Kobayashi Tetsuo (1990) 'Gaikokujin rōdōsha to dō tsukiau no ka', Narizawa 1990a:42–50.

Komai Hiroshi (1990) 'Intabyū. Sakoku, kaikoku ronsō ni piriodo o utsu! Kyūkyoku no riron, gaikokujin rōdōsha "hitsuzenron" to wa nani ka?', Ishii 1990:260–270.

——(1992a) 'Gaikokujin rōdōsha jittai chōsa hōkokusho – kaidai', Tezuka A.O. 1992:283–291.

——(1992b) 'Tan'itsu minzokushugi wa koerareru ka. Nihon ni okeru tabunkashugi no kanōsei', *Sekai* 572/9, 88–96.

——(1993) 'Imin shakai no iriguchi ni tatte', *Sekai* 580/4, 185–199.

Koyanagi Nobuaki (1989a) 'Gaikokujin dekasegi rōdōsha to yoseba', Genki magajīn henshūbu 1989:127–136.

——(1989b) 'Yoseba no Ajiajin rōdōsha', NKK 1989:2–3.

——(1990) 'Kamagasaki ni okeru iryō mondai', *Yoseba* 3, 61–77.

Kremer, Manfred and Helga Spangenberg (1980) *Assimilation aus-*

ländischer Arbeitnehmer in der Bundesrepublik Deutschland. Forschungsbericht. Unter Mitarbeit von Lothar Jäger und Stephan Schnitzler. Königstein/Ts.: Hanstein (Materialien zur Arbeitsmigration und Ausländerbeschäftigung 5).

Kurahashi Masanao (1989) *Kita no Karayuki-san.* Tōkyō: Kyōei shobō.

Kürzinger, Josef (1985) 'Gewaltkriminalität', Kaiser A.O. 1985: 145–151.

Kuwahara Satoru (1993) 'Tōtō Nihonjin ga nerawarehajimeta! "Gaikokujin no hanzai" 93nen kamihanki jitsuroku dēta', *Sapio* 16/102 23. September 1993, 26–27.

Kuwahara Yasuo (1989) 'Gaikokujin rōdōsha mondai no keizaiteki sokumen', Hanami and Kuwahara 1989:123–179.

——(1991) *Kokkyō o koeru rōdōsha.* Tōkyō: Iwanami shoten (- Iwanami shinsho <Akasaka-ban> 196).

Lamnek, Siegfried (1990) *Theorien abweichenden Verhaltens. Eine Einführung für Soziologen, Psychologen, Pädagogen, Juristen, Politologen, Kommunikationswissenschaftler und Sozialarbeiter.* 4. ed. München: Fink (UTB für Wissenschaft: Uni-Taschenbücher 740).

Latza, Berit (1989) *Sextourismus in Südostasien.* Frankfurt a.M.: Fischer (Fischer Taschenbuch 3891).

Lau, Christoph (1989) 'Die Definition gesellschaftlicher Probleme durch die Sozialwissenschaften', Ulrich Beck und Wolfgang Bonß (eds): *Weder Sozialtechnologie noch Aufklärung? Analysen zur Verwendung sozialwissenschaftlichen Wissens.* Frankfurt a.M.: Suhrkamp (suhrkamp taschenbuch wissenschaft 715), 384–419.

Lee, Yonghwa (1989) 'Zainichi Chōsenjin to "shutsunyūkoku kanri". Gaikokujin rōdōsha mondai no genten', *Shohyō* 88/6, 36–53.

Leiris, Michel (1985) *Die eigene und die fremde Kultur. Ethnologische Schriften Vol. 1. Transl. by Rolf Wintermeyer. Ed. a. with an introd. by Hans-Jürgen Heinrichs.* Frankfurt a.M.: Suhrkamp (suhrkamp taschenbuch wissenschaft 574).

Leitner, Helga (1983) *Gastarbeiter in der städtischen Gesellschaft. Segregation, Integration und Assimilation von Arbeitsmigranten. Am Beispiel jugoslawischer Gastarbeiter in Wien.* Frankfurt und New York: Campus Verl. (Campus Forschung 307).

Lenz, Ilse (1987) 'Zwischen fremden Spiegeln ... Zur Figur der wandernden Prostituierten in ostasiatischen Gesellschaften', *Peripherie* 27, 51–72.

——(1989) 'Die unsichtbare weibliche Seite des japanischen Aufstiegs: Das Verhältnis von geschlechtlicher Arbeitsteilung und kapitalistischer Entwicklung', Ulrich Menzel (ed.): *Im Schatten des Siegers: Japan. Vol. 3: Ökonomie und Politik.* Frankfurt a.M.: Suhrkamp (edition suhrkamp 1497), 227–271.

Ludwig, Wolfgang (1983) 'Selektion und Stigmatisierung. Kriminalpolitische Aspekte der Produktion von Jugendkriminalität', Schüler-Springorum 1983:50–62.

Ludwig-Boltzmann-Institut für Kriminalsoziologie-LBIK (1976) 'Materialien zur Kriminal- & Sicherheitsberichterstattung', *Kriminalsoziologische Bibliografie* 4/11–13, 52–67.

Mansel, Jürgen (1985) 'Gefahr und Bedrohung? Die Quantität des "kriminellen" Verhaltens der Gastarbeiternachkommen', *Kriminologisches Journal* 17, 165–185.

——(1986) 'Die unterschiedliche Selektion von jungen Deutschen, Türken und Italienern auf dem Weg vom polizeilichen Tatverdächtigten zum gerichtlich Verurteilten', *Monatsschrift für Kriminologie und Strafrechtsreform* 6/12, 309–325.

Mansel, Jürgen (1990) 'Kriminalisierung als Instrument zur Ausgrenzung und Disziplinierung oder "Ausländer richten ihre Kinder zum Diebstahl ab" ', *Kriminalsoziologische Bibliographie* 69, 47–65.

Marx, Gary T. (1993) 'Ironies of social control. Authorities as contributors to deviance through escalation, nonenforcement, and covert facilitation', Pontell 1993:8–22 [first published in: *Social Problems* 28/2 (Feb. 1981), 221–233].

Matsuda Mizuho (1990) 'Baishun sareru Ajia no onnatachi', Narizawa 1990a:30–41.

Matsunaga Kensei (1990) 'Kotoba no kabe no mukō ni "kangoku" ga atta', Ishii 1990:138–148.

Merton, Robert (1968) 'Sozialstruktur und Anomie', Fritz Sack und René König (eds): *Kriminalsoziologie.* Frankfurt a.M.: Akad. Verl. Ges., 288–313.

Mills, Wright Charles (1993) 'The professional ideology of social pathologists', Pontell 1993: 127–141 [first published in: *American Journal of Sociology* 49, Sept. 1943, 165–180].

Mishima Tetsu (1988) 'Rainichi gaikokujin hanzai no genjō to taiō', *Keisatsugaku ronshū* 41/5, 85–104.

Miyajima Takashi (1989) *Gaikokujin rōdōsha mukaeire ronri. Senshin shakai no jirenma no nana de.* Tōkyō: Akashi shoten.

Miyajima Takashi A.O. (1987) 'Tōron. Gaikokujin rōdōsha to Nihon no taiō', *Hōritsu jihō* 59/7, 6–23.

Mizuno Ashura (1990) 'Kamagasaki no rōdōsha no atsumari kara', Narizawa 1990a:186–187.

Miyazawa Setsuo (1990) 'Learning lessons from Japanese experience in policing and crime: challenge for Japanese criminologists', *Kōbe University Law Review, international edition* 24, 29–62.

Morawetz, Inge K. and Wolfgang Stangl (1991) 'Zur Entwicklung der Untersuchungshaft in Österreich in den 80er Jahren', *Kriminalsoziologische Bibliografie* 72/73, 5–15.

Mori Hiromasa (1989) 'Nihon ni okeru gaikokujin rōdōsha mondai no genjō to gyōsei no taiō', *Ōhara shakai mondai kenkyūsho zasshi* 386/7, 1–18.

——(1990) 'Nihon ni okeru gaikokujin rōdōsha mondai no genjō', *Ōhara shakai mondai kenkyūsho zasshi* 379.380/6.7, 61–73.

Morishita Katsuhiro (1992) 'Rainichi gaikokujin hanzai no genjō, mondaiten to sōsajō no ryūi jikō', *Keisatsugaku ronshū* 45/5, 1–23.

Mouer, Ross E. and Sugimoto Yoshio (1986) *Images of Japanese society. A study in the structure of social reality.* London etc.: Routledge & Kegan

Müller, Monika (1985) 'Die Wohnsituation von Ausländern: Diskriminierung oder Ghetto als sicherer Ort', Schulte, Trabandt and Zein 1985:55–84.

Murashita Hiroshi (1990) 'Rōdōhō–jō no mondaiten', GSK 1990: 107–122.

Naikaku sōri daijin kanbō kōhōshitsu-NSDKK (ed.) (1989) *Yoron chōsa nenkan. Zenkoku yoron chōsa no genkyō.* Tōkyō: Sōrifu.

——(1990) *Yoron chōsa nenkan. Zenkoku yoron chōsa no genkyō.* Tōkyō: Sōrifu.

Nakajima Satoshi (1990) *Tanshin seikatsusha. Zoku doyamachi Kamagasaki.* Ōsaka: Kaifūsha.

Narizawa Yoshinobu (ed.) (1990a) *Gaikokujin rōdōsha to jinken.* Tōkyō: Nihon Hyōronsha (Hōgaku seminā zōkan. Sōgō tokushū shirīzu 42).

——(1990b) *Hanzai hōdō no genzai.* Tōkyō: Nihon hyōronsha (Hōgaku semina zōkan. Sōgō tokushū shirīzu 45).

Naruse Takeo (1990) 'Gaikokujin rōdōsha mondai – Nikkeiren no kangaekata', *Ōhara shakai mondai kenkyūsho zasshi* 376, 25–27.

Nihon Bengoshi Rengōkai-NBR (ed.) (1988a) *Jinken no kokusaiteki hoshō. Kokusai jinken kiyaku no Nihon kokunai ni okeru jitchi jōkyō. Dai 31kai jinken yōgo taikai shinpojiumu daiichi bunkakai kichō hōkokusho.* Tōkyō.

——(1988b) *Jitsujō ripōto. 'Daiyō kangoku', Japan's Daiyo-Kangoku. Dai 31kai jinken yōgo taikai shinpojiumu daiichi bunkakai (dai 2bu).* Tōkyō.

Nihon kirisuto kyōdan shakai iinkai und Nihon kirisuto kyōdan zainichi-nikkan rentai tokubetsu iinkai-Nihon kirisuto kyōdan-NKK (ed.) (1989) *Ajiajin rōdōsha – Nihon no naka no.* Tōkyō: NKK.

Nishikawa Atsushi (1981) 'Japanese transnationals & Asian trainees', *AMPO* 13/4, 53–59.

Nishina Kyōsuke (1991) 'Ajia kara no shūgakusei-tachi [jō]', *Sekai* 2, 373–380.

Nishio Kanji (1989a) *'Sakoku' no susume. Gaikokujin rōdōsha ga Nihon o horobosu.* Tōkyō: Kōbunsha (Kappa bijinesu).

——(1989b) ' "Rōdō kaikoku" wa dō kentō shite mo fukanō da', *Chūō kōron* 9, 312–330.

——(1989c) 'Ukeire zehi ni Beikoku no kanshō o yurusu na', *Chūō kōron* 11, 144–153.

——(1990a) 'Intabyū. Sore de mo watakushi wa "rōdō sakoku" o shutchō suru!', Ishii 1990:184–196.

——(1990b) 'The danger of an open-door policy', *Japan Echo* 17/1, 51–56.

Nishitani Satoshi (1990) 'Gaikokujin rōdōsha to rōdōhō', Narizawa 1990a:128–135.

Niwa Masao (1993) 'Gaikokujin keiji jiken bengo no mondaiten', *Jiyū to seigi* 44/1, 80–85.

Noda Akio (1990) 'Rōdōryoku fusoku no kōzō – Mukaerugawa no jijō', KNK 1990:245–267.

Nomura Susumu (1989) 'Yakuza in Firipin. Firipin no jânarizumu wa yakuza o dono yō ni hōdō shite iru ka?', Ishii 1989:188–193.

Noro Yoshimitsu (1987) 'Nanbei kara no Nihonjin imin U-tān genshō no jittai', *Kikan Pan* 5, 36–45.

Nozaki Rokusuke (1990) 'Kokui no hanayome', Okaniwa 1990:32–33.

Nyūkan tōkei kenkyūkai-NTK (ed.) (1990) *Wagakuni o meguru*

kokusai jinryū no hensen. Shutsunyūkoku, zairyū tōkei ni miru kokusaika no genjō. Tōkyō: Ôkurashō.

Obata Kazuyuki (1990a) 'Chūgakusei-tachi ga imēji suru "gaikokujin" ni matsuwaru uwasa o ou', Ishii 1990:104–109.

——(1990b) 'Gaikokujin o ukeireru "hito" to "machi" ', Ishii 1990:120–129.

Odagiri Makoto (1990) 'Ajia wa yowashi Nihon wa tsuyoshi', Ishii 1990:149–159.

N.N. (1990) 'Gaikokujin rōdōsha ni kansuru ILO jōyaku, kankoku/ Sōhyō no kenkai', *Ōhara shakai mondai kenkyū zasshi* 376//3, 51–58.

Okaniwa Noboru (ed.) (1990) *Tōkyō nanmin sensō. Gaikokujin rōdōsha mondai ga kanki suru mono.* Tōkyō: Seihōsha (Dōjidai hihyō bukkuretto 3).

Ōiwa Yuri (1991) ' "Nihongirai" o umu nyūkan', *AERA* 15. October, 24–28.

Okazaki Kei A.O. (1989) 'Zadankai. Gaikokujin keiji jiken no ninaitetachi', *Hō to minshushugi* 242/11, 30–49.

Okuda Akihisa (1992) 'Kabukichō keisatsu vs kokusai hanzai', *Shūkan Asahi* 2 October, 33–35.

Ōmae Ken'ichi (1990) 'Gaikokujin rōdōsha ga issenmannin ni naru hi', *Gekkan Asahi* 1, 46–51.

Onizuka Tadanori (1988) 'Gaikokujin rōdōsha no hogo ni kakawaru hōteki mondaiten', *Kikan rōdōhō* 149/10.25, 68–73.

Ōnuma Yasuaki (1991) 'Gaikokujin rōdōsha mondai o kangaeru ue de zainichi Kankoku-Chōsenjin mondai no jūyōsei', Tezuka A.O. 1991:67–76.

Ōnuki Kensuke (1990a) 'Bizai de "shobatsu" sareru rainichi Ajiajintachi', *Asahi Jānaru* 9. March, 92–96.

——(1990b) 'Gaikokujin higisha ni tekisei tetsuzuki wa hoshō sarete iru no ka', *Hōgaku seminā* 35/8, 44–47.

——(1990c) 'Oni no sumu kuni Jipangu. 'Fuhō shūrōsha zōkachian akkaron no uso', Ishii 1990:253–257.

——(1992) 'Saiban to gaikokujin', Ajiajin rōdōsha mondai kondankai (ed.): *Okasareru jinken, gaikokujin rōdōsha. Nihon e no dekasegi rōdōsha o meguru genjō to teigen.* Tōkyō: Daisan shokan, 337–345.

Ortmann, Rüdiger (1985) 'Prisonierung', Kaiser A.O. 1985: 341–345.

Ōsaka bengoshikai-OBK (ed.) (1990) *Gaikokujin jinken gaidobukku. Nihongoban.* Ōsaka: Ōsaka bengoshikai.

——(1991) *Shinpojiumu. 'Gaikokujin to keiji tetsuzuki'*. Ōsaka.

Ōshima Shizuko and Carolyn Francis (1988) *HELP kara mita Nihon*. Tōkyō: Asahi shinbunsha.

Pfeiffer, Dietmar K. and Sebastian Scheerer (1979) *Kriminalsoziologie. Eine Einführung in Theorien und Themen*. Stuttgart etc.: Kohlhammer (Urban-Taschenbücher 291).

Pilgram, Arno (1982) 'Was es mit Kriminalitätsentwicklungen auf sich hat. Zur kriminalpolitikwissenschaftlichen Analyse von Kriminalstatistiken', *Kriminalsoziologische Bibliografie* 36/37, 93–115.

——(1984) 'Ausländerprobleme, dargestellt in der kriminologischen Literatur. Bericht und Ergänzung zur Theorie der Ausländerkriminalität', *Kriminalsoziologische Bibliografie* 43/44, 16–41.

——(1986) 'Ausländerbeschäftigung und Kriminalität', Wimmer 1986:349–380.

——(1990) 'Zur Sicherheitsinformation in Österreich. Wie das polizeiliche Definitionsmonopol über die "innere Sicherheit" hergestellt wird', *Kriminalsoziologische Bibliografie* 69, 3–36.

Plasser, Fritz and Peter A. Ulram (1991) ' "Die Ausländer kommen!" Empirische Notizen zur Karriere eines Themas und der Bewußtseinslage "im Herzen Europas" ', Andreas Khol, Günter Ofner and Alfred Stirnemann (eds): *Österreichisches Jahrbuch für Politik 1990*. Wien: Verl. für Geschichte und Politik & München: R. Oldenbourg, 311–323.

Pohl, Manfred (1981) *Presse und Politik in Japan. Die politische Rolle der japanischen Tageszeitungen*. Hamburg: Inst. für Asienkunde (Mitteilungen des Instituts für Asienkunde 122).

——(1991) 'Arbeitsmigration und Ausländerprobleme: Das "Wunderland Japan" lockt', *Japan Magazin* 10, 22–24.

Pontell, Henry M. (ed.) (1993) *Social deviance. Readings in theory and research*. Englewood Cliffs, N.J.: Prentice Hall.

Pörtner, Peter and Ulrike Schaede (1990) 'Von der Schwierigkeit, über den Schatten zu springen, in dem man steht. Zur Methodendiskussion in der deutschsprachigen Japanologie', Peter Pörtner (ed.): *Japan. Lesebuch II*. Tübingen: konkursbuch Verl. Claudia Gehrke, 408–412.

Richter, Helmut (1981) 'Kulturkonflikt, soziale Mängellage, Ausländer-Stigma. Zur Kriminalitätsbelastung der männlichen, ausländischen Wohnbevölkerung', *Kriminologisches Journal* 3, 263–277.

Rōdōshō (1990) ' "Gaikokujin rōdōsha mondai ni kansuru chōsa kentō no tame no kondankei" ni okeru iken no chūkanteki seiri', Narizawa 1990a:215–220.

Ronzani, Silvio (1980) *Arbeitskräftewanderung und gesellschaftliche Entwicklung. Erfahrungen in Italien, in der Schweiz und in der Bundesrepublik Deutschland*. Königstein/Ts.: Hain (Schriften des Wissenschaftszentrums Berlin 15; Internationales Institut für Management und Verwaltung).

Ruhrmann, Georg (1991) 'Zum Problem der Darstellung fremder Kulturen in der deutschen Presse', *Zeitschrift für Kulturaustausch* 41/1, 42–53.

Sack, Fritz (1985) 'Selektivität, Selektion, Selektionsmechanismen', Kaiser A.O. 1985:387–395.

——(1988) 'Wege und Umwege der deutschen Kriminologie in und aus dem Strafrecht', Helmut Janssen, Reiner Kaulitzky und Raymond Michalowski (eds): *Radikale Kriminologie. Themen und theoretische Positionen der amerikanischen Radical Criminology*. Bielefeld: AJZ.

Saitō Ichirō (1991) 'Gaikokujin rōdōsha koyō no benpō?', *AERA* 30. Juli 1991, 22–24.

Saitō Yuriko (1990) 'Tai josei Noi-san ni tsumetai hanketsu', *Yoseba* 3, 150–159.

Sakaiya Taichi (1989) 'Shin-Nihon kaikokuron. "Nanmin shūrai de otaota suru na" ' *SAPIO* 12. Oktober 1989, 8–15.

Sakanaka Hidenori (1989) 'Gaikokujin rōdōsha mondai to nyū-kanhō no kaisei', *Jiyū to seigi* 40/6, 18–27.

Sasaki Shinrō (1990) 'Heisei ninen keisatsu hakusho no gaiyō. Gaikokujin rōdōsha no kyūzō to keisatsu no taiō', *Keisatsugaku ronshū* 43/8, 1–22.

Sassen, Saskia (1991) 'Die Mobilität von Arbeit und Kapital: USA und Japan', PROKLA 83, 222–248.

Satō Kunio (1988) 'Wives for farmers, a critical import', *Japan Quarterly* July–September 1988, 253–259.

Sawahata Takashi (ed.) (1989) *Jipangu. Nihon o mezasu gaikokujin rōdōsha*. Tōkyō: Mainichi shinbunsha.

Schneider, Hans Joachim (1977) *Kriminologie. Standpunkte und Probleme*. 2 überarb. Aufl. Berlin und New York: de Gruyter (Sammlung Göschen 2804).

Schüler-Springorum, Horst (ed.) (1983) *Jugend und Kriminalität. Kriminologische Beiträge zur kriminalpolitischen Diskussion*. Frankfurt a.M.: Suhrkamp (edition suhrkamp 1201).

Schulte, Axel, Cornelia Trabandt and Abudin Zein (eds) (1985) *Ausländer in der Bundesrepublik. Integration, Marginalisierung, Identität.* Frankfurt a.M.: Materialis-Verl. (Materialis-Programm; MP 29: Kollektion Psychologie, Pädagogik, Soziologie).

Seno Nobuyuki (1989) 'Kenri ni kansuru isshikiron', *Hō to minshushugi* 242/11, 10–15.

Sessar, Klaus (1985) 'Tötungskriminalität', Kaiser A.O. 1985: 489–494.

Shakai bunka hōritsu sentā (ed.) (1989) *Kaiseian ni taisuru ikensho.* Ōsaka.

Shibuya Eichi (ed.) (1990) *Asa made nama terebi. Gekiron. Gaikokujin rōdōsha.* Tōkyō: Terebi Asahi.

Shikita Minoru and Tsuchiya Shin'ichi (eds) (1990) *Crime and criminal policy in Japan from 1926 to 1988. Analysis and evaluation of the Shōwa era.* Tōkyō: Japan Criminal Society.

Shimada Yukio (1987) 'Nyūkoku hōsei no rekishiteki keii to gaiyō', *Jurisuto* 877/2, 26–31.

Shimokawa Yūji (1991) ' "Fuhō shūrō" shindoromu. Jisatsu, yukidaore, seishin shōgai . . . gaikokujin rōdōsha o mushibamu', *Shūkan Asahi* 16–23. August 1991, 162–164.

Smaus, Gerlinda (1978) 'Funktion der Berichterstattung über die Kriminalität in den Massenmedien', *Kriminologisches Journal* 10, 187–201.

Stein-Hilbers, Marlene (1976) 'Kriminalitätskontrolle durch Buwußtseinskonstitution', *Kriminalsoziologische Bibliografie* 4/ 11–13, 77–89.

Steinert, Heinz (1981) 'Widersprüche, Kapitalstrategien und Widerstand oder: Warum ich den Begriff "Soziale Probleme" nicht mehr hören kann (1) Versuch eines theoretischen Rahmens für die Analyse der politischen Ökonomie sozialer Bewegungen und "Sozialer Probleme" ', *Kriminalsoziologische Bibliografie* 31/32, 56–89.

——(1988) 'Phasen der strafrechtlichen Kontrollpolitik. Ansatz und wichtigste Ergebnisse eines internationalen Vergleichs', *Kriminalsoziologische Bibliografie* 60, 3–15.

Sugano Kiyosuke (1989) 'Gaikokujin no fuhō shūrō "Mafia" no me ni mo', *Yomiuri shinbun* 13. Augúst 1989 (KNK 10, 25).

Suwa Masaru (1990) 'Yonjūhachinichi no "jiyū" no hate ni', *Hōgaku seminā* 35/8, 52–55.

Suzuki Shingo A.O. (1990a) 'Rainichi gaikokujin ni yoru hanzai. 1.

Hanzaisha oyobi hanzai no tokuchō', *Kagaku keisatsu kenkyūjo hōkoku (Bōhan shōnenhen)* 31/2, 48–55.

——(1990b) 'Rainichi gaikokujin ni yoru hanzai. 2. Fuhō shūrōsha no rainichi katei to honkoku oyobi Nihon de no seikatsu jōkyō', *Kagaku keisatsu kenkyujo hōkoku (Bōhan shōnenhen)* 31/2, 56–65.

Taguchi Sumikazu (1984) 'Iminzoku, ibunka no mondai to masukomi', Isomura Eichi and Fukuoka Yasunori (eds): *Masukomi to sabetsugo mondai*. Tōkyō: Akashi shoten (Kaihō shakaigaku sōsho 1).

Takafuji Akira (1990) 'Hogo to kintō taigū o megutte', *Ōhara shakai mondai kenkyūsho zasshi* 376/3, 9–15.

Takada Keiko (1991) 'Dekasegi Iranjin no a' Ueno-eki' *AERA* 25. Juni, 16–18.

Takahashi Hidemine (1989a) 'Tōkyō gaikokujin saiban 1. Kesareta shōgen', *QA* 9, 101–105.

——(1989b) 'Tōkyō gaikokujin saiban 2. Bengoshi no fuzai', *QA* 10, 101–105.

——(1989c) 'Tōkyō gaikokujin saiban 3. Hō no moto no fubyōdō', *QA* 11, 101–105.

——(1989d) 'Tōkyō gaikokujin saiban 4. Naze Shinshia wa keimusho e okurareta no ka', *QA* 12, 91–95.

——(1990) 'Tōkyō gaikokujin saiban. Saishūkai. Kōsei na saibansho wa doko ni aru no ka', *QA* 11, 82–87.

Takeoka Yaeko (1990) 'Dekasegi josei o hi no ataru basho e', Narizawa 1990b:136–146.

Tamura Tateo (1993) 'Baishunpu o ōbasutei de taiho shite mo, sugu "hōmen" to wa nanigoto da', *Sapio* 16/102 23. September 1993, 25–27.

Tanaka Hiroshi (1988) 'Nihon ni okeru rōdōryoku inyū no rekishi to genjitsu', *Kikan rōdōhō* 149, 17–25.

——(1990a) 'Ajiajin rōdōsha to gaikokujin sabetsu no rekishi', Narizawa 1990a:88–95.

——(1990b) 'Fukamaru "fuhō shūrō" no genjitsu to hōshin no kairi', *Hōgaku seminā* 35/8, 20–25.

Tanaka Kiyoshi (1990) 'Fuhō shurō o megutte', Okaniwa 1990:34–37.

Tenmyō Yoshiomi (1991) 'Iryō genba kara no teigen', Tenmyō 1991:17–28.

Tenmyō Yoshiomi (ed.) (1991) *Gaikokujin rōdōsha to rōdō saigai. Sono genjō to jitsumu Q & A.* Tōkyō: Kaifū shobō.

Tezuka Kazuaki (1988) 'Chotto matte gaikokujin rōdōsha no dōnyū', *Chūō kōron* 2, 274–285.

——(1989a) *Gaikokujin rōdōsha*. Tōkyō: Nihon keizai shinbunsha.

——(1989b) 'Gaikokujin rōdōsha mondai no shinkyokumen', *Chūō kōron* 11, 154–166.

——(1990) *Waga kuni ni okeru gaikokujin shūrō genjō to mondaiten*. Chiba: Chiba daigaku hōkei gakubu.

——(1991) 'Doitsu to Nihon no jōkyō hōkoku', Tezuka A.O. 1991:40–55.

——(1992a) 'Gaikokujin rōdōsha no shūrō jittai. Shutoken to Ōsaka no jittai', Tezuka A.O. 1992:3–66.

——(1992b) 'Shindankai ni haitta gaikokujin rōdōsha no ukeire', *Asahi shinbun (yūkan)* 18. Juli 1992, 7.

Tezuka Kazuaki A.O. (eds) (1991) *Shinpojiumu. Nihon to Doitsu no gaikokujin rōdōsha*. Tōkyō: Akashi shoten.

——(1992) *Gaikokujin rōdōsha no shūrō jittai. Sōgōteki jittai chōsa hōkokushū*. Tōkyō: Akashi shoten.

Tōkyō–to rōdō keizaikyoku-TRK (ed.) (1988) *Gaikokujin mondai manuaru – Gaikokujin rōdōsha mondai o kangaeru*. Tōkyō: Tōkyō–to rōdō keizai-kyoku rōsei-bu rōdō kumiai-ka.

Tōkyō–to Shinagawa rōsei jimusho-TSRJ (ed.) (1989) *Gaikokujin no koyō ni kansuru ishiki, jittai chōsa*. Tōkyō: TSRJ.

Toshiro Kazuo (1989a) 'Gaikokujin rōdōsha mondai no genjō to gaikokujin rōdōsha ni kakawaru koyō kankei jihan no sōsa o meguru shomondai', *Keisatsugaku ronshū* 10, 89–105 (*jō*).

——(1989b) 'Gaikokujin rōdōsha mondai no genjō to gaikokujin rōdōsha ni kakawaru koyō kankei jihan no sōsa o meguru shomondai', *Keisatsugaku ronshū* 12, 121–146 (*ge*).

Traulsen, Monika (1988) 'Die Kriminalität junger Ausländer nach der Polizeilichen Kriminalstatistik', *Monatsschrift für Kriminologie und Strafrechtsreform* 1, 28–41.

Trotha, Lutz von (1985) 'Kultur, Subkultur, Kulturkonflikt', Kaiser, A.O. 1985:286–294.

Ueda Takashi (1987) 'Gensō no Japayuki o motomete', Ishii 1987: 232–259.

Umetani Shin'ichirō (1989) 'Fuhō shūrō gaikokujin no jittai', Hanami and Kuwahara 1989:73–104.

Villmow, Bernhard (1985) 'Gastarbeiterkriminalität', Kaiser A.O. 1985:127–132.

Vogel, Ezra F. (1989) 'Pax Nipponica?', Ulrich Menzel (ed.): *Im*

Schatten des Siegers: Japan, vol. 4: Weltwirtschaft und Weltpolitik. Frankfurt a.M.: Suhrkamp (edition suhrkamp 1498), 197–216.

Wada Hitoshi (1990) 'Arusu no kai. Gaikokujin rōdōsha no nagashita namida no omosa o kamishimenagara', Narizawa 1990a:182–185.

Wakaichi Kōji (1988) *Ajia to fureau machi de.* Ōsaka: Burēn sentā.

Watanabe Hidetoshi (1990a) 'Ima, kinkyū ni surubeki koto', Narizawa 1990a:148–155.

——(1990b) 'Kuiyaburareta nyūkan taisei', KNK 1990:165–179.

——(1990c) 'Kurumaisu no kikoku', KNK 1990:26–41.

Wimmer, Hannes (1986a) 'Zur Ausländerbeschäftigungspolitik in Österreich', Wimmer 1986:5–32.

——(1986b) 'Wohnverhältnisse der ausländischen Arbeiter in Österreich', Wimmer 1986:281–306.

Wimmer, Hannes (ed.) (1986) *Ausländische Arbeitskräfte in Österreich.* Frankfurt a.M. & New York: Campus.

Wodak, Ruth (1991) 'Der Ton macht die Musik. Öffentliche Diskurse über Fremde', *Werkstattblätter* 1A/4, 16–21.

Wodak, Ruth and Bernd Matouschek (1993) ' "We are dealing with people whose origin one can clearly tell just by looking": critical discourse analysis and the study of neo-racism in contemporary Austria', *Society & Discourse* 4/2, 225–248.

Wolter, Otto (1984) 'Befürchtet – und gewollt? Fremdenhaß und Kriminalisierung ausländischer Jugendlicher', *Kriminologisches Journal* 16, 265–286.

Yabe Takeshi (1991) 'Gaikokujin o ijimeru Nippon keisatsu no ōbō', *Asahi Jānaru* 20. December, 18–21.

Yamada Ryōichi and Kuroki Tadamasu (1990) *Wakariyasui nyūkanhō.* Tōkyō: Yūhikaku (Yūhikaku ribure 26).

Yamada Toshie (1990) 'General trends of the Japanese press in 1989–1990', Gonda 1990:13–20.

Yamaguchi Masanori (1990) 'Nyūsu kachi handan kijun no kenshō', Narizawa 1990b:94–115.

Yamanaka Ichirō (1989) *Heisei Yakuza.* Tōkyō: Chūō āto shuppansha.

Yamatani Tetsuo (1988) *Japayuki-san.* Tōkyō: Jōhō sentā.

——(1989) 'Kochira Japayuki-san kanrikyoku', Ishii 1989:200–201.

Yamazaki Tetsuo (1991) 'Nihon no gaikokujin seisaku no jittai', Tezuka A.O. 1991:137–155.

Yashiro Atsushi (1989) 'Tekihō nyūkokusha no shūrō jittai', Kuwahara und Hanami 1989:31–71.

Yashima Yukihiko (1989) 'Gaikokujin rōdōsha no nyūkoku kanri to chianjō no shomondai', *Refarensu* 10, 8–29.

Yonekura Manabu and Ikoma Iwao (1989) 'Gaikokujin keiji tetsuzuki no sōsa dankai ni okeru mondaiten', *Hō to minshushugi* 242/11, 7–10.

Yonemoto Kazuhiro (1990) 'Watakushi ga tsukiatta okashina Pakisutanjin-tachi', Ishii 1990:30–48.

Yorimitsu Masatoshi (1989) 'Nihon wa gaikokujin rōdōsha o dō mite iru no ka', Hanami und Kuwahara 1989:1–32.

Yoshimen Mitsuaki (1988) 'Gaikokujin rōdōsha mondai no kentō jōkyō to kongo no taiō', *Kikan rōdōhō* 10, 57–67.

——(1990) 'Gaikokujin rōdōsha mondai o kangaeru', *Ōhara shakai mondai kenkyūsho zasshi* 376/3, 39–50.

Yoshino Kosaku (1992) *Cultural nationalism in contemporary Japan. A sociological enquiry*. London & New York: Routledge.

Zhaò Haichéng (1990) 'Fuan ni obieru ryūgakusei. Ryūgakusei kara mita nyūkanhō', *Hōgaku seminā* 35/8, 30–32.

Newspaper Articles (not naming the author)

A specification in parentheses after the article indicates that it was drawn from the newspaper clipping collection of Karabao no kai (KNK 1988–). The first number indicates the respective volume, the second the page number in the volume. The organization Karabao no kai does not give the original page number in the newspaper from which the collected articles were taken, so I cannot provide this information. The newspapers are listed in alphabetical order and the articles therein chronologically.

N.N.
'Dekasegi burūsu. Rupo. Gaikokujin rōdōsha 11. Rantō jiken shinsō. Pinhane tehaishi kainyū. Tōbō Bikki kuchi o hiraku', *Asahi shinbun* 13 April 1988 (KNK 3, 14).

'Japayuki-san. Kodoku no byōshi. Shizuoka no apāto shigo tōka amari. Sunakku tenten. "Hi ni kodomo, kaeru..."' *Asahi shinbun* 20 April 1988 (KNK 3, 6).

'Pakisutanjin shūdan nagurikomi. Adachi no dōkokujin-taku e', *Asahi shinbun* 9 May 1988 (KNK 3, 152).

'Bangurajin koroshi wa dōkukujin futari no hankō. Hitori saitaiho, hitori tehai', *Asahi shinbun* 26 May 1988 (KNK 3, 155).

'Fuhō shūrō no 1.371nin o tekihatsu', *Asahi shinbun* 6 June 1988 (KNK 4, 75).

'Bangurajin koroshi de tehai no dōkokujin taiho', *Asahi shinbun* 9 June 1988 (KNK 4, 4).

'Gaikokujin rōdōsha no rōsai hoshō fueru. Fuhō shūrō de mo kyūyo, *Asahi shinbun* 19 June 1988 (KNK 4, 91).

'Gaikoku kara no dekasegi kyūzō. Kensatsu ga taisakuin mōkeru', *Asahi shinbun* 24 June 1988 (KNK 4, 80).

'Minami Ajia-kei? Gōtō. Banguradeshujin 12nin higai', *Asahi shinbun* 27 June 1988 (KNK 4, 10).

'Honkonjin no hōseki gōtō. Yonin tehai', *Asahi shinbun* 6 August 1988 (KNK 5, 5).

'Taiō ni kurushimu kaku-seitō', *Asahi shinbun* 3 September 1988 (KNK 5, 72).

'Hijinra sannin-gumi yonhyakuman en gōdatsu. Saitama, Toda no kaisha', *Asahi shinbun* 6 November 1988 (KNK 6, 12).

'Nise no "zaigaku shōmeisho" uru. Gaikokujin shūgakusei aite ni hyakken', *Asahi shinbun* 5 December 1988 (KNK 7, 99).

'Banguradeshujin tetsu paipu de nagurareru. Jinzai haken no motsure?', *Asahi shinbun* 24 December 1988 (KNK 7, 15).

'Keihōhan ga sengo saita. Kotoshi settō ya gaikokujingarami ga zōka', *Asahi shinbun* 24 December 1988 (KNK 7, 159).

' "Kakekomi nyūkoku" Narita ni sattō. Fuhō shūrō mokuteki wa taikyo ni', *Asahi shinbun* 23 April 1990 (KNK 15, 82).

'Yonin-gumi no gōtō ni nijūgoman en ubawareru. Funabashi no Pakisutanjin-taku', *Asahi shinbun* 21 February 1989 (KNK 7, 52).

'Pakisutanjin sashikorosareru. Itabashi, apāto ni rannyū', *Asahi shinbun* 8 March 1989.

'Marēshia no dansei korosareru. Takasaki, kankō biza de nyūkoku', *Asahi shinbun* 14 March 1989 (KNK 8, 5 and 8).

'Pakisutanjin rokunin taiho. Itabashi no shisatsu. Kei nijūnin ijō ga kan'yo?' *Asahi shinbun* 15 March 1989 (KNK 8, 8).

'Dōryō o taiho. Marēshiajin ōsatsu bakuchi ni make hankō', *Asahi shinbun* 19 March 1989 (KNK 8, 8).

'Chūgokujin sannin o hōchō? de osou, Ikebukuro, hannin mo Chūgokujinfū', *Asahi shinbun* 3 April 1989 (KNK 8, 20).

'Nyūsu sanmenkyū. Kyōakka suru kyūzō gaikokujin hanzai. Shutoken ni fukusū gurūpu hotondo gizō ryoken de nyūkoku', *Asahi shinbun* 4 April 1989 (KNK 8, 24 and 134).

'Itabashi no Pakisutanjin koroshi. Dōkokujin hachinin o saitaiho', *Asahi shinbun* 4 April 1989 (KNK 8, 24).

'Gaikokujin gakusei. Biza kōshin ni shorui gizō. Seiseki nado kasaage', *Asahi shinbun* 6 May 1989 (KNK 9, 37).

'Tetsu paipu? Hakuchū gōtō. Ajia-kei ka, 128man en ubau. Pachinko tenin kega', *Asahi shinbun* 28 May 1989 (KNK 9, 128).

'Hōsekiten de 2.000 gōdatsu. Tōnan Ajia-kei? no sanningumi. Fukuoka', *Asahi shinbun* 12 July 1989 (KNK 10, 174).

'Chūkokujin ryūgakusei no heya ni gōtō', *Asahi shinbun* 16 August 1989 (KNK 10, 59).

'Chūgokujin shūgakusei-taku ni hamono gōtō. Dōkokujin? yoningumi 40man en ubau. Hitori o tehai', *Asahi shinbun* 21 June 1989 (KNK 9, 64).

' "Kaikoku" e genjitsuteki na koe. 45% ga gōhōka motomeru. "Kanzen sakokuha" wa niwari', *Asahi shinbun* 6 September 1989, 9.

'Pakisutanjinra gonin taiho. Kankin jiken', *Asahi shinbun, Saitama-ban* 21 September 1989 (KNK 11, 149).

'Shūgakusei gōtōdan. Fukkenshō–gumi, Shanhai shusshinsha osou. "Barenai" to tsugitsugi. Bukkadaka de tokōhi kaesezu', *Asahi shinbun* 6 October 1989 (KNK 11, 150).

'Tehai no Pakisutanjin taiho', *Asahi shinbun, Saitama-ban* 15 October 1989 (KNK 11, 24).

'Hōseki settōdan no Chūgokujin o taiho', *Asahi shinbun* 25 October 1989 (KNK 11, 154).

'Shigoto nakama o sashi tōsō. Chūgokujin no shūgakusei dōshi kōron', *Asahi shinbun* 3 November 1989 (KNK 11, 21).

'Chūgokujin shūgakusei osowareru. Yokosuka no jūgyōin-ryō', *Asahi shinbun* 5 November 1989 (KNK 12, 21).

'Jikkōhan ni chōeki hachinen. Pakisutanjin sasshō jiken', *Asahi shinbun* 8 November 1989 (KNK 12, 21).

'Futari o saitaiho. Hitori o tehai. Chūgokujin shūgakusei gōtō', *Asahi shinbun* 3 December 1989 (KNK 12, 32).

'Yaku niwari ga dekasegi mokuteki. Chūgoku, Taiwan de ryūgaku ishiki chōsa', *Asahi shinbun* 7 April 1990 (KNK 14, 31).

'Nihonshiki no ginō kenshū. "Taerarenai" ', *Asahi shinbun* (*yūkan*) 27 April 1990, 3.

'Taikyo tetsuzuki kyūzō. Hō kaisei de kaiko aitsugu', *Asahi shinbun* 23 April 1990 (KNK 14, 19).

' "Taiho iya" nyūkan ni sattō. Mizukara kyōsei taikyo nozomu', *Asahi shinbun* 29 May 1990 (KNK 15, 820).

'Gaikokujin sabetsu no hyōgen ga kōmoku ni. Jinkōken, "chō-sahyō" haki', *Asahi shinbun* 7 June 1990 (KNK 15, 118).

'Gaikokujin rōdōsha ukeire. 71% ga sansei. "Hitode busoku" 6wari', *Asahi shinbun* 9 June 1990 (KNK 15, 63).

'Chūgokujin futari o taiho. 4.500man en gōdatsu. Gōtō keikaku shi rainichi', *Asahi shinbun* 16 July 1990 (KNK 16, 118).

'Gaikokujin kenshūsei. Ukeire kijun kanwa e. Hōmushō: 20nin miman no kigyō OK', *Asahi shinbun* 25 July 1990 (KNK 16, 70).

'Gaikokujin no fuhō shūrō, hanzai kyūzō', *Asahi shinbun* 7 August 1990 (KNK 16, 127).

'Keisatsu hakusho. Otoko no gaikokujin rōdōsha ga kyūzō. Sat-sujin, gōtō . . . kyōakuhan wa saikō, *Asahi shinbun* (*Ōsaka-ban*) vom 8 August 1990 (KNK 16, 16).

'Nananin-gumi? Gōtōdan. Chūgokujin no heya osou', *Asahi shinbun* 7 September 1990 (KNK 17, 89).

'Pakisutanjin dōkokujin osou. Rōsai hoshō 110man gōdatsu', *Asahi shinbun* 13 September 1990 (KNK 17, 92).

'Dōkokujinra nerai renzoku gōtō no utagai. Pakisutanjin gurūpu taiho. Keishichō', *Asahi shinbun* 2 October 1990 (KNK 17, 94).

'Dōhō no Chūgokujin shūgeki yōgi. Rokunin o taiho, tehai. Fuhō shūrōchū', *Asahi shinbun* 9 October 1990 (KNK 17, 96).

'Fuhō nyūkoku ni "kyohi" kyūzō. Chūtō no eikyō mo. Kyonen no bai chikaku ni. Ōsaka, Narita kūkō', *Asahi shinbun* *Ōsaka-ban* 5 November 1990 (KNK 18, 4).

'Iran ni "Nihon dekasegi netsu" ', *Asahi shinbun* 19 November 1990 (KNK 18, 9).

' "Nihon was suri tengoku". 420ken 970man en kasegu to kyōjutsu. Taiho sareta Kankokujin 3nin', *Asahi shinbun* 22 November 1990 (KNK 18, 87).

'Dema ga machi o osen. Kairan mawashi keitai beru', *Asahi shinbun* 28 November 1990 (KNK 18, 12).

'Josei no eizu 20nendai ga hansū. Rainichi gaikokujin no kansen mo kyūzō', *Asahi shinbun* 28 November 1990 (KNK 18. 43).

' "Fuhō zanryū" 16mannin. Sakunen gogatsu Hōmushō suikei. 10kagetsu de 1.5bai', *Asahi shinbun, internat. ed.* 5 February 1992, 22.

' "Iranjin ga shufu osou" akushitsu dema hirogaru. Tōkyō', *Asahi shinbun* 5 July 1992, 31.

' "Koyō sentā" setsuritsu e. Konshū, San Pauro ni. Seiki rūto de funsō bōshī, *Asahi shinbun* 20 July 1992, 3.
'Nichiyō sukūpu. Nikkeijin rōdōsha 15mannin kosu. "Shūshoku chizu" ni henka ari. Fukyō de kaiko, shoku motome idō', *Asahi shinbun* 23 August 1992, 24.
'Keikan futari utare kega. Gaikokujin futari o taiho. Shinjuku no rojō, *Asahi shinbun* 16 September 1992, 23.
'Koyō zensen ihen ari', *Asahi shinbun* 4 October 1992, 6.
'Uikuendo keizai. Nikkeijin rōdōsha fukyō no "yaomote" ni. Hitode busoku no kirifuda itten, akikaze ga . . .', *Asahi shinbun* (*yūkan*) 9 October 1992, 5.

'Fuhō shūrō gaikokujin 1.870nin tekihatsu. Gogatsu no tokubetsu gekkan. Afurikajin mo 14nin', *Hokkaidō shinbun* 6 June 1988 (KNK 76).
'Hōseki nado nioku en gōdatsu. Chūgokujin sannin-gumi? Mise ni shachō oshikome. Tōkyō, *Hokkaidō shinbun* 9 July 1988 (KNK 4, 21).
'Honkon kara "shutchō" gōtō. Sannin-gumi, kaisha yakuin shisatsu', *Hokkaidō shinbun* 9 January 1989 (KNK 7, 30).
'Chūgokujin shūgakusei ga gōtōdan. Tokō hiyō henzai ni komari, Shanhai shusshinsha o osou', *Hokkaidō shinbun* 9 October 1989 (KNK 11, 42).
'Dekasegi nanmin haijo. "Sukurîningu" dōnyū', *Hokkaidō shinbun* 2 September 1989 (KNK 11, 77).
'Pachinkoten ni tanjū gōtō. 400man en ubai hitori jūshō. Ajia-kei no 4, 5nin. Fukuoka', *Hokkaidō shinbun* 4 January 1990 (KNK 13, 107).
'1man 404nin ga "nyūkoku dame". Nyūkan de sakunen. Dekasegi būmu izen', *Hokkaidō shinbun* 19 March 1990 (KNK 14, 12).

'Pakisutanjin jūsūnin ga osou. Dōkokujin no futari jūshō', *Kanagawa shinbun* 9 May 1988 (KNK 3, 152).
'Kankokujin dansei no fuhō shūrō kyūzō. Nyūkan ga zenkoku issai tekihatsu', *Kanagawa shinbun* 19 December 1988 (KNK 7, 114).
'Chūgokujin dansei? no shitai. Rinsetsu no apāto isshitsu kara', *Kanagawa shinbun* 3 January 1989 (KNK 7, 164).
'Chūgokujin ryūgakusei o koroshi hōka. Kubi shimerareru. Kao mishiri no hankō ka', *Kanagawa shinbun* 4 January 1989 (KNK 7, 81).

'Aitsugu gaijin-garami no kyōaku jiken. "Taisakushitsu" o shin-setsu e. Keisatsuchō', *Kanagawa shinbun* 19 January 1989 (KNK 7, 37).

'Apâto dōji hōka wa naze? Kao mishiri no hankō tsuyomaru', *Kanagawa shinbun* 3 February 1989 (KNK 7, 91).

Gaikokujin rōdōsha. Tanjun rōdō kaihō o. Chūshō keieisha no 4nin ni 3nin', *Kanagawa shinbun* 21 July 1989 (KNK 10, 168).

'Kenshū meimoku no shūrō 58%. 81nin o kyōsei shukkoku ni', *Kanagawa shinbun* 14 August 1989 (KNK 10, 26).

'3.013nin o kyōsei shukkoku. Shūchū tekihatsu de saikō. Kokuseki, chiiki tomo kakudai', *Kanagawa shinbun* 21 August 1989 (KNK 10, 29).

'Chūgokujin shūgakusei no gōtō shōgai. Shimei tehai no dōhō taiho. Taurasho', *Kanagawa shinbun* 8 November 1989 (KNK 12, 23).

'Gōtō kankin de Chūgokujin futari taiho', *Kanagawa shinbun* 3 December 1989 (KNK 12, 119).

'Shōgai chishi de Hi-kokunin taiho. Kenka no chūsaisha sasu. Yokohama', *Kanagawa shinbun* 3 January 1990 (KNK 13, 3).

'Rojō ni gaikokujin dansei no shisatsutai. Tōnan Ajia-kei nakama dōshi de kenka?' *Kanagawa shinbun* 24 January 1990 (KNK 13, 111).

'Hikokujinra futari taiho. Yokohama no rojō dansei satsujin. Kei-kakuteki na hankō jikyō', *Kanagawa shinbun* 6 February 1990 (KNK 13, 116).

'Pakisutanjin hachinin genkin to yubiwa o ubau. Sagamihara. Yonin taiho', *Kanagawa shinbun* 13 September 1990 (KNK 17, 92).

'Rōdōshō. Burajiru Nikkeijin shūshoku sōdan e madoguchi', *Kanagawa shinbun* 20 September 1990 (KNK 17, 38).

'Gaikokujin yonin nanaman en gōdatsu. Yokosuka', *Kanagawa shinbun* 17 October 1990 (KNK 17, 100).

'Eizu hokinsha to kakunin. Yokohama de baishun no Taijin josei. Tekihatsu uke kokugai taikyo', *Kanagawa shinbun* 18 October 1990 (KNK 17, 30).

'Chūgokujin sannin ga settō misui', *Kanagawa shinbun* 28 November 1990 (KNK 18, 88).

'Dekasegi Pakisutanjin dōshi. Genkin ubaware, hōfuku shūgeki. Adachi, gonin taiho', *Mainichi shinbun* 9 May 1988 (KNK 3, 152).

'Dōkukujin-taku ni gōtō no Pakisutanjin futari taiho', *Mainichi shinbun* 11 June 1988 (KNK 4, 5).

' "Bakusetsudan" 22nin o taiho, yonin tehai. Honkonjin gurūpu', *Mainichi shinbun* vom 13 Oktober 1988 (KNK 6, 6).

'Gaimushō. Biza menjo o ichiji teishi. Pakisutan, Bangura ryōkoku. Fuhō shūrō no gekizō de', *Mainichi shinbun* 27 November 1988 (KNK 6, 63).

'Kikinzoku 4.500 man en sōtō nusumu. Bakusetsudan no betsu-gurūpu ka', *Mainichi shinbun* 12 December 1988 (KNK 7, 10).

'Kikinzokuten senmon ni hassenman en. Gaikokujin sannin o taiho', *Mainichi shinbun* 15 February 1989 (KNK 7, 47).

'Pachinko-dama settōdan. Hōseki dorobō taiho no sannin "ippat-sudai" arashi mawaru', *Mainichi shinbun* 18 February 1989 (KNK 7, 51).

'Kankokujin suridan sannin o taiho', *Mainichi shinbun* 11 March 1989 (KNK 8, 127).

'Hachinin o satsujin nado de saitaiho. Pakisutanjin koroshi', *Mainichi shinbun* 4 April 1989 (KNK 8, 136).

'Kawaguchi de yonin-gumi Chūgokujin gōtō. Dōhō osou', *Mainichi shinbun* 25 June 1989 (KNK 9, 135).

'Gizō mimoto hoshōsho "sanman en de". Biza kōshin de mitsubai rūto', *Mainichi shinbun* 16 July 1989 (KNK 10, 44).

'Fukkenshō shusshin no gōtō sannin tehai', *Mainichi shinbun (Saitama-ban)* 20 September 1989 (KNK 11, 149).

'Dōkokujin o osoi kankin. Pakisutanjin sannin taiho. Kinsen tora-buru de', *Mainichi shinbun (Saitama-ban)* 20 September 1989 (KNK 11, 149).

'Nikkei Burajirujin-ra haken. Pinhane 50oku en', *Mainichi shinbun* 1 November 1989 (KBR 12, 100).

'Gaikokujin rōdōsha. Ukeire sanseiha 51% ni. Honsha yoron chōsa. Zenkai kara ichinen de tenkan', *Mainichi shinbun* 5 February 1990 (KNK 13, 10).

'Nyūkanhō ihan "kiso" medatsu', *Mainichi shinbun* 17 March 1990 (KNK 14, 11).

'Gaikokujin shūgakusei shimedashi. Nisennin zairyū enchō mito-mezu', *Mainichi shinbun* 29 April 1990 (KNK 14, 35).

'Gaikokujin rōdōsha korosareru. Gunma no tōsō kōjō jūgyōin-ryō. Hikokujin o osoi gyaku ni', *Mainichi shinbun* 12 May 1990 (KNK 15, 105).

'Firipinjin osotta Pakisutanjin taiho. Gunma, yonin', *Mainichi shinbun* 14 May 1990 (KNK 15, 103).

'Soshiki no kyoten wa Honkon ka'. Tai ni bosu no sonzai ukabu',
Mainichi shinbun (Saitama-ban) 5 July 1990 (KNK 16, 46).
'Gaikokujin rōdōsha. Kenshū–go, ichinen shūrō mitomeru', *Main-
ichi shinbun* 8 July 1990 (KNK 16, 62).
' "Fuhō shūrō" tsukekomu soshiki. Gaikokujin rōdōsha mondai o
tokushū', *Mainichi shinbun* 7 August 1990 (KNK 16, 88).
'Bangura dansei shisatsu sareru. Kashigaya', *Mainichi shinbun* 11
October 1990 (KNK 17, 100).
'100gumi kosu gisō kekkon. Kankoku, Taiwan josei ni assen',
Mainichi shinbun 30 October 1990 (KNK 17, 31).
'Gaikokujin ga rojō gōtō. Kōkyū tokei nado ubau. Chiba, Noda',
Mainichi shinbun 18 November 1990 (KNK 18, 84).
'Dōkyo no Banguradeshujin taiho. Saitama no shisatsu jiken',
Mainichi shinbun 27 November 1990 (KNK 18, 87).
'Tōnan Ajiajin chūshō dema. Henken ga uwasa zōfuku. Higai
todoke issai nashi', *Mainichi shinbun* 8 December 1990.
'Gaikokujin fuhō shūrō no genba de. Heranu shūgaku gisō no
dekasegi', *Mainichi shinbun* 6 July 1991, 3.
'Gaikokujin fuhō shūrō. Deguchi miezu ni kuryo suru seifu. Kontei
ni aru keizai kakusa, tekihatsu taisei ni genkai', *Mainichi
shinbun* 25 January 1992, 3.

'Jijitsu no jinshin baibai. "Kasegi tsuki 30man' to sasou" ', *Nihon
keizai shinbun* 3 February 1988 (KNK 7, 45).
'Pakisutanjin, shūdan shūgeki. Adachi-ku, gonin taiho. Dōkokujin
futari ga jūshō', *Nihon keizai shinbun* 9 May 1988 (KNK, 3,
152).
'Chūgokujin shūgakusei futari-gumi ga suri. Ueno de taiho', *Nihon
keizai shinbun* 26 December 1988 (KNK 7, 78).
'Pakisutanjin o shūgeki, shisatsu. Tōnan A-kei? no satsujin-gumi',
Nihon keizai shinbun 7 March 1989 (KNK 8, 122).
'Pakisutanjin koroshi. Dōkokujin hachinin o taiho. Itabashi no
apāto shūgeki', *Nihon keizai shinbun* 4 April 1989 (KNK 8,
136).
' "Kenshūsei" de rainichi, jitsu wa tanjun rōdōsha. Fuhō shūrō
itachigokko. Hōmushō ga chōsa', *Nihon keizai shinbun* 22 May
1989 (KNK 9, 65).
'Machibuse gōtō. Uriagekin ubau. Tōnan Ajia-kei no futari-gumi',
Nihon keizai shinbun 28 May 1989 (KNK 9, 126).
'Nyūkan moto kanbu ga tetasuke. Mimoto hoshōsho o tairyō gizō',
Nihon keizai shinbun 21 September 1989 (KNK 11, 10).

363

Foreign Workers and Law Enforcement in Japan

'Nyūkanhō kaisei-an o kaketsu. Shūin. Fuhō shūrō no kisei kyoka', *Nihon keizai shinbun* 18 November 1989 (KNK 12, 79).
' "Dekasegi suri" no Kankokujin sannin taiho. JR Ueno-eki', *Nihon keizai shinbun* 23 October 1990 (KNK 17, 101).
'Pakisutanjin ni chōeki hachinen. Dōkokujin koroshi ni Tōkyō chisai "Nihon no seisaku mo okure" '. *Nihon keizai shinbun* 8 November 1989 (KNK 12, 6).
'Banguradeshujin migimune o sasare shibō. Kashigaya', *Nihon keizai shinbun* 12 October 1990 (KNK 17, 100).
'Chūgokujin ryūgakusei ga shūgakusei nakama o sasu. Josei meguri kōron', *Nihon keizai shinbun* 11 November 1989 (KNK 12, 22).
'Chūgokujin dōshi no toraburu. Biza ni hitsuyō na shorui meguri. Shūgakusei ratchi no gonin o taiho', *Nihon keizai shinbun* 27 February 1990 (KNK 13, 19).
'Chūgokujin sasare shinu. Aichi-ken, Handa-shi. Nakama dōshi de kenka?', *Nihon keizai shinbun* 16 March 1990 (KNK 14, 81).
'Tanjun rōdōsha. Eijū o zenin. Daishō ga gaikokujin koyō de "yōbō". Ukeire sansei. Kuni ni setchi yōkyū', *Nihon keizai shinbun* 25 May 1990, 10.
'10sha ni 1sha, gaikokunin koyō. Inshokuten wa 4wari kosu', *Nihon keizai shinbun* 13 June 1990 (KNK 15, 10).
'Gaikokujin rōdōsha mondai. Kenshūseido jiku ni chōsei', *'Nihon keizai shinbun* 25 July 1990 (KNK 16, 71).
'Gaikokujin futarigumi 1200man en gōdatsu. Ōta-ku no kensetsu kaisha', *Nihon keizai shinbun* 26 July 1990 (KNK 16, 120).
'Marēshia kokuseki no otoko tehai. Kamata no senman en gōtō', *Nihon keizai shinbun* 27 August 1990 (KNK 16, 131).
'Gaikokujinryō osoi genkin ubau. Tochigi. Pakisutanjin? goningumi', *Nihon keizai shinbun* 12 November 1990 (KNK 18, 85).
'Iran no 12sai shōnen ga jikoshi', *Nihon keizai shinbun* 11 December 1990 (KNK 18, 14).

' "Bakusetsudan" no menbā tsukamaru. Nagoya de manbiki, tenchō ga toriosaeru', *Nikkan supōtsu shinbun* 22 December 1988 (KNK 7, 163).
'Nikkan sukūpu. Anyaku suru gaikokujin gōtōdan. Nerawareru kinman Nippon. Hanemūn yosoi jōriku. Hitto endo ran Kukubatto, Pakisutan. Hakuchū dōdō hōsekiten arashi. Fuhō taizai nakama kara ryakudatsu', *Nikkan supōtsu shinbun* 12 October 1990 (KNK 17, 97).

'Gisō kekkon kyūzō. Gaikokujin hosutesu shutoken de 200gumi', *Nikkan supōtsu shinbun* 12 November 1990 (KNK 18, 42).

'Yokohama no Nanbei Nikkeijin haken jiken. "Hanzai" ishiki usui tōjisha. 400nin ga nao ihō shūrō, *Ryūkyū shinpō* 1 November 1989 (KBR 12, 98).

'Dekasegi ijū ga mokuteki ka. Haigo ni burōka kainyū', *Ryūkyū shinpō* 24 August 1989 (KNK 10, 113).

'Gaikokujin hanzai ga tahatsu. Fukuoka Ajia-kei bōryokudan no hyōteki', *Ryūkyū shinpō* 5 January 1990 (KNK 13, 107).

'Shinnyū no gaikokujin o shisatsu. Gunma', *Ryūkyū shinpō* 12 May 1990 (KNK 15, 102).

' "Dekasegi mondai" apīru e', *Ryūkyū shinpō* 4 September 1990 (KNK 17, 50).

'Nikkeijin yosoi dekasegi. Perū: Ryoken gizōdan ga anyaku', *Ryūkyū shinpō* 20 May 1991 (KNK 20, 89).

'Chūgokujin ryūgakusei-taku ni yonin-gumi no gōtō. Naifu de kiritsuke genkin ubau', *Saitama shinbun* 17 August 1989 (KNK 10, 64).

'Dōkokujin ni bōkō, kankin. Pakisutanjin gonin sōken', *Saitama shinbun* 21 September 1989 (KNK 11, 12).

'Fuhō zanryū de taiho. Pakisutanjin rokunin', *Saitama shinbun* 24 January 1990.

' "Josei ga gaikokujin ni osowareta..." Dema ga machi ni jūman', *Saitama shinbun* 29 November 1990 (KNK 18, 13).

'Maruko. Pakisutanjin dōshi satsujin? Kōjō ryōnai ni itai o hōchi. Kubi ni kirikizu. Dōshitsu no otoko sugata o kesu', *Shinano Mainichi shinbun* 22 November 1989 (KNK 12, 10).

'Fuhō shūrō no utagai. Maruko satsugai Pakisutanjin. Kankō biza mo kigengire. "Kenshūsei' kaishagawa wa setsumei', *Shinano Mainichi shinbun* 23 November 1989 (KNK 12, 11).

'Pakisutanjin jūgyōin satsugai. Hinin no mama dōryō sōken. Marukosho: "Hankōji futari dake" ', *Shinano Mainichi shinbun* 28 November 1989 (KNK 12, 12).

'Hakken no hōchō' honkakuteki ni kantei. Pakisutanjin satsugai, *Shinano Mainichi shinbun* 5 December 1989 (KNK 12, 117).

'Kōryū kigen o enchō. Pakisutanjin satsugai', *Shinano Mainichi shinbun* 7 December 1989 (KNK 12, 118).

'Gekizō. Gaikokujin hanzai 10nen de 7bai', *Tōkyō shinbun (yūkan)* 7 August 1990 (KNK 16, 126).

'Gaikokujin rōdōsha ga iru shakai', *Tōkyō shinbun* 8 August 1990 (KNK 16, 142).

'Kōmyō na teguchi de arakasegi. "Koseki shiyōryō" 100man en', *Tōkyō shinbun* 8 August 1990 (KNK 16, 13).

'Naigai ni dai shinjikēto. Fuhō shūrō no kyōkyūgen o ou', *Tōkyō shinbun* 8 August 1990 (KNK 16, 12).

'Oashisu', *Yomiuri shinbun* vom 3 Mai 1988 (KNK 3, 41).

'Japayuku dōshi no satsujin. Sangatsu no jiken. Hitori taiho, hitori tehai', *Yomiuri shinbun* 26 May 1988 (KNK 3, 155).

'Pakisutanjin shūgeki jiken shuhan. Chūkosha hyakudai ijō fusei yushutsu. Nihonjin gyōsha to kunde. Ryoken akuyō, kanzei nogare', *Yomiuri shinbun* 29 May 1988 (KNK 3, 158).

'Fuhō shūrō gaikokujin. 1.371nin shūchū tekihatsu', *Yomiuri shinbun* 6 June 1988 (KNK 4,76).

'Nyūkan misu, assari sainyūkoku. Kyōsei sōkan no Pakisutanjin. Ryoken namae yomikae', *Yomiuri shinbun* 16 June 1988 (KNK 4, 9).

'Gaikokujin rōdōsha. Keisatsu ga bunseki, taiōsaku', *Yomiuri shinbun* 20 June 1988 (KNK 4, 81).

'Gaikokujin rōdōsha no jiken, jiko ga kyūzō. Kensatsu ga taisakuin setchi', *Yomiuri shinbun* 24 June 1988 (KNK 4, 80).

'Gaikokujin rōdōsha. Keisatsuchō ga bunseki, taiōsaku', *Yomiuri shinbun* 20 June 1988 (KNK 4, 81).

'Gaikokujin hanzai ni mizugiwa sakusen. Sora no genkan ni "Kokusai sōsa jōhō sentā". Kensatsu ga ritsuan sagyō. Rainendo no setchi mezasu', *Yomiuri shinbun* 29 November 1988 (KNK 7, 158).

'Narita kūkō robî ni goyōjin. Futari-gumi gaijin suri shutsubotsu', *Yomiuri shinbun* 12 May 1989 (KNK 9, 115).

'1.000man en hittakuri. Chūgokujin ryūgakusei "biza kōshin ni kane hitsuyō" ', *Yomiuri shinbun* 29 June 1989 (KNK 10, 40).

'Suri no Chūgokujin taiho', *Yomiuri shinbun* 17 June 1989 (KNK 9, 137).

'Dōkyō no Chūgokujin o taiho. Yokohama no shūgakusei gōtō shōgai jiken. Hitori o tehai', *Yomiuri shinbun* 9 August 1989 (KNK 10, 25).

'Chūgokujin shūgakusei gōtō shōgai jiken. Moto shūgakusei taiho, kyōhan o tehai. Dōshū sanken to kanren?', *Yomiuri shinbun* 9 August 1989 (KNK 10, 56).

'Kenshō. Kyūzō suru rainichi gaikokujin no hanzai', *Yomiuri shinbun* 16 August 1989 (10, 175).

'Tehai no moto shūgakusei taiho. Chūgokujin shūgakusei gōtō jiken. Chikaku kyōsei sōkan e. Taihosha sannin ni', *Yomiuri shinbun* 31 August 1989 (KNK 10, 68).

'Sara ni futari shimei tehai. Chūgokujin gakusei gōtōdan. Shanhai-kei fūfu kara 68man', *Yomiuri shinbun, Saitama-ban* 20 September 1989 (KNK 11, 148).

'Nihon shūgakusei. Dekasegi mokuteki ja arimasen. Baito yonwari jaku. "Seikatsu dekinu"', *Yomiuri shinbun* 9 October 1989 (KNK 11, 46).

'Shūgakusei-ryō ni sannin-gumi gōtō. Hannin Chūgokujin ka', *Yomiuri shinbun* 5 November 1989 (KNK 12, 23).

'Tōsō no Hikokujin taiho. Kōbe no bōnasu gōtō', *Yomiuri shinbun* 24 December 1989 (KNK 12, 122).

'Fuhō shūrō no gaikokujin jiko. "Rōsai" de hiroku kyūzai', *Yomiuri shinbun* 29 March 1990 (KNK 14, 60).

'Tōnan A-kei dansei shisatsu sareru', *Yomiuri shinbun* 31 May 1990 (KNK 15, 112).

'Nakama dōshi no toraburu? Matsuto. Shisatsu no dansei wa Hiko-kuseki', *Yomiuri shinbun (Chiba-ban)* 1 June 1990 (KNK 15, 112).

' "Satsugai wa hitori de" to jikyō. Unpan kyōhansetsu mo arau', *Yomiuri shinbun, Chiba-ban* 29 June 1990 (KNK 15, 116).

' "Gaikokujin-garami no hanzai ni taiō o". Kyōakka mo ichidan to susumu', *Yomiuri shinbun* 7 August 1990 (KNK 16, 87).

'Fueru gaikokujin rōdōsha to chian', *Yomiuri shinbun* 10 August 1990 (KNK 16, 144).

'Chūgokujin seinen futari o taiho. 100ken kosu nusumi jikyō', *Yomiuri shinbun* 7 September 1990 (KNK 17, 89).

'Shinte no pachinko arashi. Tōnan A-kei gaikokujinra. Kennai de higai aitsugu', *Yomiuri shinbun* 13 September 1990 (KNK 17, 92).

'Marēshia gōtōdan "kuromaku" o kokusai tehai e', *Yomiuri shinbun* 8 October 1990 (KNK 17, 100).

'Gaikokujin hanzai ichidan to kōmyō shūdanka. Namae yottsu motsu Tai onna. Marēshiajin ga honkaku gōtōdan', *Yomiuri shinbun* 10 September 1990 (KNK 17, 91).

'Hoka no sū–daigaku de mo nise shorui. Chūgokujin no 2 soshiki.

Ryokō dairiten nado kakuremino', *Yomiuri shinbun* 3 October 1990 (KNK 17, 19).

'Ikka no biza kigengire. "Fuhō shūrō" de shachō chōshu', *Yomiuri shinbun (Tochigi-ban)* 11 December 1990 (KNK 18, 14).

'Gaikokujin no hanzai kyūzō o kangaeru', *Yomiuri shinbun* 17 November 1991.

' "Shimin ni ranbō" dema sawagi. Gaikokujin rōdōsha ga jinkō no 4%. Kyūzō e fuan haikei', *Yomiuri shinbun* 7 December 1991 (KNK 23, 20).

'Kokoro nai dema kennai de mo. "Gaikokujin ni osowareta..." Gokai ni ohire', *Yomiuri shinbun* 13 December 1991 (KNK 23, 32).

Glossary and Index of Japanese Terms

(Japanese nouns can designate singular as well as plural)

369

Index

Index

Index